INSIDE
STORY

A
History of
British Assemblies of God

William K Kay

To Philip Taylor

best wishes

William Kay

INSIDE STORY
© 1990 by William K Kay, Assemblies of God Bible College

First UK Edition November 1990

Data conversion, Typesetting and Design by Technograffix,
Stourport-on-Severn, Worcs.

Printed and bound in Great Britain.

- Table of Contents -

Preface

The pentecostal movement in Britain is as old as the century. There are people still living who can just about remember the 1920s. But there is probably no one still alive who can remember the Sunderland Conventions (1908-14) with any clarity. The very first generation has nearly disappeared. This is the time, then, before memory fails, to try to find out what those early days were really like.

Some time late in 1983 or early in 1984 Keith Munday, then General Secretary of Assemblies of God in Great Britain and Ireland, phoned me and, on behalf of the AoG Executive Council, and asked if I would be willing to write a history of the pentecostal movement, focussing on AoG. He promised me access to confidential minutes and any other support I needed. I hesitated and asked how long the text should be and what the deadline was, and when he gave me assurances on these matters I agreed. In the summer of 1984 my family and I moved north 200 miles because I had been offered a lecturing post at Mattersey Hall, the Assemblies of God Bible College in Britain.

Amidst the duties of lecture preparation and preaching I began to lay plans for this piece of writing. From the start, it seemed foolish to indulge in nostalgia. History must have a purpose and, indeed, the various historical books of the Bible are all written so that readers can draw lessons from the past and apply them to the future. Moreover the historical books of the Bible do not hide the failures of their characters. We read about the sins of the saints as well as the sinners who became saints. Biblical history, therefore, does not hide the truth. It is selective to the extent that the writers follow certain themes - the prophetic interaction with the monarchs in the Books of Kings or the promises to the patriarchs in Genesis. I decided that there could be no better model of historical writing than the Bible itself and thought that, so far as possible, it would be wise to tell the story of the pentecostal movement, and Assemblies of God in particular, as it was without trying to put the pioneers on pedestals.

There are two main historical works on Assemblies of God in Britain. The first is Donald Gee's *Wind and Flame* (originally published under the title *The Pentecostal Movement* in 1941; later revised and enlarged for publication in 1967). Gee was intimately involved in much of AoG's development not only in the British Isles but also overseas. There are, however, three things which Donald Gee fails to do and which I decided to attempt in the history which follows. First, and very properly, Gee underestimates his own contribution to the shape of British pentecostalism. A natural modesty prevented Gee from seeing all the value of his own efforts. Second, Gee very rarely gives the source of any information he cites. There is a complete absence of footnotes, references, printed materials and the like in his book. We simply do not know what and whom he consulted when he wrote. And, third, Gee fails to make any mention of the immense social and technological changes which took place in his life time. He gives us the foreground without the background, and yet the background was important. It matters, for example, that ordinary commercial air travel opened up after the 1939-45 war or that telephones became common in the 1950s. The pentecostal movement did not develop in a vacuum and sometimes successful events are explicable by reference to forgotten factors. For example, the success of the great Stephen Jeffreys crusades makes more sense when one knows that, at one stage, he moved from town to town, each within easy travelling distance of the others; this allowed those who had been attracted by one set of meetings to travel to the next. Or that these crusades took place when the national health service in Britain did not exist and people *were more desperate in their search for healing.*

The second main work is Walter Hollenweger's *The Pentecostals* (SCM, 1972). This sets British pentecostalism in a world wide context and allows comparisons with pentecostal churches in Latin America, Canada, Australia, New Zealand, the Continent and North America. Inevitably, therefore, Hollengweger's book paints on a broad canvas and omits many events within British Assemblies of God.

Luke 1.3 reads, "Since I myself have carefully investigated everything from the beginning, it seemed good to me to write an orderly account for you". We have two clues here about Luke's method of procedure in the composition of his Gospel. He made personal investigations and he set his findings in order. At the end of this book a list is given of all the people I interviewed or consulted by phone. Not listed, however, because references are given at appropriate places in the text or notes, are the various documents which became available to me. These included letters, handbills, newspaper cuttings, minute books, diaries, reports submitted to the General Conference, accounts, short-lived magazines and, of course, all the volumes of *Redemption Tidings*. Undoubtedly *Redemption Tidings* proved to be the richest source of information. It was published continuously from 1924-85 and contained a whole variety of articles, crusade reports, letters, editorials, stenographically recorded sermons, advertisements and the like which, more than any other single source, recreate early pentecostalism. *Redemption Tidings* was published monthly 1924-33 and then fortnightly 1934-1956 and weekly 1956-1985.

So far as the ordering of the following history is concerned, I have simply moved forward decade by decade and with little attempt to group subjects together thematically. This rather unimaginative approach has the virtue of being systematic and it was used by Adrian Hastings in his excellent *A History of English Christianity: 1920-1985* (Collins, 1986). At the start of each major section, I have briefly outlined the economic and political events of the era. The account goes right up to the start of 1990, and this has posed a slight problem. Perspectives become flattened when recent events are considered. It is not easy to sort out the significant from the insignificant or to discover exactly what lies behind some contemporary decisions. Furthermore, living people do not want their mistakes or misjudgements paraded before public attention, and this inevitably introduces the danger of blandness into the text. Equally, it seemed inappropriate to commend every living person in this account in order to be kind. I have tried therefore to apply the same standards to the modern pentecostals as to the earlier ones.

It is also necessary to point out that this history pays particular attention to pentecostalism in Britain and only mentions missionary work overseas to the extent that this it is relevant to what was happening in Britain. In some respects this is unfortunate, but to do justice to the extraordinary work of men and women in various continents of the world would require a separate study of comparable length.

My sincere thanks are due to the Executive Council of Assemblies of God in Great Britain and Ireland both for asking me to undertake this task, for supporting me through it and for making available the minutes of all their meetings. Without this help (and the cheerful efficiency of Basil Varnam), this history could not have been written. I am also grateful to friends and colleagues at Mattersey and in Assemblies of God as a whole for their interest and encouragement. I should also mention Desmond Cartwright, the Elim historian, who has provided several bits of recondite information from his personal library. I should also like to record my thanks to Dr Douglas Davies of the University of Nottingham who helpfully supervised the academic version of this book. The academic version, which includes an element of sociological comment omitted here, is lodged as a doctoral thesis in theology (accepted in 1989) in the university library. Finally, my wife, Anthea, and my two sons, Matthew and Samuel, have put up with my enthusiasms, absences from home and distractedness with a love and patience for which I am profoundly grateful.

William K Kay,
Mattersey Hall.

TWENTIETH CENTURY PENTECOST

Initial Overview

Since the dawn of the twentieth century it is estimated that 327 million people in almost all sections of the Church world-wide have been directly influenced by a personal experience of the Holy Spirit similar to that described in the second chapter of the Book of Acts. This revolutionising experience has been received by Christians both inside and outside the historic denominations. What is remarkable about this phase in the life of the Church as a whole is that both Protestantism and Roman Catholicism have been affected - and yet the human beginnings of this spiritual movement were small, humble and with few notable exceptions on the borders of the institutional structure of Christianity. In essence it was the reality of the experience of a baptism in or with the Holy Spirit accompanied by speaking in tongues (or glossolalia) which was at the heart of the movement. Christians who had spoken in tongues began to expect other supernatural manifestations, especially miracles of healing. In practice a reciprocal relationship between experience and doctrine developed so that spiritual experience has been sought on the basis of doctrine and doctrine has been modified in the light of experience. In the initial stages of what came to be called the "pentecostal movement" separate and distinct occurrences in places as far apart as Wales, the western United States and Norway began to interrelate and eventually to issue in something new. A religious revival in Wales in 1904 and the pastoral work of a young black preacher, W J Seymour first in Texas and later in Los Angeles, were to be the object of interest in the mind of a preacher from Norway called T B Barratt who, because of his ancestry, was fluent in English. Seymour began to "advocate glossolalia as a sign attending baptism in the Holy Spirit" (Nelson, 1981: 187) and Barratt, hearing of exuberant crowds and rapid growth in Seymour's congregation, went to the United States to see and hear for himself[1]. Barratt received, in his words, "the full Pentecostal Baptism...my being was filled with light and an indescribable power, and I began to speak *in a foreign language* as loudly as I could" (Barratt, 1927: 128-9, original italics). Alexander Boddy, an Anglican Vicar in Sunderland, who had attended some meetings of the Welsh Revival, invited Barratt to England and the pentecostal results of Barratt's visit were perpetuated and disseminated by Boddy for many years afterwards. In particular Boddy's influence was to be felt, though infrequently acknowledged, by what became the main pentecostal groupings in the United Kingdom: Elim and the Assemblies of God.

Preamble

Christian history is an exploration of providential occurrences. The outpouring of the Holy Spirit in the British Isles at the beginning of the twentieth century is associated with a small group of men and women whose faith in God and whose sensitivity to the life of the church overseas enabled them to recognise, even at a distance, events which they wished to see repeated in their own circumstances and situations. As the following pages will show, it is clear that the original doctrinal characteristics of the pentecostal movement were formulated by Bible teachers and preachers outside the British Isles and that they, by invitation, came to speak to waiting groups of Christians whose hopes and prayers were set upon holiness and revival - hopes which had been kindled by the widely reported and publicised revival in Wales. The Welsh Revival demonstrated a variety of things to the acute observer of the ecclesiastical scene in Britain. First, that the doctrinal disputes which had riven the Baptists could be superseded and swallowed up in a fresh experience of Christianity and so relegate doctrinal controversy to a secondary place[2]. Indeed, *The Times* correspondent of 2nd Jan 1905 specifically referred to the "growing bitterness which has accentuated our unhappy divisions" in an article which airs the possibility suggested in the Bishop of Bangor's pastoral letter that the revival is "God's answer to many prayers". Second, that evangelicalism itself could be expressed without overdue reliance on plain forms of worship which dated back, with minor alterations, to the Puritans. Third, and perhaps most important, the Anglo-Catholic or Oxford Movement in the Church of England could not be seen as the only body of Christians who took seriously the call to personal holiness and consecration[3], for the Welsh Revival was marked by services where sins were openly confessed by distraught people in crowded congregations.

> Presently a young man pushed his way through the crowd and, kneeling in the rostrum, began a fervent prayer of penitence and for pardon. Once again, in the midst of his prayer, the whole congregation break forth into a hymn, repeated with amazing fervour and vigour eight times. A man in the gallery raises his voice to speak. The people listen, and meanwhile Mr Roberts has resumed his seat and watches all with a steady and

unimpassioned gaze. The man confesses his past - he has been a drunkard, he has been a Sabbath-breaker, he had known nothing of a Saviour, but now something has entered his heart and he feels this new power within him compelling him to speak. While he is speaking the people give vent to their feelings in a hymn of thanksgiving, repeated as before again and again. Thus the hours creep on. It is long past midnight. Now here, now there, some one rises to make his confession and lays bare his record before the people or falls upon his knees where he is and in loud and fervent tones prays for forgiveness. (*The Times*, Jan 3rd, 1905, p 12)

The connection between the Welsh Revival and the pentecostal movement is to be seen in terms of people rather than doctrines. Alexander Boddy, as the next chapter will show, played a crucial part in bringing the pentecostal experience to England but, before he did so, he had visited the Revival in Wales and observed both the fervour of its converts and unpredictable behaviour of its main catalyst, Evan Roberts. Boddy's own conduct of pentecostal meetings in the years which followed was always dignified and disciplined; whether such a bearing and poise was a consequence of his Anglican heritage or whether it resulted from an appreciation of the rapidity with which the untaught converts of the Revival began to drift away, it is impossible to say. Certainly Boddy took pains to avoid both the emotional excesses of the Welsh Revival and the reliance on experience, however spiritual, which Evan Roberts tended to promote. In another way, too, the connection between the Welsh Revival and the pentecostal movement was in terms of people: large numbers of small churches in Wales began to affiliate themselves to the Assemblies of God in the early 1920s, and these churches were, in many instances, the product of the Revival of 1904. According to Evans (1969: 192) "speaking in tongues" was a "rare(r) occurrence and incidental feature" of those few turbulent years when the Revival was at its height[4]. It is true that Roberts in his joint publication with Mrs Penn-Lewis did contend that "the baptism of the Holy Spirit is the essence of revival" (quoted from Evans, 1969: 191) but the full description of this baptism which included the "influx, sudden or gradual, of the Spirit of God into a man's spirit" omits any reference to the gift or sign of tongues which, for the pentecostal movement in general, became an objective criterion of a completed baptism in the Holy Spirit. So doctrinally and experientially the Welsh Revival was different from the pentecostalism which Boddy began to find attractive from 1906 onwards. The character of the Welsh Revival was partly determined by the nature of the tight-knit communities of villagers and miners where Roberts spoke. A sense of group guilt or individual guilt leading to public confession of sin was evoked. Boddy's pentecostal meetings which took place at Sunderland were originally based around the life of the parish church but they took on a national and international dimension from 1908 when delegates and visitors would come considerable distances to attend. The Welsh Revival gripped communities and even contributed to a measurable decline in drunkenness and criminality[5]; the pentecostal movement powerfully affected individuals whose lives later gave evidence of ministerial gifts and spiritual capacities.

General social background

When Queen Victoria died in 1901, the British Empire, still powerful and intact, undoubtedly helped the conduct of British missionary enterprise and enabled the distinctive emphasis of the pentecostal movement to become a world-wide force. Moreover, in addition to the political stability which accompanied Imperialism, there was a breakthrough in methods of communication and travel so that the telegraph and the steamship, as well as the airplane, began to play their part in conveying the missionary message or Bible teachers to distant locations. Islam was largely confined to poorer Arab nations which were, in any event, colonised in the main by the European powers. American influence on world affairs was far less than its wealth and business acumen was to earn for it after World War I, and Russia was still held in check by internal wrangles as reforming efforts failed to remove Czarist feudalism and social inequality.

In England itself the railway system which had been established in the second half of Victoria's reign, as well as the invention of the motor car, made village life less parochial and town life less cut off from the seaside or the major centres of civic life. Women began to find greater social freedom - and even the humble bicycle improved their independence and geographical mobility - while the suffragettes pressed for access to political power. Edwardian England, perhaps inevitably, began to leave behind some of the virtues and ideals of the previous century, though the conditions for change were being created by adjustments to long established political alignments and Reform Bills which altered the extent of franchise throughout Victoria's reign. The Labour Party began to emerge, the Liberal Party began to be eclipsed.

The Education Acts of 1870 and 1902 were partly a cause and

partly a consequence of other changes. "Between 1870 and 1890 the average school attendance rose from one and a quarter million to four and a half millions, while the money spent on each child was doubled" (Trevelyan, 1944: 581). Literacy in Britain was almost 100% with the result that the popular daily press had a ready-made market of readers. So far as the pentecostal movement was concerned, magazines and tracts could easily spread accounts of miracles or doctrinal studies. In Britain probably the most important launch of the early years was *Confidence* (started in April 1908) which, as the next chapter will show, propagated pentecostal doctrine and put small and isolated groups of believers in touch with each other. In the United States W J Seymour started *The Apostolic Faith* which for some years after 1906 had the same function.

Yet, whatever re-patterning occurred to the British social fabric in the first few years of the 20th Century, its prevalent social attitudes would have struck the average inhabitant of the latter part of the 20th Century as jingoistic and unadventurous: jingoistic   because of the unbridled patriotism which was aroused by the Boer War (1899-1902) and later by the World War (1914-18)[6] and unadventurous because of the acceptance of aristocratic privilege, difficult working conditions, short holidays, the tradition of self-effacing domestic service, low public expenditure on welfare priorities and huge discrepancies in standards of living between the rich and the urban poor. Rowntree's study published in 1901 *Poverty: a study of town life* showed that 27% of the population of York lived in what he called "primary or secondary poverty".

The approach adopted in this book

Three basic considerations have guided the approach to this book. First, it has been taken as axiomatic that the views of the participants in the pentecostal movement are important and that their own interpretation of the events with which they were connected should be given prominence and, where possible, credence. In other words, it has been assumed that it is not possible for a writer distant from the phenomena encountered to produce a "truer" account of their work and lives than would have come from their own mouths. Just as Marxist accounts of the Reformation which neglect the spiritual factors and describe the upheavals in Europe from 1515 onwards as being entirely the result of economic factors seem inadequate to the present writer, so an account of the pentecostal movement entirely in terms of sociological categories, or psychological concepts, seems to omit the consciousness of people involved in the events and their own articulation of those events. Where possible, then, the pentecostal pioneers will speak for themselves and it will be assumed that they understand their own motives and experiences as well as, and probably better than, an observer writing from several decades away. The main effect of such a consideration, however, will be to introduce reference to the Holy Spirit without parenthetical explanations drawn from secular disciplines. The Holy Spirit will be present in theological rather than in sociological or psychological terms. Any attempt to explain the work of the Holy Spirit in non-theological language would savour of an attempt to debunk the pentecostal movement, and this is not the present writer's intention.

Second, an attempt will be made to place the pentecostal movement in its historical and social context. The background events of war, conscientious objection, unemployment, low wages, an absence of the welfare state and the television, and so on, will be mentioned so as to place the characters in the narrative in imaginable situations.

Notes to Pages 9 - 14

1. Barratt had travelled to the States to raise money for evangelism.

2. In 1887 C H Spurgeon, himself a member of the Baptist Union, began to suggest that some members of the Union were heretical. The issue concerned the authority of Scripture. By the end of the 19th century the nonconformist churches were faced by the arguments and challenges of German Higher Criticism so that evangelicals were acutely worried. Spurgeon's pamphlets were intended to bring the conflict between evangelicals and modernists into the open. Eventually Spurgeon seceded from the Union. See E J Poole-Connor, Evangelicalism in England, Worthing: H Walter, 1966, p234f.

3 The Salvation Army, though beginning in the late 19th Century and taking holiness seriously, could not be regarded as a normal style of Christian life and was thus not influential on ordinary local church practice or doctrine.

4. Although pentecostal histories commonly state that speaking in tongues occurred during the Welsh Revival, the main evidence for this assertion comes from a report in the Yorkshire Post (27 Dec 1904), but a recent study points out,"so far I have found no explicit reference to glossolalia in any first-hand report, either in Welsh or in English, dealing with that eventful period." Quoted from C Williams Tongues of the Spirit, Cardiff: University of Wales Press, 1981, by Cartwright (1981).

However, Clifford Rees has given me information based on first-hand accounts which affirm that speaking in tongues did occur during the Welsh Revival, though its significance was not fully realised. Only subsequently, when the pentecostal movement was established in the 1930s, did people realise they had heard speaking in tongues before - namely during the Revival.

5. "The ethical side of the movement becomes more and more apparent...the chairman of the Cardiff Licensing Magistrates last week bore testimony to the extraordinary

decrease in drunkenness in the town during the past year, apprehensions having decreased from 446 in 1903 to 217 last year". <u>The Times</u> 13 Feb 1905, p 9.

6. Lloyd George opposed the Boer War but declared himself in favour of the War of 1914. Voluntary recruitment to the army was heavy and enthusiastic.

ALEXANDER BODDY

The Man

Boddy's daughter, Jane Vazeille Boddy, wrote a biographical memoir of her father some time just before 1970[1] and gives a vivid impression of his personality and ministerial years. He was born in 1854, the son of the Rector of St Thomas' Church in Manchester, and trained as a solicitor and practised for a few years before attending a Keswick Convention where he began to review the course of his life. He decided to train for ordination, but his parents could not afford to send him to Cambridge like his brother Herbert who had died while on holiday in Italy. Alexander himself saved up enough to go to Durham University for two years and took his L.Th in 1880. The Bishop of Durham at the time was J B Lightfoot, the eminent classical scholar whose rigorously accurate and famous New Testament commentaries did much to mitigate the effects of German scholarship in Britain at the end of the nineteenth century, and whose personal influence in the see of Durham was especially felt on a group of young men dubbed "Lightfoot's Lambs" of whom Boddy was one. Interestingly Lightfoot's commentary on the Epistle to the Phillipians (1868) contained a long essay on the primitive Christian ministry which expounded the notion that the original governance of the early church was in the hands of presbyterates (on the model of Jewish elders) whose members were also called "bishops". How influential Lightfoot's exposition was on Boddy we do not know, but it is clear that Lightfoot was prepared to entertain radical ideas despite his normal caution and conservatism, and Boddy's daughter tells us that "Bishop Lightfoot was one of the great influences in my father's life" Moreover Lightfoot himself himself lectured six or eight ordinands a year at Auckland Castle[2] on a training scheme he had inaugurated. Lightfoot's successor in 1890 was B F Westcott whose evangelical leanings had prompted him to encourage the growth of Christian missions. Thus Boddy was in the care of Bishops who were neither Anglo-Catholic nor liberal in their opinions. Westcott, in addition to his other concerns, was keen to play a part in solving social problems - and this trait can also be detected in Boddy.

In 1884[3] Lightfoot sent Boddy to the parish of Sunderland. The parish was in a poor state because the previous incumbent had been an alcoholic and consequent litigation had reduced its financial affairs to chronic debt. The vicarage was derelict and the church was empty.

Boddy threw himself into the work and renovated the buildings and then, when he was about 37 years of age, married Mary Pollock, daughter of a Rector in Yorkshire and a woman who had a similar spiritual outlook to Boddy because she had attended the Keswick conventions[4]. It is evident that Boddy attacked the problems of his parish energetically and evangelically because, in fact, Mary had been invited to sing at a mission he and his curate were holding.

There is no doubt that Boddy was a man of curiosity and daring as well as of energy. He travelled widely - he had visited the Holy Land before the 1890s - and was motivated partly by the semi-academic geographical honours which he gained. In his own words

> Alas! the world became attractive and interesting things crept in and took first place. Adventurous journeys were taken in North Africa, Arctic Russia, British Columbia, etc., not in order to preach Christ, but to write books of travel and to be somewhat of an authority on the people I thus studied.

> I was made a Fellow of the Royal Geographical Society, also a Member of the Imperial Geographical Society of Russia, and the Khedivial Geographical Society and wrote a number of books on travel.

> It was not until the summer of 1892 that I could praise Him for *fully* saving me (Extract from *The Latter Rain Evangel* February 1909, p 9, original italics).

His daughter reports, "I remember, as a very small child, running out to greet my father after one of his visits to Russia and seeing him dressed in the clothes of a Russian Pilgrim" (Memoir, p 2). She also tells how meals at the vicarage were a lesson in geography because Boddy had frames fitted to the dining and drawing room windows in which he could permanently show slides of his travels. He taught his children to count in Arabic and decorated his home with mementoes of his visits. He even once rowed his children out to see a man-of-war anchored beyond the pier during a storm. He would often help the life boats when a boat was shipwrecked nearby and he was involved in the start of the Seamen's Mission in Sunderland. Sometimes he would wake his children up at night to look through a powerful astronomical telescope he had set up in the church grounds.

When the Welsh Revival broke out Boddy, being the sort of man he was, had to go and see for himself and immediately invited Evan Roberts to the parish[5]. In 1906 (the date is taken from the article in *The Latter Rain Evangel* cited above), a prayer meeting in the All Saints' Vestry began and, in Boddy's words, "for months and months they held on to God, often with little to encourage" and, he went on, "How they clung to the promises [of the Bible], and so did I and my dear wife also". Thus the picture of Boddy which emerges both from his own writings and activities and from his daughter's written recollections is of a man who was energetic - even impulsive - and possessed of insatiable curiosity, as well as committed to spiritual life and progress. He was also a communicator and a writer, an attractive personality, and a man who was willing to take on the challenge of a rundown parish. He prayed, he sang with a beautiful bass voice, he visited the sick, he organised, he wrote books and tracts and he still had time to teach his children some of the things he had learnt on his travels. Indeed Jane Vazeille visited the parish in 1954 and found that the old people still spoke of the "old vicar" - meaning Boddy - with great affection[6]. His talents and his many-sided personality were a valuable asset to the infant pentecostal movement and found full expression in promoting its cause. Photographs of him at the Sunderland Conventions (see below) show him to be grey haired, stocky and moustached, with a dignified bearing, an ordinary rather than a clerical collar and a large hat and a cape[7].

The spiritual crisis

In about 1900 Mrs Boddy was cured of asthma through prayer and this led to Boddy's interest in the work of the Holy Spirit in healing. His daughter recalls how "often when I was a in a bad mood as an adolescent I would ask my father to pray with me and when he laid his hands on my head I experienced a deep peace which lasted a long time"[8] (Memoir, p 5). The prayer meetings which began in the All Saints' Vestry in 1906 were a continuation and extension of Boddy's desire for a fuller blessing of the Holy Spirit. In his own words

> We were tarrying until we should be endued with power from on high. We were praying for a revival, and we did not know *how* God was going to answer our prayer, but we were *sure He would answer and the answer has come. And the answer is from Him.*

> How well I remember taking into their little gathering one of the first papers [probably Seymour's *The Apostolic Faith*]

telling of what seemed to be an apostolic outpouring of the Holy Spirit in the West. We praised God for this answer to prayer and took courage. (Extract from LRE cited above, original italics)

News from afar was often a signal for Boddy to travel. The account of what was occurring in "the West" was soon followed by reports that similar experiences were being noticed in Norway. Barratt (1927: 142) wrote, "the remarkable thing is how rapidly the Revival spreads over Norway....people come from far and near. ...the Swedish, Danish, Finnish, American, German papers are writing up the matter...how many meetings I have had, I cannot say. I have two, sometimes three and day, and the meetings last up to four or five hours at times". Barratt went on to say

One of the first to visit us was the Rev Alex A Boddy, vicar of All Saints parish, Sunderland, England. He came, not only to see the revival, but also to get a blessing for his own hungry soul (p 143).

Boddy put it this way

At last the Lord led me into touch with this work of God which now had traveled (sic) over the Atlantic to Norway. I prayed Him to lead me to Christiania [Oslo], and that if this was His work it might soon spread to our land.......Under the good hand of God I took the long journey overland in wintry weather and received from His own great blessing in these Spirit-filled meetings. It was a mission room in an upper chamber. Perhaps about 120 were present. I had given out the teaching about the healing of the sick, and had spoken in the power of the Holy Ghost, and then we went to prayer. I asked those who had received the holy Spirit with the sign of the Tongues to lay hands on me for a Baptism of the Holy Ghost. The blessed Holy Spirit came upon me just then, filling me with love, joy and peace.

The inflow of the blessed Holy Spirit occurred March 5, 1907, but not until Dec. 2nd, nine months later, did the Lord give me the sign of the tongues (Extract from LRE cited above).

And Donald Gee (1967:20) quotes an article Boddy sent to several English papers, "My four days in Christiania (Oslo) can never be forgotten. I stood with Evan Roberts in Tonipandy, but have never witnessed such scenes as those in Norway". In effect, Boddy compared the overtly pentecostal revival in Norway with slightly different revival in Wales and found the former greater than the latter.

Boddy returned to England, and to his faithful partners in the prayer meeting at All Saints, Sunderland and, in this long extract, continues the story

> Back in England in the months that followed, our prayer meetings were filled with power. I was mightily anointed several times. On one occasion received a special witness from the Lord of my sanctification. It was when we were adoring the Lamb that the power of God overwhelmed me, and caused me to sink helpless on the floor. It was thus that God specially met me, filling me more and more until the sign came, and the full vessel at last overflowed.

> One Sunday four of us were led together to pray at 9:30 P.M. in the Vicarage and we continued until nearly one in the morning. We had had a blessed day of worship and witness. The window blinds were not drawn down. I was opposite the window and so looked out at the church. A wonderful light suddenly filled the room and lingered over the church roof. One brother fell to the floor very suddenly, crying with tremendous vehemence, "It is the Lord, there is no deception, brothers, it is the Lord Himself." This continued on and on, the light lingering over the roof of the church, an emblem it seemed of blessing that was to be connected with this place. Only one saw the Lord, we three saw the light only. Then a brother kneeling at my right hand fell to the floor suddenly and cried in wonderful tones of awe, "It's the blood, Oh, it's the blood. *(Latter Rain Evangel)*.

There are several points of interest in this account. First, it is noticeable that Boddy separated the "inflow" of the Holy Spirit from the sign of tongues; some nine months pass between the two experiences. Second[9], Boddy uses the since-disputed terminology, "Baptism of the Holy Ghost". Third, Boddy dates his Norwegian trip quite precisely as being in early March 1907. Fourth, what later took place in the parish at All Saints, Sunderland is specifically connected with lengthy meetings for prayer, even if the number of those present was quite small. Fifth, there is a connection between an inward and personal sense of sanctification and the sign of tongues in Boddy's own experience. Sixth, there is reference to the blood of Christ. Seventh, there is reference to supernatural visions. Eighth, Boddy already believed in and taught about the healing power of the Holy Spirit before his receiving his other experiences of the Holy Spirit. Ninth, there is a close association between worship - adoring the Lamb - and an apprehension of the reality of the Holy Spirit.

Ramifications of all these nine points will appear in the account of the years which follow. Already, at this stage in the history of the pentecostal movement, it is apparent that the baptism in the Holy Spirit is seen as a sudden event in a person's life subsequent to conversion, supernatural in origin and objectively evidenced by speaking in tongues.

Boddy pressed Barratt who, because of his English parentage[10] could speak English, to come to Sunderland and so, on Saturday August 31st 1907, Barratt sailed in from Copenhagen; "what rejoicing there was at out Waiting Meeting that night, when it was found he was actually in our midst"[11]. Meetings started in earnest the next day, Sunday September 1st, and after a fortnight about 17 people had spoken in tongues (see Barratt, 1927:150). Barratt stayed only seven weeks in Sunderland: Mrs Boddy was baptised in the Spirit[12] on Sept 11th 1907 but Boddy himself continued to wait.

> On the 13th of September, in one of our large meetings in the Parish Hall in the presence of all my people, I offered myself definitely to the Lord, as the Spirit came to me causing deep breathings and laying hold of me more and more. I prayed there for those who were opposing the work of God. I asked for more love, the love of Christ to be mine....I quite hoped to receive the sign of the tongues, but it was not given that night. I must confess that I was disappointed. It seemed hard to be taking so prominent a part in this work of God and yet not to have the sign which the Lord gave to many others before He gave it to me *(Latter Rain Evangel)*

From this extract we can deduce that meetings were held in the Parish Hall and that there was room for spontaneity in them because

Boddy was led to make a public declaration of himself before the congregation. Moreover his prayer shows that even at this early stage, there was opposition to what was going on in his meetings. Indeed Barratt (1927: 153) quotes at length from an article in the London *Daily Chronicle* which rather tongue-in-cheek publicised what was going on

> I wonder if his grace the Archbishop of Canterbury has heard of the Rev Alexander A Boddy. Does he ever, I wonder, mount the watch-tower of his episcopal stronghold at Lambeth, and peer out towards the North....... Sunderland is in the grip of religious revival....on what I must accept as reputable authority, there has been something else besides. According to the Rev Alexander A Boddy, the vicar of All Saints, Monkwearmouth, Sunderland, "More that 20,000 people throughout the world are now so filled with the Holy Ghost that they are speaking in tongues". Of these, Mr Boddy informs me, about twenty are to be found in his parish - even more..... young men tell of visions, in which the Christ has appeared.... boys and girls, after the strange Pentecostal baptism, start up and sing in sweet, silvery, unearthly voices[13].

The writer in the *Daily Chronicle* went on to call Barratt the "Evan Roberts of the North" which suggests that reports of the proceedings were already, before Christmas 1907, catching the national daily press and, as Barratt (1927:155) indicates some of the weeklies as well. The media's publicity, while it may have been cast in a rather cynical light, had the beneficial result of informing large numbers of Christians about what was happening and encouraging visitors of all sorts to go and hear for themselves.

One development, unhappily, took place during Barratt's six weeks in England which must have given Boddy pause for thought. Reader Harris QC had founded the Pentecostal League in 1888 to promote traditional holiness teachings. The League was very active in Sunderland[14] and Boddy had found it helpful, particularly in his early days as a vicar. It so happened that the League was holding a Convention in Sunderland while Barratt was also there. Indeed, Boddy had actually participated briefly in the League's Convention during Barratt's stay. When Reader Harris, however, denounced the "Gift of Tongues Movement" for being Satanic and specifically mentioned "the recent extraordinary goings on in Monkwearmouth [ie Boddy's parish]"[15] then a rift between Boddy and Harris was bound to open up. Moreover the *Sunderland Echo* (2.10.1907, p4) reported on the disagreement and the anguish it caused Boddy which, unbeknown to the press, was worsened by the involvement of James Pollock Boddy's brother in law who, despite his reception of the baptism in the Holy Spirit under Barratt's ministry, was persuaded by Reader Harris's arguments to renounce his experience. Harris, had (as Robinson, 1976: 59) points out, merely been opposed initially to the view that only those who had spoken in tongues had been baptised in the Holy Spirit. Indeed Harris had said "the gift of tongues, therefore, is not unscriptural and consequently, we must not oppose or despise the gift"[16]. The dispute between Barratt and Harris had the effect of hardening and clarifying doctrinal positions and it is possible that Boddy recognised the justice of Harris's criticism of the disorderliness of the innovative meetings at which Barratt spoke. If this is so, two consequences followed from the immediate negative reaction of the Pentecostal League: first, future pentecostal meetings must be beyond reproach - decent and well regulated and, second, there was nothing further to lose by maintaining the apparently divisive doctrine that baptism in the Holy Spirit was invariably accompanied by speaking in tongues. Later, perhaps as a result of his contact with German pentecostals (see Robinson 1976: 81), Boddy modified his position in the sense that he considered that in addition to speaking with tongues he would wish to see evidence in the character of a claimant of the baptism in the Holy Spirit. To this extent, Boddy's criteria for evidence of the baptism in the Holy Spirit became more and not less stringent (as Robinson, 1976, fails to realise).

Boddy was never narrowly polemical. His desire for a greater work of the Holy Spirit was always within the context of his own quest for communion with God and the overall progress of the parish. Barratt was an evangelist and a revivalist, Boddy was a pastor, and it was the breadth of his pastoral sympathies that made him prefer to put human relationships before doctrinal controversy. Certainly there is no hint later that the Sunderland Conventions were troubled by churchmanship, despite the variety of denominational groups represented.

It was only after Barratt had gone home that Boddy was able to describe his own spiritual climax as follows

> I hope that the precious memory of the glorious Spirit-filled meeting in All Saints' Vicarage, Dec 2, 1907, will never fade away. I lay before the Lord feeling that I could not get low

enough. I had special reason to believe that at last He was going to give me the sign. So on that Monday night He took my tongue as I yielded and obeyed. First speaking quickly but quietly and then more powerfully. The whole meeting at this point was adoring and praising God with great joy. The Lord was raising His hands in blessing above the meeting as we were conscious of His presence. My voice in tongues rose with theirs as a torrent of words poured out. So far it had been between me and the Lord, and I was indeed grateful that after nine months the sign I had hoped for had come at last[17]. Hallelujah to the Lamb! *(Latter Rain Evangel)*

At the time Boddy had just enjoyed his 52nd birthday. He was to live another 23 years, but for the next ten he was to be the most influential pentecostal leader in the British Isles.

The Work

There were two major ways in which Boddy was to be instrumental in leading the budding pentecostal movement: the first was by the founding and distribution of a magazine entitled *Confidence* which ran from April 1908 to 1926, 141 issues in all; the second was to organise and chair the Sunderland Conventions which were held at Whitsun from 1908 to 1914 inclusive. Each Convention lasted six days and most of the men and women who were later to be prominent in pentecostal gatherings attended either as speakers or listeners. The formative years of the pentecostal movement were therefore providentially in Boddy's hands. What he taught, and the way he taught it, was to become normative and those problems which he faced were, by and large, similar to those which recurred in later years.

Since *Confidence* carried reports of the Conventions, it will be convenient to examine these two aspects of Boddy's work together. Of course, as time went on, and the pentecostal experience was dispersed to a greater number of people, there was a sense in which Boddy's role became more diffuse, and he himself would almost certainly have regarded the spread of pentecostalism as being directly due to the Holy Spirit rather than the agency of any man however dedicated he might have been.

The first copies of *Confidence* (subtitled on the front cover "A Pentecostal Paper for Great Britain") were sent out free of charge and the title was clearly linked with two verses of Scripture, 1 John 5.14-15 and Proverbs 3.16, which were quoted on the front cover of the first issue : "This is the confidence that we have in him, that if we ask anything according to his will, he heareth us: and if we know that he hear us, whatsoever we ask, we know that we have the petitions that we desired from him" and "the Lord shall be thy confidence, and shall keep they foot from being taken". The magazine's title was neither eschato-logical nor revivalistic in tone, but simply stressed prayer and its an-swers. The first issue contained an invitation to the first Sunderland Convention, which was held from June 6th to 11th 1908 at All Saints', Monkwearmouth and stated

> As these meetings are for Conference and not for controversy, we admit by ticket, which will be freely given to those who can whole-heartedly sign the following (which is printed on the Admission Card):-

DECLARATION
> *"I declare that I am in full sympathy with those who are seeking 'Pentecost' with the Sign of Tongues. I also undertake to accept the ruling of the Chairman"*

Underneath a Conference Programme was given. On the Satur-day two prayer meetings and a welcome meeting were to be held; on Sunday (Whit-Sunday) there were two celebrations of Holy Commun-ion at the parish church, an afternoon meeting for greetings from "friends from a distance", a service at 6.30 and just after 8pm an after-meeting with "testimonies from visitors". The remaining four days were to contain further reports from visitors and four talks on: Bible Study and Pentecostal Literature, Tongues as a Sign of Pentecost, The Coming of the Lord, and Divine Life - Health and Healing in Christ. In addition there was to be a "Conference as to the Conduct of Meetings". These titles illustrate the seriousness with which the visitors took both prac-tical topics like Bible study and the conduct of meetings in which spiritual gifts were to be exercised and the biblical themes with which they were most concerned - the Second Coming and Divine healing.

Boddy had obviously previously given thought to the conduct of meetings because underneath the Conference Programme were the words

> Prayer and Praise should occupy at least one-third of even our meetings for Conference. It is suggested that everyone should make a point of being very punctual, and, if possible, to have

a quiet time of prayer before the meeting, and that there be as little talking as possible in the room before the meetings, but silent prayer only while waiting.

As to choruses, etc., it is suggested that, as far as possible, they should be left to the Leader to commence or control, and friends are asked to pray (silently) that he may be led aright. Confusion is not always edifying, though sometimes the Holy Spirit works so mightily that there is a divine flood which rises above barriers.

The Chairman's ruling should be promptly and willingly obeyed in cases of difficulty. There should at those moments, if they occur, be much earnest prayer (in silence) that God may guide aright and get glory through it all.

The tension between liberty and control, which has always existed in pentecostal meetings, is nicely conveyed in these paragraphs. Boddy expected to be obeyed as he led the meetings, but he conceded that a divine flood can rise "above barriers". Jane Vazeille Boddy's memoir carries a description of the Convention which gives an idea of how closely these guidelines were followed.

The Meetings were held in the parish hall and my father conducted them, though he was never a formal Chairman. All he did was to introduce speakers, sometimes speak himself, and give out hymns. Otherwise the meetings were controlled by the Holy Spirit and there were long periods of prayer, some speaking in tongues with interpretation. In between the prayers choruses were started by anyone who felt moved to do so.....I never remember seeing anything "sensational". My father kept firm control and if, occasionally, someone fell prostrate, one or our workers took that one to a room at the back for a talk and spiritual help.....the singing was always impressive.....on the wall of the platform was an enormous text, stretching right across, with the words "Fervent in Spirit" in very bold lettering.....at times I remember hearing what some people called the "heavenly choir", It started during a time of prayer, very softly, by one or two voices; others joined in and the voices rose higher....there were no words, just glorious harmonies....once at least during the Convention there was a Missionary Collection....ladies were asked to put jewellery in the plates, if they could not afford much money. (p 7)

The first issue of *Confidence* also carried some biblical teaching, though some of this was slightly oblique. For example, in an article entitled "The Bridegroom Cometh" there was reference to the "latter rain" which typologically identified the outpouring of the Holy Spirit in the 20th century with the second period of rainfall in Israel which was given to fill out the crops just before the harvest. A period of rainfall earlier in the year softened the ground before planting and the latter rain prepared the grain for the autumn harvest; the early rain corresponded to the outpouring of the Holy Spirit in the days of the first century apostles and the latter rain corresponded to pentecostal manifestations from 1907 onwards. The latter rain was therefore a signal that Christ, as Lord of the harvest, was about to return. Hence the pentecostal movement was intimately connected with millennial expectations from its outset. Smith Wigglesworth, of whom more later, wrote "we fully believe that we are in the last days, and before the Lord comes we trust to see the mightiest Revival the world has ever seen or witnessed. We have seen demons cast out, and the very devil of disease rebuked...".

Boddy wrote a brief article in which he enunciated the belief that there was a distinction between "(1) the Seal of Tongues as a sign of the indwelling of the Holy Ghost (given very specially at one point in the Spiritual experience), and (2) a *continuous* Gift of Tongues" (p 18, original italics), and he went on to state that, so far as he was concerned, "Pentecost means the Baptism of the Holy Ghost with the evidence of Tongues". His distinction between two functions of tongues was taken up and applied to 1 Cor 12.29f where Paul asks rhetorically, but expecting the answer no, whether all Christians should speak in tongues. Boddy effectively replied, yes all Christians speak in tongues when the baptised in the Holy Spirit, but they do not all thereafter continue to speak in tongues either in their private devotions or in public meetings[18]. According to his daughter's memoir "my father spoke in tongues very occasionally and my mother much more often at meetings which were then held regularly" (p 6).

Three other matters stand out from the opening issue of *Confidence*. First there were letters and communications from a wide range of places - Wales, of course, and Sunderland, Yorkshire, Lancashire, Carlisle, London, Scotland, Holland, Sweden, Switzerland, Egypt and India. Second there is evidence of criticism of the pentecostal experience. Wigglesworth put it bluntly "one of the clear proofs that Pentecost with Tongues is of God is that all the Scribes and Pharisees of the present day condemn it" (p 7), while in a note on p 13 there is warning that "there are those who, under pressure, have gone back from the Lord's own Sign of the Tongues". The editorial says of the "pentecostal blessing" that "it is a work which arouses Satan's opposition in the least likely quarters"[19].

Third there is some indication of the number of people involved in the incipient movement. Boddy's editorial says "a year ago the writer only knew of some five or six persons in Great Britain who were in the experience. At the time of printing this there are probably more than 500." And in a section entitled 'News of Pentecost', details of what was happening in Sunderland come to life. "Since the beginning of September about 70 have received a Baptism of the Holy Ghost with the Seal of Tongues.....the Lord has graciously used Sunderland as a centre for free literature....scores of thousands of testimonies and other publications have been sent for, [to some of the places mentioned above] ...two faithful secretaries ...are daily at work". If Boddy's figures are correct, it is clear that between September 1907 and April 1908 some 500 people were baptised in the Holy Spirit, and most of them, presumably, through contact of some kind with the congregation at Sunderland. According to Cartwright (1981:5)

> it was to Sunderland that many workers and leaders travelled (usually by invitation).....the majority of those who came were laymen. A high proportion had links with undenominational missions that had mushroomed around the turn of the century.

Reports of the first Sunderland Convention are sparse. *Confidence* (no 4) contains an article by Mrs T B Barratt in which she says

> a large part of the meetings was spent on our knees, praying, singing, or in silence praying to God's Lamb, whose Blood was so precious, in that the Spirit's Light fell over it, and we experienced that it cleansed us wholly.

> Many came forward and testified how God had healed them, in that the Fire fell over them, and now they are quite strong and well...a deep solemnity pervaded through it all (p 5).

Throughout the years which followed Boddy was super-abundantly active. He travelled extensively to almost any location where he heard of pentecostal gatherings and was in touch by letter with those beyond his journeying range. Among the places he visited was Kilsyth, just north of Glasgow, where an outpouring of the Spirit had taken place in February 1908. Moreover the Sunderland Conventions continued to attract people from different parts of the world and inspire other convocations of similar character in Bradford, Bedford and London. A photo in *Confidence* for July 1913 shows the speakers, delegates and visitors to Sunderland to amount to some 83 men, many of whom are in early middle age and dressed in suits with stiff white collars. Many carry hats and Bibles. Smith Wigglesworth was baptised in the Spirit in Sunderland in 1907 and Thomas Myerscough[20] in 1909 at the Convention. John and Howard Carter attended the Conventions for three years from 1912 to 1914, Stanley Frodsham, later an editor of the *Pentecostal Evangel* in the USA attended in 1912, and the 1913 photograph shows George Jeffreys[21] in attendance, along with Cecil Polhill, one of "The Cambridge Seven", and later important in the ministry of the Pentecostal Missionary Union. John Carter (1979: 26) was happy to admit that the Sunderland Conventions made a profound impression on him and his description of the meetings - "tongues were uttered and tongues were interpreted to the edification of all" - testify to the orderly operation of spiritual gifts (see 1 Cor 12 and 14) in the meetings; it was the dignified conduct of spirituality which struck the young John Carter because, as he reminisces, "in those early days 'tongues of men and tongues of angels' were freely exercised by those Pentecostal saints without regard to order or interpretation" (1979: 25). Moreover, an incident which he remembered all his life underlined the validity of tongues as being genuine languages supernaturally inspired whose meaning could be conveyed through the gift of interpretation which was itself equally supernatural. He was present in one of the Sunderland meetings

> I was on the end chair of our row next to the aisle. Across the aisle sat a Scotsman and my attention was arrested when I saw him begin to shake under the power of the Spirit. Then he gave vent to a loud utterance in tongues. I can hear it now, the unknown tongue was so distinct and clear. It sounded like this, "Ding-a-la, ding-a-la" and then went on into a series of sentences. Mrs Crisp, the lady-principal of the Women's Training School in London, interpreted the message by the Holy Spirit. On the platform was a lady missionary from the Congo Inland

Mission and this is what she publicly related:-

"As soon as that brother began to speak I whispered to the German pastor beside me 'It is a real language'. I recognised it immediately as the language of the Kifioto tribe among whom I have been labouring. This lady (pointing to Mrs Crisp) has given an excellent interpretation of that message. Had I translated the tongue naturally, I would have employed different words, but let me say that the interpretation by the Spirit has embodied in a most beautiful way all the underlying thoughts that were contained in the message" (Carter, 1971:24; and *Confidence* July 1913)

The basic guidelines which have obtained to this day in pentecostal/charismatic circles regarding the utility of spiritual gifts were already grasped by Boddy in 1907. In *Confidence* (No 7, p 22) he considers the events at Caesarea when the household of Cornelius (Acts 10) was filled with the Holy Spirit. Boddy pointed out that the gift of tongues seems "primarily to have been for the edification of the Spirit-possessed person himself" and not for preaching to the heathen. *Confidence* (no 4, p 3) contains a letter from Wales saying that "since returning from Sunderland...the 'gift of prophecy' has been wonderfully poured out in our midst". The implication must be that tongues, interpretation and prophecy (1 Cor 12) were functioning in Sunderland.

The Last Two Conventions
By 1913 the Sunderland Conventions had become well established and, because a very full account of the preaching and discussion of the 1913 Convention is given in various issues of *Confidence* for that year, the examination of the pentecostal movement six years after its inception in the British Isles is straightforward.

By 1913 *Confidence* cost a penny a month and gave discounts to pentecostal assemblies taking a dozen or more copies. Printing costs are given in the inside page of the issue for July 1913, and these amount to £17-17-6^d, plus £1-4-0^d for blocks (presumably for the printing of photographs) and £5-2-7^d for postage. Subscribers received their copies post free and the discount given to assemblies taking more than a dozen copies was 33%, so that a dozen copies cost 8^d rather than one shilling. If bulk subscribers bought at cost, then we can suggest that the £17-17-6^d represents a print-run of at least 6000 copies[22]. This figure is rough-and-ready because the magazine was aided by gifts as well as strict subscriptions. What the inside page also shows is where many of the orders were sent; while the largest financial contribution came from London, Washington, New Zealand, Australia, Los Angeles, Johannesburg, Liberia, India and places in the UK all had regular orders.

The third page printed a short history of the magazine and a statement of basic beliefs. These included a synopsis of common evangelical emphases (like regeneration and sanctification) but also made a point of stressing "identification with Christ in Death and Resurrection" which would imply a stress on holiness; and there was, as might be expected, mention of the Baptism in the Holy Ghost, divine healing and the "Soon-Coming of the Lord in the air." Prominently displayed in the July 1913 issue is a "Declaration" from the International Advisory Pentecostal Council which apparently met during the 3rd Session at Sunderland in 1913. The declaration is careful to warn against a book and a teaching which had troubled, or threatened to trouble, pentecostal groups in Britain and elsewhere. From a sociological point of view it is clear that the Sunderland Conventions were beginning to act with charismatic authority to stem potential abuses. The erroneous doctrine from America to which the declaration averred concerned the idea that "we will not be prepared for the rapture if we are not living an eunuch life". In a few calm paragraphs the unscriptural basis for this idea is refuted. *War on the Saints*, a book by an unnamed lady writer (in fact, Jessie Penn-Lewis (1861-1927)), argued that the pentecostal phenomena were caused by evil spirits and not by the Holy Spirit. The signatories of the declaration, who included Boddy and Polhill from England, and two Germans, a Dutch and a Swiss had no difficulty in disposing of Penn-Lewis's attack.

The 1913 Convention addressed itself to "The Task of the Pentecostal Movement" and to "The Conditions of Apostolic Revival"[23]. In brief, it saw the task of the pentecostal movement as being

> a) to stir up the people of God for the edification of the Body of Christ
>
> b) to bring the restoration of apostolic gifts
> c) to preach the Gospel to the world as a last call of the Lord
>
> d) to sound the midnight cry: "Behold the Bridegroom! come ye forth to meet him"

This analysis and agenda carries no hint of denominationalism; the first tasks of the pentecostal movement are within the church, the Body of Christ, and then in the realm of evangelism. The preachers were, in the main, from Germany and the record of their sermons[24], as is often the case with sermons, is not striking, except insofar as their content is surprisingly akin to much of the pentecostal preaching of the 1980s. "We cannot move on in this Pentecostal Movement without this unity in the Body of Christ"[25]; spiritual gifts were to be an integral part of the corporate life of the church and not for the aggrandisement of individuals. Moreover, the danger the pentecostal movement faced was similar to that encountered by the believers in Galatia who, having known a release from the burden of the mosaic law, risked a new form of legalism. The conditions of "apostolic revival" amounted to a realisation of "living fellowship with Christ"[26].

As it turned out, the Convention of 1914 was the last to be held at Sunderland under Boddy's chairmanship. The Convention took place from the 29th of May till the 5th June. The Archduke Francis Ferdinand was assassinated three weeks later on the 28th of June and war broke out a month afterwards, though the imperialistic ambitions of the Kaiser had for a long time been matter of public record. By the the 12th of August[27], Belgium was swept aside, England had declared war on Germany and seven German armies were invading France and the conflict which was meant to be "over by Christmas" turned, within a year, into a murderous stalemate that killed nearly a generation of young men and destroyed the ideals of the survivors. Boddy was a few months off his 60th birthday[28]. Neither he, nor anyone else, seems to have been prescient of the horrors that were to come, and when it was clear that the war was not going to be short-lived, Boddy unhesitatingly, though with an initial note of resigned sadness, defended the British government's interpretation of events - a decision which did not endear him to those of his pentecostal brethren who became conscientious objectors. The final Convention is well documented in *Confidence* both because General Booth's son-in-law, Arthur Booth-Clibborn who had a journalistic flair, was asked to record his overall impressions and because a short summary of every address at the Convention was given in addition to verbatim (and presumably stenographically reproduced) accounts of the longer sermons.

The German brethren again did much of the preaching, and their sense of grave responsibility was perceived by their listeners. Booth-Clibborn wrote one of the words frequently uttered with intense solemnity during the Convention (and chiefly by our beloved Pastor Paul) was the "sense of responsibility" which rested upon the hearts of the leaders, and which they sought to convey to the gathering; responsibility in view of the incomparably grave character of the present time in the world's history, the consummation of the ages, the "last hour" before the coming of the Lord, and the imperative call now needed to *entire sanctification* of *spirit, soul and body*. (*Confidence* June 1914, p 103)

Attendance at the Convention was "much larger than in past years"[29] and "the light, the life, the love, and the (true) liberty have steadily risen, and have come to highest expression in this the Seventh"[30] - certainly no feelings of nationalism prevented genuine friendship between English and German delegates, whatever the posturings of their governments. The millennial expectations of the Convention were fuelled by political events in Europe as well as by theological understandings of the outpouring of the Holy Spirit in the history of the Church. The political and the theological perspectives might combine (as they did in some Welsh pentecostal churches in the 1930s when Mussolini was identified with anti-Christ) or remain separate. In practice the call to personal holiness was an answer to both perspectives. The preaching at the Convention included a series on "The Resurrection Life" which explored the believer's identification with Christ as the basis and means of personal holiness and "The Present Time in the Light of the Coming of the Lord" which explored an interesting set of themes suggested by the parables of the Kingdom in Matthew's Gospel, namely, scriptural teaching on "night", on "the midnight cry", "the time of awakening" and the "time of expectant waiting". Interwoven with these subjects were talks on more practical topics - healing, women's ministry and the regulation of the gifts of the Spirit in the congregation.

The effects of the 1914 Convention were sustained by the publication of its sermons in the autumn issues of *Confidence*. As the war crisis in Europe deepened, it became necessary to comment on what was taking place. The September issue showed bereavement had struck close to home as several boats had been sunk by gunboats or mines near Sunderland and 200 to 300 people had lost their lives, and letters were printed from French Christians who were caring for the wounded; but there was one from an English soldier (dated Aug 16th 1914) containing the phrase "I don't think the war can last very long, maybe a few months at the most". An article by Albert Weaver entitled "Antichrist and His System" gloomily, but perhaps more accurately, said "we are in the fringes of Tribulation Days...the beginnings of sorrows"[31], and an editorial by Mrs Boddy on Zechariah's Horses asserted that "we feel assured that this terrible time of war is the Word of God going forth in judgment, and therefore we are assured that there will be a triumphant victory of the Holy Spirit of our Christ over the Spirit of Antichrist, which is so evident in the arrogance, cruelty and vandalism that are being exhibited. It is a spiritual warfare, the instruments being nations, men and women". Boddy himself was touring in the United States, but a note in the October issue calling people to a night of prayer showed how he was thinking. "We British Pentecostal people", he wrote, "should pray very earnestly that Militarism may come to an end through this war; that our Empire should learn its lessons soon through humiliation and penitence, and come out refined and purified to serve the cause of Christ more loyally than before".

Boddy quoted approvingly in the November issue a long extract from a piece by Graham Scroggie. In the first instance he defended the actions of the British government which had honoured its treaty with Belgium and entered the war without preparation. He saw the war as a chastisement from God which Britain fully deserved, but he considered the British action as equivalent to that of the necessary restraint of the village bully: however "it is not the Church of God that has gone to war, but the British Empire, and both are fulfilling divine purposes." After a discussion of the duties of Christian citizenship which, according to Scroggie, weighed in favour of accepting a part in the fighting, he spelled out the grounds for divine judgement as he saw them: "Belgium for her Congo atrocities; Russia for her anti-Judaism; France for her infidelity; and Britain for her pleasure-loving, sabbath-breaking, and intemperance".

No one could accuse Boddy of not caring about the war or the church. He went to work in the war zone[32] for two months in 1915 and continued to fulfil all the duties of his thriving parish, as well as his editorial responsibilities; his congregation had risen to 420 on a Sunday evening and a huge Sunday school demanded his attention[33]. After his death two stained glass windows were placed in the All Saints church in memory of Boddy and his wife[34]. When the Sunderland Conventions ceased[35], he used *Confidence* to inform his readers about similar occasions elsewhere - there was no sense in which he was jealous of what other Christians were achieving. His daughter says he was very "ecumenically minded"[36] and the Conventions were certainly interdenominational. He was pressed to start a recognised pentecostal grouping after the 1914-18 War was over but, by then, he was in his late sixties and remained "firm in his allegiance to the Church of England"[37].

The pentecostal movement did begin to organise itself as a separate fellowship of churches in the 1920s, and Boddy's influenced waned. In two areas, though, the line he had adopted was more or less absorbed by the vigorous young men who launched the Assemblies of God and the Elim Foursquare Alliance. The use of spiritual gifts in a pentecostal meeting is always potentially disruptive and modern studies of the early church have viewed the development of Christian ministries against the polarisation between the charismatic gifts and the institutional forms and structures in which they are contained. If the charismatic gifts are unregulated, there is a danger of subjectivism and therefore doctrinal error; if the institutional offices predominate the church loses a sense of organic unity and spiritual liberty. Boddy chaired a discussion on the subject at the last Convention and it was taken down by a visiting journalist. A Mr H Mogridge of Lytham argued that there was no place in the meeting of Christians for tongues followed by interpretation. Tongues, he argued, had a purely private function and it was clear from Paul's discussion of the matter in 1 Corinthians that prophecy was to be preferred to tongues. By speaking in tongues in a public meeting, Christians were simply demonstrating immaturity. If speaking in tongues was absolutely necessary, it must be interpreted but in general there should be strict control.

Not unnaturally, there were far more speakers who took a different point of view. Yet the reasons the speakers gave for disagreeing indicate the wide diversity of views which were held about the nature of the gifts of the Spirit and their purpose. One speaker considered that an utterance in tongues during a period of prayer or worship could be a prophecy: in fact, prophecy in tongues with interpretation was more powerful than prophecy without the preceding tongues and examples were given of conversions which had taken place as a result of "prophecy in tongues". However one speaker pointed out that he never interpreted an utterance in tongues unless he "realised in his own spirit that God was in the message" - in other words, he said that some public utterances in tongues could be ignored because, as another speaker put it, they were "soulish" rather than spiritual. The nice distinction between the soulish and the spiritual was not further elucidated by the speakers, but it appeared, from what was said later, that some utterances in tongues were left uninterpreted for the very practical reason of discouraging speakers who interrupted meetings too frequently or unhelpfully. An American delegate, Robert Brown, thought that there were two quite different types of utterance in tongues: the first was the "seal of God" demonstrating that a believer had been baptised in the Holy Spirit - and in this case the tongues were irresistible and could not be restrained by the person who was experiencing a pentecostal baptism - and the second was the "gift of tongues" which was only for interpretation in the public meeting. What Mr Brown did not make clear, though, was whether he thought the gift of tongues was conferred independently of baptism in the Spirit and whether this gift was also for private devotions (as Mr Mogridge had contended). The implication of what he said was that tongues should only be heard either in connection with a baptism in the Holy Spirit or as an utterance for interpretation in the public meeting. He therefore appeared to rule out a general speaking or singing in tongues in the worship of Christians either collectively or privately.

Another contributor took a more relaxed view of the matter and thought that, if the Holy Spirit came upon "a brother or sister so that they gave utterance and could not be restrained, he was sure that same Power would hinder the powers that be (the leaders of the meeting) from interfering"[38]. Cecil Polhill was less sure that speaking in tongues was the necessary accompaniment of a baptism in the Holy Spirit and considered that tongues were a sign, but not an evidence, of baptism in the Holy Spirit.

The other area where Boddy's influenced may be discerned is that of women's ministry. Boddy certainly felt that his wife had a right to preach or exhort and her contributions to Conventions and to *Confidence* were manifold. The 1914 Convention discussed women's place in the church and Boddy chaired the meeting[39]. Pastor J Paul (from Berlin) thought that while Scripture forbade a woman to teach, she could encourage and testify and be expected to manifest spiritual gifts, particularly prophecy, though he distinguished between two kinds of prophecy, one which was very much a statement from God to his church - "Thus saith the Lord", and the other which was related to encouragement and admonition. It was the second kind which he expected women to develop. The governance of an assembly should be in the hands of a bishop or overseer or elders, and deaconesses could serve within the context of this governance. Only in exceptional circumstances should women take control of a church (and here he cited the Old Testament example of Deborah), but because he thought that women tended to be more inclined to allow their hearts rather than their heads dictate to them, there was a danger that women who prophesied might be carried away by the spiritual impressions implanted in them. A man with a gift of spiritual discernment should guide women with prophetic gifts to prevent the excesses of over-enthusiasm.

Mr Walshaw (of Halifax) disagreed with the view that it was forbidden for women to teach (1 Tim 2.12-15) on the grounds that the context of St Paul's interdiction was domestic and not ecclesiastic. Boddy intervened at this point and suggested that one should draw a distinction between the gathering of the church, which would be a large group, and a smaller gathering in a home or elsewhere; the boundary between home and church was therefore not as hard and fast as it might seem. Thomas Myerscough accepted what Pastor Paul had said, but with the proviso that a "distinct call from God" could overrule accepted procedures, moreover, of course, there might be exceptional circumstances, for example an assembly composed entirely of women, where exceptional female roles might quite rightly exist. Mr Mogridge, partly on the basis of his experience of Brethrenism and its veto on any female participation in public worship, reasoned that as women might prophesy, and as prophecy implied the ministry of the Word of God, women, if gifted in this direction, might also teach. The discussion was concluded by Pastor Paul with reference to the general oversight of churches. He pointed out that any revelations from the Holy Spirit by whatever means to any member of the congregation had to be "proved by other members of the church", especially the leaders of the congregation. Ephesians 4.11 speaks of apostles, prophets, evangelists, pastors and teachers and the influence of such leaders had to be respected. The prophet would not necessarily be the leader of a church; thus the more charismatic and revelational gifts within the body of believers was to be counterbalanced by the contributions and approval of the other ministries which God had given to the church. If, initially a prophetic directive seemed out of God's will, then, the prophet, should be prepared to submit to the guidance of the leadership. Equally, a spiritual person would be prepared to wait while the leadership of the church prayed over what had at first seemed an unacceptable revelation.

It was without doubt the reasonable and balanced discussion of potentially explosive issues at Sunderland which enabled the pentecostal movement to cope with the new burst of spiritual power which its people were enjoying. The full implications for church order and life of the pentecostal blessing were beginning to be realised. The division between laity and clergy was in theory to become nearly irrelevant; the variety of Christian ministries was seen to be much greater than traditionally understood; the supernatural dimension of Christianity was to become part and parcel of every believer's experience; study of the Bible helped in the solution of practical questions. The legacy of the Conventions which Boddy initiated was very considerable. In Assemblies of God there has always been a place, even if it is a small one, for women pastors. Likewise the relationship between the gifts of the Holy Spirit and the ministry gifts of Ephesians 4 has been maintained in equilibrium; and both of these have been measured against the objective standard of Scripture. As a result the dangers of subjectivism and fanaticism have largely been avoided. The Christian ministry has been seen as a divine calling but, at the same time, it has been recognised that every Christian is, to some extent, a minister. Moreover, the priority given to missionary projects, and the liaison between the Pentecostal Missionary Union (the PMU) and the Sunderland Conventions, was established. Boddy's own travels were, in a sense, transmuted into an organised missionary concern, and his friendship with Cecil Polhill, one of the original Cambridge Seven who went to China, were a bequest to the Assemblies of God when it was launched in 1924. The PMU was taken over by the fledgling AoG fellowship and both prospered together.

Boddy himself continued to be vicar of All Saints, Sunderland till 1922 when he was offered the living of Pittington, five miles away. He visited his parishioners, who were mainly miners, and so soon built up his congregation. His ministrations to the sick and those hurt in pit accidents were much appreciated but until 1926, when he was over 70, he still found time to bring out *Confidence*. After the Balfour Declaration of 1917 he saw the return of the Jews to their homeland as a further sign that the return of Christ was near and he continued to maintain the validity and reality of the baptism in the Holy Spirit. The immediate post-war years were difficult for the pentecostal movement "leadership wavered and disappointed" (Gee, 1967: 110) but Boddy's rejection of the pacifist position during the 1914-18 War and his adherence to Anglican views on infant baptism[40] distanced him from the up and coming generation of pentecostal leaders who were beginning to emerge; this was especially so after 1916 when conscription became compulsory. Nevertheless His gracious personality and his ministry at the Conventions, as well as the forum he provided for a rational and harmonious discussion of the problems and possibilities of a church where every member had experienced the baptism in the Holy Spirit, enabled the young men 40 years his junior to avoid some of the pitfalls which would have destroyed and divided them as they set out into the unknown; an unknown which was to lead to the formation of Elim and Assemblies of God.

Notes to Pages 17 - 40

1. The final (9th) page of the undated memoir contains the phrase , "although it is nearly 40 years since he died". Since Boddy died in 1930, the memoir must have been written just before 1970. It is a typewritten document and was found in the archives at the General Offices of Assemblies of God at Nottingham. It was originally written for Martin Robinson, who was doing research on Boddy (see bibliography). Mary Boddy was then at the Anglican Convent in Grahamstown, South Africa.

2. See The Oxford Dictionary of the Christian Church (1984), OUP, p 1470

3. Boddy was sent to All Saints, Sunderland in 1884, but did not become its vicar till 1886 because the previous incumbent refused to resign.

4. This is a point made by Jane Vazeille Boddy's memoir, p 2.

5. Jane Vazeille Boddy's memoir dates this invitation after 1906, but this seems a year or two later than one would expect. The prayer meeting seems to have been an indirect result of the Welsh Revival. As Donald Gee in Wind and Flame p15 pointed out "When that eventful year 1906 drew to a close the Pentecostal Movement had not yet commenced in the British Isles, but there were, as we have already seen, prayer meetings being held all over the country for a yet deeper Revival than that which had so recently visited Wales".

6. See Jane Vazeille Boddy's memoir p 9.

7. Original photographs of the Sunderland Conventions are to be found, among other places, in the vestry of Hebron Church (in fellowship with Assemblies of God), North Bridge Street, Sunderland.

8. Boddy had written a book entitled The Laying-on of Hands in 1895, probably published by SPCK who, according to Jane Vazeille Boddy (p 2), were responsible for other books by Boddy, like Christ in His Holy Land, in 1897.

9. See, for example, S Tugwell (1971), Did You Receive the Spirit?, London: DLT, who because of his sacramental theology, prefers to speak of the manifestation of baptism, ie the manifestation of the Spirit who is received during Christian initiation.

10. Barratt (1927) tells how his father, a Cornishman and ardent Methodist, accepted the offer a job as manager of a new mine being sunk in Norway. The young T B Barratt was educated at the Wesleyan College at Taunton and went home to Norway in the summer holidays.

11. quoted from Tongues in Sunderland a pamphlet by Boddy, which is included on p 149, 150 of Barratt (1927)

12. Unless otherwise indicated in the text, the term "baptised in the Spirit" will be assumed to mean "baptised in the Spirit and spoke in tongues". This usage is common in the pentecostal movement, especially the Assemblies of God, but is less common in other

sections of the charismatic/pentecostal movement where a variety of positions are adopted ranging from that outline by Tugwell in note 9 above to that accepted by the Elim Pentecostal Church which contends that the "baptism of the Spirit" takes place after conversion and will be accompanied by "signs following", but not necessarily by tongues. The terminology of "filled with the Spirit", "baptised with the Spirit", "receiving the Spirit" is sometimes used in theological literature to designate the same experience and sometimes to differentiate between distinct experiences.

13. Reports also appeared in the Morning Leader (Oct3rd, 4th and 5th), the Edinburgh Evening Dispatch (8th Oct), Lloyds Weekly News (Oct 6th) and the local North Mail.

14. According to Robinson (1976) the League had five centres in Sunderland and sold nearly 800 copies of its magazine Tongues of Fire in the area.

15. See November 1907 issue of Tongues of Fire.

16. See Harris's editorial in Tongues of Fire April 1907, p 9.

17. Boddy refers in the same article to "the anniversary of my baptism in 1892" and the implication must be that he had undergone some form of believer's baptism because he must already have undergone infant baptism in childhood at his clerical father's hands.

18. Robinson (1976) suggests that Boddy modified his views on the function of speaking with tongues as an indicator of the baptism in the Holy Spirit. In 1910 Boddy wrote in Confidence (Vol 3, no 11) "The experience of these years of Pentecostal fellowship with many at home and abroad, fellowship with some of the Lord's best has caused the writer to feel thus: He could not say of a stranger who came to him 'speaking in Tongues', 'This man is baptised in the Holy Ghost because he speaks in Tongues'. He would also have to see DIVINE LOVE".

19. "Bishop Handley Moule, who was Bishop of Durham during those years was always friendly towards my father and probably sympathetic in his own mind, though he warned him that he could not promote him or send him to another parish, as the clergy, as a whole, were antagonistic, and none of them came to the Conventions" (from Jane Vaizelle Boddy's memoir, p 7). More to the point, the Reader Harris of the Pentecostal League attacked the work at Sunderland and occasioned a public reply from Boddy in the Sunderland Echo; see Cartwright (1976).

20. Thomas Myerscough, a local estate agent, taught at what Donald Gee (1967:54) described as a "pentecostal centre" in Preston. Among his pupils were W P F Burton, James Salter, George Jeffreys, Percy Corry and E J Phillips (see Boulton, 1928: 13). Myserscough was for a short time in charge of the official Bible School of the Pentecostal Missionary Union. According to Donald Gee, Myerscough was an "outstanding expositor of the Holy Scriptures". Gee himself was, according to Robinson (1976), one of the only later pentecostal leaders who did not attend Sunderland; Gee's writings, though, read as if he had first hand impressions - he must have talked closely to those who did attend.

21. According to Boulton (1928:15) George Jeffreys was one of the speakers at the 1913 Sunderland Convention.

22. Printing costs given in the April and September issues are £13-9-2^d and £13-15-0^d respectively and these would suggest print-runs of just about 5000 copies. The high figure given in the July issue could be accounted for by visitors to the Convention.

23. See Confidence for April 1913, p 74.

Cornelis van der Laan analysed the proceedings of the leaders' meetings (1908-11) and of the International Pentecostal Council (1912-14) in a lucid article in the EPTA Bulletin (VI.3) (1987). He shows various pastoral, apologetic, doctrinal and organisational topics were discussed/decided. He suggests that the "German position" which minimised the importance of speaking in tongues eventually prevailed. As a result Barratt, who took a line which emphasised tongues, turned towards a more denominational view and began to think in terms of pentecostal churches.

24. These are given consecutively in the autumn issues of Confidence for 1913.

25. See Confidence for Sept 1913, p 183.

26. See Confidence for Sept 1913, p 177.

27. See Liddell Hart, B (1970), History of the First World War, London: Pan, p49.

28. He was born on November 15th 1854.

29. See Confidence (June 1914) p 106.

30. See Confidence (June 1914) p 104.

31. See Confidence (Sept 1914), p 167.

32. See Confidence (June 1915), p 107.

33. See Confidence (June 1914), p 106.

34. See the Centenary Magazine 1849-1949, p 18

35. According to Gee (1967:93) the north east coast was considered dangerous during the war and this rendered Sunderland unsuitable for Conventions.

36. Jane Vazeille Boddy's Memoir, p 6.

37. Jane Vazeille Boddy's Memoir says "My father told me that considerable pressure had been brought to bear on him to start a Pentecostal Movement, but he was firm in his allegiance to the Church of England and felt he could not conscientiously leave it; also he was too old" (p 8). The editorial for Confidence March 1911 is more explicit and emphatic, "The Editor...does not feel that the Lord's leading...is to set up a new Church".

38. See Confidence (December 1914) p 236.

39. See Confidence (November 1914), p 208f.

40. See Donald Gee (1967: 76) "all visitors to the Conventions did not accept the beloved Chairman's Anglican views concerning baptism in water".

WIDER THAN SUNDERLAND

The Jeffreys brothers and Elim

Sometimes as a result of the spiritual impact of Boddy's ministry at Sunderland, and sometimes independently of it, there were signs of new life and developing leadership in other parts of the British Isles. George and Stephen Jeffreys, two brothers who were "children of the revival" from Maesteg, Wales, were not connected with the pentecostal movement until Edward, Stephen's ten year old son, unexpectedly spoke in tongues while he was on holiday with his family in 1910. The young Edward was heard to speak in tongues by his father and uncle and quoted Scripture in Welsh with a "quite unwonted" facility[1]. A few days later George Jeffreys found himself singing in tongues one Sunday morning, though not long before he had preached against the experience. All accounts agree that both the Jeffreys brothers were gifted speakers and that, quite soon after they were launched on their ministries, extraordinary miracles followed their preaching. George was the younger and the better planner of the two, and it was George who began to gather a band of men and women around him who became the nucleus of the Elim Alliance.

George's Bible training was given as an indirect result of the formation of the Pentecostal Missionary Union. The PMU (as it was usually called) began at a meeting chaired by Alexander Boddy on January 9th, 1909, in the Vicarage at All Saints' Sunderland. Cecil Polhill became the president and held the post until 1925 when the PMU was merged into Assemblies of God. The work of the Union entailed the training of missionaries and, to this end, various homes and schools were established[2]. Soon after 1910 the PMU sent its male candidates to be taught by Thomas Myerscough in Preston and the young George Jeffreys, after being given satisfactory references - presumably by those who had heard his evangelistic sermons, was taken on from November 1912 till January 1913[3] and then asked to give a series of Gospel addresses at the 1913 Sunderland Convention each evening[4]. One of the visitors to the Convention was William Gillespie and, after hearing Jeffreys preach, he and his brother, enclosing three ten shilling notes with their letter, invited George Jeffreys to their home at 22 Pine Street, Belfast, in 1913 with the intention that he hold an evangelistic campaign in the area. Jeffreys made the sea crossing and, while war was raging in Europe, started to forge the principles and gain the practical experience which was to stand him in good stead for the next twenty or thirty years. Essentially Jeffreys was a powerful and logical preacher who prayed for the sick at the end of his meetings, but his administrative flair and commanding personality led to the founding of a network of several hundred new churches which became one of the main expressions of pentecostal life in the United Kingdom.

A souvenir booklet surveying the first 21 years of the Elim Foursquare Gospel Alliance[5] gives a brief year by year account of the growth of the Elim movement under George Jeffreys. After the 1915 campaign in Monaghan in Ireland, 1916 saw the introduction of a 275 seater tent for meetings in other parts of Ireland and, as evidence of the seriousness with which foundations were laid, a statement of beliefs was published. 1917 "a year of national gloom" saw the continuance of Jeffreys's tent work in Lisburn and Ballymena and the opening of a Hall in Hunter Street, Belfast, which became the first permanent Elim assembly. In 1918 the name "Elim Pentecostal Alliance" was changed to "Elim Foursquare Gospel Alliance" apparently to emphasise the evangelistic nature of the work and to formalise its message. The "Foursquare" Gospel proclaimed Christ as Saviour, Healer, Baptiser and Soon-Coming King; both the present power of Christ to heal and the ministry of Christ as Baptiser in the Holy Ghost were underlined by this new name - as were millennial expectations. As a mark of the growing property holdings of the Elim movement, 1919 saw the first church buildings placed under the protection of a special legal trust. The intention of this legal enactment was to safeguard buildings from exploitation by dominant or wealthy individuals within a local congregation, but as we shall see the other side of this coin prevented local congregations owning the buildings they had paid for and therefore removed control of property to a more central agency. As another sign of the establishment of the Elim work, a quarterly magazine described as a "record of spiritual life and work", started in December 1919. Within a few years the magazine became monthly, then fortnightly and then weekly. Until 1921, Jeffreys had concentrated his evangelistic attention in Ireland, Wales or the Channel Islands, but that year he began a crusade in Leigh-on-Sea, Essex, and from there, in 1922, he prepared to work in London, starting at Clapham. Between 1922 and 1936 altogether 36 buildings were taken over for use by Elim congregations in the London area. The next year, 1923, marked the beginning of overseas missionary efforts in both Congo and Mexico and later Spain. In 1924 a publishing house was established, and this grew rapidly till, in ten years, it required a three story building.

Boddy, of course, knew George Jeffreys and realised that the evangelistic campaigns were resulting in the creation of entirely new groups of believers. While Boddy was looking east towards the war in Europe, Jeffreys was looking west to the spiritual needs of Ireland. When the war finished, and a new normality returned, Jeffreys was already half way to begetting a fresh and entirely pentecostal denomination. Before looking at the foundation of a second pentecostal grouping - made up of congregations and leaders who were outside Jeffreys's orbit - it is necessary to consider a third pentecostal grouping, the Apostolics, which had begun to emerge.

The Apostolics

The Apostolic Church began in Wales among Christians who had become committed to Christ during the 1904 Revival. D P Williams, who became one of the Apostolics' leading figures and founding fathers was baptised in the Spirit some time in 1909 at Aberaenon, presumably as an indirect result of Sunderland's influence. Williams heard prophecy given in the Mission Hall at Penygroes and Turnbull (1959: 18) quotes the exact words which Williams heard. Such was the immediacy and force of the prophecy, and its relevance to Williams's own life, that he began to teach that the nine gifts of the Holy Spirit spoken of in 1 Corinthians 12 must also be accompanied by the five ministry gifts of Christ in Ephesians chapter 4; in other words, while he concurred with the majority of the pentecostal movement as to the contemporary function of the Holy Spirit in the life of a congregation, he also insisted that modern church government should install the offices which had been recognised in the New Testament. Williams, however, came to teach that the prophetic office in the church should be expected to "give governmental words of prophecy" and, indeed, "the prophet reveals doctrinal truths to the Church". The Apostolic Church admits that "it is in regard to governmental callings that have come through the prophets, especially in regard to the calling of certain persons for certain positions in the Body of Christ, and to certain spheres of labour, that there have [sic] been great opposition today" (Turnbull, 1959: 176,177). Similarly, the role of apostles is publicly defined and those men designated apostles are to be set apart for their authoritative tasks. This practice is briefly discussed by Hollenweger (1972: 193) in his massive study of pentecostalism and he concludes by quoting Donald Gee (of Assemblies of God) that

to bestow New Testament titles of office upon men and women

and then to consider that by doing so we are creating apostolic assemblies parallel to those in the Primitive Church is very much like children playing at churches

and a German Pentecostal pastor, Arnold Hitzer

the system of ministries in the Apostolic Church hinders the true power of ministries truly instituted by God.

The thrust, then, of the majority pentecostal criticism of the Apostolics was that those men designated apostles and prophets were not in fact and reality of the calibre their titles implied; for their part the Apostolics attempted largely successfully to surmount criticism by avoiding bitter arguments. During the 1914-18 War the Apostolics began to organise themselves as a separate and distinct group of churches in the British Isles. As the quotations above show, the rest of the pentecostal movement did not accept the Apostolics' understanding of apostolic and prophetic offices with the important result that Elim and Assemblies of God drew up their constitutions in such a way as to emphasise the roles of pastors and evangelists; by and large the Assemblies of God tended to see apostolic labours as being demonstrated overseas in the planting of new churches and any similar work in the British Isles was regarded as pioneer evangelism. As we shall see only in recent years has there been a widespread reconsideration of prophetic and apostolic functions.

Smith Wigglesworth
In addition to the pentecostal denominations which were in the process of being formed during or before the 1914-18 War, there were also numerous individuals who were active one way or another in the widening pentecostal circle. One of the most colourful and respected of these was Smith Wigglesworth who became an almost legendary figure in his own life time. At one stage he seemed to epitomise pentecostalism. He was poorly educated, gruff, uninhibited somewhat unpredictable and said to have read only one book all his life - the Bible. Yet he travelled all over the world, possessed an amazing faith in Christ's power to heal and was reputed to have raised the dead.

Wigglesworth was born in Yorkshire in 1859, the grandson of an active old-time Wesleyan Methodist who took the lad along to chapel. His family were poor and industrious and he began to work long hours in the turnip fields at the age of six, and when he was only nine years old he got a full-time job at the local textile mill where he had to keep going for twelve hours a day. Throughout his childhood he prayed, indeed he said "I can never recollect a time when I did not long for God"[6]. His schooling was cut short by the need to help his family's finances and when, at about 23 years of age, he married a Salvation Army girl who was a fiery preacher, he was more or less illiterate. One of the first things she did was to teach him to read though, as he pointed out, she never made much progress in helping him to spell! While she worked at the Bowland Street Mission, Wigglesworth carried on a prospering plumbing business in Bradford but also became active in the Mission especially as he was impressed by its emphasis on the "prayer of faith" and divine healing. Polly Wigglesworth frequently preached and Smith "was often by the penitent form to lead souls to Christ"[7]. Despite his continued uncertainty about his ability to preach, he zealously talked to individuals in their homes while doing their plumbing or in the street and would often take ill and infirm people along to meetings for prayer. In the absence of any of the leaders of the Leeds Healing Home (who were attending the Keswick convention), Wigglesworth found himself asked to conduct the service there and was as amazed as anyone else when he prayed for a man on crutches who was instantly healed. His own faith was later strengthened when, after prayer and the laying on of hands, he survived an acute attack of appendicitis; his theology became very simple and straightforward: any sickness whatever was from the devil and could be resisted and removed by aggressive faith. Not even when several years later he suffered painful kidney stones would Wigglesworth budge from this position.

Whilst it is true that Wigglesworth was in many respects a simple man, his simplicity was profound, and the stenographic   records of his later sermons show him to have had a fine command of English, which was, of course, based almost entirely on the King James Version of the Bible. His theology, though it centred on faith, was enlivened by spiritual experiences of unusual power. His description of his baptism in the Holy Spirit is given in *Confidence* (Oct 15th 1908, p 15)

> At about 11 am., Tuesday morning, at All Saints' Vicarage, I asked a sister [Mrs Boddy] to help me to the witness of the Baptism of the Holy Ghost. She laid hands on me in the presence of a brother. The fire fell and burned in me till the Holy Spirit clearly revealed absolute purity before God. At this point she was called out of the room, and during her absence a marvellous revelation took place, my body became full of

light and Holy Presence, and in the revelation I saw an empty Cross and at the same time the Jesus I loved and adored crowned in the Glory in a Reigning Position. The glorious remembrance of these moments is beyond my expression to give - when I could not find words to express, then an irresistible Power filled and moved my being till I found to my glorious astonishment I was speaking in other tongues clearly.

One almost immediate result of Wigglesworth's pentecostal experience was that he began to preach. Indeed, his wife challenged him to do so straight after his visit to Sunderland and when he spoke during the next Sunday meeting at Bowland Street, she exclaimed afterwards "that's not my Smith, Lord, that's not my Smith"! The tongue-tied plumber became an unusual orator. All accounts agree[8] that Wigglesworth needed "the anointing" as a preacher, but that when he was inspired he was remarkable. He would sometimes speak in tongues during a sermon and then give the interpretation himself with the result that "the preacher himself probably little understood the sheer theological depth and insight of his own words"[9].

When assessing the origins of the pentecostal movement in the United Kingdom, it is important to realise that those early recipients of the baptism in the Holy Spirit, especially those who had travelled to Sunderland in search of the power of God, were mature Christians. In Wigglesworth's case, he already believed in divine healing before his own Spirit-baptism and he was an ardent personal evangelist as well as a man of prayer. In some ways, therefore, it is no surprise that almost immediately after his enduement with the Holy Spirit, he became a force to be reckoned with[10]. *Confidence* for April 1913, December 1914, May 1916, March-April 1917, April-June 1919, July-September 1919 and April-June 1922 all mention Wigglesworth in one way or another. By 1913 Wigglesworth was holding annual Easter Conventions at Bradford which were occasions for healing as well as exposition of Scripture by speakers like Thomas Myerscough[11]. By 1914 he was in California and saw "not less than 1500 people healed"[12]. The Bradford Conventions continued despite the constraints imposed by the Great War, and to this extent the absence of the Sunderland conventions was less felt. After the war, Wigglesworth continued to convene at Bradford and saw that money was raised there for foreign missions (£1,200 was raised in 1919). He was preaching in Australia in 1922 and reports of the meetings were given in the Melbourne "Argus"[13].

Donald Gee

The life of Donald Gee is probably better documented than that of any of the other pentecostal pioneers of his generation because Gee was, from quite early in his ministry, a diligent writer and several times combined autobiography with teaching[14]. Gee was born in 1891[15] and was the only child of a widowed mother, a circumstances which may explain his later tendency to solitariness[16]. Mother and son attended the thriving Finsbury Park Congregational Church in North London and Gee heard the Welsh evangelist Seth Joshua preach in October 1905[17] and "personally accepted Christ as his Saviour"[18]. For two years Gee was more interested in the social side of his church than any other and avoided the Christian Endeavour Society which his mother attended because he shrank from its consecration and missionary connotations. In 1907, however, after a CE meeting he went up to his attic-bedroom at home and prayed till he had a sense of peaceful resolution that he would, if necessary, be prepared to forsake the security and comforts of home for the foreign mission field. His mother's transfer of affiliation to a Baptist church in 1912 annoyed him and her decision to undergo baptism by immersion in water infuriated him but he soon followed her example while retaining his membership at Finsbury Park and his job as assistant organist. Water baptism threw him into a panic - "I felt as if my very reason would snap as a result of the intensity of the spiritual conflict", he later wrote[19]. His mother continued to search for more real communion with God and she began to attend late night prayer meetings at a Missionary Rest Home with the result that her son felt obliged to accompany her because she walked back to her own home after midnight. The prayer meeting had a pentecostal element and for three months Gee and his mother attended until, in March 1913, Gee experienced a new fullness beyond words,

> and found it becoming increasingly difficult to adequately voice all the glory in my soul. This went on for about two weeks, and then one night, when praying all alone by my bedside before retiring, and when once again finding no English adequate to express the overflowing fullness of my soul, I found myself beginning to utter words in a new tongue. I was in a condition of spiritual ecstasy and wholly taken up with the Lord[20].

A year later he married a girl from the Finsbury Park church who had followed the same path as he had. She had been baptised in water by immersion and then in the Holy Spirit. The young couple moved in with Mrs Gee senior and Gee followed the family business (of signwriting) while devoting their spare time to their new pentecostal fellowship. When conscription was introduced in 1916, Gee had to make a difficult decision about his attitude to pacifism. He chose conscientious objection and in July 1916 came before a tribunal which was empowered to send him to prison if it found against him. A clergyman sat on the bench opposite him and the very last question to be flung was "young man, would you be willing to be a foreign missionary ?"[21]. Gee was able to given an honest affirmative answer and, twenty minutes later, he was told that he was exempt from military service on the understanding that he take up any work of "national importance". His wife's uncle owned a farm in Buckinghamshire and within a fortnight he was able to become a farm labourer. He transferred to a neighbouring farm when the uncle died a year later. He found his duties onerous, exhausting in the extreme because he had to be active for sixteen or seventeen hours a day, and socially agonising because, belonging to a small group of "conchies" (as conscientious objectors were derisively called), he was ostracised and the object of venomous insults and threats from the locals. Moreover he perfectly understood the grounds for which he was hated by people whose fathers and sons were in imminent danger on the western front. "I could not but appreciate their point of view, though it made my mental suffering all the harder"[22]. He began to speak in a local mission hall on the Sundays and, ever afterwards, he looked back at his war years as a time when God put iron into his character while, at the same time, giving him a ministerial initiation.

Returning to London after the war, he tried to resume his old trade, but with the growing conviction that he should enter the ministry. The Gees went through about two years of extreme poverty and were forced to sell some of their wedding presents to make ends meet. At last an invitation to become the pastor of an assembly at in Edinburgh arrived and, after a journey northwards to inspect the situation, he accepted and moved his young family once more. The summer of 1920 dawned fair.

Gee later wrote about his pastorate in *Bonnington Toll* [23] which is an almost unique document of the life of a pentecostal pastor in the 1920s. Gee was not a typical pastor (as his later life and ministry showed) but the expectations of his people probably indicate the sort of pattern many other pastors followed. The assembly building was an "unattractive low-roofed, double-fronted shop in the poorest part of Leith"[24] and the congregation numbered thirteen people the first Sunday morning. In the evening, before the service, a short open-air gathering (at which the Gospel was presumably preached) was held just outside the front doors, and the evening attendance was rather larger the morning's.

During the week he worked punctiliously at his desk every morning between 9 and 12 and in the afternoons he visited members of his congregation in large tenement buildings and would usually read some verses of Scripture and then pray.

Gee's problems were significant. He had, as was common then, a low income and he also had to cope with members of the assembly who had "previously enjoyed almost unlimited opportunity for self-expression, however unedifying to others"[25]. His own position seemed insecure because when he began to give some leadership to the congregation, there was a temptation to regard him simply as an employee to be dismissed at will. Gee therefore devised a system for supplying his own salary which allowed him to be seen as "the servant of God before being the servant of men"[26]. He arranged for a box to be placed at the door and for the amount of money given each week to be notified on a small blackboard. There were no collections and he undertook to pay the running costs of the assembly first before taking the remainder of the money to support his wife and children. Members of the assembly were expected to draw their own conclusions about whether what was given each week was sufficient. This system gave Gee control over what would, in later years and in other pentecostal churches, have been delegated to a group of deacons. It is perhaps no surprise that he felt that considerable resistance to his leadership developed and he was driven to desperate prayer and a fortnight in London to restore his sense of calmness and equilibrium. The most wealthy family in the assembly, and the family which had originally invited Gee to Edinburgh, were the Berulsdens[27] and their financial support was crucial in the early days. When they announced that they were emigrating to Australia, it was a bombshell to the assembly as a whole and to Gee in particular. It seemed that he would be starved out of the pastorate because it would leave in the ascendancy those who had previously dominated the meetings. At the hour of trial, however, Gee's wife inherited several hundred pounds and the drop in the weekly offerings caused by the departure of the Berulsdens was off-set from this private store of capital. As things settled down and the months passed the assembly and the weekly offering began to grow again steadily. Then, to Gee's dismay, trouble loomed from a completely different direction as a rival and "aggressive sect" opened its doors in direct competition with the work at Bonnington Toll; Gee's congregants were canvassed to join the newcomers. Gee defended his system of church government - which was the bone of contention - and grew, as he admitted, acrimonious in the controversy to the extent that the ordinary meetings of his flock became hard and metallic[28] until he realised what was happening and then put matters right by praying for his "enemies".

These three areas of difficulty: financial stringency, undisciplined dominant individuals within the church and spiritual rivalry outside it are probably typical of much nonconformist activity. They have certainly persisted throughout much of the twentieth century. In one respect Gee's handling of the situation was made easier by the fact that he was the first pastor his congregation had ever had. He had no constitutional challenge to his leadership and no tradition to break, but he did have to work out all his answers freshly from biblical first principles and some of his later writing on church life and its problems show how sanely and systematically he applied himself to the Scriptures.

Gee went to Edinburgh in 1920 and the fellowship of Assemblies of God was not formed till 1924. The church grew steadily as Gee kept to an exhausting routine with meetings almost every night of the week and monthly conventions on selected Saturdays to which neighbouring churches were invited. George Jeffreys began to build the Elim Alliance up and Gee was interested in joining. There is an extant set of letters between Gee and members of the growing Elim organisation in which the whole matter is discussed[29]. The letters reveal Gee as both spiritually sensitive and cautious. The matter was complicated by the ownership of the building at Bonnington Toll which, under the terms of the Elim constitution, would have had to be handed over to Elim. On April 10th 1923 Gee wrote "I have written Bro Henderson seeking for myself and the Assembly here to become associated with the Elim Alliance" and he went on to give a partial account of what must have been a change of heart "I scarcely know what explanation to give you of my taking such a step in view of my past attitude, but three years in Scotland has been a hard school in which I have perhaps learnt one or two lessons". He went on, "Pray for me. I am pressed on every hand". The exact nature of the affiliation with the Elim Alliance that he wanted is made clearer from a letter written on the same day to Mr Henderson in which he says,

> For the present my wish is for myself and the Assembly to become *associated* with the Elim work, - as your second proposition.

This could always lead to a complete merging of the work here with the Alliance, - as your first proposition, - as the Lord makes His will and time clear. [original underlining]

The hard lessons of Scotland must have shown Gee that he would have been well served by some kind of support and fellowship exterior to the local church. Jeffreys was, however, revising his constitution, and one of the trustees at Bonnington Toll had reservations about handing the deeds of the building over to the Alliance Council (which had been set up specifically to hold property in trust for the Elim movement as a whole). The trustee's reservations - as well as the incompetence of the solicitor handling the assembly's affairs - delayed the transaction long enough for Gee to wait until he should have an opportunity to see the provisions and obligations of the new constitution. When he saw it, he decided to retain the assembly's independence. In a letter of the 18th July 1923 he wrote to Mr Phillips expressing his disappointment. "It is with considerable disappointment that I feel unable to join the Alliance by signing the pledge.....much as I have come to see the value and legitimate place of organisation in the Church of God, - I feel at present that this Constitution exceeds that which I am prepared to subscribe to....I feel personally that I ought not tie myself up to this extent". Gee backed graciously away from the restrictions, as he saw them, of the Elim constitution. A year later he was to join the rather looser structure of Assemblies of God.

John Nelson Parr
The early life of Nelson Parr is told in his autobiography *Incredible* (which he he published and distributed himself). Parr was born in 1886, educated at Ross Place Council School in Manchester where he passed the scholarship examination that opened the door for him to continue to the next stage of schooling. But because his home was "impoverished by drink" he was forced to go out to work in textile engineering at the age of thirteen. He was full of energy and liked both football and cross-country running. In April 1904 he went to a Young People's Club where, after a sermon , he gave his life to Christ and soon became involved in open-air preaching and the distribution of tracts. After passing the qualifying examinations in Latin and Greek, he nearly entered a theological seminary, but on the advice of an evangelist in the Manchester Holiness Church, he gave that plan up and began to think of missionary work in Tibet. He continued ceaselessly to consecrate

himself to all kinds of evangelistic activity while absorbing all he could from the preachers who came to Manchester and from visits to the Keswick Convention. News of the pentecostal outpouring at Sunderland generated great excitement in the Holiness Church where Parr worshipped, but because the leadership of the church were suspicious of all that was associated with "speaking in tongues", Parr left and joined himself to a group of Plymouth Brethren in Stanley Hall, Manchester, who were praying to receive the pentecostal baptism. At a Christmas Convention in 1910, a number of people who had spoken in tongues as a result of visits to Sunderland, were invited from Preston and Kilsyth to minister at Stanley Hall and in the evening of a service on Christmas Day Parr spoke in tongues and continued to do so until 2 am the next morning. For the next four years "revival fire was burning gloriously" (Parr, 1972:24).

Because many of pentecostal leaders were imprisoned for conscientious objection during the Great War, the pentecostal movement faltered and, when in 1917 Parr, who then held a senior management post at Crossley Bros, became part-time pastor of his assembly in Longsight, there were only about fifteen people in attendance. The church itself had relapsed into traditional Brethrenism in that it refused to allow musical instruments during the communion services and vetoed any female participation. Parr set about restoring the situation and, by 1923, the Manchester Pentecostal Church was beginning to thrive[30].

The Carter brothers

The two Carter brothers had quite different personalities. Howard, the older, was a man of remarkable faith whose character included the contradictory traits of meticulous tidiness and unpredictability. John was orderly and organised in all that he did, predictable, reliable and gracious and, in his early years, a fine evangelist with a gift for thorough expository preaching[31]. Because they did not marry until relatively late in life (John was about 35 and Howard was 65), the two brothers were able to work together on many occasions.

Howard was born in 1891 and John in 1893. Howard had a speech impediment all his life - though in later years the only sign of this was a deliberateness in his choice of words while he preached. John's strength of resolve in later life probably stems from his childhood determination to minimise his own speech difficulty[32]. Their godly mother took both boys to the Church of England and Howard sang in the choir. Their father was employed as an "inventor" with a large firm of gun-makers (one of his inventions is still in the Science Museum in South Kensington) and his hobby was bellringing, which prevented him from attending church. Howard inherited his father's inventive and artistic faculties and set his heart on becoming an art teacher. When he was about eighteen years old, and while he was training to fulfil his ambition, he became a Christian at a small informal "Church of Christ" in a suburb of Birmingham and, after tussling with his conscience for several months, walked out of the art school leaving his paints, brushes and palette behind for ever. He never allowed himself to take up painting again.

The two brothers heard about the Sunderland Conventions and went there in 1912 with their mother. A few weeks later, when she was at home alone, Mrs Carter spoke in tongues and, soon afterwards, was healed of chronic arthritis when Howard suggested she should specifically pray for to this end. The faith of both brothers was encouraged by the miracle in their home, but neither received the baptism in the Spirit immediately. They went to Sunderland again each year at Whitsun and were impressed with what they saw and heard. In 1914 a pentecostal convention was arranged at Bedford. Howard spent four days in prayer and fasting "until I was so faint I could hardly walk about. I let everyone put their hands upon me but I did not experience the least scrap of power"[33].

A year later at the 1915 Bedford Convention, Howard Carter found what he was looking for

> To describe a spiritual experience is as impossible as to define the sweetness of an apple or the beauty of a flower. I may simply state that the spiritual blessing received that day met the great yearning of my soul, and satisfied me that the experience which I had sought so long was now actually real. The Lord granted me the Gift of the Holy Spirit and the manifestation as on the Day of Pentecost...a definite experience of boundless love and joy filled me[34].

Howard managed to persuade the electrical firm which was employing him as a designer to allow him to work for half the day only. A pentecostal assembly of about ten people was meeting in an upper room in Birmingham and, just before the 1914-1918 War started, Howard assumed leadership of the group. Numbers grew and the pioneering efforts of the two brothers allowed them to begin a second congregation in a different district. Howard left his secular employment completely and felt (typically!) strongly that he should trust Christ for his financial support. Despite a benevolent offer of fees for training in the Church of England ministry, Howard stuck to his decision and continued to look after his little flock.

In 1916 conscription became compulsory. John, who was working in the head office of Lloyds Bank in Birmingham, was exempted on conscientious grounds, but Howard, at another tribunal, was granted exemption on the condition that he undertook medical service. He agreed to this so long as the men he nursed were not returned to the fighting. His request was refused and was about to be dismissed when it was discovered that he was a minister of religion. A civil judge heard the case, but rejected Howard's plea when he learnt that Howard belonged to no recognised denomination. The military police ensured he was taken to Wormwood Scrubbs Prison and nine months later to Dartmoor[35].

While in prison Howard devoted his spare time to the Bible and began to delve into the subject of spiritual gifts. He felt like an explorer looking at uncharted territory. "Here was an important subject which had been strangely neglected by the Church of Christ as a whole"[36]. He began to understand that spiritual gifts were entirely supernatural in their origin, and he later influenced the pentecostal movement very directly by his teaching on 1 Corinthians 12 and 14. His own mature ministry had a clear prophetic element and his ventures of faith - as when he took on the running of a Bible School single-handed, are explicable in terms of his apprehension that faith is a gift imparted by the Holy Spirit and given for special circumstances and occasions. Howard returned to Birmingham after the war, but soon felt a divine calling to London, where he started a new church. A business man gave him over £2000 and he bought a building known as the "People's Hall". The call to London and the supply of a large sum of money were both linked with manifestations of charismatic gifts. Howard was not simply a man who spoke in tongues occasionally. He expected the Holy Spirit to give him prophetic guidance, or healing, or faith, or whatever was required to do God's will. Yet, as his writings show, he was scrupulously orthodox in his understanding of the Person and work of Christ. He was not eccentric or mystical. The result was that the new church at Lee in south London began to grow, particularly after the opening campaign which George Jeffreys and Ernest Darragh conducted in 1920. A new twist in events was to occur, however, when a solicitor named T H Mundell invited Howard to take on the running of a Bible School in

Hampstead which had been used to train missionary candidates accepted by the PMU (Pentecostal Missionary Union). The burden of the Bible School and the new church proved too heavy and so Howard sent for John, who arrived and shared the pastorate.

During Howard's absence in London, John took charge of the assembly in Birmingham and invited Jeffreys and Darragh to hold a campaign there in 1919. This was successful, but an unexpected outcome of it was that John joined the Elim Evangelistic Band in Ireland at the end of the year. There he accepted two short pastorates until he went to join Howard in March 1921.

Between them therefore, and before the formation of Assemblies of God, the Carter brothers had pioneered three new congregations and pastored in another two. They had seen George Jeffreys at work first hand and knew him personally. Howard's insight into spiritual gifts was uniquely comprehensive for its time and supported by a number of personal experiences which confirmed his understanding of the way the Holy Spirit operated. Both of them had seen miracles of healing attend their ministries and both had learnt from Boddy at the Sunderland Convention. Howard had been through the fire of social ostracism and imprisonment and John, perhaps a more cautious younger brother, had proved his own faith during the period of Howard's absence. Moreover, their contact with A E Saxby, who had been a Baptist minister in north London, alerted them to wider doctrinal issues than those connected with the baptism in the Holy Spirit. Saxby had spoken in tongues, but then became a strong advocate of universalism with the result that the younger men under his influence (including Donald Gee), broke free and left him alone.

The Pentecostal Missionary Union

On January 9th 1909 Alexander Boddy and Cecil Polhill[37] met in the All Saints' Vicarage at Sunderland and started the Pentecostal Missionary Union. Cecil Polhill had been one of the original "Cambridge Seven" who went out to China in the 1880s and his presidency of the Union ensured that its eyes were turned firmly to the mission field he knew best. The principles of missionary organisation adopted by the PMU were similar to those established by the China Inland Mission which Hudson Taylor had pioneered so courageously in the 19th century. The task of the Council at home was to distribute the funds, collected in the churches, to those overseas. The missionaries were expected to live "by faith", that is, without a guaranteed income, but to trust that donations would be sufficient to provide for their food, accommodation and travel. The supervision of missionaries was minimal and decisions about what should be done at local level on the field were left with them. They were free to adopt whatever system of church government they wished in any congregations which came into existence as a result of their ministries.

The first three PMU missionaries sailed for India in February 1909[38], and these were followed a year later by four more who, after specific PMU training, left for China. The recognition that missionaries needed preparation and teaching before launching into the unknown led, by degrees, to pentecostal Bible schools in Britain. Before the 1914-18 war Mrs Crisp trained female missionary candidates in London and Thomas Myerscough, in Preston, trained the men[39]. By 1913 there were 8 PMU missionaries in India and 9 in China[40]. By 1922 there had been an increase to 21 men and women in China, 6 on the Tibetan border, 8 in the Belgian Congo and three in Brazil[41]. But according to a later analyst[42] the PMU made slow progress in the years 1909-24 because the pentecostal movement as a whole was uncoordinated and donations for missionary work tended only to be raised at large Conventions or through a system of collecting boxes. Both Polhill and Mundell were relatively wealthy men, and they gave generously, but they were unable to fund the whole enterprise and there are signs that the post war depression stretched resources very thin. The sixteen paid missionaries in 1912 were supported by an income of £1,532; the 30 missionaries of 1921 were supported by an income of £5,000[43]. It is very difficult to calculate prices for the period 1912-21, particularly to estimate the value of the pound sterling against foreign currencies, but retail prices in Britain in 1921 were 2.25 times their 1913 level[44]. If financial support in 1921 had attained its pre-war level, about £6,900 would have been supplied that year. There was thus an obvious shortfall and, reading between the lines, it is likely that missionaries made serious sacrifices on the field while, at the same time, the giving which was directed abroad had the effect of diminishing the payment of pentecostal ministers at home. Moreover, the founding of the Congo Evangelistic Mission in 1919 had the unintentional result of deflecting missionary finance to that field and away from PMU workers in China, India and the Tibet area.

Two important results followed from the exertions of the PMU: firstly, the pentecostal movement as a whole had, from its earliest days, a zeal for missionary work and for world-wide evangelism. The danger of becoming a holy enclave or a religious ghetto never affected the pentecostals seriously because they were constantly reminded of their responsibilities to preach the Gospel to every creature. Secondly, the training of ministers became a priority. If the United Kingdom was a mission field, then it was logical to train men and women for that field as it was for any other.

Sion College

Cecil Polhill was also started meetings at Sion College on the Thames embankment from March 1909 onwards. The College itself was, as Donald Gee describes it, like a "club without an entrance fee" which had been founded as an almshouse by the charity of a 17th century clergyman. The weekly meetings gave pentecostal preachers a regular opportunity to encourage the London assemblies, and a good number of people were healed and baptised in the Holy Spirit over the years. In 1925, the gatherings had dwindled to a mere thirty or forty people and Howard Carter was asked by Mr Mundell to take over responsibility for all the arrangments[45], and the number of people soon rose again.

It was Polhill[46], too, who had the foresight to arrange annual Whitsun meetings at the Methodist Kingsway Hall. Before the Sunderland Conventions were stopped by the war, visiting foreign preachers would often address a London crowd before travelling to the north of England. After 1914 the Whitsun Convention in the capital became a natural platform and rallying point for pentecostal speakers.

Notes to Pages 43 - 58

1. Cited from Desmond Cartwright's article "Echoes from the Past" in the Jan 22, 1983 issue of Elim Evangel. Cartwright is quoting a Church of Ireland clergyman, Thomas Hackett of Bray, who was connected with the Elim movement during its early days in Ireland.

2. Donald Gee in Wind and Flame, p 60f gives details.

3. Cartwright (1981:8) gives information drawn from the PMU Minute Book.

4. Cartwright (1981:9) says that Jeffreys took an active part in the Open Air services which occurred during the week of the Convention.

5. The booklet is entitled 1915-1936 Coming of Age Souvenir of the Elim Foursquare Gospel Alliance and contains accounts of the various departments of the Elim work as well as a page devoted to the main event(s) of each of the 21 years.

6. See S H Frodsham's Smith Wigglesworth: apostle of faith, London: Assemblies of God Publishing House, p 3. Much of the information on Wigglesworth comes from this source.

7. see note 6 p 10.

8. For example, in a tape-recorded interview with Tom Woods (b 1901) at Beford on 21st September 1985.

9. See Donald Gee's These Men I Knew, 1980, London: Assemblies of God, p 90.

10. Donald Gee Wind and Flame, Croydon: Assemblies of God Publishing House, makes this point emphatically, p 44f.

11. Myerscough spoke at the Bradford Convention in 1916, Confidence May 1916.

12. Confidence Dec 1914, p 228.

13. Confidence April-June 1922, p 27.

14. Gee wrote voluminously and some of his books appeared with different titles on either side of the Atlantic. Bonnington Toll: the story of a first pastorate London: Victory Press, 1943, contains information about Gee's early life as also does the unpublished Pentecostal Pilgrimage: World Travels of a Bible Teacher which runs to 32 typewritten pages and is kept in the archives of the Assemblies of God at Mattersey.

15. 10th May.

16. Paul Newberry, who knew Gee when he was Principal of the Bible School at Kenley in the 1960s, described him in conversation as a "lonely man". Gee's first wife died and he only married again towards the very end of his life.

17. B R Ross wrote a doctoral thesis *Donald Gee: In Search of a Church; Sectarian in Transition,* unpublished PhD, Toronto, Canada, 1974, from which some of this information is taken.

18. See Gee's Wind and Flame, p 34.

19 See Ross (1974: 7).

20. See Ross (1974: 11).

21. See Gee's unpublished Pentecostal Pilgrimage, p 3.

22. See Gee's unpublished Pentecostal Pilgrimage, p 6.

23. See note 14.

24. See Bonnington Toll p 6.

25. See Bonnington Toll p 15.

26. See Bonnington Toll p 15.

27. Mrs Berulsden wrote to A A Boddy and her letter describing her healing and baptism in the Spirit at Sunderland was printed in the first issue of Confidence in April 1908. The Berulsdens were a fairly wealthy family of ship chandlers and their son later went to the mission field. They were a mature couple and the assembly at Edinburgh owed its early existence to their hospitality as well as to a visit by Boddy on 1st and 2nd January 1908.

28. See Bonnington Toll p 15.

29. The letters are kept at the Assemblies of God Bible College, Mattersey Hall, Nr Doncaster.

30. Most of the information from this section comes from Parr's autobiography, "Incredible" distributed by J Nelson Parr of 16 Coniston Ave, Fleetwood FY7 7LD and copyrighted in March 1972, when Parr was in his eighties.

31. John Carter lived to be 86 years old and continued working until the very end. He lectured at the Assemblies of God Bible College (Mattersey Hall) and died in one of the rooms at the College in April 1981. On his death all his personal papers were left to the College and contribute to the Mattersey archives. He was known to the third generation of pentecostals and he wrote a life of his brother, Howard Carter - Man of the Spirit , Nottingham: AoG Pub House, 1971, and his own autobiography, A Full Life, Nottingham: AoG, 1979. Much of the material from this section is taken from these two books. For an insight into Howard Carter's character I am indebted to Peter Snook of the Assemblies of God Book Room, Nottingham, who worked with Howard Carter in the Bible School at Hampstead. Carter was always smartly dressed, often with a bow tie, and had beautiful handwriting and a comprehensive but unique filing system which was a mystery to the uninitiated. Nevertheless he could do some utterly unpredictable things because of his simple faith in Christ and his understanding of spiritual gifts.

32. See J Carter (1971:9,10).

33. See J Carter (1971:25).

34. J Carter (1971:28).

35. John Carter's account of their lives mentions that A E Saxby went with John to visit Howard in prison. Saxby became identified with the doctrine of "ultimate reconciliation" and so it is no surprise that the two brothers were later firm in their rejection of that doctrine, despite the favourable impression given by Saxby's dignified and warm personality.

36 J Carter (1971:44).

37. Other members of the Council of the PMU were T H Mundell, a solicitor, W H Sandwith, Pastor Jeffreys (who appears to be no relation to Stephen or George), H Small, Andrew Murdoch, Thomas Myerscough, James Breeze and Mrs Crisp. Details of the formation of the PMU and its Council, as well as its missionaries, were regularly given in Confidence and later, when the PMU merged with Assemblies of God, Redemption Tidings took over the function of publicising missionary needs and successes.

38. See Gee (1967:47). These were Miss Lucy James of Bedford and Miss Miller, who were later joined by Miss Boes. Miss Boes had worked with the Indian Village Mission, but returned to India under the auspices of the PMU.

39. A photo in Confidence (October 1913), p 205, shows six Preston students.

40. See Confidence (July 1913) pages 146 and 147.

41. See Confidence (April-June 1922) page 29.

42. See Alfred Misson, General Secretary of Assemblies of God 1963-1978, who wrote The Sound of a Going (1973), Nottingham: Assemblies of God Publishing House, p60-61.

43. See <u>Confidence</u> (April-June 1922), page 31.

44. See Stevenson, J (1984: 117) <u>British Society</u> 1914-45, Harmondsworth: Penguin.

45. See Carter J (1979:91).

46. Gee (1980: 73-75) gives a portrait of the wealthy "Squire of Howbury Hall" who used his money generously to further the pentecostal cause. As a chairman and speaker, Polhill was sometimes tedious - "his continual repetition of Beloved Friends became a byword and a joke. Audiences that had come to hear Stephen Jeffreys squirmed with impatience as he inflicted on them his little homilies from the chair".

NEW BEGINNINGS

Social conditions after the Great War

The economic and human costs of the 1914-18 War were immense. Britain, had depended for its huge wealth on advantageous trading conditions within the Empire, but hostilities with Germany immediately imperilled overseas investment and shipping. Government expenditure, expedited by the emergency administrative centralisation Lloyd George had been forced to create, rose sharply; government income was levied partly by taxes, which also rose sharply - roughly by a factor of six, and partly by expensive loans with the net result that, until the last eighteen months of the war, financial policy was inflationary: the purchasing power of the pound dropped by two thirds of its 1914 value (Hill, 1966:376; Thomson, 1981:58). Moreover, the cost of pensions and benefits to ex-servicemen and widows prolonged the war debt. The effect of inflation is always to reduce the prosperity of those with savings or fixed incomes and, if as was the case in the 1920s, organised occupational groups are able to demand and obtain higher wages, a redistribution of national wealth ensues. Dean Inge wrote in 1921 "a new class of rich people has arisen, who took advantage of their country's necessities to make exorbitant profits, and who are now spending their ill-gotten gains with an ostentation as vulgar and tasteless as it is politically insane"[1]. But the situation changed rapidly within a short time. Immediately after the war a short boom followed the removal of price restrictions and trade controls but then, between December 1920 and March 1921, unemployment more than doubled, and soon passed the two million mark. Throughout the inter-war period, it never dropped below one million[2]. Housing had been vigorously attended to before 1921, and it was profits of bricklayers against which Inge inveighed before the general fall in wages that took place in the early 1920s. The "roaring twenties" only roared for the jazz fans and upper middle classes of Noel Coward comedies. For the rest of the populace times were hard and industrial unrest surfaced. The intellectual mood was caught by T S Eliot's Waste Land which begins with a section on "The Burial of the Dead" and breathes an air of desolation in a world of "broken images". Trade Unionism struggled against the obstinacy of employers whose prejudices were strengthened by revelations of the horrors of Bolshevism and whose economic strategies were, in the main, limited by an inability to see beyond their own bank balances. Capital investment was diverted away from those industries which most needed modernisation. Strikes and threats of strikes marked the start of the decade. The police struck in 1918 and 1919; there was a railway strike in 1920; the miners, railway and transport unions formed a "Triple Alliance" in 1921, though it came unstitched and the miners struck without support until they were forced back to work "to the general rejoicing of the educated, prosperous classes" (Taylor, 1975: 196). The militancy of the trenches was transferred to industrial relations, but the emergence of the Labour Party stimulated hope that the condition of manual workers might be improved by democratic and constitutional means rather than by revolution. Lloyd George had introduced a scheme to insure against unemployment in 1911 and the 1920-2 Unemployment Insurance Acts extended this and provided "uncovenanted benefit" or what came to be called "the dole". The pains of post war disillusionment - of an unfulfilled desire for a country "fit for heroes" - were palliated, and wages gradually crept upwards until the mid-decade crisis.

Attitudes to Germany immediately after the war were harsh. Lloyd George had spoken of squeezing the orange till the pips squeaked. Ramsey Macdonald and a minority of the Labour Party had incurred nearly ten years of unpopularity by declaring themselves to be against the Great War and in the 1920s, when there was a revulsion against "super-patriotism", the tables were turned. Lloyd George lost power and Ramsey Macdonald gained it. The stigma of being anti-war, or even pacifist, vanished and, for what it was worth, the young pentecostal leaders found themselves on the side of public opinion.

Religious Conditions after the Great War
The effects of war on religious faith are literally incalculable. When two nations with Christian heritages are engaged in conflict and when their priests and padres invoke the same God for blessing on their respective guns and armies, it is easy to become cynical or to embrace the Shavian conclusion that "God is on the side of the big battalions". When millions die, and when thousands meet their deaths horribly in the course of a single afternoon, as in the Somme offensive, for the sake of a few miles of mud or when mutilation or annihilation comes suddenly from an unseen artillery battery many miles away, fatalism and superstition cloak the meaninglessness of thoughtless patriotism; indeed the war poets most poignantly exposed the "old lie" that it is "a sweet and noble thing to die for one's country"[3].

The Church of England by and large supported the entrance of

England to the war. Indeed the Bishop of London became "one of the most successful recruiting officers in the country"[4]. Some clergy joined the forces as combatants while the 3000 Anglican chaplains who served as non-combatants found themselves completely unprepared and untrained for their unexpected ministry. Their pastoral theology was not designed to cope with the constant personal crises of bereavement and shell shock and, in addition, they were frequently appalled by the ignorance of basic Christianity which the majority of soldiers displayed. After the war, as Norman (1976: 239) notes, the chaplains were more ready than ever to support social reform and the better distribution of wealth. Some of the most distinguished churchmen, like Gore and Temple, had long been supportive of calls for social change and the war provided them with a groundswell of agreement.

Inge (1926: 304) analysed "religion in England after the war" and commented on the increase in necromancy and spiritualism which had been occasioned. "Large numbers of sorrowing parents and widows...[attempted] to establish, by various forms of occultism, communion with the spirits of those whom they had dearly loved". Church attendance seemed to Inge to have remained at its post war level, though figures quoted by Argyle and Beit-Hallahami (1975:9) show a steady decline in Easter communicants in the Church of England between 1914 and about 1923. In part this was due to the absence of servicemen in fighting or by death. The underlying trend of church attendance between 1914 and 1965 was downward and affected Anglicans and Nonconformists almost equally (Argyle and Beit-Hallahami, 1975:11). Martin (1967: 39) says, "the Free Churches present a picture of continuous erosion. Initially they seem to have maintained themselves while the Church of England began to decline, but once their own decline set in it was quite rapid". Moreover, because of changing social customs and habits, nonconformity began to look old fashioned: sabbath observance could hardly be switched on and off like a tap depending on whether the nation happened to be at war or not; illegitimacy rates increased as did the number of divorces (Thomson, 1981: 87). Contraceptives were sold by "every village chemist" (Briggs, 1983: 264) and, though the broadcasting of religious services on the newly formed BBC was popular, there was a general feeling that the church as a whole had failed to "hold the loyalties of the younger generation" (Thomson, 1981: 119). Both abroad for those who had lived in the trenches among the unburied dead and on the larger diplomatic and international scene of what had once been European Christendom, Christianity appeared to have failed. At home Christianity was on the defensive. Few of the intellectuals of the day found it attractive. Surreal art and dadaism, which gloried in the randomness of existence, expressed the feelings of the age. The ideal of human progress was shattered. Christian theology began to grapple on the one hand with issues of citizenship and its proponents were roundly condemned by the more right wing   commentators, like Inge and Hensley Henson, as being "armchair socialists." On the other hand, there was an upsurge of "modernism" which reduced the influence of the Evangelical party in the Church of England and whose main opponents were Anglo-Catholics.

Inge (1926:313) layed the blame for the war at the door of Hegel's philosophy of of the state which he was at pains to show has no connection with Christianity. The effects of the war on the Church in England, and indeed world-wide, are described by Johnson (1976: 479) as producing a "mood of pessimism" and an abandonment of triumphalism, both Protestant and Roman Catholic, as "visions of a Christianized world faded". Tensions within the Anglican Church were expressed in the wrangle over the 1928 Prayer Book which was defeated in Parliament largely because of the rubric which would have permitted the practice of the "reservation" of the consecrated bread and wine[5]. The practice of "reservation" was favoured by Anglo-Catholics, and Gore[6] decided to make enquiries in other dioceses because of pressure for open access to the reserved sacrament for devotional purposes. Public prayers for the dead became common during the 1914-18 War and it was clear to Inge that, while the Evangelical party had declined, the Anglo-Catholics and   Modernists were struggling for preeminence in the Anglican fold. Gore belonged to the Anglo-Catholic party and defended the doctrinal position which the Church had reached in the historic creeds - an intellectual stance which Inge found incomprehensible because it prevented any sort of revision of dogma. Barth's famous commentary on the Epistle to the Romans (1919) had not yet brought an injection of strength to the Evangelical Anglicans who were seriously weakened by Old Testament German scholarship in the 19th century which had undermined the traditional concepts of biblical inspiration and inerrancy; in addition the philanthropic causes that had won sometimes grudging admiration for Evangelicalism in the days of Wilberforce and Shaftsbury had been subsumed in the social thrust of the growing Ecumenical Movement. Evangelical Anglicanism seemed to have no distinctive voice or banner[7].

The finer points of established churchmanship did not concern the early pentecostals. They were not bothered by disputes over the sacraments, the reservation of the host, the establishment or the disestablishment of the Church of England or the wisdom or otherwise of the appointment of Hensley Henson to the See of Hereford in 1917. Their roots were nonconformist and though, as Boddy and even Gore showed, it was quite possible for Anglicans to think highly of nonconformist liberty and zeal, it was never the case that nonconformists for their part found the arguments for episcopal church government convincing. Gore himself (Prestige, 1935: 377) accepted that the "necessity of the episcopal" carried with it the invalidity of nonconformist ministry. Of the later leaders of the pentecostal movement in the United Kingdom only the Carter brothers had been in regular attendance in the Church of England in their boyhood. Smith Wigglesworth had been taken by his grandmother to the Wesleyan Methodists; Donald Gee was a Congregationalist; John Nelson Parr came from a holiness group; Thomas Myerscough was rumoured to be from the Plymouth Brethren; A E Saxby was among the Baptists and Fred Watson the Methodists; the Jeffreys brothers were brought up in the Welsh Congregational Church and Harold Horton and Tom Woods were Methodist local preachers.

Notes to Pages 63 - 67

1. W R Inge (1926) Lay Thoughts of a Dean, London: Putnam's Sons, p305. Over one million acres of land were sold in 1919. England was "changing hands" Asa Briggs (1983) A Social History of England, London:Book Club Associates, p264.

2. A J P Taylor (1975) English History 1914-1945, Harmondsworth: Penguin, p195.

3. See Wilfred Owen, Isaac Rosenberg and Siegfried Sassoon. Both Owen and Rosenberg were killed in action in 1918, Owen being one of the most promising poets since Keats.

4. See J H R Moorman (1980), A History of the Church in England, London: Adam & Charles Black, p 416.

5. See The Oxford Dictionary of the Christian Church ed F L Cross and E A Livingstone, Oxford: OUP, p 1177.

6. See G L Prestige (1935).The Life of Charles Gore, London: Heinemann, p390.

7. Inge in The Church in the World (1928). London: Longmans, Green & Co, p 18, wrote "the younger Evangelicals read the critical and philosophical works of the German Protestants, and are in process of reconstructing their party on new lines. Thought within the Church of England is freer than ever before." The essay from which this extract is taken was first published in January 1925.

ASSEMBLIES OF GOD IS FORMED

Churches, denominations and sects

In discussing the distinction between churches, denominations and sects, there are various starting points. Theological premises drawn from the Gospels and from the Acts of the Apostles show that the Church has a local expression (for example "the church at Corinth", or the "church at Ephesus") and a universal expression which refers to all those who, whether physically alive or dead and whatever their racial origin and geographical location, belong to Christ. Subsequent theological reflection has produced divergencies of opinion about the nature of Christian initiation, and therefore about membership of the Church both local and universal so that, by the fifth century it was possible for Augustine to argue that Donatists were not genuinely within the Church of Christ even if they were within an institutional structure that called itself a church and which administered sacraments in exactly the same way as believers outside Africa[1]. Sociological premises usually start from Weber's distinction between a church as "a sort of trust foundation for supernatural ends, an institution, necessarily including both the just and the unjust" while a sect is the "believer's church...solely as a community of personal believers of the reborn, and only these"[2]. The Church, in sociological analysis, is distinguishable from a sect by its attitude to "the world". Whereas a church accommodates to the world, a sect is anti-world and otherworldly. Denominations stand mid-way between sects and churches so that sociologists would expect to trace the movement of an exclusive and cliquey sect, through a broadening denominational phase to a final stage where the denomination becomes a church. Each step of this gradual series of transitions is marked by alterations in doctrinal emphases, internal organisation and relationships with the political powers that be[3].

In general English usage the word "sect", like the word "cult", has a pejorative connotation and is rarely used self-descriptively by any religious group. In many Christian circles the word "denomination" is also coming to have a distasteful meaning since it implies narrow traditionalism and an unwillingness to consider afresh the impact of biblical truths. Moreover, from a perspective drawn from ecumenicism (which stresses the union of churches), denominationalism is equally reprehensible because it hinders Christian co-operation. Those who took a lead in the formation of Assemblies of God specifically disavowed the notion that they were sectarian. In a letter dated 20th

February 1924, E W Moser wrote to G Tilling of the proposals which were adopted as a basis for the constitutional framework of Assemblies of God

> The scheme is a very simple one and certainly has not the objection to it that many other denominational unions have. It does not constitute a "sect", nor does it constitute a breach with any other community of Believers who do not wish to join us.[4]

Incubation

When the 1914-18 War ended, the most obvious leaders of the pentecostal movement in the British Isles were Alexander Boddy and Cecil Polhill. Both these men, however, were unwilling to take the lead in establishing a new Christian group. Their expectation was that the hundreds who had been baptised in the Holy Spirit from 1907 onwards would return to their home churches and infuse spiritual life into their religious peer groups. Neither Boddy nor Polhill suffered any real social or religious rejection because of their pentecostal experience - Boddy because of the excellent work he had done in Sunderland under sympathetic bishops and Polhill because of his independent financial means and "squire" status. Those who had been imprisoned, like Howard Carter, or ostracised, like Donald Gee, were less inclined to take so sanguine a view. Moreover George Jeffreys had from 1915 onwards begun to organise the Elim Foursquare Alliance and so demonstrate that a purely pentecostal network and fellowship of churches was perfectly feasible.

A two-day conference of leaders at Sheffield in 1922 calling for "more concerted action among the assemblies of Spirit-filled Saints"[5] resulted in three resolutions. The first two concerned the setting up of a Provisional Council "for the advice and assistance of the Assemblies in the United Kingdom and Ireland" and that this council should submit a plan for fellowship, business and co-operation to the assemblies for their judgement. The third resolution is, in many respects, the most interesting because it agreed that

> a solemn note of warning be sent to all assemblies concerned against the practice, not found in New Testament Scripture, of "enquiring of the Lord" for guidance through gifts of tongues, interpretation or prophecy, a practice that has caused and is causing such havoc among the saints.

One motive for calling the leaders of assemblies together, therefore, and an important clue to the state of affairs in pentecostal circles prior to the mid-1920s is revealed by this third resolution. There were obviously abuses of the gifts of the Holy Spirit and, indeed, possibly an oblique reference to the practices growing up or troubling in "Apostolic" churches. The vocal gifts of the Spirit were being used for guidance with the result that very subjective pseudo-divine directives could be given to individuals who were naive enough to ask for them.

The 1922 Conference was a disappointment to its organisers. Although a Provisional General Council (of nine men)[6] was elected by the 38 people present and although a Constitution of "The General Council of The Assemblies of God in Great Britain and Ireland" was produced and circulated to local assemblies (with a tear-off slip to be signed by those which accepted it), only 10 in England and Scotland and one of the twenty in London felt they could sign[7]. The reasons for reluctance to identify with the General Council's Constitution are unclear: it may be that suggestion that the General Council "be empowered to exercise any needed discipline as required by Scripture over the recognised workers of the assemblies" smacked too much of an authoritarian central government. Certainly the constitutional framework which was later adopted by the Assemblies of God - the identical nomenclature shows the continuity between the efforts in 1922 and the successes of 1924 - was careful to safeguard local church autonomy.

Birth

Some years before Howard Carter died in 1971 he and his brother John had discussed the early days of the pentecostal movement and a typescript of their conversation survives[8]. They recalled the visit of Archibald Cooper, a preacher from South Africa, to the Hampstead Bible school towards the end of 1923. Cooper's itinerant ministry had given him an insight into the fluid and uncertain state of British pentecostalism and he proposed some sort of unity be attempted. Howard remembered "we were fanatically opposed to any form of denominationalism. We had been brought up to believe that any organisation would lead to central government, and our spiritual freedom would be imperilled...the two previous attempts to create unity, made at Sheffield and Swanwick...had proved abortive".

Cooper nevertheless got in touch with Thomas Myerscough and Nelson Parr. After the apparent failure of the Sheffield Conference, Nelson Parr (who had not attended) took the initiative and wrote a gracious circular letter on the 23rd November 1923 to several pentecostal leaders asking them if they would lend their names to a further attempt to "establish a union of Assemblies". Parr made it clear in his final paragraph

> In closing may I give you my sincere and earnest assurance that the supreme desire filling my heart is to see that Union established which so many are longing for; and my joy will be to retire into the background when it is an accomplished fact.

Parr's efforts culminated in the formation of Assemblies of God about a year later. When we ask why Parr should have been successful where others, by roughly the same methods and only a short time previously, had failed, the most compelling clue lies in Howard Carter's recollection that the early pentecostals felt their spiritual freedom would be put in jeopardy by organisation of any kind which, they thought, would lead to central government. Parr as a pastor himself clearly guaranteed and understood the desire for local autonomy. The Sheffield Conference had included the powerful and organising personality of George Jeffreys. Jeffreys is notably absent from the list of those involved with the circular letter which was sent to independent pentecostal meetings (ie presumably those which did not have links with Elim)[9].

Thus the steps which Parr took were, first, to gain the agreement of a number of prominent pentecostal leaders to his suggestion for a union, and second, with these leaders as signatories, to circularise independent pentecostal assemblies and, third, to call together the signatories for a face-to-face discussion of what to do next. The response to the circular letter would enable the thirteen signatories to gauge the likely scale of their activities.

Parr's circular letter must have been sent out in November or early December of 1923 and gives five reasons for greater cooperation and union among local assemblies. These, in his words, were:

1. To preserve the testimony of the full Gospel including the Baptism of the Holy Spirit with signs following and to save the work from false teaching.

2. To strengthen the bonds of fellowship and to obtain a fuller degree of co-operation among Assemblies.

3. To present a united witness to those outside.

4. To exercise discipline over those who walk disorderly. To fail to recognise authority of those who have the rule over us in the church throws the door open to lawlessness.

5. To save a number of Assemblies from falling into unscriptural organisations.

Moreover he went on

> there can be union without Legislative Authority, without "Centralization" and without interference in local church government from any council or committee that the assemblies may see fit to appoint for advisory or executive purposes.

After giving these reasons for union and co-operation, Parr suggested to the assemblies that 30th December[10] be set apart for a special day of prayer and fasting and asked for any further suggestions. On 23rd January Parr sent out "a rough draft of a few proposals" which he wanted the signatories of his circular letter to consider at a Conference he called at Birmingham on 1st February 1924. In fact twelve men and one woman made their way to a room over a garage in Aston that day[11]. They were J Nelson Parr, R C Bell of Hampstead, Charles Buckley of Chesterfield, Howard and John Carter of London, Mrs Cantel, the only woman, who also travelled from London, J Douglas of Stratford, Donald Gee from Edinburgh, Tom Hicks of Crosskeys who came as a representative of a block of Welsh assemblies, Arthur Inman of Mansfield Woodhouse, E W Moser from Southsea, Fred Watson of Blackburn and Arthur Watkinson of York. Thomas Myerscough was absent through illness[12].

The reminiscences of Howard and John Carter relate how Parr was elected Chairman of the gathering and how he assured those present that "the autonomy of the local Assembly would be strictly observed. What he had in mind was the formation of a British fellowship based upon the pattern of the American Assemblies of God". The draft proposal which lay before the Conference had been sent out a week previously, and was open to amendment. Parr was not asking the Conference to rubber stamp his prayerful thinking. The basic structure the document envisaged was divided into three sections corresponding with three levels of union. The level ensured that local assemblies adhered to the same fundamental truths; the second level ensured that local assemblies would be in fellowship through a system of District Presbyteries, each of which should be made up of local pastors or elders; a General Presbytery (made up of itinerant and overseas ministers and members of the District Presbytery) should also be convened annually.

This three-layer structure was accepted and continued in Assemblies of God for some sixty years without any serious modification. The balance between local, district and national authority has persisted, sometimes uneasily, sometimes creatively, and given Assemblies of God its characteristic shape. In general the District Presbytery, or District Council (as it came to be called), was only to be summoned in to help a local assembly in direst emergency. Whereas Parr showed that he expected the District Presbytery to appoint evangelists and other workers who would function in a particular geographical region (since this function was included in section 7F of his draft document), shortage of funds tended over the years to limit the effectiveness of locally-funded ventures.

The gathering in Birmingham decided to publish a quarterly magazine to be called *Redemption Tidings* - on Howard Carter's suggestion[13], and much of the information about the early stages of Assemblies of God in Britain can be gleaned from its pages. The *Elim Evangel* was already covering what was happening in the Elim churches and so, between them, these two publications give the best public record of what was taking place in the largest British segments of the pentecostal movement. It was agreed that Parr should be the editor of the new periodical. Parr's dynamic energies found ample scope for expression: he was chairman and secretary-treasurer of the new fellowship of churches, as well as the editor of a 20 page quarterly, the active pastor of a growing church - and, in addition to all this, held down a responsible job in business.

By March 1924 about 70 assemblies had agreed to become part of the newly formed Assemblies of God. Approximately half of these were in Wales[14]. Thus, although in a letter dated January 1924 E W Moser mentioned that over 20 assemblies were in agreement with the draft proposals, by March the total number of congregations was far in excess of this[15]. Moser wrote in February 1924 commending the scheme to Mr Tilling of Southampton and emphasised that the General Council or Presbytery would be made up of elders and pastors who would have equal authority. No one individual or group of individual would have authority over groups of local churches and leaders. And, he went on,

All Elders of Assemblies form a General Council which will be a tribunal to help and decide questions which affect the welfare of the whole Community. At present there is no such tribunal as we read of in Acts 15.2. The consequence is that false teachers and teaching have had the free run of the weaker assemblies and very much harm has been done which cannot now be undone but which might well have been avoided if there had been a constituted Presbytery to take the oversight and act for the general welfare of the whole.

I do not regard this scheme as something that we are asked to join, but rather as a recognition of the Eldership of true assemblies of God already in existence and an acknowledgement of our obligations towards them.

Moser's stress on freedom is balanced by the realisation that immense harm had been done by allowing false doctrine to spread unchecked. Moreover he saw the annual convention (or General Presbytery) as being thoroughly representative of the whole community and "on much sounder lines than any of the large Conventions at Sunderland and London, although we have no wish to unkindly criticise those good works".

Moser's role in the formation of Assemblies of God has been explored (by R D Massey, 1987) and there is evidence that, as a behind-the-scenes worker, Moser was very effective. What Moser, as an old Pentecostal Missionary Union man, knew was that it was very difficult to raise and sustain funds for missionary work without an organised home base. Assemblies of God, therefore, was an answer to the prayers of those who had seen PMU funds drop drastically as a result of financial conditions in the early 1920s.

Events moved quickly after the Conference in February 1924. Not only did 70 assemblies quickly join themselves to the new affiliation, but, striking while the iron was hot, a Conference in May was rapidly arranged for the pastors or elders of these churches[16]. This altogether larger gathering was interrupted on the first morning by a telegram from George Jeffreys asking why, in a discussion of unity among pentecostal people in Britain, he had not been invited to attend. According to the Carter brothers' reminiscences many of those present

were eager to invite him immediately to join us in our discussions, but I (Howard) cautioned them to wait until we ourselves knew exactly where we stood. We had only just come into existence as a new Fellowship, and I expressed the fear that, if such a strong personality were present in our midst, there would be a danger of us being swallowed up by the Elim organisation, which had already been in existence several years and was rapidly growing. If this happened, the principle of local autonomy might be gone for ever[17].

Jeffreys was invited to attend on the second day and brought with him a contingent of Elim personnel including E J Phillips who made the "breath-taking proposal"[18] that the Elim workers become the evangelistic arm of Assemblies of God. This idea was held in abeyance until December when the Elim Evangelistic Band reviewed its own year's progress. They concluded that they believed it to be God's will that each section of the pentecostal movement, Elim and Assemblies of God, continue on its own lines. If either side floundered, the movement as a whole would not be wrecked.

Despite the ultimate failure to unify pentecostals in Britain, the May meeting did ensure that a large London Convention was arranged for August 2-8th 1924 at Peniel Chapel for all and sundry[19]. Special railway excursions and accommodation ensured that the three meetings a day were well attended. There was a missionary meeting and a missionary speaker but all the other eight speakers except one were drawn from those who had attended the Birmingham Conference. Parr reports that "there was a tremendous outpouring of the Holy Ghost upon this Convention and scores of people were Baptised in the Spirit and spoke in tongues"[20] and the Percy Corry wrote "many souls were blessed and filled with the Holy Spirit, many were healed and saved, but the outstanding memory of the Convention is the sweetness of the anointing and the goodness of the unity that came with it"[21]. Corry was to become the Dean of the Elim Bible College; despite the lack of Elim preachers in London that summer, at least one prominent member of the Elim movement was happy to attend.

Examination

Analytical scrutiny of the train of events leading to the formation of Assemblies of God, and a look at the formation itself, is necessary to see exactly what was achieved and why. First, and most obviously, the new fellowship did weave a network of communication and contact between pentecostal assemblies in various parts of the British Isles. The Sunderland Conventions had long since ceased, and so there was no forum for discussion or centre for the dissemination of information. Congregations had tended to work in isolation from each other, and many of them, after the Great War, were in a bad way. Secondly, the lack of communication made congregations prey to false teaching of various kinds. The "gifts of the Spirit" were open to abuse because it was supposed that divine direction could be given to private individuals by those who had prophesied or interpreted tongues in a church meeting. Spiritual gifts were taken out of the context of the "body of Christ" which 1 Corinthians gives them and removed from the primary function of exhortation, edification and comfort (1 Cor 14.3) and given a role in personal guidance which, so far as Scripture is concerned, is very rare. Thirdly, and perhaps most important in the long run, a basis for future expansion was reached. The evangelistic campaigns of the final years of the 1920s and the 1930s would hardly have been possible had local assemblies not been in contact and informed about the crowds which flocked to hear, for example, Stephen Jeffreys. In the sphere of missionary activity, too, the collaboration of assemblies made it possible to raise funds and provide encouragement for those who felt an overseas vocation. Fourthly, a system of church government which was defensibly scriptural had been attained. The churches of the New Testament were incontrovertibly largely self-governing under the pastors and elders who led them because apostolic direction and instruction, although rightly enforced by Paul and the church at Jerusalem was, by virtue of slow travel and postal delays, frequently absent. Only in recent days has the issue of apostolic authority become a burning question (as we shall see later). Fifthly, and more intangibly, Nelson Parr, by his gracious appeals, undomineering spirit and organised approach set an example to others of what could be accomplished by brotherly co-operation[22]. Sixthly, the formation of Assemblies of God marked a self-consciousness of difference from other Christian groups with a lower view of the Bible and a more limited view of the work of the Holy Spirit - it was like friends meeting each other in a crowd - the rapid affiliation of so many scattered congregations was only possible because in many respects they were like-minded and faced the same problems. Their coming together was an implicit recognition that the existing churches failed to meet the challenge, as they saw it, of the hour. The formation of Assemblies of God therefore was an achievement of *identity*.

Although there were positive reasons for the formation of Assemblies of God, and positive gains as a result of its formation, it is also clear that what transpired in the first half of 1924 was a reaction *against* an existing situation. This in itself does not detract from the very human co-ordinating efforts of the men involved, but it does cast light on their ultimate vision, their short-term goals and their perception of the direction in which they were facing.

Firstly, in the latter part of 1923 or thereabouts the pentecostal assemblies in South Wales felt the need for safeguards against the "full brunt of the many local divisions caused by the rapid advance, at that time, of the 'Apostolic Church'"[23]. The Welsh assemblies therefore considered an application for recognition as a separate District Council within American Assemblies of God[24]. As Donald Gee expressed it, "this stung the English brethren into action"[25] and the call to the independent pentecostal assemblies which Nelson Parr issued in the autumn of 1923 can be see as a reaction against undue and unnecessary American domination of British believers.

Secondly, Nelson Parr saw the treatment meeted out to pentecostal conscientious objectors as evidence of the need for a denominational registration of some kind. As he said

> The brutal treatment received by some of the Pentecostal preachers when they entered prison was one of the major reasons why, at a later date, I took steps to organise the Assemblies of God in Great Britain and Ireland, and also when I prepared the draft of the first Constitution made sure a clause was included which set forth our attitude to war. This constitution and the clause referring to war proved invaluable when the Second World War started in 1939 and we had no difficulty in obtaining exemption for our Ministers, Ministerial Candidates and Bible School Students.[26]

Assemblies of God was therefore formed to combat the jingoism directed against pacifists who belonged to no established religious grouping.

Thirdly, as is apparent from the first issues of *Redemption Tidings* the early pentecostals took sharp issue with modernistic trends in the field of biblical interpretation and they consciously stood against the spiritism with which they were sometimes confused. In an article in *Redemption Tidings* (vol 1, no 1 page 18), the writer stated

> Thousands of church members and others have been seduced into the appalling errors of Spiritism (or Spiritualism), Christian Science (which is neither Christian nor Scientific), Millen-

nial Dawn (or Russelism) simply through ignorance of the truth revealed in Scriptures concerning the supernatural manifestations and operations of the Holy Spirit, the power of Christ to heal sickness and the future of the human race.

Bible study sections of *Redemption Tidings* dealt with the question,"Where are the dead?" in great detail. Teaching about "ultimate reconciliation", that is, the doctrine that the abode of the dead is a place of purgation through which the wicked may pass on their way to heaven, had been associated with A E Saxby[27] (who was known in pentecostal circles at that time) and was, of course, propounded in a modified form, by Anglo Catholicism. Spiritism appeared to support similar beliefs. Millions of people bereaved by the Great War very naturally looked for comfort and solace in religion. Any doctrine of hell and of judgment seemed to make matters worse, but the early pentecostals were determined not compromise what they took to be the plain teaching of Scripture - for this reason the very first of the Fundamental Truths published in the first issue of *Redemption Tidings* affirms "the everlasting punishment of all who are not written in the Book of Life" (Rev 20.10-15) - and offer a false hope. When Assemblies of God came into existence, it came with a definite sense that it should stand for biblical truth in a time of uncertainty and religious error[28]. This sense of standing *against* the religious and cultural currents of the age, is well illustrated by early articles against women wearing men's garments[29] (the writer takes exception to women "who have donned men's knee breeches for cycling, mountain climbing, etc") and against smoking[30]. It was given a wider frame of reference in W F P Burton's articles on "Babylon" and the necessity for the joyful separation of Christians from the false church and whole world system[31]. But its noblest and most profound expression was in a desire to preach the Gospel as fully and as widely as possible[32]. If sinful mankind was careering to hell, then the only remedy was fiery and fearless evangelism, at home and overseas. Nelson Parr continued to preach "the old time Gospel" until he was in his eighties and the two Jeffreys brothers filled the largest halls in the towns where they campaigned throughout the dismal thirties.

The most prominent and distinctive doctrinal note struck by the early pentecostals concerned the baptism in the Holy Spirit, and the gifts of healing which were unlocked by it. Corry's article in 1925[33] refuted arguments that (i) the baptism in the Holy Spirit was a seal of Christian perfection and (ii) that contemporary "speaking in tongues" was "soulish" and therefore spurious. Donald Gee in an open letter headed "reply to a friendly suggestion" revealed that

> if I would only drop "tongues" and my connection with this movement, there are waiting for me open doors, which are at present rigidly closed, of useful ministry and blessed fellowship among some of the Lord's most faithful, spiritual and evangelical saints.

He went on to say "to stand for the supernatural element in the Gospel, not theoretically merely, but actually, - this is our privilege.....he (Christ) IS going to get all those nine gifts of the Spirit back into the Church somehow or other, we are persuaded of that"[34].

The preachers and pastors who affiliated themselves and their churches to Assemblies of God in the 1920s were, in almost every instance, mature and stable individuals. Their characters had been tested during the Great War and their beliefs had been hammered out against the conventional evangelical wisdom of the day. They were young enough to be visionary and old enough to avoid the pitfalls of novices. There were negative elements to their vision: they did not want centralised church government or modernistic Christianity, nor did they care for the fashions of the age; there were also positive elements to their vision: they wanted men and women to come to Christ and be healed and be baptised in the Holy Spirit - in a word, and it was a word which appears again and again in the first issues of *Redemption Tidings*, they wanted revival. They achieved a genuine fellowship, a unity of interests and aims combined with co-operation in prayer and hope. In a few years they had broken new ground in urban evangelism and articulated an exciting alternative to the prevalent view that church life should be liturgy-centred or socially orientated. They began to believe that the East End could see a church as successful as that at Ephesus or that Preston could have as much missionary enterprise as Antioch. What had been lost to the church could be restored to the church which once again experienced the outpoured Spirit.

Notes to Pages 69 - 80

1. So far as possible I have tried to use a capital "C" to refer to the universal Church and a small "c" to refer to the local church. Augustine also developed the doctrine of the "visible" church, which was the socially observable institution, and the "invisible" Church which was made up of all true believers and was known only to God. According to Augustine the "invisible" Church existed only within the Catholic fold and under the Pope.

2. Quoted from Andrew Walker (1985) <u>Restoring the Kingdom</u>, London: Hodder & Stoughton, p 203. For a fuller discussion, see "The origins and functions of sects" (chapter 11) of Bryan Wilson's (1966) <u>Religion in Secular Society</u>, London, C A Watts & Co Ltd. In Wilson's view "sects are normally lay movements, which practise their religion without an established professional ministry" p 180. It should be noted that sociologists are not concerned to define sects and churches by reference to doctrinal orthodoxy.

3. See Walker (1985:205 f).

4. Most of the documents quoted in this section are held in the archives of the Assemblies of God Bible College at Mattersey. Some of the documents were originally preserved by the Elim headquarters at Cheltenham (since they relate to Elim personnel) and were made available for the present research by the general courtesy of the Elim Executive and by the good offices of Desmond Cartwright, himself an Elim minister.

5. This quotation is taken from an advertising poster/broadsheet which was issued by eleven pentecostal leaders including George Jeffreys, W P F Burton, T Myerscough and E W Moser. Burton's name heads the list and, according to Desmond Cartwright (1981:12). Burton, on returning from his apostolic endeavours in the Congo, had been concerned about the disarray of the pentecostal churches in Britain.

6. Or eleven men if one includes the Welsh representatives who were asked to select two leaders from among their own number.

7. See a letter from E W Boulton to G J Tilling dated 11 Jan 1923. The letter is in the archives at Mattersey Hall.

8. See "Those Early Days" in the Mattersey Hall archives.

9. The circular letters are re-printed as appendices in Parr's autobiography <u>Incredible</u>. Copies of most of them are available in the Mattersey Hall archives.

10. On page 76 of <u>Incredible</u> Parr's letter suggests that December be "set apart" for "special prayer and fasting". The original letter, of which there is a copy in the Mattersey Hall archives, simply gives 30th December. However spiritual the early pentecostal were, it is unlikely they would have observed the entire Christmas period in fasting!

11. Not all those who attended were signatories of the original circular letter to the independent assemblies. Parr was obviously not inflexible in his plans. Massey (1987; 88f) gives a great deal more detail about these events than there is space for here. He deduces that the number of people present at the initial meeting in the garage was more likely to have been fifteen. Massey's thesis is well worth reading for the light he throws on these formative events. Occasionally his speculations run ahead of the evidence, but generally he pieces together the interconnections between the personalities and the consultations and conferences with great skill. I wrote this section before reading Massey's account. Massey's account discloses the hitherto unrecognised contributions of E W Moser and Mr Mundell to the formation of AoG.

12. Myerscough was absent though illness but later signed the circular letter issued by the Conference. Donald Gee, who was present, felt unable to sign without first consulting his own assembly in Edinburgh which had, of course, already been in negotiation about joining Elim.

13 See the typescript of John and Howard Carter's reminiscences (p3) in the Mattersey Hall archives.

14. See <u>Incredible</u>, p 32. Parr states that 34 meetings decided to become Assemblies of God but that, with the South Wales block, the total number of assemblies amounted to

about 70. According to Moser's letter of the 20th February (quoted above), Parr had received 50 sympathetic replies from assemblies in England. There were obviously at least 16 assemblies which showed interest, but which did not immediately join in the first wave.

15. See his letter to Mr Mundell dated 30th January 1924, p2. The letter is in the Mattersey archives.

16. The Conference was held at Mrs Cantell's missionary home at 73 Highbury New Park on 8th and 9th May.

17. See Those Early Days (Mattersey Archives) p 5.

18. This is Howard Carter's word in Those Early Days p 5 (Mattersey Archives).

It is important to note that the "breath-taking proposal" came from E J Phillips in a later dated 8 May 1924. The two Jeffreys brothers and most of the leading members of the Elim Alliance were in Canada and the USA from June to October 1924.

19. These dates are taken from the first issue of Redemption Tidings. Parr's autobiography Incredible, p 32 gives the 24th August. Presumably the advertisement in the first issue of Redemption Tidings is correct.

20. According to Incredible p 32.

21. See the report on p 16 of the second issue of Redemption Tidings in October 1924.

22. Donald Gee (1967:128) rightly assesses Parr's contribution: "It must remain an abiding source of wonder as to however he managed the terrific amount of work involved in pioneering this new venture, while at the same time continuing for the next few years in his important business position in industry. His devotion was beyond praise, and undoubtedly was the supreme factor under God in ensuring that, at last, an organisation had arisen which should remain, and function."

23. Quoted from D Gee (1967:126).

24. See J Carter (1971: 72).

25. See D Gee (1967:127).

26. See Incredible p 26.

27. Donald Gee (1980) in a series of articles printed as These Men I Knew Nottingham: AoG Publishing House, wrote "The annual Convention (1919) at Kingsway Hall was vacant, and A E Saxby took the great step of faith for the leader of a little assembly in North London of hiring at considerable cost for the whole week the famous venue for a thoroughly Pentecostal Convention. God vindicated him and it proved a milestone in the history of the British Movement...after that Convention A E Saxby was in constant demand all over the British Isles". Saxby wrote several books, including God's Ultimate (undated), London: Stockwell Ltd, where he set out his views and, among other things, looked forward to the salvation of Judas.

28. See the scathing remarks about Peake's Commentary in Redemption Tidings Vol 1.1, p 17.

29. See Redemption Tidings vol 1.1, p 15

30. See Redemption Tidings vol 1.5, p 8,9

31. See <u>Redemption Tidings</u> vol 1.6 and 1.7

32. See A B Simpson's article in <u>Redemption Tidings</u> vol 1.3, p10-12.

33. See <u>Redemption Tidings</u> 1.4, p2,3.

34. See <u>Redemption Tidings</u> 1.4, p 9,10.

GIANT STRIDES:
THE FIRST SIX YEARS

Numbers

The number of local assemblies affiliated to Assemblies of God grew extraordinarily in the first six years.

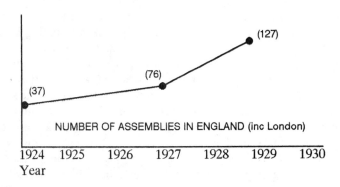

A tabular presentation culled from *Redemption Tidings* for October 1924, July 1927 and July 1929 gives more detail. The July issue of *Redemption Tidings* was published soon after the Whitsun Convention when there would have been a meeting of the General Presbytery and it would therefore have been possible to gain an accurate picture of current affiliation.

NUMBER OF ASSEMBLIES	1924	1927	1929
England (exc London)	30	61	112
London	7	15	15
Wales & Monmouth	36	59	62
Ireland		3	4
Scotland		1	6
TOTAL	74	139	200[1]

The table shows how between 1924 and 1927 almost every area of the United Kingdom saw a doubling in its number of assemblies, whereas between 1927 and 1929 the greatest growth took place in the the main part of England excluding London. What these figures do not reveal, of course, is exactly how many of these assemblies were completely new and how many had been founded soon after the initial outpouring of the Spirit in Sunderland and were then brought into fellowship with Assemblies of God. Nor do the figures give any real indication of the total adult membership of Assemblies of God. Some of the local congregations were very small, and some only lasted for a short time before closing down because of internal difficulties.

There are three other indicators which give clues about the number of people involved in the early days of Assemblies of God. The first is the circulation figure for *Redemption Tidings*. The April 1925 issue contains the note, "We are trying to increase the circulation to 5,000 before the end of the year. Subscriptions are coming in from Canada, USA, China, Palestine, India, and other countries. When you have read your copy, PASS IT ON with prayer for blessing upon it". This would suggest that the circulation was somewhat less than 5,000, though it is impossible to say exactly how much less. If, for the sake of argument, we assume that the circulation ran at 4,000, and if we suppose that readers did indeed pass their copies on to others, then, after subtracting a small overseas quota, we might conservatively estimate the total readership of the magazine was something over 6,000 people. This figure does not give a total membership of Assemblies of God, but it would point to the size of the hard core or to those members who could afford the cost of a quarterly magazine.

The second indicator is given by the number of assemblies. If we assume that each assembly had on average 50 people in attendance[2], then the total number of people involved with Assemblies of God would have been 3700 in 1924, 6950 in 1927 and 10,000 in 1929. These figures seem to tally reasonably with the estimates of circulation for *Redemption Tidings* in 1925 when we should have expected around 4,500 in attendance at Sunday meetings.

The third indicator is given by the size of the annual Kingsway Conventions in London. The July 1925 issue of *Redemption Tidings* contained an article by Donald Gee on the Convention that June. "Approaching 2,000" was the figure bandied about, though Gee himself wrote "1,500 to 1,600 would be a sober estimate". The report the following year recorded "the numbers must have hovered around 2,000 (the Press said 3,000)"[3]. The total size of Assemblies of God is only hinted at by these figures. People living in the north or west of England would have had difficulty in reaching London, and many of the attenders may have been associated with the Elim churches - especially as the Jeffreys brothers were both made "heartily welcome" in 1925[4] - or have been driven by curiosity or reports in the national press.

The size of the meetings at the Kingsway Hall probably more

accurately reflected the strength of Assemblies of God in the country in the mid-1920s. By the end of the decade, as we shall see, there had been numerous campaigns and conventions up and down the land, and, for example, the report on the 1928 gathering was placed alongside a report of a similar event at Crosskeys in Wales. The Kingsway Conventions ceased to be the main forum of pentecostalism in Britain by the end of the 1920s. The most well-known preachers could be heard locally at Easter, Whitsun or Christmas Conventions and the District Presbyteries were usually active in making the necessary arrangements.

Preaching at the Conventions

Many of the Kingsway Convention addresses were printed in *Redemption Tidings* and give an insight into the spiritual state of the pentecostal movement in the late 1920s. Smith Wigglesworth's unpredictable and powerful healing ministry, as well as his extraordinary sermons, were in great demand. He was a generation older than nearly all the other pentecostal preachers of the time - he was about 65 years old in 1924 - and listened to with great respect. Later writers have tended to dismiss his preaching as the effusions of a simple but godly soul[5], but an examination of what he actually said shows him to have had a substantial grasp of the realities of difficult passages in the Pauline epistles. Moreover, his sermons, unlike those of many other preachers, still make an impact from the printed page[6]. The theme which constantly inspired Wigglesworth was that Christ dwelt in the heart of the believer. When Wigglesworth laid hands on the sick, he expected the divine life to provide healing; when he preached, he was quite ready for an utterance in tongues and an interpretation to be included in the sermon. "We do not have to go down to bring Him up nor up to bring Him down. He is nigh thee, He is in thy heart....I am here to-night to say it does not matter how many times we have failed, there is one key note in Pentecost, Holiness unto the Lord. I find the association with my Lord brings purity, and makes my whole being cry out after God, after holiness"[7]. Time and again, Wigglesworth proclaimed that Christians should enjoy a relation of sonship with God and that this sonship stems from a personal acceptance of Christ. The acceptance of Christ results in a new birth - see John 3 - which places within the Christian a completely new principle of life quite different from ordinary human life. Wigglesworth's preaching was often laced with illustrations from his colourful life and there were, at the end of a meeting, nearly always well attested cases of healing as a result of the faith he imparted[8]. The overall impact of his ministry was to stir the congregation to greater consecration and to greater faith. Wigglesworth never delighted in denominationalism, and by common consent[9] he was not a teacher. He believed that the power of God could be manifested at any time to meet any need. While he was alive he ensured that pentecostalism never degenerated into empty formalism or smug complacency. Though he had views on eschatology and the gifts of the Holy Spirit, these never assumed a central place in his message. He expected "mighty revival"[10] rather than tribulation and was insistent that genuine manifestations of the Holy Ghost would lead to an exaltation of Christ.

Wigglesworth preached at the Kingsway Conventions in 1925, 1926 and 1928. The other evangelist who preached there - because Wigglesworth was often billed as an evangelist - was Stephen Jeffreys. He spoke in 1926 on the apostle John who, at the Last Supper was leaning on Christ, and at the crucifixion was standing beside Christ, and after the resurrection was following Christ. Donald Gee's memoir of Jeffreys reports both how tender and how thunderous he could be. In speaking of "leaning on Christ", he instilled a sense of calm and godly trust; in speaking of the power of the cross or, as he did the following year of the shipwreck of the apostle Paul, he summoned a sense of impending divine judgement. Gee said he was like one of the Old Testament prophets proclaiming doom for the impenitent, though in personal conversation he never lost his sense of Welsh humour and repartee[11].

Wigglesworth and Jeffreys kept the eyes of pentecostal Christians looking at the world around them. The other speakers tended to be more devotional or expository. In the six years between 1924 and 1930 approximately 25 people spoke at the Kingsway Convention; the platform was by no means a closed one. Donald Gee spoke in 1925, 1926, 1927, 1929 and 1930. Three of his sermons were reported in *Redemption Tidings*[12]. In 1926, he said

> When waiting on the Lord for a message, knowing that there would be a great many speakers, I thought this will be my only opportunity to speak so I must make the most of it. I thought it would be a fine opportunity to start on a real controversy on the Pentecostal Movement, and answer some of these dear people who write these articles in certain papers warning you against the so-called "Tongues Movement", but I did not get any liberty to speak on any of it. I am not here with controversy, I am here with testimony, and I believe testimony will win where controversy will fail.

Gee's theme, taken from John 7, was the satisfaction of "spiritual thirst" which the infilling of the Holy Spirit gave the Christian. He recounted his own mediocre experience in a Congregational Church and went on to ask rhetorically, "Why is it that Churches are empty ? Because people are not satisfied". He asserted the value of the fulness of the Holy Spirit while, at the same time, showing that it was the absence of this fulness which was rendering inadequate the other Christian groupings which tended to attack pentecostalism. Gee returned to this theme in a later sermon during the same Convention. In an almost prophetic vein he declared

> Last year I was listening for it, and the note I caught then was the note of a new hope, a new expectation, I heard it running through all the while, and although twelve months have rolled by it has been confirmed that it was of the Spirit. What is the note I have heard this time ? A rising tide, a rising tide...God has given us a vision of a rising tide.

For himself he was able to say "I am surprised these days to find that I have come into the experience which I longed to possess years ago". The pentecostal experience satisfied and, so far as Gee was concerned, it fitted squarely with the teaching of the New Testament. Yet, as a realist, he knew that many of his audience would return to the kitchen or the workshop and he was keen to assure them that what God had imparted to them could withstand the rough and tumble of everyday life. The previous year Gee had sensed "new hope" to dispel the gloom which had threatened the still isolated and small pentecostal churches. Within twelve months of hectic activity, he had begun to sense an incoming spiritual tide. As an analysis of the number of assemblies shows, a lot of people were being swept into a new phase of spiritual life. Pentecostal preachers who had hitherto addressed small back-street congregations suddenly found themselves looking at a sea of two thousand faces.

Because the Conventions were occasions of celebration - it was encouraging to be in a large crowd instead of a small congregation - they were rarely analytical. It was in this function that Gee excelled. He wrote quite quickly at this time two series in *Redemption Tidings*, one on spiritual gifts and one on local church life. It was he who began to understood the complementary function of evangelists and pastors or prophets and teachers, and he was able to harness such functions to an explanation of the charismata of the Spirit. Jeffreys and Wigglesworth, perhaps unconsciously, saw the Conventions as a prelude to a huge evangelistic effort. The saints had work to do; God's judgement was ready to fall on godless cities. In the latter part of the 1920s, as we shall see, there were scenes of almost unprecedentedly powerful Gospel preaching. The dynamism of the pentecostal movement in the 1920s is specially evident if one compares the Kingsway Conventions of that decade with a report of the 1936 Convention which merely says "2000 Happy Saints at Kingsway Hall"[13].

Revival campaigns

As the distribution of Methodist Churches shows, even Wesley found urban evangelism difficult. Discussions of secularisation often link it with the industrial revolution and the building of vast conurbations. Considering these unpropitious precedents, the pentecostal campaigns of the late 1920s were remarkably successful. A section for "Home News" in *Redemption Tidings* charted their progress and readers associated with Assemblies of God could hardly open their magazines without being delighted by yet another packed town hall or miraculous healing, or the opening of a new assembly. In 1926 and 1927 the campaigns in the south-east of England were deliberately arranged so that news of miracles in one town could be spread by word of mouth to another one nearby.

Stephen and George Jeffreys were temperamentally very different and matters came to a head in 1926. Stephen left the Elim churches and became free to accept invitations to preach from any quarter. Most invitations came from the Assemblies of God and for two golden years Stephen worked tirelessly on evangelistic campaigns. He was then about 50 years of age[14] and at the height of his powers. His lack of organisation (which contrasted so strongly with the tidy mind of his younger brother George) did not matter so long as someone made sure he was at the right place at the right time. Once presented with a congregation he preached with zeal and humour, and the newly formed Assemblies of God were only too willing to book him up and hire the largest halls in town for him to minister in.

Photographs show him to be a stocky man - he had worked as a miner for twenty-three years - and usually dressed in a slightly rumpled dark suit with a clerical collar[15]. He spoke with a Welsh hwyl and sang with a fine tenor voice. In 1926 he campaigned in Plaistow, Ramsgate, Hackney, Dover, Bedford, Edinburgh, Wales, Margate and Chelmsford[16]. That year the meetings in Bedford were the most well-attended. The *Bedford Record*[17] contained a picture of the packed Corn Exchange where the meetings were held. The crowd is large, seated and, judging by the number of hats visible, more than half female; in fact given the casualties among young men in the 1914-18 war young men would have been less numerous in the population as a whole[18].

> During the hearty singing of some of Alexander's rousing chorus hymns (much of which was accompanied by hand-clapping), cripples and other sufferers were carried in. Pastor Jeffreys led the singing with a typically Welsh tenor voice evidently suffering from over-use....the Pastor's address showed him first of all as an Adventist, believing that the coming of the Lord was at hand...the last great revival, the last great visitation of the Holy Ghost was at hand, and those who were saved that afternoon could count themselves as lucky...from this the Pastor led on to the unnecessarily large burdens most people carried, and reminded his listeners that the little sparrow woke up every morning without knowing where his breakfast was coming from. But someone shook a tablecloth and he was supplied.....after the address came the healing. Those who had tickets mounted the platform on the right and sat in a chair. When the Pastor had done his work they crossed the stage in the full view of the audience and came down from the platform on the left. There was a long queue of sufferers and for nearly an hour until the service closed they followed one another into the chair.

On the last Sunday morning of the fortnight's campaign at least 600 people broke bread together[19], and the local assembly began to flourish.

The next year (1927) Jeffreys was as active as ever. He was in Kent at the beginning of the year and in the north of England at the end of the year[19]. The meetings in Sunderland were the most extraordinary - perhaps the high point of his crusading - and we have account both of what was accomplished there and a detailed diary of his meetings in Bury. Sunderland, of course, had been the home of Alexander Boddy when the Holy Spirit was first outpoured in Britain with charismatic signs. The ground, therefore, was well prepared and huge crowds flocked to the hear the preaching and be healed. Boddy had remained in Sunderland until 1922 and, in addition to his charismatic ministry, a small independent pentecostal meeting existed at a mission hall in the area[20]. Most of those who attended were ex-Methodist or Salvationist, though there were some who had come out of Anglican and

Catholic backgrounds.

The Victoria Hall, which could hold approximately 3000 people, was hired for the campaign and, within three days, was packed to capacity. Crowds began to line the pavements at 9am so as to gain a seat at the 3pm service and mounted police were needed to keep order. Invalid carriages and stretchers brought in the sick by the hundred and there were numerous miracles. "On one day six people wheeled into the hall in carriages were healed, rising, walking and leaving their carriages, and in some cases wheeling them away themselves"[21]. The local newspaper reported that an Alderman presided at one of the "Sunshine Services" where Jeffreys spoke on the Prodigal Son. The presence of civic dignitaries was an added bonus to the crusade because it was more difficult for religious or journalistic comment to deride pentecostalism as the delusion of cranks. On the second Sunday of the crusade over 950 people gathered for the Breaking of Bread while hundreds more waited outside for the afternoon service[21].

The campaign continued for a month and over 3000 people made decisions to follow Christ. On one occasion Jeffreys preached after midnight to a queue waiting for the next day's meetings. The evangelist was enthused by his message and the people were eager to listen. Nothing like it was seen in Sunderland until Billy Graham filled the local football stadium during Mission England in 1984. It was not generally known, however, that Jeffreys was beginning to feel the pace of his constant evangelistic activity. His son reported that "it was a real venture of faith for him to get out of bed each day to minister to the sick...he preached at the Victoria Hall with amazing power. You could hardly believe that this was the same man who an hour before in his own bedroom was prostrate with weakness...in the interval between the afternoon and evening services he would go home and rest in bed to be in readiness for the next meeting. He would get up and sit on the bed completely exhausted"[22].

In December Jeffreys went to Bury in Lancashire. Agnes Adams visited the meetings for the last 10 days and published her account[23] which, because of its detailed diary-like nature, gives a unique insight into the general texture of the campaigning.

<u>Friday afternoon, Dec 9th 1927</u>
The Drill Hall is a vast place: one man told me that four thousand people can dance on the floor. It is a fine hall, but the congregation, although large for a weekday afternoon, was rather lost, and the voices of the speakers resounded with a

hollow echo from the back of the room. Also the hall was cold... Mr Nelson Parr preached - in order to give Pastor Jeffreys a rest. The Pastor was very tired, and had such a bad cold that he found it hard to speak. Nevertheless he gave the personal call to the penitent after the sermon. A considerable number stood, and they repeated after the Pastor a short prayer of self dedication.

The sick were then led to the platform. As always some were healed and some not, the great majority said they felt better, but not quite well "yet." All these not healed added that "yet".

There were many bath chair cases, and no complete healing from the bath chairs, though many said they felt better and tried to rise.

Friday evening

The meeting began as usual with the singing of hymns. Dear Mrs Jeffreys was there...Mr Nelson Parr preached.

Two deaf people were healed, one them a little girl of fourteen...it is remarkable how absolutely joyful most of the unhealed people are.

Saturday afternoon

This afternoon the Pastor was again in fairly good voice and able to conduct the service. There were about three times the number of people that were there the afternoon before, and the place was warmer. Pastor Jeffreys preached from John 5 - the story of the Pool of Bethesda, the healing of the impotent man.... And He asked him a very simple question, "wilt thou be made whole ?" And the man answered, "Sir, I have no-one to put me into the pool". "Dear me!" the Pastor exclaimed, "He hadn't asked him anything about the old pool!"...He spoke of the troubled waters of the pool - how the Spirit of God troubles the waters of the soul - it cannot leave them stagnant or frozen or still. "And whosoever went down first into the waters was made whole of *whatsoever disease he had*". People often ask me "Can cancer be cured ? Can fits be cured...Jesus can cure you of whatsoever disease you have"...the Pastor then gave his direct call to the penitent and a large number stood....people were cured so quickly this afternoon I could not keep pace with them. He always tells those who are not healed - and their friends - to keep on trusting in Jesus, and to believe that God has touched them. Often he reminds them of the lepers who as they went were cleansed.

Saturday evening
There were (at a rough guess) about three thousand people in the hall to-night.

It was the testimony meeting. [Here follows a series of detailed account by people who had been healed from a variety of diseases]

Sunday morning
[This was a communion service attended by about 150 people]

Sunday afternoon
[The hall was about three quarters full. Agnes Adams herself spoke at the meeting and refuted the charge that the healings were produced by "mesmerism". She recorded, though, that her contribution seemed to deaden the meeting. After a sermon on David and the Philistines, "the Pastor gave the call to the penitent, and many stood".]

Sunday evening
There was no sermon...the testimonies of Nellie Welford and her sister took the place of a sermon, and many were in tears as this girl and her sister told their story...I never knew such a night of miracles...the place resounded with hallelujahs and clappings as one after another the blind saw, the deaf heard...one elderly and decidedly portly Lancashire woman seemed to lie back in her chair like a shapeless lump. In a moment after the Pastor's prayer, she swung her arms. "Eeeee! Ay!" she cried, and leapt to her feet, and jumped all about the platform.

Everyone burst out laughing, and clapping. It was impossible not to laugh, indeed it was impossible to stop laughing for a long while. The whole hall rocked. It was one of the most humorous things I have ever seen in my life, and one of the happiest.

These extracts demonstrate some important and often overlooked features of these meetings: firstly, that Jeffreys himself was often under considerable physical strain; secondly, that Jeffreys always was more concerned about the forgiveness of sins than the dramatic manifestation of healing - he was and remained an evangelist at heart; thirdly, the whole matter of the unhealed was a live issue at the time and accounted for some of the criticisms of Jeffreys' ministry, but Jeffreys himself simply said "There has never been a service where everyone was healed. There has never been a service where not one was healed. I go on doing what the Word of God tells me to do - the healing is not mine, but God's"[24]. Local newspapers often contained angry debates in their letter columns. In June 1928 *The Newcastle Chronicle* printed a letter from a "licensed missioner to the Northumberland and Durham Mission to the Deaf and Dumb" who argued that he knew of no authentic healing which had taken place and that apparent healings resulted from the ability of the deaf to lip read. *John Bull* (18th Aug 1928) published an aggressive piece under the headline "Bogus Parson's Wicked Hoax: A Miracle-Monger Unmasked" and suggested that the particular cruelty of Jeffreys' campaigns was that they raised false hopes in the incurably sick and that, when challenged to produce evidence for the healing of organic diseases, "Jeffreys' answer was to flee the city". These criticisms were largely met by Agnes Adams' book to which the *John Bull*[25] article sceptically referred. A photograph in *Redemption Tidings* (Sept 1927) shows Stephen Jeffreys standing beside a man carrying a placard with the words "My answer to all critics. ONCE I WAS BLIND. NOW I CAN SEE. G W Harding, 8 Elm Road, Dartford". Above the photograph is a letter giving details of the industrial accident which had caused the blindness ("I was discharged incurable, and received compensation for the same") and the precise date and circumstances under which vision was restored.

From time to time Jeffreys attacked nominal Christianity, and was accused of laying the blame for the powerlessness of the churches at the door of education. He retorted, "I never had many privileges, not of schooling. I saw in the paper on Saturday that someone said I ran down education. I never did it. I never ran down education - I just wish I had more of it. What I did say was that education without the grace of God makes nothing but educated sinners"[26]. Modernistic interpretations of the Bible did, however, come under Jeffreys' condemnation, "here we have modernists and higher critics swarming the country with ideas and trying to tear the Word of God to pieces"[27]. A general impression of secular and Christian reports of the period suggests that Jeffreys was attacked more often than he attacked; in the main he shrugged off the innuendos and slanders which were directed at him and pressed on with the next campaign. There undoubtedly were genuine healings in his ministry[28] and, nearly 60 years later, he is still remembered with affection while those who criticised him have been largely forgotten.

The success of Jeffreys' campaigns in Kent was intensified by the rapidity with which news of healing and powerful gospel preaching was passed from town to nearby town. In the north east of England the region had already been prepared by the lingering influence of A A Boddy and the Sunderland Conventions. In Manchester the impact of Jeffreys' ministry was preserved and multiplied by the work of J N Parr who, as a result of Jeffreys' visits to his city in December 1927 and March 1928, left his secular employment and devoted his enormous energies to being a full-time pastor. Parr eventually built up one of the largest single congregations in Britain. By the time he retired in 1964 he expected a Sunday night gathering of about 1000 people. Parr's own preaching was fervently and traditionally evangelistic, but his methods were unconventional and had a touch of showmanship about them. On 28th June 1928 Jeffreys sailed for the USA. Though no one knew it then, a chapter had been closed. Other, younger men attempted to do what Jeffreys had done, but they lacked his drive and stamina. Hubert Entwistle was an excellent Gospel preacher and so was Hugh Horler. W J Thomas, another fiery Welshman, showed promise in this direction and, between them from 1926-8, these men held about 10 campaigns in various parts of the country. Horler died tragically young, Entwistle settled into the pastorate at Sunderland - for which it turned out he was not temperamentally fitted - and Thomas eventually became an excellent shepherd to the growing flock at Doncaster. It was not obvious that Jeffreys' early and unobtrusive years had prepared him for his later eminence, nor was it immediately clear to his contemporaries to what extent the geographically fixed ministry of pastor (or local presbyter or elder) was quite distinct from that of the itinerant evangelist. The physical and mental cost of continuous evangelism was high, whereas pastoring a large congregation seemed more secure and less strenuous. And, of course, the new congregations which were springing up all over the country did require looking after. Willie Hacking (b 1902)[29] recalled how he was asked to care for the assembly at Canterbury in about 1927 and shortly afterwards telephoned by Jeffreys and asked to take over a congregation of about 400 people in Southend. Hacking went and stayed there three years before settling in Blackburn for eight years from 1930-8. The congregations were not consulted about their future ministers - the pastoral office seemed to be in the gift of the evangelist. The peculiarity of the situation was that the evangelist might often choose a man to succeed him who was also an evangelist because it was by evangelistic activity that young men demonstrated their sincerity and spirituality. The result was that congregations were nurtured on a diet of soul-stirring revivalism and that ministers changed churches frequently.

In 1933, as we shall see, Nelson Parr resigned from all his offices within Assemblies of God as a result of a slur on his financial probity. The loss of both Parr and Jeffreys within the space of five years blunted the evangelistic edge of the pentecostal movement in the British Isles. George Jeffreys, who was working in Elim, did not conduct any major campaigns after 1934 and so the initial wave of exciting new growth collapsed in the mid-1930s and was followed by a trough of debilitating disagreements[30], alternating with periods of consolidation.

Notes to Pages 85 - 97

1. Including one assembly on the Isle of Man.

2. Nelson Parr in Incredible, p33 gives the membership of Manchester Pentecostal Assembly in 1927 as forty-five people. Membership is usually lower than attendance, so its weekly attendance would probably have been more than forty. Parr's congregation may have been bigger than usual but, as we shall see, there were quite large numbers of people who were interested in pentecostal meetings even if they were officially and technically connected with other denominational groupings. An average of 50 people in attendance, rather than in membership, seems accurate (see below on personal impressions). It is certainly unlikely to have been higher than this figure.

3. Redemption Tidings (June 1926, p 7).

4. Gee's report in Redemption Tidings (July 1925, p 3).

5. Michael Harper's (1965) As At The Beginning tends, but only tends, to do this.

6. This is obviously a subjective judgement.

7. See Wigglesworth's sermon 4th June 1925, Kingsway Hall. Redemption Tidings (July 1925, p 5).

8. See Redemption Tidings (August, 1925, p4) where 11 separate cases of healing are itemised after Wigglesworth had preached on "Faith".

9. Interview with Tom Woods in Bedford in 21st Sept 1985.

10. See Redemption Tidings (December 1925, p 3) "Mighty Revival, I feel it coming, my whole being moves towards it. I dare to believe in simplicity of faith".

11. See Gee (1980), These Men I Knew, p 53 and a long quotation from Gee in Edward Jeffreys' book on his father Stephen Jeffreys: The Beloved Evangelist published in April 1946, London: Elim Publishing Co Ltd, p81.

12. See Redemption Tidings for October 1926, February 1927 and August 1927.

13. See <u>Redemption Tidings</u> vol 12, no 13 (July 1st 1936), p13. This issue also carried an Open Letter from Howard Carter entitled "Keeping the Movement Pure". He warned against the "tares" that had been sown in the pentecostal movement.

14. Jeffreys married on December 26th 1898 and the certificate shows him to have been 23 at that date. Twenty-eight years later in 1926 he must have been 50 or 51 years old.

15. See Cartwright, D (1986) <u>The Great Evangelists</u>, Basingstoke: Marshal Pickering. In some respects Jeffreys' career is like that of the Nottinghamshire fast bowler Harold Larwood. They both emerged from the pits to national prominence and they were both gluttons for hard work.

16 This list come from Cartwright (1986) chapter 10. <u>Redemption Tidings</u> (for July 1926) also mentions a campaign at Southend and the issue for October 1926 mentions a three day convention at Rayleigh in Essex.

17. Presumably a local newspaper. It was quoted at length in the July issue of <u>Redemption Tidings</u> for 1926.

18. W R Inge (1926) in <u>Lay Thoughts of a Dean</u>, London: Putnam's Sons, suggests that there were roughly 600,000 fatal casualties among English and Welsh men as a result of the Great War. The influenza epidemic immediately after the War killed about 112,000, but women would presumably have been as susceptible to the disease as men.

19. D W Cartwright (1986) mentions Jeffreys' visits to Folkstone in January, Canterbury in February, Bishop Auckland in March, then visits to Louth, Maidstone, Gravesend, Sunderland, Spennymoor, Chesterfield in October, and then Bury and Manchester.

20. A visit to the Sunderland area and a weekend in autumn 1985 where the congregation of the existing Assemblies of God were invited to share "all our yesterdays" elicited a large amount of information on the groundwork for the Jeffreys crusade. I suspected that there had to be a nucleus of people in Sunderland before Jeffreys arrived to have issued the original invitation to him. This proved to be the case. Alderman Walker, a wealthy man who owned a flour mill, probably agreed to underwrite the costs of the crusade. Certainly Mr Walker's wife supported the 50 or so people who met at the more or less pentecostal holiness mission in Hinds Bridge upper room from about 1914 onwards.

21. See <u>Redemption Tidings</u> October 1927.

22. See E Jeffreys (1946) <u>Stephen Jeffreys: The Beloved Evangelist</u>, London: Elim Publishing Co, p 73,74.

23. See A Adams (1928) <u>Stephen Jeffreys</u>, London: The Covenant Publishing Co. The date of publication is given at the end of the preface and not on the flyleaf.

24. See A Adams (1928), <u>Stephen Jeffreys</u>, London: The Covenant Publishing Co, p 52.

25. Alan Wilkinson (1986), <u>Dissent or Conform?</u>, London: SCM, p 43, "Horatio Bottomley, the editor of <u>John Bull</u>, who used the war to feather his own nest, often employed the type of patriotic rhetoric with biblical undertones which proved so popular". D Cartwright (1986) The Great Evangelists Basingstoke: Marshall Pickering, p 100, points out that Bottomley had served seven years of imprisonment for fraud.

26. See A Adams (1928), <u>Stephen Jeffreys</u>, London: The Covenant Publishing Co, p 87.

27. See A Adams (1928), <u>Stephen Jeffreys</u>, London: The Covenant Publishing Co, p 80.

28. The sister of S E Petts (a retired headmaster) of Mattersey, Nr Doncaster, was deaf

and dumb from birth and healed during a Jeffreys campaign. I know S E Petts personally.

29. Willie Hacking was 82 years old on 14th November 1984 when the writer and Mr David Allen interviewed him at his home in Morecambe, Lancs.

30. As we shall see, the relatively trivial matter of clerical attire became a major bone of contention.

THE THIRTIES

Social and economic conditions of the 1930's

Light fiction presents a simple picture of the 1930s. Bertie Wooster and Jeeves bumble their way through the intricacies of upper class etiquette and romantic intrigue; Bulldog Drummond and Biggles, slightly more alert to the dangers of the international situation than their comic counterparts, would nevertheless have attended the same London clubs and played on the same golf courses. Whereas Drummond solved life's problems with a straight left to the chin, Jeeves found a diplomatic solution to his master's predicaments. There was a lazy assumption that the products of the British public school would beat the rest of the world. Indeed, the 1930s were a decade of excellent cricket as Hobbs and Sutcliffe[1] regularly opened England's batting. After the match, at a large country house, the "bright young things" who populated Noel Coward's comedies danced to a jazz band or a rhythmic charleston. All was right with the world. The "war to end war" had been fought and won. The Oxford Union debate of 1933 expressed a common mood by voting for the motion "this House will not fight for King and Country". Beneath the escapism and the languid *joie de vivre*, however, there were darker realities.

The most obvious and crippling reality was the poverty to which a large proportion of the British Isles was condemned. Unemployment was the cause of poverty, and unemployment hit the large industrial regions whose goods were undercut by cheaper manufacturing abroad. The Empire had subsidised British prosperity and the loss of the Empire implied Britain's impoverishment.

A Labour government was formed in 1929 under Ramsay MacDonald and a committee was set up to deal with unemployment. By the autumn of 1930 the unemployment figures had risen to more than two million but the cabinet was unable to agree on an effective course of action. Economic orthodoxy demanded that the budget be balanced and that, so far as possible, Britain continue on the gold standard to fortify international confidence in the value of the pound. But so far as the social effects of a financial and banking crisis was concerned, the predominant attitude in Parliament and the Stock Exchange was, "we have done nothing. There is nothing we can do"[2]. When drastic cuts in unemployment benefit (the dole) were proposed by Snowden, the Chancellor of the Exchequer, nine members of the cabinet were prepared to resign, though most of them had no comprehensive alternative strategy. A National government was formed in the summer of 1931. Ramsay Macdonald continued as Prime Minister, but Labour opinion gradually hardened against him and, indeed, accused him of betraying the interests of those who had elected him. The new cabinet contained four Conservatives, four Labour and two Liberals. The main bulk of the Labour party felt that they had been cheated by unscrupulous capitalists and that the financial crisis was somehow engineered by bankers and financiers to destroy the credibility of the previous Labour government.

Payment to the unemployed was regulated by a Means Test which was intended to ensure that only the "deserving" poor received monetary help from the public purse. The effect of the Test was appalling: it penalised the families with savings (because no dole was paid to unemployed men who had frugally banked small sums); it broke families up (because elderly relatives with savings who lived with their children also disqualified the home from receiving dole payments); it was often not paid to families who had furniture worth small amounts of money (with the result that married couples had to sell their sideboards and beds before being allowed to draw their weekly benefit). The Means Test therefore created bitterness, a bitterness made all the worse by the expectation that after 1918 when the Great War had finally been won Britain would be a country "fit for heroes". Two and a half million disabled received inadequate government pensions and were forced to seek work at a time when even the able bodied were struggling to hold down any of the jobs on offer. Moreover, a bureaucratic mentality had devised a system of payments to the disabled based on the number of limbs or joints lost. A right arm missing from the shoulder realised a pension of 16s a week. If the arm was missing from below the elbow, the pension was only 11s 6[d] per week, and left arms were costed 1s less for each joint. A skilled man who had lost three fingers might be as unemployable as a man without an arm, but the assessment of injury was not based on potential loss of earnings. At the worst stage of the depression in the winter of 1931-2, almost three million workers were officially classed as unemployed - 25% of the working population[3]. For each man unemployed, a family was usually affected and Orwell estimated that over ten million people in the nation as a whole were underfed[4].

Of course the unemployment and hunger were regional. The worst areas were in Wales (37%), Scotland (30%) and the North-East and North West of England (about 27%). Ship building, iron works and coal mining were drastically reduced and most writers of the period agree that a sense of apathy and hopelessness laid heavily upon the once thriving industrial towns[5]. The Labour government had not improved the lot of the working man, and therefore it was assumed that the lot of the working man was beyond improvement. The Communist party never totalled more than 18,000 members, and that was at the end of the thirties when the worst of the depression was past, partly because of the detestation of the Soviet Union which most British people instinctively felt. It is true that the New Left Book Club publicised Marxist solutions to economic problems which appealed to middle-class intellectuals. When the Spanish Civil War broke out in the mid-30s, the conscience of the younger generation was aroused and Auden, Spender, Orwell, Macneice and others made their way - sometimes by taxi - to the front line. The international dimension, then, whether it was fighting Franco's fascism or worrying about Hitler or the problems of the British Raj, distracted politicians and thinkers from the plight of large numbers of poor at home. Extreme right-wing solutions to domestic poverty were propounded by Oswald Mosley but they were as generally unacceptable as extreme left-wing solutions. Gradually, as the thirties proceeded, unemployment fell and those fortunate to keep their jobs throughout the decade found a distinct change for the better in their standard of living. Real wages rose by about 11% between 1929 and 1933 and by a further 5% up till 1937[6]. By this time the threat of war was acute enough to cause a strong peace movement in Britain. The worst of the depression was over. In considering the history of the pentecostal movement, however, it is important to bear in mind that many of the new assemblies came to life in the areas where unemployment and hunger were worst. The lively singing, often setting catchy spiritual songs to music hall tunes, and the powerful preaching coupled with an expectation in divine healing, gave hope to the hopeless.

Money

"A survey of about 800 families in Stockton-on-Tees in the early 1930s revealed that the average income of families where the wage-earner was unemployed was 20s 2½d a week, compared with 51s 6d for families where there was no unemployment"[7]. Orwell calculated that "the mineworker's average earning throughout Great Britain in 1934 should really be something nearer £105"[8], which is almost exactly £2 per week. This figure tallies with the table given by Cole and Postgate[9] who conclude that "in the autumn of 1935...in a number of fairly typical industries men's earnings averaged from £3 to £3 10s a week". Women earned about half the male wage and apprentices might expect about 5s a week[10]. Computations about the minimum necessary requirements for a family in the mid-1930s varied considerably. Orwell (1937: 214) quotes an estimated budget of 3s 11^d as sufficient for food for one person for a week. Cole and Postgate (1938: 620) quote the minimum amount needed in 1937 for a family with three children as being 53s a week, this amount containing a small allowance for fuel, rent and miscellaneous items. An unemployed married man in 1933 drew 25s per week on the dole[11]; a typical family might draw 30s per week, of which a quarter could be written off in rent[12]. Again it needs to be emphasised that "enormous groups of people, probably a third of the whole population of the industrial areas, are living at this level"[12]. What, then, did the pastors of pentecostal assemblies receive at this time ? How well were assemblies funded ? How much did students at the Bible School have to find ? What sorts of sums were given for missionary work ?

Most of the information in answer to these question is impressionistic. Only the Elim churches collected centralised records of Sunday and weekly offerings and these allow a precise base line to be drawn. Nevertheless there were great variations in what individual ministers received (for example George Jeffreys himself paid over £5000 for the purchase of Kensington Temple[13]) and a pastor's wages might suddenly plummet if his large assembly split because of internal disagreements.

A married Elim minister at the top of his pay scale received 65s per week and a supplement of 30s for his rent allowance in 1933. Probationary Elim ministers received £1 per week as well as their board and lodging. In the same year a committee at the Elim Conference recommended that married ministers should receive £5 per week (which included a housing allowance). By February 1936 this recommendation had been carried and married men on the top rate received £5 per week[14] (or £260 per year) and a single man £180 per year. When these figures are compared with the average wage for the period, it is clear that Elim ministers, who were all paid centrally, received comfortably in excess of the norm for the working man. Even after having to take a reduction in pay in 1937, Elim ministers on the highest rate received 10s a week more than the average wage in the last year of the decade.

On the other hand wages in Assemblies of God varied a great deal. Aaron Linford put them at about 30-40s a week in the early 1930s. As a married man he himself averaged 22s 6^d between 1931-6 while he was pioneering a church in Norwich whose congregation grew from 8 to 24 people in the six year period[15]. W Hacking earned £6 per week in 1927 while pastoring in Southend after a crusade by Stephen Jeffreys had left a congregation of 450 people[16]. W J Thomas was paid the same amount 1928-32 while he was pastoring at Doncaster. Jeffreys himself was paid whatever came in at each offering during the campaign meetings. The sums involved must have been substantial, though Jeffreys had a staff of about six people who travelled with him and for whose welfare he was responsible[17].

Social norms

The 1930s were a period of social change. Young men and women born in 1910, who had been too young to fight in the Great War, attained an age of majority in the 1930s, and, as with the post-war generation which came of age in the 1960s, there was a tendency to throw the shibboleths and restraints of an earlier era to the winds. The older generation had failed, it had not built a better world and its maxims and precepts were discredited. Orwell in a typically insightful essay of the period reviewed the modern tends in literature and distinguished between the older writers like Wells, Shaw and Galsworthy who were basically pre-war in their attitudes and the newer wave which included Auden, Spender and the Bloomsbury group[18].

Contraception, an increased divorce rate, holiday camps, the appearance of the family motor car, Sunday sport, Greyhound racing, the BBC, cinemas and building societies all came into some prominence in the thirties. Politically, it has been called "the age of Baldwin"[19]; extremism of the left and right failed to capture the public imagination or a large following and, while intellectuals fought Franco, the basic desire of most people was dictated by a desire to avoid war at any cost. Contraception, of course, tended to limit the size of families and therefore to raise the standard of living of those couples where one or both was employed. Divorce was twice as common in 1939 as in 1922[20], but had not reached epidemic proportions. The new opportunities for travel and entertainment, however, had a noticeable effect on most nonconformist religion and forced the pentecostal movement to decide one way or the other whether it wished to endorse or reject the symptoms of modernity. Alan Wilkinson has a chapter entitled "The Assimilation of Dissent" in *Dissent or Conform?* - a revealing title - (SCM, 1986) and he shows how the Methodist evening class (which was often purely educational in character) was simply superseded by the burgeoning attractions of cultural pursuits fostered through secular institutions of various kinds.

Pacifism

Conscientious objectors had been unfavourably treated in the 1914-18 War. During the 1930s a number of ex-army chaplains expressed their conversion to the pacifist cause, the most famous of these being "Dick" Sheppard and Charles Raven[21]. When the 1939 war began, Temple who was to become Archbishop of Canterbury in 1942, certainly recognised the pacifist position as a genuine Christian vocation, though one he did not share[22]. Pacifism in the thirties was expressed by the 50,000 signatures Sheppard received in 1934 pledging "we renounce war, and never again, directly or indirectly, will we support or sanction another"[23]. When war broke out in 1939 there were 59,000 Conscientious Objectors and Wilkinson estimated that no more than 15,000 of these were Christians. As we shall see, the pentecostal churches took two basic positions with regard to war: the Assemblies of God and the Elim churches took a pacifist stance, but accepted the conscience of individual members might lead them to bear arms; the Bible Pattern group, which was formed by George Jeffreys after he had left Elim, was also pacifist, but tended to accentuate nationalistic feeling by way of compensation for non-combattance.

Church preoccupations in the 1930s

The preoccupations of the Church of England and of Nonconformity in the 1930s provide two areas of thought and activity against which the concerns of the pentecostal movement can be measured. The Church of England was presided over by Cosmo Gordon Lang, a man compared by Neville Chamberlain to an excellent civil servant, and one who developed "an unctuous and patronizing paternalism" because he was unable to distinguish between dignity and pomposity[24]. Lang supported appeasement, was remarkably unconcerned at the crises of conscience provoked by the 1930 debate at the Lambeth Conference on birth control, and he seemed distant from the   perplexities and agonies of the ordinary (unemployed) man in the street.

Perhaps the most vocal and influential group within the Church of England was epitomised by William Temple. The COPEC movement[25], of which he was the chairman, created a climate of opinion within Anglicanism and, indeed, the ecumenical movement, which was pervasive and important. It was socialist in outlook, though its basis was definitely Christian, and it was criticised by ecclesiastical figures like Inge and Henson who tended to find themselves isolated on the more conservative wing of politics. The temper of COPEC was reformist rather than revolutionary. It was typical of Temple's approach that, in attacking the major social issue of the day - that of unemployment, he first directed his attention to practical schemes to alleviate the boredom and sense of uselessness which many of the long-term unemployed felt. Later, in 1936, he secured funds from the Pilgrim Trust to enquire into the conditions, causes and types of unemployment more accurately. The 450 page report was published in 1938 and praised on all sides, but the practical results of Temple and his committee's enterprise were seen in the prior setting up of occupational centres, classes and the like[26].

Education has long been a concern of the church. Temple's most productive energies in the 1930s were directed to adult education. In general there was an acceptance, fostered by Temple that secondary education was not the province of an elite. There were altogether 174,000 secondary pupils in 1913 and the comparable figure for 1935 was 457,000[27]. When one considers that the birth rate declined during the 1930s, it is evident that more children were receiving a longer period of schooling than their parents.

Despite the increase in the numbers of pupils and the opportunities for educational advancement, there were children who, because of the poverty of their families, either deliberately failed exams which would have enabled them to pass to the next stage of education or passed the exams and then refused to take up the Grammar School places reserved for them. Melvyn Bragg's interviews in Cumbria discovered elderly men whose lives had been largely relegated to unskilled work for these reasons[28]. The tempo and mode of education on offer in the 1930s (apart from the few experimental schools founded by individualists like Betrand Russell or A S Neil) would have struck a modern observer as rigid and authoritarian. You did what you were told, or you were caned; you chanted your multiplication tables or the spellings of difficult words; you were a passive recipient of numerous facts rather than a discoverer of the riches of a cultural heritage. Schools were often architecturally unpleasant - cold, with poor plumbing and crowded playgrounds[29]. Schools reflected the stratification and orderliness of society.

Because Anglo-Catholicism tended to be powerful in the higher reaches of the Church of England (there were only about three evangelical bishops in the decade before the 1939-45 War[30]) evangelical Anglicans tended to express their affinity with Free Church believers at the interdenominational Keswick Conventions. As a group, evangelical Anglicans were inclined to avoid contact with non-Christians as much as possible - they were a "separated" people who did not go cinemas or theatres - and who lived moral and disciplined lives. There was little in the way of evangelical scholarship, though the founding of the IVF (Inter-Varsity Fellowship) in 1928 gradually came to remedy this lack. Pentecostalism, which later came to identify with and draw upon the general fund of scholarly evangelical writing about the Bible, found little in the 1930s to emulate or covet. Pentecostal Christians also lived disciplined and moral lives. They, too, travelled long distances to hear sermons and made every effort to be separated from the entertainments and values of the world. Pentecostal conventions were felt to be better any than others not only by virtue of the standard of preaching but also because of the healings and other miraculous signs which attended them.

At first sight it seems odd that Nonconformity in the 1930s has less in common with pentecostalism than evangelical Anglicanism. The roots of pentecostalism were by and large Methodist, Salvationist or even Brethren. Yet, of course, nearly all the leaders of the pentecostal movement had attended the Sunderland Conventions and it was style and outlook of these, as well as the roots of the Carter brothers in the Church of England and Donald Gee in Congregationalism, which made evangelical Anglicanism a natural point of comparison. Moreover, though George Jeffreys came from a background which was thoroughly Nonconformist, the criticisms of pentecostalism which he encountered would have tended to make him model his ministry on the convention style which was above reproach. Thus, for example, during some of his huge meetings in the Royal Albert Hall Jeffreys ensured that the programme was worked out precisely to the second[31]. There was no "pentecostal liberty" for anyone to jibe at.

Yet pentecostalism and Nonconformity were on divergent paths in the thirties because the latter was beginning to lose its traditional reason for existence. Nonconformist leaders began to be minor figures of the establishment. They dined at the high tables of Oxbridge Colleges, ecumenical conferences took note of their views and in terms of theological scholarship they began to boast men who could be considered on a level with the evangelical Anglicans of the previous decade[32]. Even the traditional connection between Nonconformity and pacifism became less clearcut[33]. But it was the social and educational side of Nonconformity which seemed a betrayal of Christianity to the early pentecostals. The custom of evening class lectures on Victorian poets or band practice in Methodist halls seemed an irrelevance to Christians who had embraced the reality of the Holy Spirit. Nonconformity had been used to providing a complete cultural, social and recreational environment for its members. When these provisions could be obtained as cheaply and as readily elsewhere, there was little left for dissent to offer[34]. Cars and bicycles made concerts and lectures within reach; the sealed Nonconformist atmosphere was blown away. Across the dissenting spectrum membership dwindled: Methodist, Baptist and Congregational figures shrank by more than 40% between 1910 and 1980[35]. Pentecostals drew the conclusion that a departure from the primacy of scriptural preaching led inevitably to decline. When others looked in other directions for answers (for example there were high hopes among the Anglicans that "Parish Communion" would revitalise grassroots religious faith), the pentecostals never had any doubt that campaigning and praying were the only solutions which the New Testament church would have countenanced.

Notes to Pages 69 - 109

1. They regularly opened for England. Hobbs scored 197 centuries between 1905 and 1934. Frank Wharton's Billie Bunter with cap, caning, Latin, and gowned teachers depicts the public school, and incidentally the grammar school, of the period.

2. This is how A J P Taylor (1975), p 361, summarises the view in Whitehall. Keynes had not yet worked out his economic theory to demonstrate how Government spending could mitigate the worst effects of trading slumps.

3. These figures are taken from J Stevenson (1984), British Society 1914-45, Harmondsworth: Penguin, p 266f.

4. See G Orwell (1937) The Road to Wigan Pier, p 201 of the edition published in 1983 as The Penguin Complete Longer Non-Fiction of George Orwell.

5. See G D H Cole and Raymond Postgate (1938), The Common People: 1746-1938, London: Methuen, p 606.

6. See G D H Cole and Raymond Postgate (1938), The Common People: 1746-1938, London: Methuen, p 617.

7. See John Stevenson (1984), British Society 1914-45, Harmondsworth: Penguin p 282.

8. See G Orwell (1937), The Road to Wigan Pier, p 180 of edition previously cited.

9. See G D H Cole and Raymond Postgate, The Common People: 1746-1938, London Methuen, p 619.

10. See M Bragg (1976), Speak for England, London: Book Club Associates, p 153

11. See note 10 p169.

12. See note 4 p 203.

13. See Desmond Cartwright (1986), The Great Evangelists, P 120.

14. Desmond Cartwright the official Elim historian supplied these figures. I am not sure what the tax position was on housing allowances. Pastoral salaries can usefully be compared with payment of teachers. If this comparison is made, teachers certainly come out ahead. In 1923 the average male certificated teacher earned £310 per year. [S J Curtis (1961) History of Education in Great Britain London: University Tutorial Press, p 346]. I have not discovered what sort of salaries teachers received in the 1930s.

15. In an interview conducted by David Allen and myself on 9th November 1984.

16. In an interview conducted by David Allen and myself on 14th November 1984.

17. In an interview conducted on with A J Lucas by Ken Healey and myself on 25th June 1986.

18. See G Orwell (1962) Inside the Whale and other Essays, Harmondsworth: Penguin. The essay referred to is "Inside the Whale" which was written in 1940.

19. See R Blake (1985) The Conservative Party from Peel to Thatcher, London: Fontana

20. See Randle Manwaring (1985) From Controversy to Co-existence, Cambridge: CUP, p 46.

21. See Alan Wilkinson (1985) Dissent or Conform ? London: SCM, p 104.

22. See note 21 above, p 290.

23. See note 21 above, p 136.

24. See note 21 on previous page, p 138,139.

25. Conference on Politics Economics and Citizenship, 1924, and better known thereafter by its acronym.

26. See F A Iremonger (1948) William Temple, London: OUP.

27. See G D H Cole and Raymond Postgate (1938), The Common People, London: Methuen, p 631.

28. See Melvyn Bragg (1976), Speak for England, London: Book Club Associates, passim.

29. See note 28 above, p 316.

30. See R Manwaring (1986), From Controversy to Co-Existence, Cambridge: CUP, p 43, 102.

31. Personal communication from D W Cartwright.

32. C H Dodd is a clear example of a Nonconformist scholar whose work was respected in Anglican circles just as the opinions of Wescott and Moule had been listened to by Nonconformists a generation previously.

33. Lloyd George knew how to manipulate Nonconformist opinion and it was he, as much as anyone else, who mobilised the chapels behind the war effort from 1916 onwards.

34. A Wilkinson (1986), Conform or Dissent?, London: SCM. 13f.

35. See note 3 above, p 56. These figures are supported by trends discussed in M Argyle & B Beit-Hallahmi (1975), The Social Psychology of Religion, London: Routledge & Kegan Paul, Chapter 2.

The Condition of Typical Assemblies:
Royston and Doncaster

The revival campaigns of the 1920s often produced new pentecostal assemblies or numerically strengthened the small groups which had issued invitations to Jeffreys or the other evangelists. There are still people alive who have a clear recollection of the life of these new or growing assemblies and an interview with Aaron Linford[1] (b 1909) conveys much of the atmosphere and format.

> Now one thing about those early days that lives in our memory and will forever was the *intensity* of the experience we enjoyed. We really were wholly in it. Mind you, it was something new then. Today there is such a widespread charismatic atmosphere, but then it was something new.

Members of the assembly wrapped their lives round the activities of the assembly. There were two mid-week meetings and two Sunday services. There were also regular occasions when the Gospel was preached in the open-air. At holiday times - Easter, Whitsun or Christmas - people flocked to multiple meetings at Conventions.

> At our Royston Christmas Convention we would have three or four full days. We would spend most of the entire time in the church; we would have dinner and tea there, we would go home to sleep but we would go in the morning for the morning meeting, we would stay for dinner, afternoon meeting, stay for tea, then night meeting.

The absence of television and radio, and the bleak economic conditions which most people in the late 1920s and 30s faced, made thriving church life one of the few attractions in an otherwise drab existence.

Each Sunday morning the congregation would Break Bread and there would be unaccompanied singing using a hymn book compiled by the (Plymouth) Brethren.

> As we got to a certain point of fellowship and intense feeling, there'd be singing in the Spirit [ie singing in tongues/glossalalia] and I have never heard singing with the Spirit anywhere like I heard in those days. It wasn't just a few notes you know, kind of a few chords struck, somebody going up and somebody

going down. We were in perfect harmony, and the greatest thing was that when you were caught up in the Spirit of this thing you fitted in.

The unity of the congregation was expressed in the seating because all the believers were arranged in a circle around the table on which the bread and wine stood. Yet, despite certain fixed features about the communion, nobody knew what course the meeting would take. People spoke as they felt they should.

We would come to the meeting and we would sit quietly. There was no starting off straight away, so we would sit quietly for a bit, then somebody might strike a chorus, someone would go to the front and read a scripture, somebody else might say 'shall we sing hymn number so-and-so'.

Several people would stand up and deliver a short sermon (or "message" as it was usually called). At sixteen years of age Linford was quite at liberty to preach briefly to everyone else present, and he felt the acceptance of teenagers as full and active members of the body contributed to the success of the church. The congregation grew to about 100 people and came to influence the life of the mining village where it was situated.

There were traces of Methodism and Brethrenism in the new assemblies because it was from these two roots that much of the weekly life of pentecostalism sprang. Each Sunday evening the Gospel was preached and church members were encouraged to bring their unconverted friends to this meeting. During the week there was a Bible study which was held by the pastor. Members were discouraged from reading any other books than the Bible (or a Concordance) and there was little contact with other Christians. At Royston Linford recalls that the pastor and some of the older men had been Methodist lay preachers, but Methodism was then inclined to feel that it had outgrown its evangelistic heritage with the result that its attitude to the Bible was modernistic. Even the Salvation Army's view of the inspiration of Scripture had moved away from the traditional position held by William Booth. "We were very largely despised and persecuted by the other churches. Now we earned some of that. We probably asked for it because we would go down the street shouting 'glory hallelujah'". In fact there were strongly anti-denominational elements in the early Assemblies of God. The denominations were regarded as "the harlot daughters" of Babylon, the apostate church. "The trouble is we classed them all alike and of course they reacted against us and it did create bad feeling".

The impression given by the early pentecostal assemblies was that they were ruggedly individualistic. Many of the leaders had been imprisoned for conscientious objection during the 1914-18 war and had been ejected from their childhood denominations for believing that speaking in tongues was the sign of the baptism in the Holy Spirit. Having been forced to leave their original denominations, it is not surprising that these pentecostal leaders reacted strongly against most forms of denominationalism; and having been socially rejected because of their refusal to support the war with Germany, they resisted the blandishments of secular culture. Horizons were narrow and most doctrinal positions were held with extreme tenacity. "We were firm almost to bigotry on divine healing. We would not go to a doctor. In fact if anyone went to a doctor they'd failed the Lord". And so "if you had anything wrong with you, you would always be anointed with oil by the elders - that was the first thing you did". This willingness to believe that a miracle would meet every reasonable need was expressed by the custom of going to kneel at the front during any prayer time in a meeting. Reliance on God - whether in preaching, in sickness or in financial straits - was a hallmark of early pentecostalism. Moreover reliance on God was fundamental to the basic experience of baptism in the Holy Spirit. People were taught that there was little or no human component in this spiritual baptism, and many Christians wanted to feel that they were overwhelmed and constrained by the Holy Spirit. The usual procedure for receiving the baptism in the Spirit was to attend a "waiting meeting" (a term derived from Acts 1.4) and to expect that, during prayer, one would be filled with the Holy Spirit and speak with tongues. At Royston "every meeting", Linford said, "could become a 'waiting meeting'...it was looked upon as part of the situation...I remember it was on a Friday night when I went out, well I'd been out several times really, but this Friday night I went out and received the Holy Spirit and spoke in tongues".

The ministerial work of the assembly was originally done by a "working pastor", that is, a pastor who had a secular job, and the elders. The pastor was the preacher and the elders presided at meetings, dealt with minor disciplinary matters and went to the homes of those who were too ill to travel. Clashes between the elders and the pastor seem not to have occurred in the earliest assemblies because the pastor, having been appointed by the people or having founded the church, appointed the elders. Only later, when there was a generation gap between the younger pastors coming from the Bible School and the older men who had functioned as elders since the 1920s, were there disagreements which would often cause the pastor to look for another flock. At Royston Joe Richardson "was a great powerful, strong emphatic preacher. He would not only teach us the Word very strongly, he would also tell us, especially as young men, 'hammer it out on your own anvil, go to the Bible for yourself, look it up, work it out'". Preaching was imbued with an expectation of the Second Advent and so the Gospel was communicated urgently.

> We really felt the coming of the Lord was near. There was hardly a convention that went by but that there was at least one message on the Second Advent and among the fundamentals [the credal statement] of Assemblies of God that was indeed possibly, together with the initial evidence[2], the most prominent. And healing of course, we were keen on that. But the Second Advent we always rejoiced in that. Oh joy, oh delight, should we go without dying ?!

Royston was typical of many assemblies in that it grew up steadily in a small industrial area. The outlook of its members was enthusiastic and parochial. Linford himself was even strongly advised not to go to the Assemblies of God Bible School by one of the elders, "if you go there, you will lose your ministry". But there was another class of typical assemblies which had grown more rapidly by the influx of numerous converts during a crusade. Doncaster is an example of this second kind of assembly[3]. Very gradually between 1912 and 1920 a small pentecostal prayer meeting began to grow and to take on some of the functions of a local church. A Bible study for young people was initiated, a regular place for public meetings was eventually bought or hired and itinerant pentecostal preachers - many of those who had attended the Sunderland Conventions years before - began to be invited. The church was small and there does not appear to have been a full-time pastor, but in 1924, with the formation of Assemblies of God, the church entered a new phase because it felt more confident and less isolated. Its own identity became clearer and it was less frequently dubbed "Christian scientist" or confused with the "spiritualists"[4]. It grew to about 40 adults and was led by two elders, Mr J Parkinson and Mr A J Lucas, who, after prayer and fasting, decided to ask Stephen Jeffreys "to stir up the people of Doncaster"[5]. Jeffreys was a hard man to pin down and was eventually booked on May 14th 1928.

Jeffreys duly arrived and the Co-operative Hall, with a capacity for 500 people, was soon full[6]. The crowd was a mixed one. Some came expecting miracles, others were sceptical and thought Jeffreys was a quack who used hypnotism or concealed electrical appliances[7]. The evangelist, though, knew his job large numbers of people committed themselves to Christ[8]. The *Doncaster Chronicle* (May 1928) published an article detailing some of the healings and gave the names and addresses of those who had been healed. Two meetings a day were held for a fortnight (with three on Sundays and one on Fridays) by the end of which time the regular Doncaster congregation had increased from forty to two hundred. It was at this point that the elders of the Doncaster assembly showed their foresight. They immediately invited W J Thomas, another Welshman who been a coal miner but had become an experienced preacher, to be their full-time pastor. Thomas started his pastoral duties on July 17th 1928 and, within a year, the assembly had a membership of around four hundred and fifty. The original publicity for the August campaign was not withdrawn (partly because the deposit for the Guildhall had been paid) and so Thomas preached once or twice a day that month. Altogether, therefore, Doncaster had six weeks of crusading and both Thomas and Jeffreys saw remarkable attestations of their ministries by means of miraculous healings. The congregation eventually assembled under Thomas' leadership was a mixed one. It contained completely new converts who had been plucked from the pubs and the dance floors, and it also contained families which had been Anglican, Salvationist, Spiritist, Methodist, Brethren, Nazarene and so on. Thomas had to mould the disparate believers into one new flock. In this he was successful. When a split took place a few years later, it was more along family or geographical lines than along lines corresponding with previous denominational loyalty. Though we do not have records of what Thomas taught, it is clear from Lucas's recollections (he was born in 1894 and was still alive and sharp-witted in the summer of 1986 when I went to interview him) that adult baptism by immersion was emphasised. Within a year or two about 300 people were baptised in a Baptist Church building which had been borrowed for the occasion. Thomas proved to be an able and hard-working pastor: he preached four times a week and "could open the Scripture for an hour"[9] without anyone stirring or wanting to go home at the end. The meetings would often continue till 10 pm when the caretaker would appear outside the doors shaking his keys.

For three years no serious trouble arose and then, from a clear sky, a dispute arose between Thomas and the elders, of whom Lucas was one. Thomas was receiving £6 per week but asked if he could be have whatever was left over from the offerings after the church's expenses had been paid. It is difficult to see what Thomas's motives were. It has been suggested that he thought he was underpaid in relation to the total income of the church; on the other hand, if the church expenses rose as a result of expenditure on a permanent building, Thomas would have taken a drop in salary. It may well have been that the Doncaster elders were unaware of Thomas's willingness to give his own money to the poor in his congregation[10], and that they therefore thought he was being avaricious. Alternatively Thomas's motive may have simply have been based on a desire to gain a measure of independence from the control of his elders. Donald Gee, in a similar position in Edinburgh, asked if he could be paid whatever was in an offering box at the back of the church rather than at a level set by his Oversight. At any event Thomas left Doncaster and began a new assembly in Bentley, a village just outside the town.

Bad feeling was engendered by what happened. Various members of the congregation went to Bentley with their pastor, while others stayed in Doncaster. Families were split up and the whole matter had to be taken to the Executive Presbytery of Assemblies of God for a solution. J N Parr of Manchester met representatives from Bentley and Doncaster and suggested to them that a member of the Executive Presbytery hear both sides of the case and then make an authoritative and binding decision on what should happen next. Bentley, however, did not agree to this suggestion, and so the Executive concluded that nothing further could be done[11]. Three months later the two assemblies seemed more ready to forget their differences. The Executive Presbytery minutes for May 2nd 1932 record that a reconciliation had been effected and that both parties agreed for forgive the other for any wrongs they had suffered. No transfer of membership was to be allowed unless endorsed by the pastor and elders and everyone had a month to decide which assembly they wanted to settle in. The whole episode illustrates the explosive nature of the early years of the pentecostal movement. W J Thomas did not stay long at Bentley because of illness and returned to north Wales where he died. Before he did so, though, he went to see A J Lucas and admitted that he had made a mistake in leaving Doncaster. When Thomas had gone, some of the members at Bentley drifted back to Doncaster. But the friction created by the circumstances leading to the founding of the assembly at Bentley showed that miraculous healings in no way obviated the need for graciousness of character or wisdom in leadership. Pentecostal churches, which came into existence with extraordinary manifestations of spiritual power, had to learn by bitter experience how essential were the less dramatic charismata of the Spirit. Over the past 60 or so years, the pentecostal movement has known periods of miraculous evangelism and others of discipline and busy church life. The obverse of miraculous evangelism is outspoken criticism of fellow Christians; the obverse of disciplined church life is mechanical routine without love or fire. The departure of Thomas put the leadership of the Doncaster assembly firmly in the hands of the Oversight, and this was confirmed by a visit from Smith Wigglesworth who, during a fortnight's stay, prayed for the deacons to become elders. In a typically unorthodox manner Wigglesworth got the Oversight to stand on chairs with their hands held out in an arch. The congregation then walked under the arch and some fell down under the power of God[13]. Thereafter Doncaster was governed by its elders and its pastors were expected to preach and visit, but to do little else[13]. In other large assemblies, notably J N Parr's in Manchester, it was quite clear that the pastor governed the church and the elders were expected only to give advice. Parr was a man who "would brook no opposition"[14].

The next man to be pastor at Doncaster was GeorgeNewsholme, who stayed for six years. He fulfilled a punishing schedule each weekend. Indeed, in retrospect, Mr Lucas recognised that he was treated harshly by the church[15]. His stipend was £4 10s per week and he was expected to keep in touch with his large congregation without the use of either a car or a telephone. He had to preach each Saturday evening and then be ready for a 7am prayer meeting on Sunday morning. He preached at a Breaking of Bread service at 10.45 and again at a Bible Class for some 60 men at 3pm in the afternoon. At 5.30 he was expected to conduct an open air evangelistic meeting before the Gospel Service at 6.30 pm. Once this had finished, he was expected to conduct another open air meeting. He had little help in carrying the burden of preaching except when the occasional missionary speaker or renowned visiting minister came. Nevertheless, he accomplished a great deal. He started branch meetings in the pit villages round Doncaster and sent the young men he trained at the Bible class to preach at them. He even went once a week himself to preach at Bentley. By common consent he was an excellent pastor.

Notes to Pages 112 - 118

1. Aaron Linford was editor of <u>Redemption Tidings</u> for many years, a member of the Executive Council of Assemblies of God and gave a lively interview to David Allen and myself on 9th November 1984. All the quotations in this section, unless otherwise specified, are taken from that interview.

2."The initial evidence" is a shorthand way of referring to the view that speaking in tongues is "the initial evidence" of a believer's baptism in the Holy Spirit. The Assemblies of God refused, and still refuse, to compromise on this issue. They believe that God has sovereignly given clear and objective evidence of the baptism in the Holy Spirit and that any attempt to by-pass this evidence would lead, in a generation, to the disappearance of pentecostal manifestations within the church.

3. The story of the Doncaster assembly up to 1929 is told in W J Croft (1929), <u>The Lord Working With Them</u>, Stockport: The Edgeley Press, from which most of the information given here is taken.

4. These two groups both believed that health and healing could be obtained without recourse to medical science. To this extent it is clear that the Doncaster pentecostal church emphasised divine healing and that this emphasis governed public perception of the church's nature. Before 1928, it is also relevant to note that the church met in a building also used by the Spiritists.

5. See W J Croft (1929) p 30, 31.

6. A J Lucas went to see Jeffreys in London and made arrangements for the campaign to occupy the month of August 1928. After the booking had been made and leaflets announcing the meetings had been distributed, Jeffreys told Lucas that he would be in Africa in August and that therefore he could not come to Doncaster. Lucas went to see Jeffreys again and pressed him to come. Jeffreys agreed to come in May, although he had been booked to go to Newcastle for the whole month. He gave the first half of the month to Newcastle and the second fortnight to Doncaster.

7. See W J Croft (1929), p 32.

8. He preached on Zacchaeus the tax collector (Luke 19). As Croft (1929) p 33 explains "whether our sins were such as to be punishable by law, open or hidden vices, great or small, or acts of trickery practised in the name of business, all were so vividly put before us that it would seem almost impossible that any could fail to see themselves as sinners in need of salvation".

9. With Ken Healey I interviewed A J Lucas on 26th June 1986. Lucas was born on 1st July 1894. The phrase is Lucas's.
10. Mr Harrison, one of the elders of the Assembly at Bentley, near Doncaster, told me this on 22nd June 1986. Mr Harrison was then 76 years of age.

11. See Minutes of 20th Executive Presbytery meeting dated January 22nd 1932.

13. Interview conducted by David Allen and myself with Alfred Missen on 3rd June 1985. Alfred Missen (b 1916) came from a Salvationist background to the Doncaster assembly as a teenager. He grew up in the Doncaster assembly and later became General Secretary of Assemblies of God.

14. A telephone call to Alfred Missen on 5th December 1985. This is Missen's verdict.

15. Interview conducted by Ken Healey and myself on 26th June 1986.

THE BIBLE SCHOOL

The Pentecostal Missionary Union established a Bible School in July 1909 at a house in Paddington, London. The School's Principal was A Moncur Niblock and there were about ten students in residence. In 1910 a similar home in Hackney, East London, was opened by Mrs Crisp for the training of pentecostal lady missionaries. The same year the men's home moved to Preston under the oversight of Thomas Myerscough, but in 1913 the home was re-established in London at 60 King Edward Road, Hackney, not far from the ladies' School. The men's home closed briefly during the 1914-18 War, but re-opened soon afterwards in a large house in Hampstead at 12 South Hill Park Gardens. When the PMU's funds were dwindling, its Secretary, Mr Mundell, asked Howard Carter to take over the training of young men, and, soon afterwards, the financial responsibility for the house; on February 14, 1921 the school began a new era. Howard Carter was the School's Principal till 1948[1].

Some of Howard Carter's scrupulous records and analyses of the student intake have survived and show how many students he had, which parts of England they came from (or which country they came from) and how long they stayed. From the beginning, it was made clear that each student had to pay £1 per week for their board[1] - a sum that persisted for the next ten years or more despite a rise and a fall in the value of money. The School was not cheap and its students were expected to learn to exercise faith if they lacked funds. Carter himself had very definite views about money (which will become clear later) and was strongly of the opinion that Christians should learn to live by faith, and act in faith - as, indeed, he had done when he took over responsibility for the running of the school at the age of thirty-one.

Student enrolment certainly increased once Assemblies of God was formed and the figures show that 40 students came and went in 1932, though by 1934 there were about 30 in residence.

Student numbers are most easily set out in a table:[2]
(table (a) - next page)

table (a)

Year	Term	Male Students	Female Students	TOTAL
1922	3	9	0	9
1923	1	4	1	5
	2	6	2	8
	3	5	3	8
1924	1	4	3	7
	2	2	5	7
	3	7	12	19
1925	1	11	11	22
	2	14	11	25
	3	8	12	20
1926	1	7	7	14
	2	8	8	16
	3	10	9	19
1927	1	10	10	20
	2	19	16	35
	3	22	14	36

As might be expected the students from Britain were drawn from the areas where the pentecostal movement was strongest, that is to say, from the midlands, Wales and the north. There were, for example, six male students from the north east of England, four from Wales and one from London and a miscellaneous group of others in 1929. In the same year, there was one Norwegian student, three Swedes, two Germans, and a Czech.

Many of the surviving students from those early days in the 1920s and early 30s, valued most the family atmosphere at the School and the opportunity to sit down to meals with Howard Carter and the other resident faculty. Carter had a real ability to inspire younger men with his own zeal and confidence in God[3]. He had, after all, been imprisoned for his beliefs and his pioneering and pastoral experiences, by the standards of the time, were extensive. He was able to teach young men to see every problem and difficulty they faced as a chance to learn from

God[4]. hardships and setbacks were to be embraced as divine methods of tuition or discipline. It is no wonder, then, that in the 1930s, many of Carter's proteges accepted the challenge of starting churches from nothing or taking and building up very small congregations.

An idea of the School's curriculum can be gained from three sources: the letters and articles which appeared in *Redemption Tidings*; extant copies of some of Howard Carter's notes; the correspondence courses which were written and administered from the Hampstead address. An Open Letter published in *Redemption Tidings* vol 1. no 1 in 1924 and signed by the Carter brothers says,

> Within the Home, the spirit of joy prevails at all times. Study is a delight. Family prayers are heartily engaged in by all. Meal times afford seasons for spiritual conversation, and the routine of the Home is saved from ruts by the ever abiding consciousness of the Lord's presence.

> It is important, in these days of error, to give heed to the doctrine that we teach. Special care is exercised in this direction, lest dangerous and unscriptural teaching should spoil the usefulness of those called to minister the sacred Word.

> The foundation truths of the Assemblies of God for Great Britain and Ireland are implicitly believed and taught.

In the October 1924 issue of *Redemption Tidings* the first article in a series entitled "How to Study the Scriptures" (written by one or both of the Carter brothers) began with a preamble pointing out the value of studying the Bible and the need to rely on the Holy Spirit as "the great Revealer of its treasures, the great Illuminator of its pages". They then noted seven methods of Bible study: the comprehensive (taking the Bible as a whole), the analytical (taking individual books or sections of them), the doctrinal (looking at the basis for systematic theology), the typical (looking at types and figures), the prophetical (looking at predictions and their fulfilment), the geographical (setting biblical events in their cultural settings) and the historical (dealing with chronology and biography). Folders dated March 1925 in Howard Carter's handwriting show that he made use of at least two of these methods of Bible study, and there is no reason to suppose that he omitted the other five[5]. The correspondence course material of that date which still survives shows a similar systematic application of these methods to Scripture. Indeed Donald Gee commented that the extraordinary feature of the Hampstead School was that it inculcated no fixed set of doctrines but rather concentrated on teaching students a method of study which they could to apply any doctrine or passage of Scripture[6]. Naturally, however, enough the School taught that baptism in the Holy Spirit was an experience distinct from, and subsequent to, salvation. Equally, Howard Carter's view that the gifts of the Holy Spirit were completely supernatural, and not in any way related to natural abilities, was also taught. But the impression given by ex-students and the materials which survive is that no one rode their own hobby horses; the Carter brothers (joined by C L Parker in 1925) recognised that students needed an overall grasp of the main doctrines of the Bible. Articles by John Carter in 1926 propound mainstream Christian beliefs about the Trinity and Reformed Protestant beliefs about the way of salvation through Christ's atonement[7].

The central place of the Bible School (or Schools, because homes were opened at Louth and Scarborough in addition to Hampstead) in the initial stages of the pentecostal movement was important. Young ministers were trained and formed life-long friendships at the schools. Church members were able to use the homes in the northern part of England for holidays in the summer. There was a sense of intimacy as well as excitement. Howard Carter began to buy up deserted church halls and to send his young men out to work in them. It is not clear where his funds came from, though it is probable he used the cash received from the fees charged to the students. His policy was to make no charge for tuition, but to charge quite highly for board and lodging. The lack of charges for tuition were reflected in the fact that the resident faculty received no salaries. They were expected to "live by faith" on the grounds that, unless they did so, they could not teach the students these principles. When C L Parker went to work with Howard Carter, he was told, "Your salary will be nought pounds, nought shillings and nought pence per week. And if you don't think that is enough, I'll double it!"[8]. Yet, even with these stringent conditions of service, there were by December 1927, five members of staff at Hampstead and another five at Louth.

These members of staff, in their own ways, added to the richness of the Bible Schools' ministry. They were a varied group. Howard Carter himself was the notable for his integrity and faith. His faith sprang partly from his experience of the "gift of prophecy". He believed that the baptism in the Holy Spirit was a gateway to the other gifts of the Spirit mentioned in 1 Corinthians 12 and that prophecy functioned not only as inspired utterance in an assembly of Christian believers but also personally and privately. Just as, for example, Jeremiah the Old Testament prophet received "a word from the Lord" either for himself, his king or his nation, so Howard Carter believed that it was quite possible for a Christian in the modern era to receive a similar impartation of divine truth. He did not believe that such a "word" was intended for the establishment of Christian doctrine, but he did believe that the Holy Spirit was sent by Christ to communicate the will of God to the Church and therefore to the individual believer. In *The Bible School and Missionary Association Review* for November/December 1929, Howard Carter wrote an article entitled "The BSMA in the Light of Prophecy" and in it he reported

> The first prophecy which revealed the purpose of God for my future ministry upon coming to London was given during a season of prayer with a brother in Christ one morning in November, 1929, in the North of London.....On this particular morning, the brother and I were together praying when the Holy Spirit gave him an utterance in other tongues, and I received the interpretation. The message was as follows, "Gather My people together...and build for me...and there shall be heaps of money."

That evening a Christian business man promised Howard Carter over £2000. When a cheque for £2,400 arrived, Howard used the money to buy a church hall and begin an assembly. About a month later, he reported receiving another prophecy,

> That which thou hast desired thou shalt never have, and that which thou hast longed for shall never be thine, but thou shalt be satisfied with that which I give thee.

He did not explain what he had desired (though it is possible that he had wanted an evangelistic ministry like Stephen Jeffreys' since he had returned from one of Jeffreys' meetings feeling inadequate and small), but he believed that the handing over of the Bible School at Hampstead to his care was God's particular provision for him. He later confessed himself well satisfied with all that it entailed.

In 1923 Carter had a nervous breakdown[9] and had to leave the School for a while. The cause of the breakdown was almost certainly financial anxiety because a few sentences later he records "the dark cloud lingered for some time but only to cast us upon the Lord for his interposition...after a week of prayer a cheque for £200 came by post". Thereafter he always saw faith as a quality and an active trust which could master depression and fear even if it was necessary to pass through "a gruesome night amidst the ferocious lions" before the joyful morning[10].

Once the Bible School had been established the need for staff was obvious. John Carter, Howard's brother, had an evangelistic ministry though, as the years passed, it became clear that he could turn his hand to almost anything with success. He lectured at the Hampstead Bible School, pastored the People's Hall at Lee (which had been bought with the £2,400 Howard had been given), became Principal of the Women's Bible School at Louth and conducted evangelistic campaigns in the late 1920s all over the country. He outlived most of the first generation of pentecostals and, when I knew him in later life, he was a gracious old man in his eighties, still sprightly and mentally alert, who regularly went to the Lake District on holiday and walked twelve or more miles a day. John had a high regard for Howard and seems never to have disagreed with him; he was quite happy to play second fiddle.

C L Parker had been a Fellow, Tutor and Chaplain at University College, Oxford before he was taken on as a lecturer at Hampstead. His father was the Vicar of St James', Clerkenwell and, at the end of the 1914-18 war, "C L" as he was affectionately called, was asked by the Bible League to open a Bible School which stood for the verbal inspiration of Scripture. This establishment began in the crypt of the church at St James', but later moved to Leicester and finally closed down in 1921 because of a shortage of money. Early in 1922 Parker opened another Bible School, this time in Lincolnshire, and a young man named Elisha Thompson was among the first students. The school then moved to Oxford and Parker became convinced of the reality of the baptism in the Holy Spirit as an experience subsequent to conversion. Some time before 1924, Howard Carter visited the Parkers and, when he found out that they owed £25 in rent, paid the bill for them despite his own lack of financial security. In 1925 the Parkers moved to Hampstead and joined the growing team there. They continued to live by faith, though "C L", as his wife recalled, tended to be highly strung. Their financial adventures forced him back into the Anglican ministry at one stage in the late 1930s or early 40s, but he re-joined the Assemblies of God towards the end of his life. Howard said of him, "his penetrating thoughts flashed with lightning speed from an agile brain. Those students who were privileged to sit before him in the lecture room will never forget his dynamic presentation of truth"[11]. Indeed, his wife said she could always tell when her husband had been lecturing the students: she would come in to lunch and see little groups of them in corners arguing fiercely about what he had said, and some were in tears[12]! He used to come into lectures and make a deliberately provocative and outrageous remark at the outset and then challenge the students to disprove it[13].

Elisha Thompson was refused missionary candidature because of poor health. He remained in England and joined the staff at Bible School staff in 1931, continuing as a lecturer until 1974. Everyone who remembered him commented on his humble and self-effacing disposition. The other lecturers may have led more varied and exciting lives, but Thompson's character and his willingness to do minor emergency repairs on the building at all hours of the day or night remained in the minds of generations of students. His speciality was the Old Testament but "he was just as happy wearing overalls, clearing out some drain as he was lecturing about some Pharaoh in the sixth or seventh dynasty"[14].

The other lecturer who joined the staff of the Bible Schools was Harold Horton, an ex-Methodist circuit preacher who was born in 1881. Horton was healed of a double hernia in 1925 at a meeting conducted by Wigglesworth. Thereafter Horton gave up his work as a tutor at the Duxbury Studio for Elocution in West London[15] and taught Bible Studies, French and English Composition at the Louth Bible School. He and Howard Carter were kindred spirits - both were artistic, slightly flamboyant, outspoken, even dictatorial, married late in life, and both suffered nervous breakdowns from which they soon recovered[16]. Horton combined his lecturing duties with pastoring first at Louth, and then when the Bible School moved to Scarborough, at Scarborough. In August 1933, an invitation to become the pastor at Luton, led Horton to move, and it was from there that he published what became a classic book, *The Gifts of the Spirit*, in which he acknowledged his indebtedness to Howard Carter's " schedule of private notes on the subject"[17].

Organisation beneath the surface

Howard Carter's gravestone carries the inscription "Man of Faith" and his biography is subtitled "Man of the Spirit", yet he was also undeniably a man of organisation - at least in his early years. Some of those who knew him in the 1940s described him as slightly eccentric - for example he tried to manufacture his own toothpaste and would only drink cocoa and not tea or coffee - but he had his own classification system of all the stationery and office materials at Hampstead and, in the late 1920s and early 30s, he must have attended numerous committees and groups which kept minutes of their meetings[18]. There is even a brief record of a meeting, signed by Howard Carter, in which he noted his own conversation with one other person !

Howard Carter realised that there was very little use in training men and women for the ministry if there were no congregations to which they could later go. Carter's masterplan therefore was to use the students who left the School in pioneer evangelism. He formed the Bible School Evangelistic Society (BSES) in 1926 and less than three years later in the summer of 1929 he had 67 ministers working in 17 English counties. All the members of the Society, together with the office and teaching staff of the Bible Schools, were unpaid or "living by faith", an expression which must be understood in the light of its meaning for Hudson Taylor (the missionary to China) and George Muller (the man who set up an orphanage in Bristol and expected its provisions to be supplied in answer to prayer). *The Bible School and Missionary Review,* which Carter edited monthly at the end of the 1920s contains a significant number of quotations from, and references to, these men. It is clear from an article written by Donald Gee[19] that there was an opinion bandied about in pentecostal circles to the effect that the proof of a man's call to the ministry would be given by his ability to sustain himself and his family without secular employment. Gee, in his usual balanced and thorough way, pointed out that this could not be the case since even the Apostle Paul needed, from time to time, to resort to making tents to finance his personal needs. However, unfortunately, the notion that a man who was truly called to the ministry would survive on whatever money he could "pray in" gave some young churches the excuse to be as mean as they liked with any preacher or pastor who was invited to their pulpit. Why bother to pay a minister when God would supply his needs ? Gee pointed out that the Scriptural principle was that those who preached the Gospel should live by the Gospel.

A rough calculation suggests that Carter must have had around £1000[20] per year from the £1 a week which was charged to students for board and lodging at the Bible School. Some of this money undoubtedly was spent on the capital costs of the house in Hampstead, but because he was "trusting that every city and town in this land of ours shall have a full Gospel testimony established into its midst"[21] he bought church buildings all over the country. Folders in Howard Carter's handwriting and found among John Carter's papers on his death show that at Easter 1929, there were ten separate "controlled" buildings for which, presumably, the BSES was financially responsible. Some of these buildings were pictured on the front of the BSMA and are large and imposing and of considerable value.

Minutes of monthly meetings going back to November 1929 tell the story of the growth and development of the organisation. It is a story with twists and turns in it as, for example, C L Parker was asked to draw up some Rules of Association which, in March 1934, were rescinded with the following words

> Finding that there were many complications in the Business side of the BSMA which conflicted with its spiritual aims, the members decided from this Meeting the present Constitution shall be dissolved, and the BSMA shall consist, as it was formerly, of Mr Alfred Howard Carter[22]

The Rules of Association had named the two Carter brothers and C L Paker as the first members and spelled out Howard Carter's role as the Overseer for as long as he remained in the Association. All members of the Association were to be given lifetime membership. The Rules envisaged the BSES as a subdivision of the BSMA. When the BSMA was devolved upon the person of Howard Carter the other members of the committee with which he had regularly met continued in an advisory capacity and the change in emphasis is indicated by the alteration of the title of the monthly papers from "Minutes of..." to "A Record of...". There seems little doubt that Howard Carter liked to function in his ministry with the minimum of interference from other people. He ran his Bible School without a Board of Governors or Panel of Reference and his scope within Assemblies of God, as we shall see, increased very greatly when Nelson Parr resigned from office.

It is perhaps unfair to point out that there were tensions in the arrangements which Howard Carter was making. But, to give a fully rounded picture of events, it is necessary to note, for example, that there was obviously a clash between John Carter's young wife and Howard. A BSMA Council meeting on the 18th December 1930 contains the following minute

> Owing to difficulties that have arisen in connection with Mrs John Carter and the work in general, she was invited to attend this Meeting and explain what she had against the members of the Society. In consequence of her refusal to attend, it was

regretfully decided, for the general welfare of the work, to ask her to have her meals in future in her own home with her husband, the School to make the usual allowance of 10/- per head per week for Mr & Mrs John Carter.

There are a number of interesting pieces of information here. For a start it is apparent that the allowance of 10/- per week given to residential members of staff is exactly half what students were charged. There is no question here of malpractice, but it is evident that the true cost of food and for one person for a week in 1930 was roughly 10/- and not one pound. Secondly, it is clear that, though the residential staff received no salary, they did receive a food allowance. Thirdly, it is clear that Mrs Carter found difficulty in adjusting, as a young married woman, to the communal atmosphere at Hampstead - indeed this may be a reason why later she and her husband worked at Louth. Fourthly, there is a nice combination of the gracious and the commanding in the wording of the minute. Mrs Carter is "invited" to attend the meeting, but her non-attendance is described as a "refusal". One senses that this invitation was more than an invitation. Howard Carter's power within the growing young set of assemblies was a thing to be reckoned with. He could, and did send young men wherever he thought fit, he appointed and, if necessary (as in the case of a Mr Thomas) got rid of staff at the Bible Schools, and he set the tone for the day. He combined a belief in personal prophecy with great care in the conduct of procedure laid down by constitutional lines.

Notes to Pages 121 - 130

1. See page 208 of this book.

2. All the information from this paragraph is taken from John Carter's private papers which are stored in the Mattersey Hall archives.

3. Information given during an interview conducted by David Allen and myself with Alfred Missen on 3rd June 1985.

4. Interview conducted by David Allen and myself with David Powell (summer 1986).

5. Found among John Carter's papers on his death, and now kept at the Mattersey archives.

6. See D Gee (1967), Wind and Flame, Assemblies of God Publishing House, p151

7. See Redemption Tidings for February 1926 and April 1926.

8. An anecdote passed on to me by Paul Mercy on 9th July 1986. C L Parker's widow survived into her 90s and lived in Sheffield where Paul Mercy pastors.

9. See The Bible School and Missionary Review (vol 7.4), March-April 1929, p ii.

10. See The Bible School and Missionary Review (vol 7.6), May-June 1929, p 65.

11. See the Forward to C L Parker (1969), The Mystery of God, Croydon: Assemblies of God.

12. In an interview with David Allen in 1988. She recalled that Parker always read his New Testament in Greek and did not bother with English translations. His facility in Greek, of course, would have stemmed from the Greats course at Oxford. Parker died in 1967.

13. Information about C L Parker is surprisingly scanty. The factual detail given at the beginning of this paragraph is taken from John Carter's (1971), biography, Howard Carter - Man of the Spirit, Nottingham: Assemblies of God Publishing House.

14. See his obituary notices in Redemption Tidings for 20th November, 1975, (vol 51. 47). The quotation comes from Dennis Robson.

15. See Colin Whittaker's (1983), Seven Pentecostal Pioneers, Basingstoke: Marshalls Paperbacks, p 131. Horton died in 1969.

16. See note 15, pages 134 and 141.

17. See Harold Horton (1934), The Gifts of the Spirit, Letchworth: Letchworth Printers, p 7.

18. Mr Leek, an elder at the Newark Assembly, told me about Howard Carter's home-made toothpaste, his aversion to tea and coffee and also about his refusal to wear any other foot wear than lace-up boots which had to be bought at Freeman, Hardy & illis. These boots were almost unobtainable in the war years and, whenever Elisha Thompson went out preaching between 1939 - 45, he was asked to enquire at the town to which he went whether they had such boots in stock. My conversation with Mr Leek took place on the 13th July 1986.

19. See The Bible School and Missionary Review Association Pt 1 Jan-Feb (1929), pt 2 Feb-March (1929).

20. The Bible School was open for 39 and a half weeks a year. Given that there were about 30 students in residence for this time and that each student paid £1 per week, the total income must have been in excess of £1000 per year, but this would not have represented disposable income because, of course, costs would have been incurred for food, rates etc.

21. See The Bible School and Missionary Review Association article "Seven Years Old" Sept-Oct (1929).

22. See Minutes of the 27th meeting of the BSMA on Thursday 2nd March 1933.

THE LOSS OF JOHN NELSON PARR

During the 1930s local churches who comprised the Assemblies of God carefully, and sometimes jealously, safeguarded their own autonomy. Each pastor or leader was employed by, or self-employed but connected with, his own congregation. Yet, each pastor normally attended monthly meetings of a District Presbytery at which he met the other pastors in his area. Once a year, he met with all the other pastors in the country and, from this large congregation of ministers, an Executive Presbytery was elected. The seven members of the Executive Presbytery did not have the authority to intervene when individual assemblies quarrelled or split unless, as sometimes happened, the local leadership appealed to them for help. The Executive's role was more advisory than governmental and, though it sometimes had to resolve tensions that arose between two or more District Presbyteries, a written Constitution listed its main functions as the certification of "Evangelists, Missionaries, Workers" and the general control of the Assemblies of God publishing interests[1].

Howard Carter was elected onto the very first Executive Presbytery in 1924. By 1933 only one other person had also served from the beginning: this was John Nelson Parr, the man who had issued the original invitations which resulted in the eventual formation of Assemblies of God. Both men were undoubtedly strong and dominant personalities who expressed their opinions forcibly. It was on their attitude to money that their differences came to the fore. Howard Carter was strongly anti-materialistic right up to the end of his life. He was, it is true, a bachelor and his own needs were modest. He once wrote in an article entitled, "The Call to Poverty", "We need faith a thousand times more than we need finance. Faith will produce finance, but finance will never produce faith!"[2]. Parr, on the other hand, took a more liberal view. Before he had been a full-time minister he had been a business man - and according to one account earning £3500 per year in the 1920s[3] - and he was a married with a family. In the words of Scripture, Parr believed that "the labourer is worthy of his hire".

Over the first ten years of its existence Howard Carter had attracted some of the more outstanding people in Assemblies of God round himself. C L Parker is a case in point, and Donald Gee, whose relationships with Howard Carter were not always warm, certainly lived for a while around 1930 with his family at one of the large Bible

School houses outside London. Both Gee and Parker were elected onto the Executive Presbytery and were present at its explosive meeting on June 8th 1933.

The minutes of this meeting show that it was called one evening at Whitsun Convention time to deal with an application by the Congo Evangelistic Mission for co-operative fellowship with Assemblies of God. The minutes record that there was much discussion of the matter and that eventually, after the removal of misunderstandings, unanimous acceptance of the application was reached. When the representative of the CEM had left the room, another matter, which presumably was not on the agenda, was raised. The meeting had started at 6pm and so, by that time, it must have been getting late. The wording of the minutes reads,

> The Chairman [ie J N Parr], who had taken charge of the Convention Meeting, was requested by the other members of the Executive Presbytery to give them an opportunity of laying before him their deep and unanimous disapproval of his attitude towards money, as shown in the past General Presbytery Conferences, and especially in those then sitting.

It is difficult to escape the impression that there had been an arrangement beforehand by some members of the Executive to confront Parr. The minutes do not show who first broached the subject over which they felt deep and unanimous disapproval, but the phraseology suggests that prior conversations had taken place because no unanimity could have existed without a previous exchange of views.

The minutes continue, and they must be quoted at length,

> The criticisms expressed fell under the following heads-:
>
> a) That by accepting an honorarium of £5 a week as Editor he had failed to give an example of self-sacrifice to the rest of the Pastors of Assemblies of God, and therefore, while remaining head, was in danger of losing his position as spiritual leader.
>
> b) That by publicly insisting on an honorarium, and refusing to undertake the duties of Editor unless so paid, he had allowed himself to assume the position of a hireling.
>
> c) That by accepting £5 a week for part time work in addition

to his other source of income, he had put a great stumbling block in the way of the Pastors of Assemblies of God, who laboured whole time for far smaller remuneration.

d) That his acceptance of £5 a week for part time work of a comparatively easy and comfortable nature, when so many Missionaries were giving their whole lives in dangerous and difficult circumstances for about £1 a week, was a glaring example of inequitable distribution of money.

e) That his quotation of the text "The labourer is worthy of his hire", as a justification of his attitude, was altogether out of place since-:

1. These words were spoken to men who were sent out "with nothing", and made no sort of stipulation as to honorariums, nor ever received any.

2. He had no care that others should receive a similar wage for their work, but respected only his own position in this matter.

f) By attempting to cling to all the money available for a typist, he showed the same disregard for the interests of others as before. As leader, the proposal should have come from himself; there should have been a desire to look not only on his own things, but also on the things of others.

We have here a compressed record of what was obviously a lengthy, and probably a heated, discussion. The criticisms under a-d were levelled against Parr, and section e is clearly his main reply, to which the subsections 1 and 2 are the counter arguments of the rest of the Executive. Criticism f make reference to a "typist" and must have added towards the end of the meeting after Parr had given some explanation about the use to which he put the honorarium.

Parr, amidst his numerous duties, was the Editor of *Redemption Tidings*, and employed a typist to help him produce the magazine. Before he had resigned from his secular employment in 1927, he paid the typist out of his own pocket. After he had begun his work at the Bethshan Tabernacle, his stipend was small and he was unable to afford to finance the typist himself. In 1928 a proposal at the annual Conference that the editor "should attend to these interests as a work of faith", in other words, that he should produce the magazine without any help from the churches among whom it circulated, was waived and instead an honorarium of not more than £250 per annum was recommended. It appears from what is said in the extract from the Executive Presbytery minutes above that the honorarium was regarded as a potential payment rather than a payment to which the editor had an absolute right. This would explain the phrase "by publicly insisting on an honorarium"; Parr would not have had to *insist* if the payment had been made automatically. No doubt, discontent had been held at bay from 1928 to 1933: Parr must have disliked having to claim his honorarium and those who had first proposed that the magazine be a venture of faith must have disliked seeing Parr raise money so easily. It has to be said, though the writer has no evidence on this, that the proposal to run the magazine on faith lines would have fitted in well with Howard Carter's cast of mind since, during this period, he was running more than one Bible School and a magazine without receiving any honorariums at all.

The flare up at the Executive meeting reveals a great deal about the pressures which the leaders in Assemblies of God faced. Lack of money was enforcing self-sacrifice on many ministers, and prolonged self-sacrifice had produced a critical attitude against prosperous Christians. As the years passed, there is some indication that these attitudes altered and that in the 1960s Assemblies of God ministers began to share in the higher standard of living which affected the country as a whole. But there were still paradoxical equations: spiritual men are self-sacrificing and therefore poor; anyone who can not support himself full-time through his ministerial ability is not genuinely called to Christian service; thus genuine ministers have to support themselves *and* remain poor.

The issue of missionaries which is raised in paragraph d of the Executive Minutes is a complete red herring. It takes no account at all of the cost of living in foreign countries and it assumes that missionaries will receive no income at all from the people to whom they preach. The Congo Evangelistic Mission, whose work had been discussed earlier in the evening, was careful to aim for indigenous local churches which were self-supporting and whose pastors were eventually all native. The missionaries who went to the Congo, though they received some financial help from their home assemblies in England, accepted gifts from local Christians on the field.

The accusation that Parr was putting himself in the position of a "hireling" in paragraph b was also unjustified. The accusation echoes John's Gospel chapter 10 where a distinction is drawn between a genuine shepherd and one who runs away from a dangerous wolf. Not only is the context of the passage connected with pastoral work, it is also clear it focuses on the physical dangers which might cause a pastor to forsake his congregation. This was simply not the issue in the case of Parr and the honorarium for the magazine.

The meeting ended, according to the minutes, when "the Chairman had admitted that there was something in what had been said". However, at a later date, probably at the next scheduled meeting on October 10th 1933, Parr refused to sign the minutes and so the other six men present appended their signatures. At the October meeting the rest of the Executive were expecting Parr either to accept their accusations or to produce evidence in refutation. Instead, he read the following statement,

> I have received letters from all members of the Executive Presbytery, regarding this most unfortunate matter. All these letters, except one, were sent to me by Mr Parker. Several of the letters contain very serious criticisms of my character and one or two tender suggestions.
>
> Regarding the suggestions as to the courses which are open to me, I would like to deal with two of them only.
>
> The first suggestion is that I should produce evidence which would refute your criticisms, made at the Extraordinary Meeting. Failing this, it is suggested that I should resign. One or two other suggestions were made, but I do not propose dealing with them.
>
> I had decided, after much prayer, on the first course, and intended bringing the whole matter before the General Presbytery, and was preparing facts to refute your criticisms, but while praying over this refutation of your criticisms, the Lord spoke to me, clearly revealing His path for me, and, after following the Lord for nearly thirty years, you must, I think, agree that I should be able to recognise the Shepherd's voice. From that hour I have had perfect rest and marvellous blessing.

This is the answer the Lord gave me to your criticisms, and it is my only answer to your charges.

The case against Joseph appeared to be very black and irrefutable, all were unanimous. Only one man knew it was all untrue, and he opened not is mouth.

The indictment against the Lord Jesus was terrible, and untrue, but as a sheep He submitted to the shearing, and He opened not His mouth. He answered "not a word".

Then the Lord said to me "Why do you not rather take wrong?" (1 Cor 6. 7). This is the exhortation of the Spirit of God through the great-hearted Apostle to those who sought to justify themselves, and, therefore, beloved brethren, I have decided to commit my cause to Him that judgeth righteously, or, as Weymouth writes, "When He suffered He uttered no threats, but left His wrongs in the hands of the righteous Judge."

Under the circumstances, the second course suggested in the correspondence is the only one left for me to take, and I will, therefore be glad if you will kindly arrange for me to vacate all the offices held in connection with the Assemblies of God at December 31st. This will include the Executive Presbytery, Chairman, Editor, Trust Board and Missionary Council.

I would like to make it clear that it is only the Grace of God which has made me willing to take this course. I am not being moved by an offended or bitter spirit, my act is one of willing submission. It has been a real joy to labour with you during the past ten years, and I sincerely trust that greater blessing will be poured out by the Lord Jesus upon the Assemblies of God in the future.

I have already suffered sufficiently, both mentally and physically, through this tragic affair, and I will be glad if you will kindly accept my decision as final.

Parr's words must have fallen heavily upon the ears of his six fellow ministers. The October minutes say, "After the Chairman had read a statement attributing his resignation to the direct guidance of the Lord Himself, the remaining members, whilst entirely repudiating the implications of Mr Parr's statement, had no alternative but reluctantly to accept his resignation". In many respects the tables had been completely turned: Parr admitted no wrong, accused the other six by implication of acting like Joseph's jealous brothers and, at the same time, considered that the will of God had been done.

The October minutes show that, despite the dignity of Parr's statement, there were tensions beneath the surface. They record,

> concerning the accusation made by the Chairman, that the Members of the Executive Presbytery had held a Meeting behind his back to criticise him in violation of constitutional and Christian practice, Mr Parr, after hearing the verbal denials of all the members and having read their written denials, refused either to substantiate or to withdraw his charge.

It is difficult to know what to make of this paragraph. The men concerned were all honourable and upright and if they said that "a Meeting" had not taken place, then it is certain that "a Meeting" did not take place. All that one can surmise is that either one member of the Executive had made accusations against Parr and that the others had spontaneously joined in or, perhaps, a series of casual conversations had taken place over the years between 1928 and 1933 when the whole matter came to a head.

Despite the fact that he did not resign officially resign till December 31st, Parr did not sign the minutes of the October meeting on the 6th of December 1933. Howard Carter, as the new Chairman, is chief signatory[4].

The affair rumbled on for some months. A letter from C L Parker was sent to the Chairmen and to the Secretaries of the District Presbyteries on the 23rd October 1933 in which it was said, "this resignation was a result of a complete divergence of opinion between Mr Parr and the remaining six members of the Executive Presbytery over Mr Parr's attitude to the typist's wages and Editor's honorarium". The wording here is ambiguous because it could imply that the typist's wages are one and the same as the Editor's honorarium (ie that the Editor is given an honorarium in order to pay a typist) or that the two sums of money are quite different and distinct. Parr's daughter, who was then a young girl, said it was not until 1933 that my Father asked the Executive if they could possibly see their way clear to help with the typist's wages, as it was becoming difficult for him to manage[5],

which suggests that the £250 per year was voted to the Editor in order to help with the typist's wages while not necessarily being solely for this purpose. The Editor was presumably allowed to keep some money for his own incidental expenses; such an arrangement was open to misconstruction[6].

Parr became aware of the contents of Parker's letter because, on the 27th October 1933, he wrote his own circular. With it he enclosed the statement he had read to the Executive earlier that month; he wanted to show that his resignation did not arise out of "stubborn self-will".

The Executive Presbytery minutes show continued friction, often over minor matters, between Parr and the others. Parr, for example, had used a £200 loan to help finance a "Words only" edition of the new hymnbook when he should have used some of the money towards a music edition. A year later an article on church government by Parr was refused publication in *Redemption Tidings* till its references to personalities were removed. Parr refused to receive any correspondence from Parker (presumably returning post unopened) and even in December 1934 a letter from Parr to the Executive was read out and "its tone regretted". Finally however wounds were healed. And they were healed in a remarkable way because Parr eventually took a full part in Assemblies of God and was welcomed as the co-chairman of the 50th General Conference in 1972. Around 1937 Howard Carter came to Parr's house in Manchester to apologise. Parr gives a brief account of the whole episode in his autobiography. He simply says "about four years after that day the instigator of those charges came to see me and said he had made a terrible blunder in making the infamous accusation against my character and asked me to forgive him. All the members of the Executive of Assemblies of God also sent letters withdrawing their accusations against me" (p 43).

Carter's apology is a clear indication of two things: firstly, that he was the main protagonist in bringing the charges against Parr and, secondly, that he later recognised the injustice of those charges. It is also, importantly, an evidence of Carter's stature as a Christian leader: when he knew himself to be wrong, he admitted it.

Parr was an ardent preacher of the Gospel and the loss of him and of Stephen Jeffreys within a short space of time ultimately affected the speed at which the Assemblies of God grew. Howard Carter now entered a period of prominence within AoG and his gifts flowered fully. Parr remained in Manchester and built one of the largest congregations in the British Isles.

Relationships between Parr and Howard Carter were never warm again - if indeed they had ever been warm. But Parr and Gee were reconciled (as a series of letters kept at Bethshan indicate), and the whole episode may have led Gee to be more wary of Carter than he had been.

Notes to Pages 133 - 141

1. The Constitution, or "Constitutional Minutes" were printed, revised and readily available for sale. On the role of the Executive Presbytery there was little essential difference between the 1924 and 1941 versions. The quotation above is taken from page 8 of an undated version of the Constitution issued around 1930. I have implied that all those present at District Presbyteries or the annual General Presbyteries were ministers in Assemblies of God. This is not strictly true. Local churches could send any representative of their choice (male or female) to either of these predominantly ministerial gatherings.

2. See The Pentecostal Evangel March 5 1967,p5, 6.

3. See Interview with W Hacking on 14 Nov 1984 conducted by David Allen and myself.

4. Due to the way the minutes were distributed, that is in the form of a letter from the secretary, they were also always signed by the secretary.

5. See a private letter to me from Marjorie Parr dated 12th February 1986.

6. In commenting on the honorarium voted to Parr at the 1928 General Conference I have followed Alfred Missen's (1973) account in The Sound of a Going, Nottingham, AoG Pub. House, p 29 and conflated it with the private letter referred to in note 5 above. The minutes of the General Conference (1928, no 9) seem to say that Parr was voted £250 for that year only and not annually.

HOWARD CARTER'S CHAIRMANSHIP

The condition of the pentecostal assemblies

Nelson Parr had been Chairman and Secretary of Assemblies of God as well as the Editor of *Redemption Tidings*. His departure in the sudden circumstances of 1933 was a shock. People felt sad and confused and wanted the reassurance which only steady leadership can give. At the General Conference in 1934 there were various nominations for the vacant post of Chairman, but it was soon agreed that all but that of Howard Carter should be withdrawn, and Carter was rapidly confirmed in the office in which he was to remain for the next eleven years.

After his election Carter addressed the Conference emotionally. It was his habit to spend a day each month in prayer. On the 24th May 1928 he had received what he took to be a prophetic revelation: "Mark the day, for the blessing shall come, and thou shalt be astonished. As the opening of a book, as the turning of a leaf, so shall this purpose of the Lord be revealed, even that part which thou hast not seen". Exactly a year later on the 24th May 1929, the day he had marked, he was voted as the Vice-Chairman of Assemblies of God; on the 24th of May 1934 he became its Chairman. He was later astonished to discover that, because the Conferences varied round the date of the Whitsun holidays, it was only during those two years that the 24th May fell in Conference week. He was therefore convinced that he was exactly where God wanted him to be. From the outset he made it clear that he was willing to visit any assembly which asked for him - while still maintaining the work of the Bible Schools. Before he had the chance to pick up the threads in Britain, though, he felt constrained to go abroad to encourage missionaries. He set sail on June 8th 1934 and travelled to New York before heading across North America for the Far East.

Howard Carter travelled round the world from June 1934 to the spring of 1936. It was an extraordinary voyage. He went in the spirit of the apostles who carried "neither purse, nor scrip, nor shoes" and preached in Australia, Java, China, Tibet, Japan, Poland, Nazi Germany and Scandanavia. At least two books described his mission - one entitled *New York...Tokyo...Moscow!* he wrote himself and the other, *Adventuring with Christ* was by Lester Sumrall and published by Marshall, Morgan & Scott (c 1939) - and they indicate the scope of Carter's vision for the strengthening of the Church and his desire to see Christians filled with the Holy Spirit. He spoke at the Assemblies of God General Conference in 1936 and then left the country again and went to Canada, America and South America to return for the 1938 General Conference.

During his prolonged absence, he kept in touch with the churches by writing articles in *Redemption Tidings* and through a series of monthly prayer-and-information letters. A full set of these letters was found among John Carter's papers on his death and they give a good picture of Howard's progress and concerns as well as the backbone of the Assemblies of God. In addition to the monthly letters, there is a series of weekly letters addressed to members of the Bible School Evangelistic Society. Writing more than fifty years after the events it is difficult to say how the two sets of mailing lists were compiled and whether or if they overlapped to a greater or a lesser extent. It looks, however, as though the weekly letters were primarily for leaders and therefore had a smaller circulation. Weekly letter 190 (dated Jan 4th 1933) lists 130 separate members of the BSES and it was with this scattered group of people (who met regularly at an annual conference quite distinct from the Assemblies of God General Conference) that Howard Carter shared the ministerial successes and failures of his students and ex-students. He created a sense of excitement and unity.

The Leaders' Weekly Letters carried information from the local churches as well as exhortations and articles written by Carter or others. As early as May 1933 there is a record that "backsliders have returned" with its implication that even the miracles which accompanied early pentecostal campaigns failed to prevent some Christians drifting away from the church. Evangelism was constantly emphasised and this generated an itinerant attitude among many ministers. There was always the temptation to go and preach elsewhere when life in the local congregation became difficult. Eight letters written by two pastors on the job given a clear picture of pastoral life. Four of the letters appeared in 1936 (numbered 306-9). The first described the call to pastoral ministry and stressed the difference between a sheep and a shepherd, "the shepherd is by nature a gatherer; the sheep a wanderer" and the shepherd knows "the demand on us is great. A forsaking of all: taking up the cross daily: putting near and dear ones in a secondary place seems to be the plan and rule laid down in the Gospels". In outlining the pastor's work, the writer points out that "first there is the keeping together of the body of Christ" partly by means of pulpit ministry and partly by means of visiting people in their homes.

Letter 318, in more sombre tones, supports the impressions

already created,

> When we first set sail upon the unknown sea of this ministry with the Divine breeze of spiritual fervour strong in our hearts, we imagined that there would be straight sailing - no storms, no adverse winds, nothing but clear horizons of packed halls, miraculous displays, sweeping revivals, and separated and sanctified saints ablaze for God. But we were before long disillusioned. Instead of what we visualized, the reality was in many cases a small hall upstairs in some obscure street, a remnant of an Assembly that survived a series of splits, a district hardened by prejudice, and after weeks or months of hard labour, we managed to secure one or two converts to swell the numbers. It is then when zeal is ready to flag: when Satan buffets us mercilessly as to the genuineness of our call: when we are about to give up hope, and count ourselves useless for God or man. But what was the outcome ? We desperately sought the face of God: we received marvellous sustaining and strengthening grace: new determination and enthusiasm infused into our beings by the Spirit, and we emerged from the storm wiser and better, having had the ballast of self-abasement and sobriety placed aboard.

The young pastor expects so much and works so hard and seems to reap so little. And the reason for this is contained in a clue about the condition of the church. The splitting of Assemblies had deep-seated effects on Christians in the area. It caused some members to lose their faith and, once it had happened, a precedent was set for further splits. No wonder that pastors doubted their call to the ministry or that they emphasised, almost above everything else, the unity of the flock. It was almost unknown in those days for the pastor to delegate any sphere of leadership to other men in the congregation for fear that factions would break off from the main body. Pastors, therefore, were often benign dictators who controlled the life of the church with little reference to elders or deacons and, if a pastor left a small congregation to take on a larger one, the remaining officers would sometimes feel betrayed by the man for whom they had begun to feel affection mingled with respect. In this way the new young pastor had to start from scratch to establish the authority of his calling. Part of the trouble, unfortunately, stemmed from the view, which both these tried and tested pastors propagated, that it was necessary to remain aloof from the flock so as to retain its respect - indeed "to introduce friends into the home from members of the assembly would result in calamity". No wonder that pastors found their job a lonely one or that they so valued the contact they had with other ministers in their local presbyteries. Little by little the temptations changed: pastors began to prosper and to own cars. Letter 308 says "to hear of the pastor who spends more time over his car than over his sermons, is becoming a common complaint". We begin to move into the modern era!

In a letter dated 31 May 1937 readers were told about the "decontrolling" of the "first crop" of Assemblies. This had been formally recognised at the General Conference of that year (see below). Records found among John Carter's papers on his death show two categories of control, one relating to the assembly (and therefore probably the role of the pastor) and the other relating to the building. There were 28 controlled Assemblies (of these 4 were in controlled buildings) and a further 6 controlled buildings. At the General Presbytery Conference in 1937 the BSES (or its parent organisation the BSMA) proposed that controlled assemblies be set free to affiliate themselves to Assemblies of God. Howard Carter had never intended to set up a group-within-a-group and was aware that he might invite criticism if he built up an empire of his own. Apart from five young or immature congregations and another eight with financial liabilities, all the remaining Assemblies were "pruned off" to allow the BSES to bear another harvest. The BSES did not eradicate itself and the Bible School remained at the centre of its activities: it was from here that students were sent out, and it was to here that they reported back, requested prayer or asked for practical help. According to rumour, Carter would look at the map, put his hand in his pocket and produce a one way second class rail fare and tell a young man in training at Hampstead to take over a small number of believers as their minister. It was a sink-or-swim policy and the miracle of it is that so many young men did learn to swim. Yet there were weaknesses in whole enterprise. Perhaps most obvious was the prolonged absence of Howard Carter. He did what he could to consolidate the churches on his return from overseas in 1936. His itinerary was given in letter 299 and opens with the words "we are delighted to note, what we believe is the steady improvement in the health of Mr Howard Carter" (he had caught malaria). He was to visit 39 different Assemblies between Darlington and Maidstone in three months.

A sober and perhaps pessimistic assessment of the progress to date was given in letter 332 (dated 26th June 1937),

It is fair to suppose that no one taking a general survey of our own evangelistic situation could honestly say that it was, even in a measure, satisfactory...While individualistic evangelistic effort within a small circle does not require long experience for its successful application, general efforts over large areas need to be arranged with that sagacity which only long experience can produce. Being a young movement it is quite likely we have not realized the imperative need of such directing .....Why should we not ask ourselves if we have not, in our past efforts, made the mistake of over-reaching ourselves by beginning at the top instead of at the bottom. Everyone is anxious to do the BIG thing. Experience suggests, however, that it is wiser to START with the little thing and then lead up to the larger one. In other words, to lay the foundation first, then rear up the structure. It is not wise to begin by seeking to bring on the TOP stone with rejoicing. Why not frankly acknowledge our mistake and begin again at the beginning ? (original capitals)

And the writer (G T Shearman, then working at the Bible School) went on to compare the small beginnings of the Assemblies of God missionary work and its steady growth with the over stretched and under organised work at home. When one looks at the statistics showing the number of different congregations in Assemblies of God, it is evident that the graph continued to rise steeply throughout the 1930s. At the beginning of the decade there were about 140 churches and by the end there were approximately 350 and these figures (which were compiled by Basil Varnam at the Assemblies of God General offices in the early 1980s) do not include provisional or pioneer congregations. Yet G T Shearman's assessment, even if it is only applied to the ground-breaking efforts of the BSES members, rings true, especially if a comparison is made between the progress of the pentecostal church in Britain and in Scandanavia or even, to everyone's surprise, France.

Councils and leadership
There were two, or perhaps three, men in Assemblies of God who had as much potential influence as Howard Carter. One was John Carter, the second was Tom Mercy a dynamic welshman who had seen about 40 congregations pioneered from his home base at Crosskeys, and the third was Donald Gee. Mercy tragically died of overwork in 1935. An examination of Gee's carefully hand-written sermon notes (lent to me by Jean Wildrianne) showed how extensive were Gee's travels up to

1934. From 1931 to 1933 he hardly set foot in the United Kingdom: he was in South Africa, Scandinavia, several other European countries, the USA, Canada, Syria and Jerusalem. But, after Nelson Parr's resignation from all offices in Assemblies of God in 1933/4, Gee and John Carter, who had a profound respect for one another and worked together without friction, became joint editors of *Redemption Tidings* and Gee tended to restrict his travels abroad to short bursts. Early in 1933 the Gee family had at long last moved from their beloved Edinburgh; Mrs Gee was offered the post of matron at the Louth Bible School in Lincolnshire and they began to recognise that Donald would never again occupy a pastorate. In 1934 he was in South Africa, France and Sweden, in 1935 he went to Germany and Poland, in 1937 he was in Poland, France, Canada, China and the USA and in 1938 he went to Switzerland. The magazine benefited from his international experience and, though the pentecostal movement in Britain made little obvious impact on other evangelicals, it was never allowed to be parochial or defensive in outlook. The closely guarded autonomy of the local assemblies prevented any great alteration in the overall administrative structure. Development of governmental structure occurred by the addition of councils and committees brought together for specific purposes and whose members were usually voted into office.

This tendency evidently attracted criticism either for being unscriptural or for the caution and delay engendered by its system. Gee characteristically tackled the problem head on in an editorial in *Redemption Tidings* on November 15th 1935.

Part of the price which any "chief among the brethren" have to pay for their heavier stewardship is the constant scrutiny of the multitude. The great apostle had judges in plenty among the churches (1 Cor iv:3). What is true of leaders individually is equally true when they meet in a Council; and Councils, as such, usually get plenty of criticism.

> Neither need we be to anxious to have it otherwise, if the criticism is kept within proper limits. We conclude that nothing is more foreign to a true conception of the Church as the body of Christ than a dictatorship or a bureaucracy that crushes or scorns all expression of dissent. A healthy criticism can sometimes be the finest tonic for any body.. Among Pentecostal people there has been an intense suspicion of all Boards and Councils... so many of us have had some disappointing personal experiences of Church Boards and Denominational

Councils that have all too evidently forfeited their spirituality, and substituted that which is natural and carnal.

His comments show firstly that there was, even within the first 10 years of Assemblies of God, criticism of the method of conciliar national supervision and secondly that the two alternatives - of power in the hands of an individual (which he calls "dictatorship") and of bureaucracy - had no appeal. He went on to justify the system in force:

> Yet Church government and the direction of the Holy Spirit THROUGH COUNSEL represents the New Testament revelation of the divine pattern...It is to COUNCILS that the Holy Spirit imparts guidance (Acts xv:28) and it is by the "laying of of the hands of the PRESBYTERY" that spiritual gifts are often bestowed (1 Tim iv: 14). The early assemblies were expected to keep the DECREES formulated by the "apostles and elders which were at Jerusalem", and marked blessing and increase came through their submission (Acts xvi: 4-5). (original caps)

And he ended with a description of a council at its best:

> Scene after scene in recent years come before us, as we recall a room full of just such men, sobered by a deep sense of responsibility, dropping on to their knees before the Lord, and beseeching the God of all grace to grant them heavenly wisdom. Afterwards when counsel has been given, it is enriched by a great variety of different gifts and outlook bestowed by the Spirit, and garnered from a wide and long experience. Often a decision is delayed pending that unanimity which seems specially to mark an arrival at the mind of Christ.....Those who freely indulge in continual criticism of Councils do well to consider where their pernicious activities may ultimately lead. It may well be that they are resisting, not men, but the Holy Ghost.

There are aspects of his argument and exegesis which are open to question - for example the Council of Jerusalem in Acts 15 is the only one mentioned in the New Testament and was called to deal with the specific problem of Jew/Gentile relations and not with the deployment of evangelism, missionary work or the certification of ministers. Yet, given that the men who sat on the various AoG councils were gracious and spiritual, they could indeed be expected to make the correct decisions. Where the councils degenerated into feuding committees, and where election to councils arose from adept manipulation of voting procedures, the system was liable to fail, as indeed, seems to have been the case in the 1950s.

Two new conciliar groupings were established in AoG in 1935. Gee reviewed the year in December 15th's *Redemption Tidings* and reported on the formation of a Chairman's Presbytery which was composed of the chairmen of the District Presbyteries and the members of the Executive Presbytery. The main reason for the new body seems to have been to provide a link between the centre, that is, the Executive Presbytery and the circumference, that is, the outlying assemblies. The formation of this body seems to have been eminently sensible. The other council which was formed seems to have come about as a reaction against two sets of circumstances. The first was the departure of Fred Squire and the second was recognition that the Bible School Evangelistic Society was ready to surrender its operation to a larger company. The Assemblies of God Evangelistic Council (of 11 men with Gee as chairman) was established to oversee evangelistic campaigns. It is to the matter of Fred Squire which we must turn because in many respects it highlights the problems being faced by AoG, or being faced within AoG, and the efforts made to deal with them.

One of the speakers at the 1935 Whitsun Convention was Fred Squire who was beginning to wear the mantle Stephen Jeffreys had been forced to leave behind. Squire (c 1904-62) spoke twice and delighted everyone with an account of the revival he had just witnessed in the west country. The crowds had been large and there had been miracles of healing. T B Barratt, then 73 years of age, and Wigglesworth, a few years his elder, also spoke and represented the vigour of the older generation. Gee and Squire were leaders of the younger generation, and it must have seemed that the pentecostal movement was finding men of calibre to complete the unfinished tasks which A A Boddy and the others had dimly glimpsed before 1914; but Squire, as we shall see, later had his difference with Assemblies of God, probably to the detriment of both and Gee never was, or claimed to be, an evangelist.

Fred Squire's abilities as an evangelist were just what was required by Assemblies of God. The young men from the Bible School were, in most cases, not yet mature and few of them seemed to have been able to sustain evangelistic campaigns. Squire, by contrast, was an excellent campaigner. He was musical, he could grip a large congregation with a forceful presentation of the Gospel and, when he prayed for those who were ill, miracles of various kinds usually took place. *Redemption Tidings* regularly carried snippets of news about his work and frequently reported larger attendances at his meetings than those of his contemporaries. His preaching drew the attention of the secular press and cuttings from the *Northamptonshire Evening Telegraph* (7th Feb 1933) are headed "Claims of Cures at Kettering Revival" while those from the *Daily Tribune* (Jan 5th 1933) proclaim "Remarkable Scenes in Nuneaton". Why, then, did Squire and Assemblies of God go their separate ways ? Until the middle of 1936 he was a minister in Assemblies of God, with responsibilities in the newly formed Assemblies of God Evangelistic Society.

According to Jean-Jacques Zbinden, his son-in-law, Squire and Howard Carter did not see eye to eye. Carter did not believe that churches should be large and was inclined to split any big congregation into two smaller ones, presumably because he thought that this would aid evangelism. Squire, on the other hand, often saw churches of several hundred people built up quite quickly as a result of his preaching and did not like the idea of sub-dividing them, especially when there was a shortage of pastors to look after them. As early as October 1932 Squire formed "The Full Gospel Testimony", to provide a framework of care for his churches. It seems to have been a bone of contention between Carter and Squire that, whereas Carter was willing to "prune off" the churches formed by the BSES, Squire was unwilling to let go of his Full Gospel Testimony churches so easily. John Carter said that Squire referred to them as "my" churches. But the real cause of Squire's departure seems to have been triggered by his insistence on wearing a clerical collar. Clerical attire had been favoured by Stephen Jeffreys and many photographs show him wearing a dark jacket and trousers and a "dog" collar. Squire also considered that clerical clothing helped him to gain a respectful hearing for his preaching. Other members of the pentecostal movement were strongly opposed to any outwardly distinctive mark of ministerial office because it raised the spectres of denominationalism and professionalism which seemed likely to divide congregations into lay and clerical sections. The Assemblies of God General Conference passed a resolution stating

> We entirely disagree with the wearing of any ministerial of priestly attire whatever (5th June 1936, item 20, General Conference Minutes).

Within two months Squire had resigned from Assemblies of God. He continued for nearly thirty years to hold crusades, though he was extremely concerned to help refugees after the 1939-45 war and his formation of the International Bible Training Institute in Sussex demonstrated his organisational capacity and an ability to leave behind something more substantial than the memory of his evangelistic fervour. Yet his Full Gospel Testimony had every appearance of being a rival to Assemblies of God. Salt must have poured into the wound when Nelson Parr joined Squire as the Testimony's General Superintendent. Although they never attracted more than about 20 churches, they could at least count the illustrious name of Bethshan, Manchester.

Themes in the 1930s General Conferences

The minutes of the Assemblies of God general conferences in the 1930s show the year to year concerns of the fellowship. We can classify its concerns under three headings: *growth, divisions and leadership*. First and foremost, there was continued growth, both in the numbers of ministers or representatives attending the General Conference and in the numbers of assemblies being received into membership. No figures for attendance are given until 1935 when 90 men and 11 women attended. By 1940 these numbers had risen to 143 men and 9 women. In the same period 128 extra congregations were received into Assemblies of God, and this figure represents the net gain in size after the subtraction of 45 assemblies which had closed down or resigned. This growth was paralleled by an increase in financial solvency. Money was short at the beginning of the decade but, by the end of it, the fortnightly publication of *Redemption Tidings* had risen to just over 9,000 copies per issue and profits from sales provided a healthy surplus balance of nearly £800. Of course, growth and leadership are connected, and it is apparent that the loss of assemblies, on the one hand, and the increase in magazine circulation on the other, points to the strengths and weaknesses of the Assemblies of God at that time. There was no proper way to keep small churches going, especially if they were unable to support a full-time pastor, but the overall numbers of pentecostals in the country was still on the increase because there were pastors who were able to hold large congregations and to evangelise at the same time. Some of the new assemblies (but it is impossible to say what proportion) were daughter churches of existing congregations. It is evident, too, that the administration of Assemblies of God which, from 1937 onwards, was in the hands of John Carter, and before that with C L Parker, was efficient. John Carter and Donald Gee picked *Redemp-*

tion Tidings up after Nelson Parr's shock resignation in 1934 and they quietly brought about the smooth running of many aspects of life and communication within the growing number of churches. To them must go considerable credit for the survival of the movement as a unitary whole. Howard Carter was out of country for about four of the years 1934-40 (and the Bible School seems to have suffered in his absence) but John had a genuine willingness to serve and, because of this, he was regarded by some people as the greater man.

The leadership of the movement was expressed through the functions of the Executive Presbytery. This group of men were largely those who had been active pentecostally from just before or after the 1914-18 war. They had won their spurs by their individualism and steadfastness when the vast majority of religious and secular opinion had been against them. Younger men would have liked to serve on the Executive and it is clear from propositions put to the Conferences that they were looking for ways and means to broaden the leadership within the movement. In 1933 a proposition that the Executive Presbytery be elected by a card vote of all Presbyters (and not just those present at the Conference) was defeated; in 1935 a proposal that retiring members of the Executive should not seek re-election for two years was defeated; in 1937 a proposal that the Executive Presbytery be composed of the chairmen or other representatives of District Presbyteries was defeated; in 1938 a proposal that the Executive Presbytery be increased to 12 men was rejected and in 1940 a proposal to abolish the permanency of the general Chairmanship - held by Howard Carter - was also rejected.

The presbyterian machinery set up by Nelson Parr was only capable of dealing with crises rather slowly. It could direct and coordinate, but it was not so good at initiating new ventures. Nevertheless, when Fred Squire left, it was obvious that something would have to be done. The most gifted and promising young evangelist had gone his own way and so an Evangelistic Council was founded with the remit of "shepherding our evangelistic work" (1936, minute 12). The Council had been mooted the previous year before Squire's resignation and so it got into action without its star preacher. Reading between the lines it looks as though one of its preliminary tasks was to liaise with the BSES (the Bible School Evangelistic Society) so as to avoid overlapping and competition. In 1937 it was announced that the BSES had become "a spiritual fellowship of Bible School ex-students" (G C Mins 1937.10a) and the AGEC (Assemblies of God Evangelistic Council) had a clear field of work, apart from the need to keep in contact with

District Presbyteries. Without labouring the point, it is immediately clear how the decision-making process was slowed down. In the 1920s and early 30s evangelists had been invited to towns by small groups of believers and had simply preached for all they were worth. Now it was necessary to consult and plan and there was always the possibility that an evangelistic campaign, if it was conducted without informing the AGEC, would cause friction. The danger was that committee work would replace the decisiveness of gifted individuals. This danger appears to have been fully realised when, in 1938, a brief report indicated that, after a presentation of the financial statement, the AGEC ceased to exist. It did not restart until 1941.

After unity in the 1920s, there was disunity in the 1930s - not catastrophic and not always obvious, but disunity nonetheless. Nelson Parr's departure was the most obvious instance of an individual's disagreement with his brethren and, though Parr attended the General Conference again in 1936 and 1937, he was not there in 1938, 1939 or 1940. The breach with Parr was consciously repaired and a statement at the 1936 Conference reported that "it was mutually and unanimously agreed to mutually withdraw all criticisms we have made against each other, and we are pleased to state to the glory of God that at this meeting a complete and full reconciliation was effected". The statement was signed by the surviving members of the 1933 Executive Presbytery. Then there was the loss of Fred Squire which, though it was not as sharp as the loss of Parr, was perhaps as damaging in the long run. The Full Gospel Testimony was discussed at the Conference in 1938, 1939 and again in 1940 and after a mediating attempt to allow collaborative efforts, it was finally agreed that "one cannot be a member of Assemblies of God and at the same time of the FGT" (G C Mins 1939.16), and this decision was reaffirmed a year later. It is sad to note that in Donald Gee's Conference Address for 1935 he had spoken on Philippians and had outlined the fellowship in the Gospel, the fellowship in the Spirit and the fellowship in the sufferings of Christ which the epistle describes. Gee had stressed that "fellowship rather than organisation" was the fundamental principle of Assemblies of God. It would appear that his words had fallen on deaf ears.

The Assemblies of God as a whole

Overall the British pentecostal churches came through the 1930s in better shape and size than might have been expected. True, the most visionary and optimistic hopes of the pentecostals were not realised and, by comparison with Scandinavia and North America, everything was on a smaller scale. We shall look first at the situation in the UK, and include here matters of doctrine and organisation, and then look overseas at missionary work and at the increasingly alarming situation in Europe.

Redemption Tidings carried a series of open letters and testimonies written by pastors and leaders which reveal something of the way the average pentecostal perceived his situation. Harold Horton, for example, wrote:

> There is a tendency among those dear brethren who received their Pentecostal baptism in the 'former days' about thirty years ago, to suppose that those were the palmy days; that no days can ever equal them, that the Pentecostal power has since deteriorated, that baptisms are not as real or as mighty as they were, and that the whole Pentecostal experience has fallen to a lower level and grown ordinary, or even dull in comparison with that of the 'former days'. In consequence of this attitude maintained, and even advertised, among some of our brethren and sisters in the rank and file of Pentecost, there is a growing feeling among some of our younger folk that they have come into Pentecost a decade or two too late. (June 1st, 1936)

Nostalgia had obviously begun to take root and there was a sense of decline among old and young alike and it was against this pessimism that Horton directed his letter. Looking back from the vantage point of a further fifty years, it seems very odd to discover that people hankered for the spiritual enthusiasm of the turn of the century. To us the 1920s seem to have been remarkable, and the 1930s, if not pentecostally startling, at least better than much of the 1940s and 50s.

A fortnight later Fred Watson in the same magazine slot said, "the glorious and soul-stirring wonder of this Holy Ghost outpouring in these 'latter days' has come at a time of great and increasing darkness and satanic activity". Watson saw the pentecostal movement as simultaneous with a rise in unwholesome and unchristian trends in society, a theme echoed by E H Davis of Belfast in the words "we are confronted today with a condition of things never known before in the history of the Church. Satan seems to be bringing up every reinforcement in a final onslaught, and his bitterest venom is concentrated on believers who have received the Pentecostal blessing..British-Israelism, Universalism, Buchmanism, and many other 'isms' are sucking at our life's blood" (18th Dec, 1936). In an article on the Holy Spirit, Howard

Carter pointed out, "we have fellowship with all believers who love the Lord Jesus, and yet the Pentecostal Movement is strangely ostracised in the churches" (May 15th, 1936). The pentecostals felt that they had been rejected by the denominations and though, at times, that rejection was mutual, it would not be true to say that pentecostalism in general had a detestation of everything their fellow Christians stood for; in other words, pentecostalism did not react like a sect. On the contrary there was clearly a desire to read the events of the day in the light of biblical prophecy and to measure each political and economic change in the light of its probable effect on the proclamation of the Gospel. Pentecostals felt themselves to be involved in a spiritual struggle which demanded their consecration and faith and the maturest of them saw the baptism with the Holy Spirit as a means of empowering the Church rather than as a quirk or toy for individual sensation seekers. John Carter put it this way: "we rejoice in the work done for Christ's kingdom by other evangelical sections of God's church...We ourselves maintain that God has raised up this Movement to emphasize long-neglected truths, viz. the present-day experience of the Baptism in the Holy Ghost with signs following, Divine Healing, and the Gifts of the Spirit" (*Redemption Tidings* 11 March, 1938).

Redemption Tidings carried a regular feature entitled "Revival Tidings" which collected accounts of campaigns and conventions and anything else encouraging round Britain. It is noticeable that most months included a report of the opening of new halls. May 15th, 1936, for example has subheadlines reading "Opening of new hall at East Kirkby" with the note "over 600 present on Easter Monday evening" and "Opening of new church at Mardy" with the note "Welsh-chairman conducts opening ceremony". A month later there were similar reports: "Opening of new hall at Norwich" and "Hucknall assembly enter more suitable premises" and on the 31st July "New hall opened at Motherwell", while in the middle of August an item recorded "Assembly opened at Pontypool". Three years later in July 14th 1939 a new work was opened in Essex and a new hall at Tiverton. The impression, then, is that in the 1930s the Assemblies of God was moving out of small rooms and hired halls into its own property. It was becoming established. Donald Gee, perceptive as ever, noticed what was happening and wrote an article on "Financing Assembly Property" (*Redemption Tidings* Feb 1st, 1936) in which he pointed out the disadvantages of hired halls and the methods by which funds could be raised to pay for property, bearing in mind too the need for a carefully worded trust deed. In fact a trust fund had been set up in Assemblies of God from around 1931 and functioned as a sort of Building Society after money had begun to flow in during 1932. The trustees of the fund were the Executive Presbytery and they issued a model trust deed to assemblies who wanted advice when applying for loans. Moreover, just as Assemblies of God was beginning to be a property owning group, so also the Elim Pentecostal Churches were recognising the extent of their assets. As it happened, the Elim churches fell foul of an attempt to reorganise their financial operations in the midst of other activities, and a long and painful wrangle between George Jeffreys and the Elim General Offices resulted in a damaging parting of the ways. Jeffreys came to consider the centralised ownership of Elim property as unfair to the local congregations which had put up the money for their buildings and he made an attempt to "democratise" the Elim system of church government - an attempt which raised all sorts of questions in people's minds since it was Jeffreys who had been largely responsible for constructing the system in the first place. The Assemblies of God always recognised that a local congregation owned the building to which its funds had contributed; this was part of the autonomy of local assemblies which was at the heart of the AoG Constitution. Furthermore, local assemblies appointed their own trustees and thus had complete freedom to buy, alter or sell their buildings. Only if the assembly left Assemblies of God did problems occur, especially if the assembly was a debtor to the Assemblies of God property trust.

The acquisition of property did not prevent Howard Carter and Donald Gee from some searching self-questioning. A *Redemption Tidings* (30 June, 1939, p 7) report of the 1939 General Conference had discussed "the apparent decrease of Pentecostal power" while in January of 1936, Howard Carter had asked, "How can one be satisfied with nothing more than a simple evangelistic work, when the Bible speaks of deeper experiences in the spiritual life ?" and he went on to argue that a union with Christ accompanied by sacrificial giving was the next necessary step. Interestingly Carter saw spiritual progress in terms of personal consecration and sacrificial generosity rather than in the building up of large thriving congregations; he did not want bigger churches, but more dedicated individuals. Gee asked bluntly in the title of an article in *Redemption Tidings* on the 17th June, 1938, "Can this pentecostal revival be maintained ?". His answer was taken from a study of the Acts of the Apostles and concluded that if boldness, purity, adequate church government coupled with visionary leadership and organisation were forthcoming, the revival would not falter. Gee's analysis would appear to have been borne out by events because the immediate post war decade was perhaps the least effective the pentecostal movement had known, largely for the absence of those requirements he had outlined. But Gee also put his finger on some of the weaknesses which had begun to emerge on the British pentecostal scene. He wrote about the "love of office" which was a danger to some assemblies - there were evidently men who pushed themselves forward for positions in the church out of a mistaken pride and from no genuine desire to serve (*Redemption Tidings* 15 March, 1936). And then there was the problem of ministerial jealousy which aided and abetted divisions between prominent Christians (Redemption Tidings 25 Sept, 1936). G T Shearman was even more damning in his view of the state of the pentecostal movement,

> The large number of small assemblies: the poor attendance at prayer meetings and Sunday morning services: the large number of churches which make no real progress: the widespread neglect of private prayer and personal Bible study: the almost entire absence of real care for the lost: the small number of real conversions: failure to impress the outsider, are some of the proofs of the wide extent of the need. All these things declare that in many places we are out of touch with the real power and purpose of God. Let us make no mistake here; for if we do not recognise our need we shall never get it supplied. (*Redemption Tidings,* 26 Aug, 1938)

What Shearman was acutely aware of was that the pentecostal movement was not yet a revival, and by this he meant something akin to the move of the Holy Spirit in Wales in 1904. He was looking for a change in the spiritual climate of the country, a burning up of lukewarmness so that whole communities turned to Christ. He was not satisfied with the gathering of a few hundred people to sing hymns lustily. And Gee too made the point that "the abiding, compelling, overflowing fulness of God in our midst must inevitably bring blessing to our brethren in the denominations around us; and so, even yet, fulfil the Vision of a Revival rather than a new sect" (*Redemption Tidings,* 15 Sept, 1934).

On a different front, pentecostal leaders were concerned to safeguard sound doctrine. Pentecostalism was vulnerable to false teaching whenever the utterance of charismatic message were not properly judged. The British-Israel doctrine was whispered in the Elim churches and so the Assemblies of God were alert to it. Though the doctrine was profoundly misleading, it had the advantage of being profoundly patriotic and, when conscientious objection was derided, it was a psychological counter to social pressure. Gee tackled the subject cautiously in 1936 because he feared a "quagmire of controversy". British-Israelites claimed that the ten lost tribes of Israel had come to Cornwall and that the British were therefore Israelite by blood relation. Hopes for salvation then tended to rest on being "Israelites" rather than on the atoning work of Christ. W F P Burton, a missionary to the Congo whose labours were of genuinely apostolic proportions, in a characteristically lucid and pointed article, explained "Why I do not believe the British Israel theory" (*Redemption Tidings* Feb 11, 1938). Burton rejected the Irish legends and the "irrelevant passage from the dream of Esdras" on which the theory was founded and showed that the mere fact that circumcision in Britain was not customary, invalidated any claim for British citizens to be within the Old Testament covenant. After a consideration of the biblical passages dealing with the history of the ten northern tribes, Burton then showed the folly of an additional development to British Israel teaching, namely that the Great Pyramid of Egypt, if measured in inches, provided evidence upon which the date of the second coming of Christ could be based. After predicting Christ's return in 1928, 1935 and 1936, they had brought normal second adventist doctrine into disrepute.

Evangelical Christians have generally agreed that conversion to Christ is identical with the "new birth" spoken of in John 3 and that this birth results from the work of the Holy Spirit. It seems clear that various churches - though it is not clear whether they were pentecostal churches - were depreciating and distorting the new birth, possibly in order to maximise the importance of the baptism in the Holy Spirit. For example a distinction was being made between "being in Jesus" (forgiveness of sins) and "being in Christ" (being born again); and it was argued that the new birth was always accompanied by glossolalia so that anyone who had not received this experience was unready for the return of Christ. A series of articles in Redemption Tidings in 1934 were written to set matters right and to reassert the distinction between regeneration and baptism in the Spirit, and to make it clear that the first only was necessary for salvation and that the second was impossible without the first.

The other doctrinal matters which concerned Assemblies of God were those related to its specific stance, especially on speaking in tongues. By and large, little attention was paid to other gifts of the Spirit, or even to eschatological issues, and though there was a continuing regard for miracles of healing, it was only Gee who attempted to fit various charismata into the scheme of ministry gifts - apostles, prophets, evangelists, pastors and teachers - listed in Ephesians 4. Water baptism, it is true, was studied and there were studies on the deity of Christ, but perhaps one aberration does reveal the cast of mind which pentecostalism produced in some people. A view arose that Christians need not die because they could claim exemption from the effects of sin as a result of Christ's sacrifice on the cross; since sin caused death, the full benefits of faith in Christ's atonement would indefinitely postpone physical death. Gee refuted this idea (*Redemption Tidings*, 15 June, 1936) - yet it can be seen to have a curious logic, particularly since it was generally argued that divine healing was procured by the "merits of the Atonement of Christ" (Garfield Vale in *Redemption Tidings* 15 Feb, 1935). Moody (*Redemption Tidings*, 21 Oct, 1938) contended that some people were not healed because they failed to believe that healing was part of the atonement. "Many, even in our Pentecostal ranks, have ceased to believe that healing is in the atonement", he wrote, and argued that the case can be made from Isaiah 53. Another view, however, to account for illness among Spirit-filled Christians was expressed in 1939 by Lewi Pethrus, the leading Swedish pentecostal, when he argued that there were occasions when God wished to show his power in and through human weakness (*Redemption Tidings* Jan 13, 1939).

On the matter of spiritual gifts Gee and Carter were again the two men who did most to expound what became the classic pentecostal position in a balanced way. They both took the view that spiritual gifts (mentioned several times at length in 1 Corinthians) originate in the power and ministry of the Holy Spirit. They distinguished sharply between natural abilities and spiritual gifts and held that, for example, the ability to speak in several languages was quite unconnected with the ability to speak in tongues and, equally, the ability to prophesy was unconnected with any natural insight into the pattern of events. Carter's understanding of spiritual gifts dated back to his confinement to Dartmoor prison while a conscientious objector to the 1914-18 war. Gee took a slightly different tack on the matter and argued that certain spiritual gifts were associated with certain ministry gifts so that, for example, evangelists would be most likely to manifest gifts of healing, teachers to manifest "words of wisdom", and so on. Indeed, it has been suggested that relations between Gee and Carter on the interpretation of a "word of wisdom" (1 Cor 12.8) were less than cordial. Gee was more inclined to see it as a discourse or sermon illuminated by divine wisdom, whereas Carter thought that it was a sudden fragment of divine omniscience dropped into a Christian's mind to solve a pressing problem. Gee's *Concerning Spiritual Gifts* went through five editions up to March 1935; Carter's views were expressed by Harold Horton in *The Gifts of the Spirit* in 1934.

The growth and consolidation of the pentecostal movement brought the issue of denominational government and leadership into focus. Assemblies of God had been formed with the express intention of allowing each local assembly to retain its autonomy. John Carter, at the request of the Executive Presbytery, wrote a series of articles on the Assemblies of God constitution, presumably because they felt that, as the movement grew, more and more assemblies had only a hazy idea of the principles which had been agreed on in 1924. As Carter pointed out, in 14 years the Assemblies of God had grown from 70 to 320 local congregations (*Redemption Tidings* 11 March, 1938). Carter's articles were both straightforward and persuasive: each part of the constitution was a necessary and logical addition to the original conception of a group of loosely federated churches, each subscribing to the same doctrinal position, but each exercising its own independence on non-essential matters. At one extreme the Assemblies of God wished to avoid a centralised system of government dominated by one man or a few men and, at the other, there seemed little point in a bonding which amounted to little more than an information service. Nevertheless a comparison between the Assemblies of God in Britain and the complete lack of any organisation beyond the local church among Swedish pentecostals must have caused some heart searching. Gee reported on a powerful sermon by Lewi Pethrus at the Stockholm Conference (see below) in which he repudiated all forms of organisation on the grounds that, far from creating unity, it did the reverse. Gee went on "the simplicity of such an absolute freedom from the dangerous machinery of organisation possesses a strong appeal. Its strongest argument, however, lies in the fidelity to the New Testament pattern that it embodies" (*Redemption Tidings* July 14, 1939).

Looking back at the pentecostal movement in the 1930s, it is very easy to see the shadow of the 1939-45 war lengthening over Europe and, beyond that, the other more sinister and lasting shadow of the Soviet bloc which would, in the years after the war, shroud Christians and enfold them in many years of misery. Were the pentecostal churches alert to the dangers ahead and did they use the time at their disposal as well as possible ? The answer to both these questions must be an almost complete "yes". It is very moving to realise that Donald Gee, for example, travelled in southern Russia, Danzig, Poland and China in the 1930s doing his best to encourage the Christians there and to confirm their faith. He was not to know how the doors into those countries would shut fast - indeed his trip to China was unexpected and unhoped for, but he felt that it was directed by the Holy Spirit. On the 1st January 1940 he reflected in *Redemption Tidings* on twelve years of world travel. He was not a wealthy man and yet his travels were extensive and, as he pointed out, the dollars he had been given in America helped finance his trips to less wealthy parts of the world. His practice was never to enter into any financial arrangements over ministry and he "always left that side of things to the voluntary freewill offerings of the Lord's people on a perfectly willing basis". He took the provision of his needs as an indication that he was in the will of God. Howard Carter likewise travelled extensively, though his motivation was slightly different, because he went to encourage the 120 or so young men and women who, having been to the Hampstead Bible School, were now located in different parts of the world.

Overseas missions in AOG

There was undoubtedly a strong missionary thrust in Assemblies of God. Each fortnight *Redemption Tidings* carried reports from missionaries which balanced the reports from Britain. Missionary books were advertised and missionaries home on furlough regularly preached at conventions.

Leslie Woodford was connected with Overseas Missions in Assemblies of God for most of his life. The Home Missionary Reference Council of Assemblies of God handled the applications of aspiring missionaries and directed funds from churches to serving missionaries overseas. In August 1936, because the administrative work of the Council was growing, Leslie Woodford was mooted as a possible assistant secretary. In June 1937 he was voted into the this position and so brought his methodical mind to bear on missionary problems. In fact, if the HMRC minutes prior to Woodford's arrival are anything to go by, the running of missionary work in Assemblies of God was already well conducted. E W Moser, as a solicitor who had worked with the old PMU, and G J Tilling, who had been in a diplomat, were no amateurs, and Woodford was able to learn from their style. In addition the Council benefited from the contributions of Donald Gee, the Carter brothers, F R Barnes, T J Jones and Harold Horton.

Financial statements show that in 1937 missionaries were supported in China, Congo, Brazil, India, Japan, Korea, France, Belgium,

Spain and Egypt and that about £300 a month passed through the hands of the Council. Altogether 86 missionaries carried an HMRC certificate. Missionaries received funds directly from churches and through designated and undesignated giving to the HMRC. Designated donations were obviously given with a named missionary in mind. Undesignated funds were at the disposal of the HMRC. This system resulted in inequalities in wealth among men and women serving on the same mission field. After consulting the missionaries involved the Council discovered that there was "vitually unanimous" agreement that an equal distribution system be adopted. This system would allow the HMRC to take into account the personal gifts each missionary received, and their personal needs - especially in relation to the cost of educating their children - in the allocation of undesignated funds. In effect, poorer missionaries received more from the common purse.

The relationship between the HMRC and its missionaries is illustrated by the adoption of the Equal Distribution System (see HMRC minutes 12 Nov 1937). Courtesy and common sense prevailed. The HMRC did not impose its will on the missionaries, nor did the missionaries make unreasonable demands on the Council. In May 1938 Woodford considered the question of fares for furlough. His report to the Council is an example of precision and clarity. He listed the options, weighed the pros and cons of each, and then concluded with the recommendation that missionaries continue to save their own income towards travelling home for furlough, but with the understanding that Field Councils should be encouraged to set aside funds for special needs. Any emergencies could be dealt with from a fund set up by the HMRC and amounting to 10% of the monies it transacted.

In 1937 Donald Gee travelled to AoG mission fields in the Far East from where he submitted an eight page report to the Council. His report gives an insight into the sort of problems which could arise at the sharp end of missionary operations and it also gives his candid assessment of the characters and abilities of those he met.

He takes trouble, in the first instance, to commend the constitutional and business procedures of the 13th meeting of the China Field Council and he encloses a copy of the minutes of this meeting with his report. Initially, the Field Council had met to discuss a property in Kunming which was used as an office and a missionary home. The HMRC had directed the Field Council to dispose of the property but the missionaries had dissented from this instruction and decided to maintain it out of their own pockets. Gee, after inspection, remarked "we have been spared the folly of parting with premises so necessary for the prosecution of our work in this Province". It seems that the HMRC had failed to understand that the East Gate Chapel in Kunming was maintained by the missionary on the spot out of his own funds, whereas the other property was the Field Council's collective responsibility. Personalities had impeded a correct perception of the situation: "Mr Wood's unfortunately over-detailed manner in correspondence and business has probably taken the edge off a sympathy and appreciation to which he is undoubtedly due" was Gee's verdict.

Gee then turned to other matters. The AoG missionary office in China did a great deal of postal, banking, purchasing and other business on behalf of all the British missionaries and also acted in this respect for some "very poor Continental Pentecostal missionaries", with whom Gee pleaded for a closer amalgamation. As ever denominational barriers counted for little at a distance from home, though frictions could and did occur. A dispute over a property in Amicheo was finally settled in a "constitutional" manner and "confirmed at a joint meeting of the full American and British Field Councils". The Amicheo incident had occurred when Howard Carter had authorised the handing over of a British building in China to American Assemblies of God. This had generated bad feeling and harsh words between the missionaries concerned and so Gee encouraged one of the missionary ladies to write a letter of apology to another. This she eventually did and as a consequence he asked the HMRC to renew her certificate which had been withdrawn as a discipline. Then there were problems caused by romance. One AoG missionary lady wanted to marry a man who had been refused missionary candidature by the HMRC but who had gone out onto the field with a different missionary society. A rather different problem was posed by another lady missionary who had taken a Chinese boy into her home and adopted him as her son. After consulting other missionaries, Gee was assured of the perfect propriety of the arrangements in Chinese eyes and, in any event, the boy, who was 17, was about to leave home and marry a Chinese bride.

Two other ladies on the field had been giving accounts to others of their dramatic spiritual experiences and, while most of the other missionaries were impressed, Gee was more sceptical and wanted to see the evidence of their spirituality by "fruits". Then he went on say,

> With regard to our missionary personnel: I am happy to testify to their genuine consecration and spirituality. As to general ability I fear that we must class most of them as mediocre.

Mr Colley, however, impressed him by an ability to preach fluently in Chinese and this prompted Gee to remark penetratingly,

> I was pleased to find that all of our missionaries seem to possess a workable knowledge of Chinese, but I also fear that it it not of a quality to appeal to the better class of people. Our work in Kunming is almost entirely among the poorest and most ignorant class, and probably for the above reason. This factor is calculated to hinder the realization of an Indigenous Church, in which all classes must obviously find a place.

This led him to recommend that anyone the HMRC later sent to China should have to undertake at least one year in Language School. Following this the Council discussed whether missionaries, even after their candidature had been accepted, should be asked to return to Britain if they failed to make satisfactory language progress after two years on the field of their calling. In addition, probably because Gee's visit was so beneficial, the Council decided that regular visits to the various fields should be made by Council members at the Council's expense (HMRC minutes 11 Nov 1938; 9 Dec 1938). War conditions, worsening rapidly after 1939, soon intervened and put all routine decisions on one side. There was, however, just time for Jimmy Salter to visit India and report back before travel restrictions closed in.

The iron hand draws near

None of the pentecostal churches in Britain foresaw precisely the nature or extent of the Second World War. They tended to paint the disturbances in Europe with the colours of Biblical prophecy: they saw Argmageddon itself rather than an image of Argmageddon on the horizon. Again, it was Gee who was on the spot at the critical time. He was in Germany in 1935 and reported what he saw. He attended meetings in a Leipzig public hall where over 750 people came together to hear the exposition of Scripture. In Berlin between 30 and 40 pentecostal pastors met for a convention and there was great joy and singing and a revival atmosphere as Gee preached, though afterwards Gee was interviewed by a plain clothes police officer. Although Lutheran pastors had by then been imprisoned because they refused the meddling of the Nazis, pentecostals were not interfered with any more than Baptists or Methodists - partly, perhaps, because many German Christians had "a great appreciation for Herr Hitler....the personal example of his own private life, which is rigidly self-denying and utterly 'consecrated' in the political sense, is an inspiration to the whole nation. So far our Pentecostal brethren find no conscientious difficulty in sharing to a large extent the public appreciation of the 'Führer'. Naturally there is the fear that things may go too far" (*Redemption Tidings,* 15th April, 1935). In the same issue, Gee pressed the point home,

> While we thankfully rejoiced with our German brethren in the large measure of liberty they still enjoy to preach the Gospel and conduct their assemblies, yet it was with a sigh of relief that we crossed the frontier into Holland, and later over into England. No more 'Heil Hitlers' instead of 'good morning' from ticket-collectors; no more irritating restrictions upon currency; no more flags and badges and signs on every hand; no more need for scrupulous care over every word uttered in public because of probable secret police in the meetings. We had sung quite lustily with all the rest of Berlin, 'Ich bin frei' (I am free); but we felt that our freedom was a spiritual thing only.

> Probably it is an utter impossibility for the average Britisher justly to value his liberties unless he starts to travel.

And he continued to reflect on the state of Europe, and its slide to totalitarianism.

> (In Italy) the Pentecostal Church is no longer recognised because the authorities did not like the character of its meetings.

> 'Get out of here, and quickly!' These words were recently spoken by an official in Latvia to an elder of a Pentecostal meeting asking for permission to hold a communion service. Yet not much more than a year ago we personally enjoyed some delightful united services with our Pentecostal and Baptist friends in that very town, where public Pentecostal meetings are now definitely forbidden.

> What are we doing with our present perfect religious liberty in the British Isles ?....we must seize the present opportunity with both hands, and work while it is called day. The night is coming. The iron hand draws near.

The urgency Gee felt about the situation in Europe was matched by fervent prayers for peace. Some Christians feared (as the quotation above shows) the loss of religious freedom in Britain; others hoped against hope for peace and the retention of religious freedom. There was, in any case, a widespread desire for disarmament throughout British society and, when war came, pacifists were treated with a great deal more respect than they had been from 1914-18. Certainly there was reason to fear catastrophe. Stanley Baldwin declared, "the next war will be the end of civilisation in Europe" and this was headlined in *Redemption Tidings* (1 May, 1936). R H Broughton commented in the same edition, "the outlook for the politician is indeed dark...but, thank God, the believer has glimpsed the glory through a rift in the clouds...the Peace of the Millennial reign of Christ even now calms his breast". German anti-semitism was evident in the build-up the outbreak of hostilities, and pentecostals were pro-semitic - they quoted "he that toucheth you (the Jew) toucheth the apple of mine eye" (Zechariah 2.8). On the basis of this verse alone, they had some confidence that Hitler would fall. On the other hand Broughton had no difficulty in identifying the growing power of fascist Italy with the "iron teeth" of the Roman monster described in the book of Daniel. When the German pastor Neimoller was arrested and imprisoned in a concentration camp for his Christian principles, he was applauded for his courage by *Redemption Tidings* (29 July, 1938); when war eventually broke out Gee wrote a series of articles rallying the churches and giving practical advice on the position of the Christian in time of war. Despite the evident evil against which the British people were engaged, there was no question in Gee's mind of a compromise with the militarist position - though his articles did make it clear that each individual had to make a personal decision as to his or her response to conscription. In fact, as we shall see, later pentecostal pastors were prepared to support both members of their congregations who were conscripted and those who were conscientious objectors. There was no party line. What mattered was the health of the churches and the evangelisation of the troops. Gee and Howard Carter were in England, and forced to stay there, throughout the war and they gave themselves to the fellowship of churches; their untiring efforts are still gratefully remembered by British pentecostals.

In January 1939 issue of *Redemption Tidings* John Carter wrote on "The Christian's Attitude to War" and he stoutly defended the position of the conscientious objector and argued that "in the last war voices were confused, some religious leaders maintaining that it was the duty of all young men to enlist in the fighting ranks" but, so far as he was concerned, "the soul's allegiance to God must ever take precedence over our obligation to the State". To the distinction between aggressive and defensive wars, Carter contended that modern warfare was always primarily aggressive. So far as non-combatant but semi-military duties were concerned (like working in factories producing armaments) Carter was unwilling to compromise: to make poison was as wicked as administering a lethal dose. In April of the same year, Gee tackled the issue of the Christian and the State (*Redemption Tidings* 21 April) and spelled out Christ's own relations with the civil authorities of his day. He, and the apostles after him, maintained a scrupulous regard for Roman law and, despite the revolutionary nature of their message, were never found guilty of sedition or any other less serious civil crime. Christians gave Caesar those things that belonged to Caesar; but in the quite different realm belonging to God they were equally careful to maintain their allegiance as fully as possible. Gee could see no way in which a Christian could observe the teachings of the Sermon on the Mount and participate in the killing of other human beings but "under legal obligation from the State the Christian should have not insuperable conscientious scruples where national service involves no participation in the actual military machine and the shedding of blood". Aaron Linford (*Redemption Tidings,* 22 Sept, 1939) asked the pressing question "Should a Christian Fight ?" and adduced seven biblical reasons why the answer must be, No.

As soon as war finally broke out, Gee wrote again on the practicalities of being a Christian in a country engaged in fighting. His words are pastoral and the exhortation in them is not cheap. He urged three things: first, that Christians more than ever should meet together and that they should make adjustments to the times of their services and attend to the blacking-out of buildings so as to be available for one another; second, that Christians should "walk circumspectly" and do nothing to antagonise their neighbours or the government by offensive words or attitudes; and thirdly, that they recognise the value and source of Christian joy and draw upon inward spiritual resources. On the 20th of October *Redemption Tidings* pointed out the three basic grounds for exemption and on the 15th of December Gee again addressed the issue with a view to clarifying motivation. "There ought to be some heart-searching as to whether presumed conscientious objection does really spring from deep conviction, or only from an almost unrecognised desire to take any means of escape from the danger and discomfort of military service" and, again, "the proper Christian conscientious objector disagrees with the whole business of war if he objects at all, and he ought to recognise that his principles apply equally whether the particular cause is considered to be wrong or right". Thus, although the matter was one of conscience, the consistent thrust of the pentecostal leadership in Assemblies of God was against participation in fighting.

When Gee himself told the story of the pentecostal movement in *Wind and Flame* his account of the 1930s ended not with bombs and bullets but with the European Pentecostal conference in Stockholm in June 1939. It was to be the last possible occasion for many years when pentecostal Christians from all over Europe were able to gather together for worship and to learn from each other. The Assemblies of God and Elim leaders were drawn together and the meetings themselves were larger than anything either groups had experienced anywhere in the UK. Roughly 12 thousand people gathered and the services had the effect of lifting the faith and encouraging the hearts of all those who attended - particularly when they considered the bleak war-torn years which followed. It was a glimpse of heaven before the experience of hell. It was the beginning of a growing European consciousness which continued into the post-war period.

THE WAR YEARS

General considerations

The three quarters of a million British lives lost in the 1914-18 War was confined almost entirely to servicemen. In the 1939-45 War 60,000 British civilians were killed, many in air raids, and this figure represented about 18% of all British casualties. The psychological result of this shared effect of war was to make non-combatants less exceptional because everyone who stayed in England suffered the same fears and dangers. Almost all ministers who belonged to Assemblies of God were conscientious objectors and were therefore exempt from conscription. But there was an unexpected side-effect of the situation: ministerial certificates became much more important than they had been before and consequently the Executive Presbytery, which issued the certificates, had something of a whip hand over wayward personnel.

The early days of the war were filled with a fear of invasion but, as the balance of the fighting shifted, and after Pearl Harbour and Montgomery's victories in Africa, it gradually became clear that the hour of greatest national danger was past. When the Atlantic convoys began to be more successfully organised and protected and food became more plentiful, there was a gradual equalisation of material goods between the various social classes in Britain. The rich had no luxuries, but the standard of living of the poor improved to that of the skilled artisan and wages - as opposed to salaries - went up by 18% between 1938-47 (Taylor, 1975: 623). Since the pentecostal movement was predominantly taken from the less well-off sections of society, it is not surprising, when examining some of its accounts, to observe a gradual improvement in its financial resources as the war progressed. There was, too, less opportunity to give to missionaries overseas, with the result that some funding must have been diverted to enterprises at home.

Anyone who comes to examine the war-time life of the pentecostal churches with the preconception that everything must have been difficult and unhappy soon realises that they are mistaken. In many respects, the war years in Britain had the effect of creating a sense of national unity. The Assemblies of God enjoyed both numerical growth and some excellent General Conferences in the latter part of the war. There is little trace lukewarmness, and divisiveness was promptly dealt with. The emergency put the churches on their mettle and, largely through the practical difficulties and hardships which were the experience of the whole population, Christian virtues could shine. The counter attractions of the music hall and the cinema were dimmed, and men and women were perhaps more inclined than they would be in peacetime to consider the value of a faith to live by. Moreover the Assemblies of God were fortunate in being led by mature and capable men. The two Carters and Donald Gee were in their forties when the war began. They worked well together as a team and were tough enough to cope with strenuous regular travel besides being old enough to draw on the perspectives they had acquired in the previous war. Both Howard Carter and Donald Gee had travelled extensively to many parts of the world in the 1930s, but now they gave their energies exclusively to the home churches.

Although conditions were undoubtedly restrictive from about 1940 onwards, *Redemption Tidings* continued to be published and to maintain its circulation at about 9,000 copies a fortnight. Even when paper was severely rationed and *Redemption Tidings* was reduced in its size and number of pages, no issue was missed and this allowed the leadership of the Assemblies of God to communicate with the churches and the churches to communicate with each other. Its price remained at twopence a copy and apparently its profitability improved slightly as the war continued.

The theological climate of the war is hard to assess. Some soldiers and airmen carried mascots; others carried Bibles. Winston Churchill, after the evacuation from Dunkirk, said, "there are times when all men pray". According to one survey in the 1940s only one family in ten did not possess a copy of the Bible (Briggs, 1983: 292). The one theological question which must have burned at the back of everyone's mind was, Why doesn't God intervene ? Two articles in *Redemption Tidings* (9 Feb, 1940; 16 Jan, 1942) tackled the subject. The first pointed out that God has not been invited to intervene, that if God did intervene it would be on divine terms which would entail the renunciation of evil and that, in any event, God has intervened in the crucifixion of Jesus. The second article said, "His intervention takes a form different from that which we, in our ignorance, demand. We, knowing not our ignorance, demand to be delivered from suffering. He, in his wisdom, seeks to deliver us from sin and selfishness and fear". *Redemption Tidings* also carried reports of an increase in spiritism. The report of a committee appointed by the Archbishop of Canterbury noted "the growing strength of Spiritualism in the Church of England, the increasing number of its adherents both among clergy and laymen, and the claims of mediums"

(22 March, 1940, p14). An editorial by John Carter (14 Jan 1944) stated pointedly,

> Following in the train of the present war are innumerable evils associated with warfare, and one lamentable result of the loss of life is the growth of spiritism. According to a statement recently made in a daily newspaper by the Secretary of the largest Spiritist society in this country, there are now more than a million spiritists in Britain. Speaking of the spread of this cult since the beginning of the war, he said, 'When a person comes up against bereavement, what can the Church offer ? Only hope. Whereas we spiritualists can offer communication with the lost ones on the other side'.
>
> We absolutely repudiate this boastful claim. Their offer to put the bereaved into communication with their loved ones is false.

Adjustments and responses

Very early after the declaration of war (in September 1939), the Executive Presbytery of Assemblies of God made a decision to   attempt evangelism among the troops. A committee of three (F R Barnes, George Newsholme and John Carter) was appointed and a financial offering from every assembly was solicited. Progress was reported at the General Conference in May 1940 by when two institutes had been opened in areas near troop concentrations. Regular articles and sometimes photographs appeared in *Redemption Tidings* describing what was happening. In some instances appreciative letters from the parents of volunteer soldiers from Canada were printed. In others the institutes were able to send in this sort of account of their activities,

> We had a very busy time during the Christmas week, hardly knowing which way to turn. On Christmas Day we had over 50 men of the Forces in, and the same number on Boxing Day. They really appreciated all we were able to do for them to make the first Christmas (for many) in the Army a happy one. Late on Christmas night, after some of our friends and workers had gone home, Mrs Woods and I invited a crowd of drunken soldiers in and gave them a cup of tea....During the week we had over 200 men in, and such a variety of cases too. To show

the ignorance of some in this enlightened land, I will mention two rough young soldiers, the marks of sin on their faces. They saw two copies of John's Gospel...(*Redemption Tidings*, 16th Jan, 1942).

This account is fairly typical and the story ended with the conversion of a soldier whose mother was praying for him at home. The institutes were places of practical help and hospitality as well as preaching centres. In the summer months they held open air services.

Evangelism was part and parcel of the pentecostal movement. The war years obviously made campaigning very difficult. Air raids and blackouts discouraged people from going too far from home and so the Institutes set up in Aldershot and Colchester for evangelising the troops were a thoughtful response to the needs and conditions of the time. Some campaigning, it is true, was attempted but the huge crowds which had been gathered in the late 1920s and early 1930s were simply unattainable. The war years forced the pentecostal movement to engage in new types of evangelism. This was fortunate from another point of view: the best evangelists were largely out of action in the years immediately preceding the war; Stephen Jeffreys was ill, George his brother was entangled in a dispute with Elim, Fred Squire had his hands full with the Full Gospel Testimony and Wigglesworth was nearly 80 years of age.

If evangelism was harder to organise, there were also problems for churches on the south coast. The threat of invasion was countered by evacuations and several pastors lost most of their congregation which, in some instances, had been already depleted by young men and women who disagreed with conscientious objection. Assemblies of God certainly never took a hard line with its members who decided on conscientious grounds to fight. The people at home prayed for their sons and daughters and welcomed them home if they returned alive. To meet the predicament of pastors whose congregations had vanished, a "Distressed Presbyters" fund was started and regular payments were made to the men affected while they searched for new congregations or work on the land.

By October 1940 over £300 had been collected - which represented approximately two annual wage packets for clerical or manual workers - and was given out at the rate of £7:15s per week. A local committee, which was particularly active in the south east where the needs of presbyters were greatest, helped by the John Carter, the General Secretary, administered the fund but by November 1941, it had decreased by £145 - presumably because people were donating surplus cash to other projects. The Executive Presbytery suggested reducing payments by 25%, a suggestion which was strongly resisted at local level. A further appeal for funds was therefore made through the pages of *Redemption Tidings;* by November 1942, however, the balance in hand was a mere £5. In contrast a special fund for evangelism at home had risen to £900 in the same period. Nevertheless distressed presbyters continued to receive somewhat reduced payments until the end of the war. Although it is very difficult to calculate, the impression given by these events is that, because wages were increasing and in the absence of any corresponding supply of consumer goods in the shops, there was every incentive to give charitably to good causes. After the war it was a different story.

The difficulties of presbyters who had lost their congregations were unexpectedly increased by the return to England of a reasonable number of missionaries. Missionaries in war zones came home for the duration of the war, and they continued to be paid as before. Many of them supplemented their normal incomes by occasional preaching to midweek congregations or at convention meetings; this benefited the congregations but reduced presbyters' chances of doing the same thing. *Redemption Tidings* carried an account of the sudden and rapid return of a missionary couple from Belgium in January 1940. Two years later *Redemption Tidings* carried an account of a missionary convention at Luton where a whole range of topics was discussed. "Already some are doing valuable work in home pastorates. But others, especially those recently returned, will continue to itinerate on behalf of Foreign Missions, for we cannot afford to let our missionary zeal die down" (27 March, 1942). Certainly missionary work was constantly kept in front of the pentecostal movement by articles and sermons. In fact, there was almost an idealisation of missionary work to the detriment of evangelism at home. Gee pointed out that Britain itself was becoming more and more of a mission field and that children from all sections of society only knew the name of Christ as a swear word. Gee's solution was to fund full-time workers on the same basis as overseas missionaries. He forestalled the objection that people were waiting to fund highly gifted evangelists who drew large crowds by gently pointing out that some of the men and women who had gone overseas were very ordinary people who, working in Britain, would probably not have attracted the financial support they drew by going to foreign countries.

Spiritual life

We have two accounts of ordinary English pentecostal meetings during the war. The first is by a Canadian soldier whose letter was printed in a Canadian pentecostal magazine and then reprinted,

> Whether it is because we are in uniform, I do not know, but on entering the church, we are greeted with warm handshakes, kind words and smiles that only a child of God can give. From the start we feel right at home. As we take our seats and await the commencement of the meeting, the organist plays over some hymns and choruses. Presently the pastor and his wife, and some of the elders file in and sit down in their places on the platform. Soon the meeting is under way, and the little hall resounds to songs of praise....The English people have an unique way of singing a hymn. They may get through the first verse, and then the second, but as we draw in our breaths for the third, a lady starts reading it out good and loud, so we pause and wait to see what this is all about. Then after the verse is read, everyone starts singing it, so we join in too....If they are really enjoying the hymn, someone else reads out the first verse, and we start again....we now have a prayer, and a number of people lead out. The English include lots of prayer in their diet. Then follows another hymn, after which a Scripture portion is read. One of the elders makes announcements, and then we have another hymn. Then, the Word [ie the preaching]....Then, one by one they slowly rise and start for the door where the pastor and his wife are waiting with a hand-shake and God bless you. Everyone is smiling, nodding at each other and shaking hands. 'What a friendly place - I'll sure have to come back', we say to ourselves as we grope our way home in the blackout (*Redemption Tidings*, 2 January, 1942).

Although this account is positive, it is evident that the meeting the soldier attended was not exactly an overwhelming spiritual experience. There seem to have been no manifestations of charismatic gifts, no appeals to the unconverted and no laying on of hands for the sick. The meeting may have been a small midweek Bible study, but what seems striking is the order and formality of the occasion. The elders file onto the platform, the pastor and his wife (but not the elders) shake hands with the congregation at the end of the meeting and the practice of reading verses out loud which the rest of the congregation sing again is a well understood procedure. Congregational participation seems confined to reading verses from hymns and praying aloud.

The second account is embedded in an editorial by John Carter (28 August, 1942). This time the impressions are given by a British pentecostal who visited several assemblies because of his movements as a soldier. He commented on the unattractive and shoddy exterior of some of the meeting halls "'How can you expect to get outsiders into such places ?' - poky entrances, difficult to find, no conspicuous notice outside". More to the point he found that, "after walking some miles the other week to a meeting, the welcome consisted of a perfunctory 'Good morning' as he and his companions went in, and the same as they came out." Carter agreed that "some members seem almost to regard the presence of strangers in the meeting as an intrusion...we have heard of some so praying AT strangers (that God would save the newcomers sitting at the back) that when they opened their eyes once more, the visitors had gone!"

Carter's comments reveal the unfriendly face of pentecostalism. In some places revival had settled into routine and Christian love had become superficial. It is hard to estimate the number of pentecostal assemblies which had fallen to this kind of level and which showed such insensitivity towards people they were in theory attempting to win for Christ. The best assemblies were always lively and friendly and, of course, it is possible that a some of the faults which were expressed by Carter's critic lay in the eye of the beholder. What the Canadian soldier enjoyed, the British soldier found unsatisfactory. Nevertheless these impressions both tally in their general description of the conduct of a meeting. There is a handshake at the start and prayer during the meeting. The distinctively charismatic emphasis seems notably absent.

Yet, whatever the state of some assemblies, there was general agreement that the General Conferences held in the mid-war years were excellent. Disagreements in the business sessions were kept to a minimum and the preaching was instructive and edifying. The 1942 General Conference was held at Wakefield and John Carter said in his editorial for July 3rd that it was the "best ever" and was in every way a record Conference - "in blessing, in attendance, even in finance". Altogether 18 fresh assemblies had been received into AoG, though Carter regretted the loss of another nine. A report in *Redemption Tidings* on July 17th put down the quality of the Conference to the day of prayer and the preaching by a member of the Executive at the beginning of each day. In the post-war years there was a tendency to invite "big name" preachers to address the Conference, and some of these men were quite out of touch with the situation in Britain. The Executive Presbytery were in contact with the British assemblies and they were able to preach pertinently and with concern for the problems which were being typically faced. The day of prayer was a day of rededication and even revelation. "'Give me' soon became 'Make me', and then passed to 'Show me' as we were caught up in the eternal purposes of God".

The business sessions were courteous. "Differences of opinion and perhaps misunderstandings there will always be in such gatherings, but these are of the head and not the heart, and the unity of the Fellowship was once more maintained in the bonds of peace" was way *Redemption Tidings* reported it. The 213 ministers present heard that over £10,000 had been donated for foreign missions work and £1000 for the home front. Altogether Assemblies of God had grown to nearly 400 churches supporting roughly 100 missionaries (see *Redemption Tidings* 21 April, 1944). There discussions centred on the best way to bring the Gospel to the young people of Britain. The following year 261 ministers gathered at Doncaster and Carter's editorial was able to conclude "it is generally agreed that this year eclipsed last year's Conference in every way". Again he was able to draw attention to the graciousness in the business meetings - "a lovely spirit of restrained animation prevailed throughout the discussions" - and it does not require much detective work to read into this account the fear which Carter and others had felt that the discussions might become acrimonious and hurtful. He had attempted to prevent such outbursts by an editorial the month before in which he had written,

> The early Church was not without its difficulties, and to deal with them the brethren gathered together in council at Jerusalem. In Acts 15, the problem that confronted the Church was that of circumcision as an obligatory rite, and we read that they 'came together for to consider the matter'. All were animated by one supreme motive, viz. the welfare of the church as a whole. In our Conferences, this should be our common desire, not any personal ambition or selfish incentive, but the well-being of the work entrusted to our care.

> When many men of diverse personalities are assembled together, there is bound to be a presentation of different viewpoints. Consequently we read that there was 'much disputing'

in the Council before they came to a final decision on the matter. By this it must not be inferred that the atmosphere on that occasion was acrimonious, for when the decrees were sent forth the churches described themselves as 'being assembled with one accord'.

In his sober and balanced way, Carter showed that it was quite possible to discuss and dispute without ill-feeling or factions. The very fact that he considered it necessary to write the editorial, shows how aware he was of the possibility of pique and division. As a member of the Executive Presbytery he was probably more alert than most other ministers to the undercurrents and opinions which erupt dangerously. But, be that as it may, the Conference was exceptional. David Gee, Donald's son, reported in the July 16th issue of *Redemption Tidings* 1944. The delegates had arrived on Monday and begun some introductory business. In the evening was the first public meeting, where two sermons were preached. Wednesday was reserved as the day of prayer and Harold Horton began the day by speaking on the "naked splendour of the cross", a sermon which was so highly regarded that it was soon printed as a leaflet. It laid the foundation for the intercession and praise which followed and which continued into the evening. At various stages throughout the meetings charismatic gifts were operated. The main emphasis which Howard Carter laid in his chairman's remarks was on the need for holiness, and this was a theme which was related to the concentration of the business sessions on the supervision of probationary ministers. New men were coming forward for ordination, some of them in their early twenties, and the older generation felt it important to set high standards. Each district was to supervise probationary ministers and older ministers in the districts were to visit probationers and regularly report on them. Furthermore would-be ministers must conform to certain requirements of character, doctrine, ability and experience. The order of these requirements is not especially significant, but it is apparent that moral rectitude was - and is to this day - recognised as of great importance in the pentecostal movement. Doctrine was basically protestant and evangelical but with a stress on the baptism in the Holy Spirit; ability was to be "beyond that expected in all Christians" and experience was to include "a personal baptism in the Holy Spirit accompanied by the Scriptural initial evidence of speaking with other tongues" (General Conference Minutes, item 6, 1943). It is clear that educational qualifications were not deemed vital and that the stress on the hallmark of pentecostalism, that is, speaking in tongues, was stamped into these ministerial requirements.

Doctrinal development

Pentecostal doctrine had been more or less settled in the decades before the war. Pentecostals believed in the Bible as the Word of God, in the premillennial Second Coming of Christ, in divine healing, evangelism, the new birth of John 3 and all the other doctrines which are common to evangelical Christians. Many of the articles in *Redemption Tidings* served to remind readers of what they already, in theory, knew and believed. In 1943 there was, however, a series by Harold Horton on speaking with tongues which broke new ground. It was not that Horton dispensed with the pentecostal view that speaking with tongues was an evidence of baptism in the Holy Spirit - far from it - but rather that he looked at speaking in tongues in the life of the church and the individual believer. He produced twelve reasons from the Bible for speaking with tongues and thereby attempted to move the debate out of the area of controversy and into something more useful. In his first article Horton remembered a conversation he had had with his Wesleyan Class Leader when, as a young man, he had asked about foreign languages on the Day of Pentecost. "The only reply he had for me out of the love and honesty of his uninformed heart was the evergreen one that those tongues were for an earlier dispensation and they were intended to inaugurate a new order and then fall into decay. Of course there were no scriptures given me to endorse those human views,for the simple reason that there aren't any such scriptures to give. You could of course, with similar logic, sweep away the cross itself" (15 January,1943). In the months that followed Horton outlined the following reasons for speaking with tongues:

1. Speaking with tongues is the initial evidence of baptism in the Holy Spirit.

2. It was Jesus who promised we should speak with new tongues

3. It is a means by which God speaks to people

4. It is a means by which people may speak supernaturally to God

5. It is a means of magnifying God

6.   It is a means of edification for the speaker

7.   It is a means, with interpretation, of edifying the church

8.   It allows the human spirit, as opposed to the human mind, to pray

9.   It is an avenue to singing with the spirit

10   That with the help of interpretation of tongues our understanding might be informed of the mysteries our spirit rehearses in prayer in other tongues

11   That out intellects might rest in adoration

12   That believers may profit.

By and large all these reasons have been accepted, or accepted in a modified form, by the charismatic movement that burst upon the church in the west in the 1960s. In the 1940s they were new and represent Horton's personal contribution to the development and clarification of pentecostal doctrine.

A seemingly innocuous, but in some respects more radical contribution, was made by the veteran missionary W P F Burton. Burton had gone to the Congo from Preston in 1915 and, by general consent, the fruits of his ministry were genuinely apostolic. He left behind hospitals, schools and well over a thousand churches. In *Redemption Tidings* (12 February, 1943), Burton argued for the use of the human mind in the work of God. He pointed out that some of the attitudes generated by the Welsh revival of 1904 had been detrimental to any intellectual activity,

> Indeed the most foolish things were sometimes done under the supposed guidance of the Spirit, bringing reproach and ridicule on God's work. Any who disapproved were told 'You need to cut your head off. Put your mind out of the way'.

In a few extreme cases this led to saints abandoning themselves to spasmodic impulses and excitement. One who gave a well-thought-out address was said to be 'in the flesh'. A connected Bible-study was 'letterish and not spiritual'.

Would-be preachers were told to get up and say whatever came to them, without the least premeditation, claiming the promise of Luke 21:14-15.

Having pointed out the follies of extravagant anti-intellectualism, Burton then spent a page and a half presenting the overwhelming biblical case for the use of the mind in Christian work. His case was never answered - as in the nature of things one would not expect it to be - though there were still pentecostals in the 1980s who tended to equate anything mental with a lack of spirituality.

Burton's other bombshell was an article which drew a distinction between the dominant ministry of a single pastor and the shared ministry of a variety of elders (*Redemption Tidings*, 13 April, 1945). Most of the pentecostal assemblies in Britain stressed the authority and preaching capabilities of the paid pastor, but Burton pointed out how unbiblical and short-sighted such an arrangement was. Where the congregation was turned into a bulk of passive listeners whose talents were ignored or suppressed, there was unlikely to be any extensive church growth. Despite the respect in which Burton was held, approximately thirty years passed before Assemblies of God began seriously to set up team ministries in the larger churches.

Two articles (*Redemption Tidings*, 9 April and 5 November, 1943) discussed the qualifications of church officers. Neither writer envisaged team ministry. Their concerns were with the genuine spirituality of men who took on pastoral work. They wanted the younger generation of ministers to be as dedicated as they had been - and this was also a constant theme in Howard Carter's addresses. He distinguished between a worldly estimation of "success" and what he took to be a biblical estimation of success and said that the ability to build a big church did not necessarily imply success by any divine standard (*Redemption Tidings* 3 Nov, 1944). With hindsight Carter's articles and sermons along this line, together with those on the subject of church officers, look rather negative. If preachers are not to regard big congregations as evidence of God's blessing, are they to presume that the smaller their churches the better is their ministry ? There was always a danger in British pentecostalism that the ability to endure poverty was classified as the hallmark of spirituality: but in point of fact the apostle Paul makes it clear that he had learnt to cope with the extremes of financial stringency and financial plenty at various times in his life (Philippians 4.12).

Discipline and Friction
Howard Carter was the Chairman of Assemblies of God during the war years and, as we have already seen, his ministry and personality were such as to make him a commanding figure. He had strong views on certain subjects and he expressed them strongly. He had travelled widely and seen the American Assemblies of God in action and noted the existence of a General Superintendent whose task it was to be the pastor of the pastors and to exercise an oversight across all the pentecostal churches together. Confined to England during the war years, Carter was not a man to sit idle while churches or District Councils (presbyteries) became entangled with problems. There were, however, really three types of body in Assemblies of God which were in a dynamic relationship with each other. Firstly the General Council, composed of all the ministers or delegates from the assemblies, elected an Executive Council (or presbytery - the name was changed during the course of the war) from among its members, and then, thirdly, there were also District Councils made up of the ministers or delegates of assemblies in a specified area. Both the District Councils and the Executive Council could bring matters to the General Council which had the final say in any argument. In theory the roles and duties of the District Council and the Executive Council were clearly defined by the constitution, but in practice it was possible to change the constitution and, in any event, the opinion of the Executive Council might well be upheld in debate against any opinion put forward by the District Councils. There was therefore a sort of balance. Sometimes the Executive acted as an umpire between two District Councils in dispute; at other times the Executive was in direct conflict with a District Council and both sides had to consider the possibility of appealing to the General Council. Sometimes, to avoid conflict, matters were sent back and forth like a ping-pong ball between the Executive and the District or between the Districts and the General Council.

During the war, there was a long-running disagreement between the Executive and the Kent District Council. The whole saga illustrates the complexities of church government in a presbyterian system. Matters were made more delicate by the well-established principle in Assemblies of God that each local church was autonomous. Briefly what happened was that Garfield Vale, a Welshman who had returned to England from missionary work in the Congo, took over the pastorate of an assembly in Maidstone. The church officers objected to his dictatorial manner and hot temper and split the church taking a large proportion of the congregation with them to start a new church elsewhere in the town. The District Council, which was called in to cope with the matter, had, of course, as one of its members none other that Garfield Vale. Perhaps inevitably, therefore, the District Council tended to side against the "split" and with the remnant of the church. The Executive Council who had been called in early in the proceedings were more inclined to favour the "split".

The Executive Council minutes (for July 13th, 1944) record,

> At the interview [between the Executive and the Chairman and Secretary of the Kent DC], the question was asked why the Kent DC had been ignored by the Executive....the Executive pointed out that, in the first place, the appeal from the church officers had been sent to the EC. We had sent it on to Kent with the suggestion to investigate the trouble and conduct a secret ballot. As this was not carried out, the Executive had written insisting upon a full and impartial investigation by Kent, and suggesting that two members of the EC attend. The suggestion was not acted upon, and later, the General Secretary had invited the DC Chairman to interview the Executive at the Chairman's Conference at Nottingham, but the invitation was not accepted. It was only when they realised that the DC were taking no further steps in the matter that the Executive proceeded to plan an investigation.

> Explaining the notice published in RT [*Redemption Tidings* to the effect that the split congregation was recognised by Assemblies of God], the Executive had come to the conclusion that, seeing the pastor had been engaged by the church officers, the latter were within their authority in serving notice upon him. The action of the officers in removing the church to another building was prompted by their feeling of responsibility to the flock which was being scattered.....The General Secretary was instructed to ask Brother Botham if the accusers will face Brother Vale at a meeting of the Executive, and stress their moral responsibility of seeing the charges substantiated or otherwise.

The Executive Council's recommendations seem eminently sensible. The charges made by church officers against their pastor needed answering and, in the first instance, it was deemed the task of the District Council to make the necessary investigation. The problem with this suggestion was that the District Council was, to some extent, influenced by the voice of the person whose misconduct it was meant to be assessing. A suggested joint investigation in which representatives of the Executive were present was also not acted upon. The Assemblies of God constitution did not address itself to a possible conflict between different councils. The Executive only had power to "suggest" though if its suggestion were ignored, it could act independently of the local pastors. Evidently the Kent DC was inclined to be obstructive. This is partly because it was composed mainly of full-time pastors who lacked sympathy with a precedent which that seemed to strengthen the hands of the unpaid officers and to weaken the position of the pastor. However, the willingness of the Executive to accept the dismissal of a pastor by his church officers must have sent a shiver down many spines and induced considerable anxiety among pastors who felt that their flocks were obstinate and mean. It was all very well for the Executive Council to side with church officers, three of their members (the two Carters and Donald Gee) were not in the pay of any particular congregation. The stage was set for some creative legislation in the Assemblies of God constitution.

The meeting between Vale and his accusers was arranged on the 6th of September 1944. The Executive had ensured Vale's presence by assuring him that his ministerial certificate would not be renewed if he declined attendance. Before meeting with Vale and the church officers, the Executive met with the Kent District Council. Each side explained its case and, after discussion, the gathering ended in statements of mutual confidence.

In the evening of the 6th the full Executive and all the members of the Kent DC were present to hear the case against Garfield Vale. Ten witnesses were called. The position of each in the church (treasurer, deacon, etc) was ascertained and then each stated the essence of his charge against Vale. Each witness recounted various incidents. On one occasion, when there had been disorder in a church meeting, the pastor had told one of the deacons to fetch the police; on another occasion the pastor had left the officers' meeting in a rage; another church member had been insulted in the street; another church member had been ordered out of the church "in the name of Jesus Christ". Vale defended himself by putting a different construction on events, and three church members spoke in his defence.

At the end of the hearing the Executive suspended Vale for six months. Disagreement continued for a while. The Kent DC thought the Executive's verdict too harsh, but both sides were unwilling to take the matter to the General Council. More than forty years have passed since the whole incident and the small assembly which left Vale's flock has prospered and grown; the remnant is much smaller.

There were other matters of a similar nature which the Executive Council had to deal with during the war: a minister who had committed adultery but whose DC seemed unwilling to impose any discipline upon him; a church which divided and then wrangled over the building; and churches that either came out of Elim or the Bible Pattern movement to join Assemblies of God or left Assemblies of God to join the other groups. The number of assemblies switched allegiance during the war was relatively slight because the Executive Council maintained good relations with their counterparts in the Elim movement, and both Executives wisely tended to look askance at maverick congregations. Certainly the Assemblies of God Executive took its responsibilities seriously and was able to act decisively partly because its members were confident in their ministerial authority and were physically fit and energetic and partly because the conditions of war rendered the ministerial certificate of social value. Nobody wanted to lose his ministerial certificate and face a tribunal.

Relationships with Nelson Parr continued to be prickly. Bethshan Tabernacle, Parr's church, continued in Assemblies of God although Parr himself, because of his association with the Full Gospel Testimony was debarred from inclusion on the ministerial list. In other words, it seems that, because membership of Assemblies of God operated on two levels - the ministerial and the congregational - it was possible for a congregation to be registered with Assemblies of God without its minister being in a similar position. Such a state of affairs, in fact, was common where a probationary minister took over the pastorate of an established congregation. There might well be a gap of some months before the new young minister applied for probationary status with Assemblies of God, though the congregation itself continued to take part in any activities within the wider fellowship. Parr seems to have profited from this constitutional loophole and ensured that he personally belonged to a variety of pentecostal bodies while his church remained in Assemblies of God. The Executive Council received a letter from Bethsan's Trustees saying they wished Nelson Parr to be recognised as their presbyter (Executive Meeting, 12 June 1942, item 15b). The Executive wrote back to ask whether Parr was still a member of the Full Gospel Testimony and received a reply stating,

> We do not intend allowing the Executive Presbytery, or any other Presbytery, council or committee to question or raise any queries about any appointments made in this locally-governed Church of the living God. (Executive Minutes 30th September 1942, item 3c)

Parr clearly did not intend conforming to any one else's expectations. He was his own man. His daughter's recollections of him include his visits to Lourdes and to a Bingo hall, both places which the average Assemblies of God pastor would have shunned for fear appearing unsanctified. Parr was the sort of man who wanted to see things for himself. When he preached, it was with all the conviction of his heart and Bethshan continued to grow in leaps and bounds under his ministry.

Even without Nelson Parr there were disagreements between strong personalities. The Yorkshire Presbytery (or District Council) wrote to the Executive protesting

> against the Chairman's gave breach of his official privilege in connection with matters that arose in the last General Presbytery Conference in connection with the Yorkshire District Presbytery. While they accept the apology that was made, they also feel that the gravity of the incident justifies further notice. (Executive Minutes 30 September, 1942, item 5d).

Howard Carter's comment, which is recorded in the same minutes, is interesting. He contended that "the Lord had made him more than an official Chairman, and as the spiritual shepherd of the work, he must feel at liberty to express his mind whenever he felt so constrained". In effect, he completely repudiated the criticism and more or less withdrew whatever apology he had made. He felt that his position was more than that defined by the Assemblies of God constitution. Undoubtedly he was correct. In reality he was more than a chairman. The exact point over which he clashed with the Yorkshire Presbytery (it was at the 1942 Conference that Presbyteries were renamed Councils) is not at issue. What matters is that there was a disagreement between constitutionalism and spiritual authority, even though the man exercising spiritual authority was himself no mean constitutional thinker.

Mission continues

Lawrence Livesey was doing remarkable work in the Coimbatore area of south India and the Indian churches were progressing in the establishment of indigenous leadership. Equally remarkable was the ministry of Douglas Scott. He had preached all over France and, more or less single handed in the period 1931-39, brought French Assemblies of God into existence. Just as the Nazi net was closing in, but apparently without any thought of the political and military condition of Europe, Scott felt he should move to Portuguese East Africa where he preached for a short time. He then moved to the AoG field at Kalembe in the Congo, where his ability to preach in French was utilised.

> We now have 126 villages with churches and schools with 126 native workers, as against 65 when we took over the territory in December 1939. During the year 212 have been baptised in water. We have an increase of 95 in the number of complete families, where the father and mother are both Christians. We have 3030 children coming to schools were they get teaching in the Word of God and the way of salvation, as against 1414 at the end of 1939, so you see that on every hand we have an increase and God has been graciously pleased to increase the number of those who have received the blessed Holy Spirit by 150; this being a low figure to be really sure (OMC Mins 9 May 1941)

Scott's method was to pray for a fortnight for a heathen village, go there with the Gospel, heal the sick, gather his converts, instruct them to build a meeting hut, appoint one of them as an overseer and then move on elsewhere. Years afterwards, John Carter, in a visit to Kalembe was met by men who spoke with amazement about Scott's ministry.

Administrative arrangements at home continued to be efficiently handled and arrangements had to be made for missionaries unable to proceed to their fields because of the war. So much detailed consideration of individual cases was required that the HMRC decided to meet bimonthly, but with the proviso that a smaller sub-group should meet on alternate months to decide on urgent matters.

The war affected travel most of all. The Liveseys were unable to return home on furlough despite their five years in India. Others had to be evacuated from parts of the world ravaged by the spreading military conflict. Missionaries in China were urged by the British Consul to travel to India on a passage provided by the Government. Once having decided what to do, missionaries found themselves out of physical danger but in a country for which they were not prepared. Immediate contact with the HMRC was imperative and funds had to be cabled across the world in response to urgent telegrams. The Beruldsens stayed in Peking and, after a period of anxiety, reported that relationships between missionaries of different denominations were greatly enhanced by the common danger.

Yet the minutes give the impression that the Council in England cared about their friends abroad. Of all the Assemblies of God minutes (local church, District Council, Executive Council or General Council) the HMRC minutes contain the most frequent expressions of thankfulness to God for the safety of missionaries or their successful spreading of the Gospel. Even when the HMRC minutes seem high-handed (as in forbidding a missionary to marry), they are concerned that the missionary who ignored their advice and therefore lost his missionary certificate apply for an ordinary ministerial certificate. One man, Mr Benson, was tortured by the Japanese and, perhaps to avoid unnecessary worry at home, the Council asked him to play down his dreadful experiences when speaking in churches in Britain. This was partly for Mr Benson's sake and partly to avoid generating excessive worry about other missionaries.

The war years gave the Council and opportunity to deploy its homebound missionaries in the British Isles. Those who had been evacuated from the field (for example from Belgium) or who had arrived in Britain on furlough often found travel out to the field again impossible. At least five missionaries settled down into pastoral work after two years of itineration.

So far as direct military action was concerned the Indian field was almost unaffected by the war. But immediately after the war the prospect of Indian self-government troubled some of British workers there. And there were other tensions on the field. Not only had one missionary couple returned to Wales on the basis of divine revelation - which they later admitted was mistaken - but another couple claimed personal supervision over their own section of the work, changed its name, and broke free from the Indian Field Council and Assemblies of God. Yet another missionary couple in India demanded repatriation and asked for the fares of their grown up children. In the immediate post-war period expenditure on tickets and outfitting was high and, at first, the increased amounts given through collecting boxes produced record income. For the last three years of the war there was little incentive to save money and people gave more generously than usual - in addition, of course, there were few consumer goods on which money could be spent; industry was still geared up for the war effort.

Amidst the interviewing of prospective candidates, the Council was faced with the psychological and financial needs of missionaries who had had more than their share of hardship. The Beruldsens had been to the limit. They had been forced to sell their valuables for food and Mrs Beruldsen's health had failed. On arrival in England, they had nowhere to live and no furniture or suitable clothes (OMC mins 8 Mar 1946). Also Douglas Scott and his wife, weakened by fever, returned from Congo after being unable to face the rigours of another wet season in the Congo (OMC Mins 8 Mar 1946). The Council shouldered its responsibilities and, though sometimes missionaries thought they ought to have been given more help, the minutes generally suggest the Council acted with compassion as well as wisdom. Certainly the three missionary conference organised during the war years enabled experiences to be pooled and ties between missionaries to be strengthened. Moreover, the conferences alerted the assemblies to missionary possibilities and so helped raise the level of funding.

Roots and branches

The troubles at Maidstone highlighted a weakness in the AoG Constitution. The Executive Council minutes (for 13 July 1944) record, "Brother Gee advocated the setting up of a permanent Court of Appeal to deal with appeals form local Assemblies. He pointed out that a minister involved in a dispute is often a member of the very District Council that receives the appeal". Gee was asked to go away and draft a resolution which was then circulated to the District Councils and later debated at the first General Conference in 1945 (there were two that year). His resolution was accepted by the Conference and resulted in the setting up of a permanent Court of Appeal which had five ministers as its judges. The Conference was obliged to elect twelve men by a two-thirds majority, and these twelve sat in turn so that there were only five on duty at any one time to deal with a case.

The issues raised here by the establishment of a Court of Appeal are useful in illustrating how Assemblies of God's Constitution gradually grew. A problem arises; the existing machinery attempts to deal with it; there is stress and strain because the machinery has not been designed with every eventuality in mind; someone proposes an innovation; there is discussion in each district separately and eventually the General Conference makes a decision after debate, and by voting, and a new piece of Constitutional machinery is lodged into place. The system is slow and thorough. It requires thought and discussion and its end product is a constitution which is at some distance from the apostolic simplicity of the New Testament church. There is a whiff of paradox here because the pentecostal churches stressed their similarity with the church in the Book of Acts. Nevertheless, as the pentecostal churches in the twentieth century were not slow to point out, the church in Acts and the Pauline epistles does have its councils and debates, its letters of commendation, its methods of dealing with irregularities and problems, its divisions and customs. Apostolic simplicity was not only spontaneity in the Holy Spirit; there was a measured tread and strategy in its advance, a sense of building for the future.

The bombing of London was intense at the start of the war. In a *Redemption Tidings* editorial (22 June, 1945) John Carter recalled that 120 high explosive bombs fell within a three-quarters of a mile radius of his offices at Lewisham. The Executive Council therefore made a decision to move out of the city and by November 15th 1940, he was relocated in Luton and when, towards the end of 1944, the lease was almost at the point of expiry, the owners of the accommodation offered it to Assemblies of God. Howard Carter, with typically brazen faith, personally offered to pay the mortgage of the property until the General Council authorised the purchase. Number 6 Marsh Road, Luton was bought for £2,750 and the monthly payments were £15-11-8, excluding rates. The General Conference in June 1945 ratified the arrangements and Assemblies of God became the owner of its own headquarters for the first time.

Although the new building might have implied a centralisation, in fact it did not. If anything the building indicated that the Assemblies of God was putting down roots and prepared for a long march home. Belief in the return of Christ had not waned, but it was obviously wise to make some plans for the future. Post-war property was relatively cheap and John Carter, who was the AoG General Secretary, had a background in banking which perhaps inclined him to play safe whenever given the option. His own salary was raised during the war. In January 1941 it went up to £4:5s per week (in September 1945 to £6 pw) and in January 1944 his wife was paid £1:10s per week for her work as a part-time typist; although this was not a handsome combined income, it was certainly a reasonable living wage, and would have been supplemented by gifts of various kinds for preaching at weekends.

The war seemed to have left the pentecostal movement in good shape. There was unanimity between its various sections and plans had been put in motion to ensure that the next generation of ministers were of high calibre. Moreover finances were sound and there was evidence in Bishop Chavasse's report that the Church of England, - and presumably the evangelical churches as a whole - was turning towards evangelism once again. The Executive Council had worked together harmoniously for five years and begun to re-establish contact with Nelson Parr. In a retrospective editorial (22 June, 1945) John Carter gave thanks to God that only one AoG minister had been killed. He anticipated considerable growth in the late 1940s and was prepared for the changes, constitutional and otherwise, that such growth would bring. In 1945 Donald Gee, for the first time, was elected as the Chairman of Assemblies of God and Howard Carter replaced him as Vice-Chairman. An era had ended as Howard Carter stepped away from the commanding position he had enjoyed since 1934. He was soon to leave Britain once again and, though he regularly returned and preached, his main energies were spent elsewhere. It was left to Donald Gee and John Carter to provide the continuity and wisdom necessary for the post-war decades. Smith Wigglesworth, active to the last, died in 1947.

Two articles give a subjective picture of the fervour and feelings of the pentecostals at this time. Tom Woods wrote,

> We are essentially a people with a burning passion for the Saviour, and I rejoice as I journey here and there and catch the fragrance of consecrated men and women who have left all to follow the Master. We have been enriched with good men. They pass before my mind as mighty men of valour. Men who have hazarded, suffered, triumphed. I salute my esteemed brethren who have paid the price to maintain the spirit of fellowship amongst us. I have been enriched by the ministry of all....Society is better for this blessed blood-bought fellowship. Bodies once torn by pain and affliction have felt the touch of His nail-pierced hand, and grateful hearts unite to praise Him Who has carried our sorrows in His body to the tree....the path has not been easy. I have been laid low in health until I despaired of life; but He has come to me in the sweetness of His Presence and raised me up, and taught me not to trust in

myself, but in Him Who raiseth up the dead. (*Redemption Tidings*, 24 March, 1944).

On the outside the pentecostal movement might look odd or bigoted, but to those who were on the inside it was something precious and divine which stood for long-neglected scriptural truths. Donald Gee preaching in May 1945 referred to the comradeship and love which was pentecostalism at its best,

> Let me go back a few years in personal reminiscence. First of all only six years - June 1939. On a delightful calm, June evening in Stockholm, 8,000 Pentecostal people gathered from 22 countries of Europe, sat together round the Lord's Table, broke bread, remembered His death until He come. Among that company there were British and there were Germans. Then my mind goes further back still to 1913. A little Pentecostal meeting room in North London. Cecil Polhill, one of the 'Cambridge Seven', reputed millionaire, at a memorable prayer-meeting, being short of hymn books, he, Cecil Polhill of Howbury Hall, sharing his hymn book with the kitchen maid. I came from the snobbish church of of which I was assistant organist. I said, 'Thank God, this is better, purer, cleaner'. Thank God for the baptism of the Holy Ghost, it saves us from snobbishness. Love and snobbery don't go together. I go back (not in personal experience till afterwards) to 1906. In later years I saw the building. A rough, wooden barn-like structure in Los Angeles. God was pouring out His Spirit and men and women were coming from all over the world to receive the Holy Ghost. The leader was a simple coloured man, W J Seymour, but colour bars were all forgotten when the Holy Ghost fell, and they were content to have the coloured preacher pray for them. Only one thing they saw, the Glory of God in the face of Jesus Christ. Pentecost means love, victorious love. God shed it abroad in floods! (*Redemption Tidings,* 17 Aug, 1945).

Victory on the battlefield was soon celebrated in the town halls and market squares of Europe. Bomb-damaged buildings were to remain for many years to come, but the worst was over and Britain, with a new Labour Government under Clem Attlee, began to plan for the future. The churches made their preparations. The provisions of the 1944 Education Act included some of the Christian hopes which had been kindled during the war years. The pentecostal movement, too, began to reorientate itself in a new landscape. All seemed set fair for many years to come.

THE POST-WAR YEARS

General background

Crowds gathered outside Buckingham Palace on May 8th 1945 and Churchill stood on the balcony beside the royal family acknowledging the delight and relief of the British people. In the jubilation of victory Churchill had hoped the war-time coalition government might extend its term of office into the peace. But the strong Labour Party team, headed by Attlee, was unwilling to defer a general election. Churchill's high profile election campaign made use of a motorcade, and although he drew popular acclaim wherever he went, and his photograph appeared on the publicity of more than half of Tory candidates, there was little visionary thinking in the Conservative manifesto to attract the electorate. On the hustings Conservative attacks on the evils of socialism seemed rather hyperbolic and hollow in the light of the recent fact that British munitions factories had been making bombs for "Uncle Jo" Stalin's use during the latter part of the war. The Soviet Union could hardly be depicted convincingly as a major threat to peace in the world if its soldiers had been fighting on the allied side against Germany. Attlee came to power with a massive majority and fielded a strong team (Attlee was fond of cricketing metaphors)[1].

In August 1945 a journalist travelled by train to Newcastle on Tyne. In his diary he recorded that the miserable journey took more than twice as long as it had done in peace time. "No cup of tea to be got at the stops because the queues for this remarkable beverage masquerading as tea were impossibly long...my hotel towel is about the size of a pocket handkerchief, the soap tablet is worn to the thinness of paper, my bed sheets are torn" (quoted by Marwick, 1982: 22). The gradually increasing prosperity of the second part of the 1930s, and the sense of comradeship as well as the more equitable distribution of goods and services between social classes during the war years, began to recede. The Labour Government was faced with the massive problem of providing housing for the country. Soldiers who returned from abroad swelled the numbers of people living in Britain, but war-time bombing had depleted the stock of houses. In addition 70% of the nation's properties were about 50 years old and in need of maintenance or repair (Marwick, 1982: 22). The winter of 1946/7 was the coldest for over a century and there were burst pipes and power cuts. Between July 1946 and July 1948 bread was rationed and clothes rationing did not end till 1949. The war-time factories were expanded and the north-east of England and the coal mines received fresh injections of government money. Unemployment dropped to 2.8% (Marwick, 1982: 33). Leisure activities enjoyed a boom. A shortage of commodities did not affect cinema or football attendance which, in retrospect, can be seen to have passed through a golden age. Thirty per cent of the population went to the "flicks" once a week and football, without violence, and football pools, with the prospect of sudden wealth, were extremely popular.

The divorce rate reached 60,000 per year in 1947, which was ten times the pre-war figure (Marwick, 1982: 64), and though the rate dropped to 25,000 per year in the mid-1950s, an alteration to fundamental patterns of domestic life began to emerge, especially in view of the increasing numbers of women who earned money outside the home to supplement the husband's income. A sharp rise in the birth rate, the "baby boom", took place immediately after the war, but then, as family planning methods were practised, the graph levelled off. Religious observance declined. Only about 10% of the population were regular and frequent churchgoers, and 40% never attended church (Marwick, 1982: 110; Argyle & BeitHallahmi, 1975: 11f)). The picture of a poorly housed, poorly fed, hard working, pleasure seeking, largely irreligious, materialistic, growingly affluent (by 1951 a man over 21 averaged £8.30 per week, Marwick, 1982: 118) society could be discerned. It is against this background that the efforts of the pentecostal churches in the late 1940s must be seen.

Note to Page 195

1. Much of the information in this paragraph is taken passim from The 1945 Revolution by William Harrington and Peter Young 1978, London; Davis-Poynter.

PENTECOSTALISM POST WAR

According to Manwaring (1985:76) "And so, after six years of total war, in 1945 the Churches tried to get back to normal but, as people fought their way through shortages of food, fuel and furniture, the mood of Britain was one of frustration and disappointment. Spiritual capital had run low, traditional Christian morality had steeply declined and the age of the 'couldn't care less' had arrived". Christians of all kinds soberly recognised their situation was critical. John Carter laid some of the details before the readers of *Redemption Tidings* (25 April, 1947)[1]. There were BBC radio broadcasts which assumed the truth of the Darwinian evolutionary hypothesis; there was provision in the 1944 Education Act for Religious Instruction according to locally drawn-up Agreed Syllabuses (a provision which, for fifteen years, at any rate, was almost entirely dominated by schemes of work which were largely Christian in content and outlook), but Carter feared modernistic theology; there was statistical evidence showing that cinemas were more popular than churches and that 20% of the population were hostile to religion, meaning to Christianity. It did not matter that the reasons for some of these trends were perfectly explicable by reference to the whirlwind courtships preceding war-time marriages between servicemen and women who feared they might be killed in action, or by reflecting that post-war entertainment was merely a continuation of the morale boosting escapism provided by films and showbiz personalities to battle-weary troops on leave. The social landscape confronting the thoughtful Christian demanded action. There must be some planting if there was to be a harvest.

"The need for Evangelism was commonly agreed by Christians" (Manwaring 1985: 77). Carter was not a man to make emotive appeals in *Redemption Tidings*. He expected ministers of local assemblies to take appropriate evangelistic action. But, of course, the churches needed help. Some of them would have been willing to support a famous national evangelist or a nationally organised campaign. Few of them were in a position to begin establishing daughter churches in towns or villages nearby.

Broadly speaking, Assemblies of God responded to the post-war conditions in four ways. First, there was a bold and persevering attempt, led largely by George Oldershaw, to start new churches from scratch; second the Executive Council did try to organise large campaigns, though as we shall see, these were never as successful as those mounted in the 1930s; third, there was a serious attempt to upgrade the facilities of congregations which had existed for many years in unsatisfactory premises; and fourth, there was a gradual attempt to set ministerial training on a firmer footing. Although it is possible with hindsight to isolate these four main responses to Atlee's Britain, those who were involved in the hurly burly of life in the late 1940s did not really see themselves as carrying out a masterplan. The most careful piece of thinking in Assemblies of God was produced by a Select Committee (John Wallace, Ernie Crew, Harold Horton, T S Parfitt and C Wishart) who reported on the missionary situation overseas and made recommendations to the second General Conference of 1945. Again, we will see later what sort of impact these alterations made to the AoG churches in Britain, but perhaps one of them was financial because, as sterling slipped, donations overseas had to be increased to keep their value. In addition, changes in the internal structure of Assemblies of God were brought about by Howard Carter's decision to continue his travelling ministry. He ceased to be the permanent chairman of Assemblies of God in 1945 and resigned from the principalship of the Hampstead Bible School in July 1948. John Carter, who had done the work of two men by editing *Redemption Tidings* and functioning as the AoG General Secretary, passed over his editorial duties to Robert Barrie in 1949. Finance was re-jigged so that the editor's salary was reduced and Barrie received payment from his congregation as he continued to work as its pastor; for the first time the job of General Secretary was paid. In many respects these changes within Assemblies of God were disconnected from the needs of the hour - though, no doubt, John Carter was glad to give up his punishing schedule.

Howard Carter's disentanglement from Britain had the effect of making Donald Gee the most prominent of British pentecostals. This prominence was recognised at the European pentecostal conference in Zurich in 1947. Gee was given a mandate at that conference to produce a magazine giving information about the outpouring of the Holy Spirit all over the world and, from then until his death in 1966, he produced a quarterly review of pentecostal activity across the world. The magazine - called simply *Pentecost* was of good quality and always carried photographs and numerous reports. Gee himself contributed a searching editorial which posed the difficult questions which most pentecostals preferred to duck. Gee's own leanings were mildly ecumenical and some of the attempts to establish closer working relations between European pentecostal groups and between different sections of the pentecostal movement in Britain can almost certainly be traced to Gee's influence and inclinations.

Finance in Assemblies of God

Redemption Tidings made a profit throughout the 1930s and continued to do so during the 1940s. In 1941 it just about broke even. The economies and restrictions of paper rationing and the loss of readership because of conscription began to bite that year, but thereafter there was a steady profit, and this was supplemented by the money made by the Assemblies of God book room which, in 1947 transformed itself into the Assemblies of God Publishing House. The books and the magazine were largely written by men well known in the pentecostal movement and who took neither payment nor royalties. *Redemption Tidings* never paid for articles and most of the books written by Gee, Carter and Horton brought little or no money to their authors. The men concerned gave themselves to a writing ministry and only if their books were re-printed by Assemblies of God in America did royalties begin to accrue.

The circulation and turnover figures for Redemption Tidings show an increase to a peak in 1939 and then an almost level performance during the war of roughly 10,000 copies a fortnight. After the war, when paper was no longer bureaucratically controlled, circulation began to rise, but so did costs and profits slumped again in 1947. The book room turnover climbed consistently from 1941-45 and the profit generated by these two interests amounted to about £700 per year, which was equivalent to the wage of two working men. The spare money was put to good use. It usually financed the travelling expenses of ministers and delegates to the General Conference - a bonus which encouraged good attendance and was much appreciated by struggling pastors and their congregations - or evangelism at home, or a publishing venture like a new hymn book or the purchase of the general offices in Luton.

Funding for separate ventures was usually raised separately. The careful handling of finance can probably be traced to John Carter whose background in banking would have given him a shrewd idea of how to save and where to spend. Although the magazine and booksales and their profits were dealt with by Carter, he did not influence missionary giving or the raising of money by collections and offerings. When the two years either side of the war, 1939 and 1946, are examined in detail the figures show that approximately twice as much money was spent abroad as at home. The total figure for centrally accounted expenditure at home includes all offerings centrally collected and subscriptions to *Redemption Tidings* and sales of books (it does not include the stipends paid to pastors because this figure could only be discovered by checking the ledgers of individual congregations); the total figure for expenditure abroad is made up of donations to missionary work, including passage. This ratio remained roughly constant, though assets at home increased by virtue of property holdings. Missionary giving during the war years was used to support missionaries who returned to Britain. In 1946, when mission field opened up again, £13,652 was given to overseas missions and in 1948 this had risen to £21,148.

There were over 100 Assemblies of God missionaries in 1947 and they must have received approximately £200 per year each. At home about £2000 per year was given to the evangelisation of Britain. This was an expensive business: a campaign in Crewe in 1945/6 cost £148, and the hire of halls over the course of a single year could easily reach £100. It is, of course, hard to assess the value of missionary work either at home or overseas. There is certainly no exact correlation between the amount of money spent on an evangelistic or missionary project and its eventual outcome. If it could be established that the cost of establishing a new congregation in its own building were a fixed sum of money, then very precise calculations could be made about how to proceed. But no such calculations can be made because there are several variables which are relevant in any such situation. In general the evangelism may be effective, but the initial pastor may be inadequate; or conversely, the initial evangelism may be disappointing, but the pastoral care provided may be first class and the congregation may eventually grow beyond all expectations. Furthermore, there may be beneficial results if the evangelistic campaign is prolonged a further week or two which are out of all proportion to the costs incurred by the original hirings and advertisements. Stephen Jeffreys, in his early days, simply stayed and preached in a town until a congregation was established. Subsequently, when he was in great demand, he had to give a fortnight here and a week there and trust that local organisation and preparation would be sufficient to reap a benefit from his ministry. Home missions in Assemblies of God tended to make use of pastors with evangelistic gifts. The advantage of this system was that the pastor did not have to be employed full-time as an evangelist and could conduct two or three campaigns each year while leaving his congregation in the hands of another minister. The disadvantage of this system was that the pastor/evangelist's own congregation was unlikely to grow properly, and there was very little opportunity for a successful campaign to be prolonged because the evangelist had to return to his home church by a set date. What tended to happen, therefore, was that small congregations tried to grow by injections of evangelistic and revivalistic preaching which exhausted the participants and, once the injection had worn off, left the congregation in much the same state as before. Those churches which did manage to grow in the late 1940s and early 1950s were usually on the pattern of Bethshan, Manchester, where Nelson Parr regularly and passionately preached the gospel every Sunday night and where the life of the church was focused around evangelism more than the communion service and the fellowship it implies.

In some respects an analysis of balance sheets and spending in Assemblies of God is misleading because on several occasions in the 1940s various departments received legacies which, in the nature of the case, are single unrepeatable payments. Legacies underline the age of the pentecostal movement and the gradual acquisition of property by church members. The early pentecostals were old men and women in the 1940s and some of them were glad to pass on their material possessions to the movement as a whole. John Carter as one of its founder members willed his house to Assemblies of God in the 1980s, but such forms of funding were only likely to occur where property owning pentecostals decided to leave their estates to the movement as whole rather than to sons and daughters who had backslidden or moved to other branches of Christianity. Perhaps the real lesson of these figures is simply that it was necessary to begin a fund for evangelism at home in addition to one for evangelism overseas. This new fund was a recognition of the increasing paganism of Britain coupled with the lack of any evangelist of national stature.

Home Missions

Each month *Redemption Tidings* contained a few paragraphs of news about the work of Home Missions. The format was always the same: there was an acknowledgement of individual anonymous donations followed by a few lines on each place where a campaign was being held or planned. In July 1945 John Carter, who was the Home Missions secretary, reported that there had been 26 efforts in different places and that only five of these had been abortive. Several new congregations had been added to Assemblies of God. Carter's report must have covered the four years back to 1941 when Home Missions was first began. In June 1945 a campaign was prepared in Crewe and the evangelist, Mr Read, was provided with a caravan as his base. He visited door to door and had the hire of a disused hall for meetings on Sunday, but his regular reports showed that progress was slow. Fresh campaigns were planned for Skegness and Leigh in Lancashire in the summer of 1945 and there was a campaign at Christchurch in Hampshire in November of that year. Home Missions workers were invited to a conference in Nottingham and George Oldershaw preached on winning people to Christ at the General Conference that summer. Early in 1946 a further campaign, this time with Eddie Durham, was arranged for Crewe and he also crusaded in Canterbury in the autumn of 1946. The second Crewe campaign took place in the Corn Exchange and every house in the district received a handbill while a car with a loudspeaker toured the streets. Modern electioneering methods were applied to evangelism and *Redemption Tidings* (15 March, 1946) said that "twenty-three tested and proved conversions have taken place". At Canterbury "the number of local people rose from six on the first night to 35. It settled last week at 25 except for Sunday evening when there were 34. There is therefore every possibility that a promising assembly will be established as a result of this campaign" (*Redemption Tidings* 8 November, 1946). It is clear that the campaigns were not as tumultuous and crowded as had been known in the 1930s. The hope was that momentum would gather and that there would be a peak of revival. A tent was bought to go along with the caravan so that it would be possible to hold evangelistic campaigns continuously, but a report in September 1946 which said that the tent was in need of repair and that an old Salvation Army hall had been rented instead shows that there were practical setbacks to the chosen method of producing new churches.

In 1947 the same sort of pattern continued. Foul weather depressed attendance at the three campaigns arranged for January and despite the hire of town halls and the distribution of numerous handbills, there were meagre results. The bad weather continued until the spring and, at Shanklin on the Isle of Wight, when 23 people attended a Sunday service, or when 50 children came to a Sunday school in Wallisdown, enough seemed to have been achieved to suggest that there was hope for the future. In April slow and steady growth was reported in these towns and those which had been reached the previous year, but altogether it was clear that the planting of strong new churches was going to take time. When an average attendance at Canterbury of 22 people was reported in the summer, the campaign the previous year could be seen to have had some lasting results. In October *Redemption*

Tidings reported that a campaign at Weymouth was followed by three weeks of Bible teaching and this seems to have been a step in a sensible direction. On some occasions, too, campaigns were held continuously by changing the evangelist every few weeks in an attempt to allow consolidation to take place. In Corby a large trailer was turned into a mobile church with a Sunday school of 55 children. Eddie Durham was one of the most successful evangelist in Assemblies of God at that time and he later went on to pioneer three churches which stand to this day. However, almost certainly because of a lack of pastoral care and experience, many of the campaign efforts of this period never yielded results as permanent as those which attended the exciting pioneering of the late 1920s and early 1930s.

The next three years continued the pattern. Several campaigns were held each year and typically after a fortnight or three weeks of meetings 20-30 people would form the nucleus of a new congregation. Sometimes church goers from other denominations would make a commitment to Christ at the campaign meetings but then return to the churches where they felt their roots to lie. On other occasions candidates for baptism by immersion would come forward, but would refrain from becoming involved with the pentecostal movement. When reports gave the number of converts, it was always important to distinguish what proportion were children and what proportion were adults. Certainly considering the general decline of church attendance in the 1940s, these crusades were a notable exception to the general trend of evangelical mission in Britain as a whole. Perhaps half a dozen congregations were established every two years, but the most thoughtful of the campaigners realised that pastoral work of quality was indispensable to proper church growth. Herbert Harrison and Don Walker worked as the caravan evangelists and were successful wherever they went, but Harrison found his life's work in Newcastle upon Tyne where he eventually settled and built up a large and thriving Christian centre with many offshoots into the surrounding areas.

In 1949 several Home Missions rallies were held in different parts of the country and George Oldershaw preached at the General Conference the following year on venturing for Christ. "It is in the midst of difficult circumstances that we need to venture for God" (*Redemption Tidings*, 6 Jan, 1950) and he went on to reminisce about how he and a friend had tried to establish a congregation in a town and had failed but how, with the support of the workers and finances of Home Missions, they now saw the success that had previously eluded them. Campaigning continued in 1950 and one writer pointed out the need for assemblies on the new housing estates which were beginning to spring up all over the place. About ten new halls were opened that year. The pattern developed into a cycle: a campaign was followed by a small congregation which then hired a hall and, when the time was ripe, built or bought a hall of its own.

Large evangelistic campaigns

As early as November 1946, the Executive discussed the possibility of inviting Edward Jeffreys, Stephen's son, to hold evangelistic campaigns. The name "Jeffreys" still had some lingering greatness attached to it as a result of the exceptional preaching, and the miracles, which had attended Stephen and George at the height of their powers. Edward, it is true, had held the British Israelism doctrine in the early 1930s, but by the late 1940s he was willing to make a public repudiation of it. The whole Executive interviewed him early in 1947 and the minutes of their meeting convey disappointment in discovering that Edward had apparently embraced another untenable doctrinal position, namely that the baptism with the Holy Spirit and the new birth were synonymous. Although local assemblies, being self-governing, were free to invite any evangelist they wished, the matter died a natural death and when, in May 1947, Nelson Parr announced by letter his willingness to launch a British Youth Crusade, the Executive quickly nominated three of their number to attend a preliminary conference. In fact a National Youth Rally was held at Kingsway Hall, London, in March 1950 and Parr himself preached powerfully to two packed meetings, one in the morning and one in the evening. However ticket holders found that their seats were taken by those without tickets and Carter, who attended on behalf of the Executive, found the organisation poor on other counts too. Parr showed what could be done, but Carter seemed to have wrinkled up his nose in distaste at the showmanship which was becoming Parr's hallmark.

Meanwhile the extraordinary affair of the American, "Little David", unfolded. In July 1949 Jack Walker was given an interview with the Executive. "Little David" was Mr Walker's son and the boy (who seems to have been in his early teens) was a precocious preacher who drew crowds wherever he went. Mr Walker had arranged for "Little David" to be accompanied and managed by Raymond Richey who would look after the boy while he stayed in Britain. The Kingsway and Albert Halls had both been booked and would be paid for by Mr Walker, though any money which was raised through offerings would off-set these costs and any surplus would remain in Britain. The Executive insisted that there should be no money-raising appeals and then gave their blessing. Assemblies of God would provide ushers and ministers to help in the handling of crowds and the shepherding of new converts.

The crusade itself was a great success. There were over 8,000 people in the Albert Hall on the Sunday afternoon and 360 people had become Christians, of whom 275 had been directed to Assembly of God congregations. At some stage, after one of the evening meetings, "Little David" had been visited in his hotel room by a waitress, and had written a letter to her, which had fallen into the hands of the national newspapers. Bernard Porter, an Assemblies of God minister who had been secretary to the campaign in Britain, had been offered financial inducements by the *Daily Express* for information about "Little David's" relationship with the girl, and when he refused to say anything, had been attacked by the journalist who, as was subsequently learnt, had been drunk at the time.

Bernard Porter and the girl were both interviewed by the Executive and there seemed little doubt that the published letter was genuine and that a slight romantic relationship existed between her and "Little David". To deal with the reporters who were waiting outside the building during the Executive interviews, the following statement was issued:

> At the regular bi-monthly meeting of the Executive Council of Assemblies of God held on Thursday September 8th in London, questions concerning "Little David" were discussed and inquiry was made into the matters mentioned in the public press. David Walker came to this country without any invitation from Assemblies of God and we were approached by his father on his own initiative with a request that we provide stewards in the London meetings. From reports to hand we are satisfied that real good, both spiritually and physically, has resulted in many lives from these meetings, and in this we wholeheartedly rejoice. Having examined various sources of information we are not convinced of the accuracy of some of the stories that have received wide publicity concerning these evangelists. If they were true they represent behaviour we unhesitatingly condemn. By "these evangelists" they referred to "Little David" and his manager who was not, as expected, Mr Richey.

Despite the sour taste left behind by the "Little David" episode the AoG Executive were determined not to be prevented from supporting large-scale evangelism where this was possible and in 1950 they wrote to William Branham, who was then in Europe, telling him of their willingness to cooperate should he come to England. *Pentecost* (September 1950) records two outstanding evangelistic campaigns, one at Bristol conducted by Howell Harris in collaboration with eight nearby Assemblies of God congregations and the other near Manchester where the Elim churches banded together. In fact it was at about this time that the American healing evangelists came to prominence and there was discussion in the Christian and secular press about their style as well as their doctrine. Most of these evangelists were second-generation pentecostals who had "outgrown" their parent denominations. They held distinctively pentecostal doctrines on the baptism in the Holy Spirit and believed in divine healing, but their money raising methods and their independence of any supervisory body put pentecostal people in two minds. Harold Horton, who was then visiting the USA, wrote in *Redemption Tidings* (12 May, 1950) defending healing evangelists to the hilt. He attested to the genuineness of their miracles and to their financial probity, yet with the proviso that, if these men were paid highly, they were well worth it! Gee had given space to descriptions of "renewed emphasis on divine healing" in his roundup of pentecostal news from North America in the September 1949 issue of *Pentecost*, and he returned to the subject in an editorial in 1953 when he wrote, "what all true Pentecostal hearts desire is to distinguish between the wheat of an authentic moving of the Holy Spirit and the chaff of individualistic exploitation of a popular cult for personal ends....the Healing Campaigns and the Bible Schools represent extreme wings in the army of Emmanuel. They are mutually complementary not contradictory". However, when the big campaigns did come to England in 1954, they came through the ministry of Billy Graham whose preaching was strongly evangelistic without being "pentecostal".

Building

No centralised decision was taken to buy or upgrade AoG property holdings. Once the war was over, however, there was an expansion in all kinds of building all over the country. Houses, office blocks, schools, factories and hospitals began to go up and so congregations and church leaders naturally turned their minds in the same direction. Moreover the AoG Property Trust began to have more funds available from 1947 onwards and its cheap mortgages, coupled with the large number of derelict church buildings which were waiting to be bought up and renovated, can be seen to have offered excellent conditions for ambitious building programmes. *Redemption Tidings* carried photographs of many of the new halls which were opened in the late forties and they vary greatly in quality and size. Some were stone or brick and others look like prefabricated scout huts. Once the building phase was over, and especially when property prices began to soar in the late 1960s and early 1970s, it was much more difficult to launch into building projects and there was, by that time, a question mark about the need for spending on bricks and mortar when the "restoration movement" showed that it was perfectly possible to function in homes and hired halls. Too often, it is sad to say that in Assemblies of God building a physical building took precedence over spiritual priorities with the result that ministers were poorly paid and deacons ran the church. That sort of problem was not properly aired and faced in the years after 1945; if it had been the interaction between the charismatic movement and the pentecostal movement, which took place in the 1960s, might have been very different.

The Bible School(s)

Throughout the 1930s and into the war years the Bible School continued to be Howard Carter's base. It was in Hampstead and housed in two properties. During an air raid in 1940 one of the houses was irreparably damaged by a bomb. Providentially none of the students was hurt and training and lecturing continued as before, though in slightly different accommodation. It not clear what was going on in Carter's mind at this time. He was continually active on the Executive and there was some difficulty in obtaining students since theological training was not seen as a national priority and those young men who registered as conscientious objectors were normally expected to do work of national importance. Then in 1947 John Wallace opened a Bible College in Bristol which, like Carter's school, was self-governing. Carter wrote to Wallace to wish him well. There was no reason why both schools could not function separately and train men and women for different purposes because Wallace intended his school to provide refresher courses for Christian workers. There were already several pentecostal Bible Schools in existence. Elim had one at Capel in Surrey and in the late 1930s Fred Squire had launched his own Bible Training Institute in Leamington Spa which, in 1949, was moved to ten acres of pleasant grounds in Burgess Hill in Sussex. Squire's vision was for the European countries flattened by war and he made a point of establishing a link with pentecostals in western Europe. To many people's surprise Carter handed over his school to George Newsholme in the summer of 1948 with, according to rumour[2], the express wish that at no stage should the work lose its independence. Carter had run his school without a board of governors or panel of reference and, though he allowed Assemblies of God representatives to inspect the premises and comment on the doctrinal position of the curriculum, it was always perfectly clear that he had the last word on what was done. Indeed, when AoG representatives inspected the school in the 1930s, Carter was the permanent Chairman of the fellowship and it was hardly likely that their findings would embarrass him.

In 1950 several changes happened at once. Newsholme had been running the school with some success - though according to some reports[3] without very full attendance - and had decided to move on. He looked for new premises and found a hotel in attractive grounds in Kenley, Surrey, at a cost of £10,000. John Wallace felt able to merge his school with the new enterprise and the whole new undertaking was then given to Assemblies of God. In 1951 a Board of Governors was appointed and Donald Gee was approached as the prospective Principal. To everyone's surprise he accepted. After a life of constant travel, and having previously been critical of some aspects of Bible College work, Gee directed his energies and abilities to Kenley. He was then sixty years of age and his world-wide reputation in the pentecostal movement was sufficient to guarantee a steady stream of student applications. It is not clear whether Gee had accepted the job at Kenley before or just after his wife's unexpected death late in 1950. She had been unwell for a short while beforehand and, on her death, he made his home at the college where, despite his natural shyness, the more discerning students found him to be a man for whom they could entertain affection as well as awe. Throughout his years as the Principal of Kenley, that is until 1963, he took no salary. Such income as he had must have been derived from ministerial gifts in England and preaching tours during the summer holidays.

There are unanswered questions about the new departures in the life of the Bible School after the war. It seems odd that John Wallace was willing to sink his new College into a joint venture with George Newsholme in 1950 and not to have had the same thought in 1947 when Howard Carter was in charge. Perhaps Wallace found running a Bible School altogether a tougher proposition than he had bargained for. Perhaps his student intake was low, or perhaps he felt that it was the will of God to give up his own concerns for the general benefit of a larger number of people. We have no way of knowing. Again, it is surprising that George Newsholme should make the radical changes that he did and then leave the new project to another man. There was a debt of about £3,500 on the new property and it may be that Newsholme felt unable to cope with such financial pressure. His experience as a pastor of a thriving assembly in Doncaster would not have given him a foretaste of trusting God for large sums of money. Nevertheless, as Gee knew, there were 47 pentecostal assemblies without a pastor or recognised leader (see the Executive Minutes 12 Jan 1950, item 12) and the need for ministerial training was obviously of prime importance.

Individual successes
Billy Richards

Whatever the social and economic conditions in post-war Britain, and however the pentecostal movement as a whole tried to attack the problems which it saw, it is sometimes through the achievements of individuals that the greatest long-term benefits are to be found. Individuals with a new vision which has been authenticated by ministerial success can wake a movement up and show what can be done when it has imperceptibly settled for second best.

The post-war years were at the edge of an era. The ranks of pentecostal veterans was being thinned out. Wigglesworth, Stephen Jeffreys, Tom Mercy and Wilf Richardson (an outstanding pastor in Wakefield) had died; Howard Carter was occupied mainly in the USA; Harold Horton was less frequently in Britain; George Jeffreys, despite some large meetings in Europe, never seemed at the spearhead of pentecostalism any more. Alexander Boddy and Cecil Polhill had died in the 1930s. There was a need for fresh blood and two examples illustrate what young men and women could do.

W T H Richards (Billy Richards, as he was always called) was born in 1916 and brought up in the Welsh valleys near the large and thriving assembly at Crosskeys. His family were pentecostal and miners. As a lad he was full of humour and fun and from an early age, as he went to school, he would be greeted by the shout of, "Here comes Billy Richards". His father had been a heavy drinker and there was one occasion when Billy was still at school when the teacher had asked if any pupils had ever been abroad. Billy said he had been to France (holidays were not unsual in those poverty stricken areas). He had been taken there by his mother who was feeding him at the time and they visited his father who was desperately ill in the military hospital. The teacher thought Billy was lying and had beaten him round the head. When Billy's father came home from the pit and heard about what had happened, he went down to the school, covered in coal dust and in his working clothes, and attacked the teacher in question. Such support from home could only reinforce the sense of humour that was always characteristic of Billy, even in later life. Yet a harsh note of realism broke in on the lad when he was eight years old. He and his brother were meant to go to Sunday School before the morning service but one Sunday Harold decided to miss the lessons and go climbing in a large quarry. As he reached the top of the rock wall, he fell back down to the floor and one of the boys with him rushed to the family with news of the accident. Mr Richards senior went in the ambulance with his unconscious son to a hospital in Newport. Harold died that night. Billy missed his brother terribly and was enraged and bewildered by what had happened. Just before the funeral, at a packed prayer meeting in the Richards' house, there was an utterance in tongues followed by an interpretation containing the words, "I will fill up this gap with my glory". At the graveside one of the preachers quoted from John 14, "Let not your heart be troubled" and that calmed Billy. The lesson of the tragedy, which was not lost on the boy, was that if they had both been at Sunday School, where they should have been, Harold would not have died. Only years later did they connect the interpretation of tongues with the ministry which Billy developed.

Billy went to work on the coal face with his father at the age of fourteen and took an active part in the Crosskeys assembly. Tom Mercy was the pastor, a man respected and loved both by the mining community for his Trades Union activities and by the congregation for his faith and energy. He was a man who inspired young men and encouraged them to preach or lead a meeting, and Billy did both. The young man saved up for a big Schofield Bible and studied it carefully. One night, when he was about nineteen, Billy dreamt that he would be a preacher. He saw himself on a platform with the other pentecostal preachers of the day. Taking this as a call from God, he felt he must have some training. His mother, though she thought she would miss the money he brought into the home, did not stand in his way. Both parents were glad that he wrote to Howard Carter, saved or borrowed a few pounds and went to Hampstead for a term.

He was there in 1937 and learnt as much as he could. For the next five years his hands were full with the Assemblies of God Evangelistic Society and with two small assemblies in London at the height of the blitz. In both places he learnt to gather a congregation and to preach. As Elisha Thompson, one of the Bible School tutors recalled,

> he was troubled by poverty and getting sufficient food. There was very little we in the school could do to help here, for we were hardly any better off. In many ways his greatest struggle was with loneliness. Often he would ring up to say he was 'fed up' and could we offer him a bed just for one night. When he came, we would be able to talk and pray together. On one such occasion, I was deeply moved as I realised he was up against many problems which I had seen break many outstanding men of God. That night I think we must have wept on one another's shoulders, but the Lord did hear our cry and within a few days strangely intervened. (from *Dedication*, Nov/Dec 1974)

In late 1942 he became conscious that God was calling him to Slough and he arrived in 1943 with £12 in his pocket and the intention of starting a church. He was 26 years old and seemed to be on a fool's errand. He contacted the known pentecostals in the area, hired a scouts' hut and held an opening service. A few people from three of the London assemblies travelled down and they heard the young man preach while water dripped into buckets and bowls strategically placed on the floor to catch what leaked in through the roof. The war was by no means won and it must have seemed a strange time to think of starting a new church, especially as his finances were strictly limited. Many older pentecostal pastors were finding it very hard to keep existing congregations alive and healthy. But Richards had that combination of spirituality and practicality, with a good mixture of humour and authority, as well as inventiveness and tenacity, which mark some of the best Christian leaders.

On the first Sunday morning, June 23rd 1943, there were five in the congregation and ten at the evening service. For the next few months, a handful of people gathered. In winter the hut was so cold that on several occasions the communion wine froze and the useless old stove in the corner became a health hazard because it leaked sulphurous fumes. Richards prayed hard and kept an accurate record of gradually growing attendance and finance. On one occasion, when he felt like giving up, he prayed that God would encourage him by sending £50 and, to his delight and surprise, that is the exact sum he found in the post when he returned home. By January 1944 there were 24 in the congregation and by May of that year there were 36 people present and in October he had reached 50 people. The weekly offerings climbed to about £3 and a building fund was started. They saved up and bought some land in Pitts road and then found a prefabricated structure costing £120. Richards told the owner of the building that they would buy it the following week. The night before they had to pay a note was put through Richards' door saying, "we have decided to give £100 towards the building". But the next morning the benefactor decided to give the full amount. By a combination of hard work and faith, the church continued to grow. Richards appointed elders and Sunday School superintendents. He started a magazine called *Dedication* which built up to a circulation of 6000 copies bi-monthly, launched a correspondence course which was used in Australia, South Africa, the USA, Holland, India, Canada and Switzerland and pioneered what he called "doorbell evangelism". Throughout his life he remained a man whose main desire was to see individuals converted to Christ. By 1958 Richards had 300 church members and six Sunday Schools catering for 500 children. I heard him preach in 1970/71 and he was an inspiring speaker. He would stride about the platform and work on a congregation till he felt he had imparted some life to it. I remember, in the middle of his sermon, he suddenly quoted Proverbs 4.18, "the path of the just is as a shining light that shineth more and more unto the perfect day". The words hit me and when Richards died quite suddenly, and at the height of his powers, in 1974 a ripple went through the evangelical world and the words he had quoted seemed a fitting epitaph. Dr Martyn Lloyd-Jones spoke at his funeral and Gilbert Kirby, who was then Principal of London Bible College, paid a tribute. Lloyd-Jones said, "this man was a spiritual statesman. I have rarely known a man who had a larger and clearer world view of the present situation of the Christian Church and what we all should be doing".[4]

Hockley

The other example of post-war success concerns two ladies who had originally hoped to be missionaries. Miss Fisher and Miss Reeve were born in about 1908 and both came from Christian homes. Around 1932 George Jeffreys held a huge and exciting crusade in Birmingham. "The late buses from the City Centre crowded each night with young converts, who sang all the way home" and the evidence of miracles of healing stirred both young women. Soon afterwards they met at a Police Hostel where Miss Reeve was working and where Miss Fisher had gone to speak evangelistically. As a result of a prophecy given by the Matron of the hostel they decided to work together and, since Miss Reeve felt "a definite call to India", they bought a compound in Bangalore and began to train as nurses. When they were ready to sail out to begin their work, the second world war broke out and they found themselves unable to leave England.

> We were doing whatever we could whilst waiting for our passage. We went down air raid shelters, trying to comfort terrified people and praying for them. We ministered at local Churches many of which were later destroyed by bombs. The Lord wonderfully preserved us as we were in the midst of falling bombs, many of our neighbours and friends being cut off at this time. We hired a room in Hockley where we could spend time praying but soon we gathered around us dozens of boys and girls, and their mothers came too. We told them of the love of Jesus and may came to know Him as their Saviour and Lord. Not realising fully what was happening, Hockley Mission had commenced. The Lord provided buildings for us to rent, and later a Church to purchase[5].

The church grew out of a Sunday School. The two women kept finding it necessary to hire larger and larger premises and to provide meetings for the parents of their Sunday School children and, as they liked to point out cheerfully in later years, the emigration which took place from New Commonwealth countries after the war, brought India to them - they did not need to take ship after all! At one period they had eight Sunday Schools and about 800 children in attendance. Today Hockley's congregation is as multi-racial as the Sunday Schools used to be and many of the children who made up those early classes are now missionaries in various parts of the world. One contemporary picture shows Miss Reeve, large open Bible in hand, sitting on the floor in a school gymnasium surrounded by singing Asian children.

After the war Miss Fisher and Miss Reeve found a large derelict Baptist church building which they felt God was directing them to buy. The Baptist congregation had melted away as the whole area round it became more tumbled down, but it was still necessary to get the agreement of the Baptist Union to the purchase. As it turned out Mr Daniels, the pastor, had been in prison for conscientious objection with Howard Carter during the 1914-18 war and had formed a favourable attitude to pentecostals. The cost of the building was £3,500 and so the two women, and their flock, "began to fast, not from food but from buying new clothes, just making do with such as we had. There were to be no more luxuries till the Lord's house was paid for". Old age pensioners helped, jewellery was sold and people gave money they had saved up for their holidays. Miss Fisher and Miss Reeve steadfastly observed two principles: they refused to go into debt and they took up no collections. So far as they were concerned, if God wanted the money provided, then God would provide it. Little by little the special account they had opened climbed towards the target, and when it was finally reached the cashiers at the bank all cheered. The money lay in the account for precisely one day before it had to be paid over.

The Hockley congregation grew steadily and was different in several respects from its most other pentecostal churches in either Assemblies of God or Elim. First, Miss Fisher and Miss Reeve continued to live "by faith" all their lives. They had no fixed income agreed with the church. Second, and most noticeable, the Hockley congregation emphasised praise, worship and dancing at a time when this was squashed and criticised by the majority of pentecostals. At some stage, when the Sunday night Gospel meeting became the prime means of attempting to win the unconverted, pentecostal churches forbade or strongly discouraged the exercise of charismatic gifts on Sunday evenings. Not so with Hockley! So far as they were concerned, the most vital ingredient of the Christian life was to worship the Lord and nothing would stop them raising their hands in the air, jumping, clapping and singing. They really did not care whether people thought them mad or not, or whether the Executive Council of Assemblies of God felt that they gave pentecostals a bad name.

> Critics may say that those who dance in the Spirit are merely making a show in front of others. In fact, the opposite is true. It is the hardest thing for a person to dance unto the Lord while others are looking on, instead of entering into the blessing themselves. Acts 3.8 tells us, '...he entered the temple walking and leaping and praising God'. The person who dances in the Spirit has come to the place where JESUS fills his vision. [original capitals].

Their unrestrained spiritual and emotional exuberance did not seem to have drive people away from the church. On the contrary, Hockley grew while other assemblies were having difficulties in maintaining their numbers.

In keeping with this lively style of worship, Miss Fisher and Miss

Reeve took the view that there could be more than three utterances in tongues, with their interpretations, in any one meeting. The majority of pentecostals had taken the line that 1 Corinthians 14.27 ("if any man speak in an unknown tongue, let it be by two, or at the most by three, and that by course; and let one interpret" (AV)) implied that three, and only three, utterances in tongues should be given at a service. Brash Bonsall, the Principal of the Birmingham Bible Institute, has been a worshipper at Hockley for many years and he argues against this conclusion on the grounds, firstly, that there were far more utterances in tongues than three on the Day of Pentecost in Acts 2 and, secondly, that it hardly seems probably that God would restrict himself to a small and rather arbitrary number of communications with his church in any one meeting[6]. Indeed, one of the problems with the classic pentecostal position is in deciding what actually constitutes a meeting and how one decides when it finished.

Meetings at Hockey are therefore usually occasions for a large number of prophecies and beautiful interpretations of utterances in tongues which tend to follow a theme. I remember being present during a meeting in 1986 when the manifestations of the Spirit reminded me of a firework which unfolded into blaze after blaze of coloured light. Pentecostalism as a whole in the post-war years undervalued the vocal gifts of the Spirit with a consequent impoverishment of congregational life. Oddly enough, while Billy Richards and Misses Fisher and Reeve would have agreed about Sunday Schools and evangelism, they would probably have disagreed about very many other aspects of church life. Billy Richards kept a hand on his congregation and calmed down anything resembling emotional excess; Miss Fisher and Reeve were quite clear in their own minds that the Holy Spirit cared about emotion and that, anyway, the dancing and singing which was prevalent at Hockley, was in no way exhibitionistic or unspiritual. The lesson, perhaps, is that the church of Christ will be built in a variety of ways and that human beings tend to become divided over non-essentials.

Doctrine
The end of the forties saw the restatement of pentecostal doctrine along much the same lines as before, expect perhaps in two respects. Jimmy Salter, who was famous for sailing out to the Congo in 1915 and working with Burton, returned to England in the forties and wrote a series in *Redemption Tidings* where he outlined a fuller and more

flexible ecclesiology than was common in most pentecostal churches. Donald Gee's book *Shepherds and Sheepfolds* was as far as most people had gone: the church was a sheepfold. The other respect where there was some difference concerned the question of whether Christians who had not been baptised in the Holy Spirit with the initial evidence of speaking in tongues had, in fact, received the Holy Spirit at all in any measure.

Jimmy Salter's articles began in August 1946 and asserted that "the New Testament Church polity was *multiform*" [original italics]. He developed this assertion by pointing out that "for about the first six years of its existence, the Jerusalem Church was under the absolute control of the Apostles" but that later this Church appeared to be under the control of one prominent person or president, James (Acts 12.17 onwards); in Corinth, on the other hand, the voice of the people - some type of congregational government - seemed to hold sway (13 Sept). In the final article Salter argued that "every church officer is an elder". In essence he argued that deacons are elders and that elders will function according to their gifting.

> It cannot be stated too emphatically that when Paul and Barnabas 'ordained them elders in every church' they did not commit these assemblies to any form of government, either Episcopalian, Presbyterian, or Congregational, but merely entrusted them to the care of Church officers whose duties were undefined and whose qualities were not specified. (*Redemption Tidings* 5 March, 1947)

Not surprisingly this last article drew an editorial disclaimer from John Carter because AoG had usually sharply distinguished between elders/pastors who were concerned with preaching or teaching and deacons whose duties lay in the more practical realm; the article may have been responsible for the setting up of "church boards" in some assemblies where pastors and deacons sat on a committee together to lead the church. In the 1980s, however, this system of government, which was never very widespread in Assemblies of God, was seen to be hopelessly ineffective because it tended to make financial considerations the prime factor in any decision about the life of the church. Salter's article contains a number of disputable points, as the quotation above shows. When Paul and Barnabas ordained elders, they did commit the church to some form of government, that is, to the government of the elders they had ordained. There is no difficulty in believing that the elders who had been apostolically ordained then oversaw the appointment of deacons. Salter's claim that some of the men ordained as elders were really deacons seems to rest upon a confusion between the fact the word "deacon" means servant and that elders do serve. Only about 30 years later was ecclesiology considered in greater detail in Assemblies of God. Salter's articles might have initiated a useful debate, yet they failed to do so and this was unfortunate because the pentecostal leanness that was to come in the 1950s was partly due to an incomplete understanding of congregational life.

Later Nelson Parr hammered out his conviction that only the baptism with the Holy Spirit was to be equated with the believer's first reception of the Holy Spirit. He argued vehemently that, on the basis of Acts 8, the new Samaritan believers, who had been baptised by total immersion, had not received the Holy Spirit in any measure. He did not, of course, deny that they had received Christ. Parr's argument was based on the text that Acts 8.15 says Peter and John travelled specifically so that the Samaritan converts "might receive the Holy Spirit". In order to pursue his case logically Parr made a distinction between the Spirit of Christ (Galatians 4.6) and the Holy Spirit and he insisted that the reception of Christ, though it accompanies the regenerating work of the Holy Spirit, is quite distinct from the reception of the Holy Spirit. It is not, Parr contended, that the believer receives a part of the Holy Spirit at conversion and a fullness of the Spirit at the baptism in the Holy Spirit. Rather there are two different receptions: the sinner needs a Saviour and the believer needs a Comforter (*Redemption Tidings* 23 June, 1 Sept, 1950).

Parr's views, shared as they were by W P F Burton *Redemption Tidings* (27 Sept, 1946), were hardly likely to facilitate co-operation between pentecostals and other evangelicals, and they posed questions for thoughtful pentecostals when Billy Graham, who did not claim the baptism in the Spirit, came to London and preached with great power.

European relief

As the post-war years lengthened, the mushroom cloud over Hiroshima refused to go away. Donald Gee remarked on the often expressed temptation not to do anything for the future since "we may all be blown up" (*Redemption Tidings* 22nd Dec 1950). Nevertheless whatever the long-term prospects for Britain, it was hard to neglect the pressing practical demands across the channel. Mainland Europe had suffered intensely towards the end of the war. There had been a famine in

Holland from 1944-5 and food in Germany was short. Once travel became possible, Christians in Britain did what they could to alleviate sufferings abroad. Fred Squire toured Leamington Spa with a loudspeaker van appealing to all denominations for food, clothing and soap. He was astonished at the results because, as he knew better than many, the United Kingdom was one of the worst clothed and fed countries in Western Europe. He enlisted the aid of the Netherlands Red Cross and distributed well over 10,000 garments in one consignment alone[7]. And Squire was not alone in his efforts. Assemblies of God in the UK donated £450 to Europe in 1947/8 and, as a result of encouragement from their British counterparts, Australian Assemblies of God had sent over a ton of foodstuffs to Germany that same year (*Redemption Tidings* May 21st 1948).

Unity conferences

The European pentecostal conference of 1939 brought all sorts of pentecostals together and began to reveal the possibilities of collaboration. The points of difference between pentecostals were, by and large, on the question of church government and, once it became clear that respect and love could quite easily grow, for example, between British and Swedish pentecostals despite their differences, it became equally clear that similar affection could and should be fostered between pentecostals within the same nation. A Unity Conference was held in London in 1939 "to seek to find a basis for unity without compromising any vital truths". The resumption of European pentecostal conferences after the war, first in Zurich in 1947 and then in Paris in 1949, prompted further meetings between separate pentecostals in Britain. So, in August 1948, fourteen leaders from five groups - the Elim Foursquare Alliance, the Full Gospel Testimony, the Apostolic Church, the Bible Pattern Church Fellowship and the Assemblies of God - met at the Kings Cross Central Mission for two days and the results of their deliberations were reported in an agreed joint statement which was published in their own magazines (in *Redemption Tidings* 8th Oct 1948).

John Carter, Donald Gee and Jimmy Salter represented Assemblies of God and Donald Gee seems to have suggested a mode of procedure when the delegates assembled on the first morning. They elected a chairman and secretary, one of whom turned out to be from Assemblies of God and the other from Elim. They thought of a name, "The Pentecostal Fellowship of the British Isles" and a purpose:

to keep the unity of the Spirit in the bond of peace and further the proclamation of the whole counsel by cooperative effort

A doctrinal statement was drawn up and this underlined belief in the Bible, the Trinity and the atoning work of Christ and simply stated

we believe in the baptism in the Holy Spirit with supernatural evidence and in the gifts of the Spirit.

Noticeably there was no definition of exactly what "supernatural evidence" was to accompany the baptism in the Holy Spirit because, though Assemblies of God insisted that this evidence was speaking in tongues, the Elim church accepted prophecy or other spiritual gifts as just as biblical.

The representatives also affirmed their belief in

the ministry-gifts as set in the Church by the ascended Christ and in the ordinances for believers of baptism by immersion and the Lord's Supper.

Again, it is the lack of specificity which is notable. The Apostolics called men to apostolic and prophetic roles within the church and it was on this point that the other pentecostals demurred because they were unwilling to transform what they saw as a divine gift into an ecclesiastical office. Everyone agreed that apostles and prophets existed but they disagreed on the way such men could be recognised or, indeed, on what exactly they were expected to do in the local church.

Differences in church government were accepted and protected in the words "the basic principle of the Fellowship shall be that it leaves inviolate the existing forms of church government adopted by its members".

On the practical side, they agreed to meet each year and not to speak slightingly of or to make any attack on any other member. Interchange of ministry was encouraged on the understanding that "ministerial courtesy is observed" - presumably this meant that doctrinal differences would not be aired from the pulpit. And they also agreed not to take over dissident congregations from each other without at least making contact with their opposite numbers in the pentecostal group to which the dissidents originally belonged.

Although there were few tangible results from the 1948 conference - apart from some well attended public meetings up and down the country - the main effect is probably to be assessed in terms of cordiality, removal of suspicion and mutual acceptance. Oddly enough, too, it may be that Fred Squire's contact with other pentecostals helped him come to the decision, around 1950, to disband the Full Gospel Testimony. Its 20 or so churches were all given the option of deciding where they would like to belong, and most went either to Elim or to Assemblies of God.

Perhaps predictably, there was disquiet in some sections of Assemblies of God about the Executive's contact with other pentecostals. A letter from Fred Watson (in AoG in Lancashire) questioned whether the Executive "had the authority to go so far as to take a leading line in forming the BPF [British Pentecostal Fellowship]. He also raised the question of the wording of the Fundamental concerning the Baptism in the Spirit" (Executive Minutes 13th Jan, 1949). The South Midlands District Council asked for an explanation why such a "far-reaching decision had been made without the consent of the General Council" (same minutes) and the Lancashire District Council (of which Fred Watson was a leading member) passed a proposition saying, "we disagree with the developments made by the Executive Council regarding the so-called British Pentecostal Fellowship" (same minutes). The matter came up at the 1949 General Conference where it was disclosed that the Bible Pattern Church (under the influence of the ageing George Jeffreys ?) had withdrawn. John Carter reported on discussions to date and, when it became apparent that only two district councils had any real objections, the isolationists were themselves isolated. Certainly had Fred Watson's worries been upheld, it is hard to see how Assemblies of God could have participated in the world pentecostal conference in London in 1951. In *Pentecost* (Sept, 1950) Gee, thoughtful as ever, pointed out

> It is impossible to achieve the unity for which Christ prayed by making unions out of denominations. Such unions only precipitate new divisions because of those who find it impossible conscientiously to subscribe to the basis for agreement....what, then, is possible Pentecostal unity ? An answer is offered with diffidence

and he went on to outline his belief that the early church's unity stemmed from "an acceptance of the Lordship of Jesus Christ, with all that lordship implied" and that unity ultimately "is a personal matter" between individuals and not one which can operate on any other basis. Gee retained these opinions to the end of his life.

Travel

The war had accelerated technological change in the field of transport and communications. Men like Gee and Carter, who had started life using bicycles and boats, became adept at using cars, planes and telephones. The sufferings of Europe were brought closer to home by better communications and the mission field suddenly became a great deal nearer. A journey to central Africa which had taken months in the 1920s could be accomplished in days; a problem in the Indian pentecostal church could be tackled by British pentecostals amidst other activities in their crowded schedules.

Gee and L F W Woodford were in India in 1949 and Woodford, F R Barnes and John Wallace were in the Congo in 1950. The first of these visits was probably more significant. Woodford had been the Overseas Missionary Secretary for many years with Assemblies of God and he had a mind well attuned to the minutae of constitutional detail as well as the spirituality to write memorable hymns. The OMC had long accepted the principle that British nationals who established churches abroad should expect to train native leadership to whose hands the whole undertaking could eventually be completely entrusted. At an All-India Pentecostal Conference in Madras delegates were invited to explore the possibility of forming a Pentecostal Fellowship of India and Gee chaired the meetings. To his surprise, after they had considered the foundational doctrinal statement and the constitutional machinery, there was complete agreement and a Standing Committee consisting of Indians and Foreign Missionaries was appointed and placed in an influential position to co-ordinate and guide.

Travel also facilitated an important conference nearer home the same year. A World Pentecostal Fellowship was established in Paris. There were 156 delegates and 320 observers from 30 countries and, as ever, church government was the main bone of contention. Some groups believed in a high degree of central organisation and others stood for the complete freedom of the local church. Despite an early deadlock and a divisive proposal that the Scandinavian pentecostals be excluded from a loose affiliation with whose formation they seemed unable to agree, good will prevailed and a committee was elected into existence whose task it was to ensure there was good contact between the various national churches in the three year gap between future conferences. Gee's editorial in *Pentecost* (Sept 1949) discussed three criticisms of the conference: first that it cost too much, second that it raised the bogey of a world government of pentecostal churches and, third, that it ignored pressing missionary problems. Each of these criticisms reveal something about the perceptions of the people who made them. With hindsight, we might add a further criticism: that the excitement and enjoyment of the conference obscured the lack of progress which many pentecostal churches were making among their own people.

Contemporary assessments

Balanced contemporary assessment is always difficult. It has to avoid the extremes of complacency and of gloomy panic. John Wallace, who was later to go to Australia and become an outstanding Bible College Principal, wrote a strongly argued article in *Redemption Tidings* (Jan 6th 1950) in which he defended pentecostalism against the charges of emotionalism and of "making too much of the Holy Spirit" or, from another quarter, of accepting something which had died out with the apostles. In an address to the General Conference (published in *Redemption Tidings* for Sept 29th 1950), he asked where the pentecostal movement was going. He saw quite clearly that pentecostalism had reached its third generation and, in reviewing the past, he noted the opposition through which the early Spirit-filled preachers had come, the diminution in strength which British pentecostalism as a whole had suffered as a result of fragmentation and the short-sightedness of glorying in smallness and narrowness. For the present he noted both the growing acceptability of pentecostalism and the danger that pentecostals themselves might substitute spiritual entertainment for the power of the Holy Spirit. For the future he pleaded for a rediscovery of the message, of the well understood and powerfully preached message of the New Testament. He wanted no muting of the trumpet and no tailoring of the garment of praise.

The 1950 General Conference allowed voting figures for posts within Assemblies of God to be made public for the first time. Gee commented (*Redemption Tidings* Sept 15th 1950). There was always an element in AoG who were uneasy about voting. It seemed untheocratic and likely to encourage wheeling and dealing. Gee took a different view. He distinguished between a gifting for ministry which is the prerogative of Christ and which can never be subject to the fluctuations of ballots and the opportunity to serve a fellowship of Christians on well structured elected committees. The lesson he drew from the figures was that there were a growing number of men in early middle age who were all equally acceptable for the various tasks undertaken by constitutionally defined AoG Councils. It was the pool of talent in the movement as a whole which led to indecisive voting figures since, as he pointed out, the highest vote only reached 77%. The idea that divine appointment would be confirmed by a unanimous vote seem unrealistic to Gee, and he took comfort from the fact that the men who received the highest votes were also not voted for by about 50 people. In his submission, AoG was healthier if it was not dominated by one or two overpoweringly popular individuals. As he put it,

> the grace of God has now enriched our Fellowship with an increasing number of good men who rightly enough are regarded as eligible and capable to sustain official responsibilities. If we are embarrassed at all we are embarrassed by our riches of personnel.

Gee's case was logical enough and his analysis was almost certainly correct. But there were inconsistences he smoothed over. The failure of 50 people to vote in favour of two people who topped the poll for the Executive showed that there was an element in AoG hankering for change. Ballot majorities produced the illusion of unanimity. The years to come were not set as fair as the talent in the movement seemed to indicate.

Notes to Pages 197 - 223

1. The Study Hour was a magazine produced by the Assemblies of God Evangelistic Society. The magazine begun in February 1941 and, after starting life as a duplicated typescript. became a well printed monthly booklet intended to help pastors and preachers do their job. It contained reference to "Heathenish Britain" (15th Feb 1946) and later began a series of feature articles on revival. The same evaluation of post-war Britain was made by George Newsholme, Study Hour's editor, as by John Carter.

2. This information comes from David Powell who was interviewed on 12 August 1985.

3. But judging from the student intake which Gee inherited, this also seems plausible.

4. Much of the information in this section came from typescripts of interviews which Wesley Richards, Billy's eldest son, had conducted with a view to writing a book about his father. I am grateful for access to this information. the final quotation is taken from the November/December 1974 issue of Dedication which carried numerous articles and tributes to WTH Richards and makes clear his growing stature beyond Assemblies of God.

5. The information in this section is taken from Still It Flows by H Fisher and O Reeve (undated) as well as from conversations with members of the Hockley congregation and Pastor Miles Whitherford and Vic Nicholls.

6. Taken from Still It Flows by H. Fisher and O. Reeve (undated), p66 onward. At some point, in the mid 70s, Alfred Missen, then General Secretary of Assemblies of God, had appologised to Miss Fisher and Miss Reeve for the negative view which had been officially entertained at one time by senior ministers in Assemblies of God about the conduct of Hockley Assembly. Brash Bonsall's comments are at prefatory to Still It Flows.

7. See Squire, F (1958), Operation Relief, Britain: FSP.

THE 1950's: THE WIDER SCENE

Thirteen years of unbroken Tory rule began in 1951. Attlee's Labour Government was defeated after a rapid and comprehensive reformist programme which brought 20% of the nation's industry into the public sector, established a National Health Service, introduced secondary education for all and drove hard to provide thousands of "council" houses. It was only by 17 seats that the Tories returned to power, and there is no settled answer to the question why they improved on their performance of the previous year. Blake (1985: 267) suggests, "perhaps fears of unemployment had become that much less. Perhaps the increased emphasis on Tory freedom, after another year and a half of restriction, made just the difference" or perhaps it was the Tory commitment to increased expenditure on housing or, something for which neither Labour nor Conservatives could take much direct credit, the substantial weakening of the Liberal party in the 1950 election which led to only 109 Liberal candidates being fielded in the 1951 election. Old Liberal votes tended to be split in favour of the Tories. Whatever the precise historical reasons, Mr Churchill found himself back in Downing Street and ready to preside over a government which surmounted a potential sterling crisis as a result of Butler's astute manoeuvres at the Exchequer and a sudden fall in commodity prices as a result of the Korean war. Taxes fell, living standards rose, employment remained full and the welfare state continued to function effectively.

Internationally, the cold war reached a dangerous period in the mid-50s when the Soviet Union also developed an H-bomb (Roberts, 1980: 947) and it was unclear to the West how Stalin's death would affect communist strategy world-wide. But most of the danger seemed a long way from Europe: such fighting as reached the TV screens in spreading suburbia was in Korea (the war there lasted from 1950-53) or in China (where Mao was strengthening his hold on the country) or the Middle East (when the Suez Crisis of 1956 erupted). The Hungarian uprising of the same year seemed less likely to spill over into atomic warfare, and there was a touch of self-interested comfort in the prospering cities of free Europe that the Soviet Union, though as ruthless as the capitalist newspapers said, nevertheless contented itself with tanks rather than rockets in its subjugation of the brave populace of a rebellious satellite state.

All in all international affairs seemed to have little impact on everyday life in Britain. Analysts may have foreseen Britain's industrial decline as her empire melted away, but there was enough wealth in capital and plant to disguise the need for an overhaul of the wealth-generating systems of the old industrial heartlands. Between 1950-70 Britain's economic growth was only about 50%-60% of that of other industrialised nations. Between 1960-74 investment and modernisation had risen by only 30% as compared with 90% in Western Germany (Briggs, 1983: 296). Yet, imperceptibly, standards of living continued to rise. And that seemed to be the reality which mattered most to most British people.

In retrospect, the 1950s can be seen as a period of calm before the storm - the storm of 1960s razzmatazz in fashion, music and sex. Grammar schools and Tory rule perpetuated the more obvious class distinctions of the 1930s and the, "You've never had it so good" Macmillan slogan could be seen to imply that radical social change was being bought off by offering more to the working classes while, at the same time, preserving the material privileges of the middle and upper classes. Young and Willmott's authoritative study of families in London expresses this truth metaphorically: there is a long line of marchers moving towards prosperity and eventually those at the end of the line reach the place where those at the front used to be - but those at the front are now further ahead (Young and Willmott, 1976, chapter 1).

The gradual improvement in the standard of living of the average family was coupled with increased leisure hours as longer, paid holidays became common and life expectancy gradually stretched. As part of the same trend in the years between 1951-64, ownership of television sets rose from one million to 13 million and the number of cars increased from two and a half million to eight million (Hastings, 1986: 413). Moreover, women tended to marry earlier, have fewer children and take up full or part time jobs again. Young and Willmot's sample showed the tendency clearly: for example only 31% of wives in the 40-59 age group were not working at all outside the home (p 105).

Although there were exceptions, the selectiveness of the educational system militated against working class children and in favour of middle classes. The issue was endlessly debated in the 1960s, but in the 1950s there was a general satisfaction with the Grammar schools and a belief that their excellence gave Britain an advantage in science and technology. What almost certainly the Grammar schools did enforce, however, was the general stratification of British society. In this sense the 1950s seem to have been very similar to the 1930s, only more prosperous.

The house building programmes at the start of the decade, and the planning of new towns after the war (Basingstoke and Crawley are examples) accelerated urbanisation. Rural life was rarer. City life, city lights and city values became widely known. Television played its part here, but the cinema continued to be popular among the affluent young and the musical success of rock 'n' roll created its own Teddy boy subculture. The problems associated with extensive immigration from the new commonwealth did not arise forcefully (with the exception of the 1958 Notting Hill riots) till the 1960s.

The Churches

The Church of England entered an era of "ecclesiastical social conservatism" (Hastings, 1986: 423) after reforming tendencies of the Temple era and before the theological radicalism of the sixties. Fisher, as Archbishop of Canterbury until 1961, had little interest in social questions and most of the demands of the previous decades had been granted in the arrival of the welfare state. There was little to agitate for perhaps because the Tory cabinet was populated with personally committed Anglicans like Macmillan, Butler, Hailsham, Home, Salisbury, Heath and Powell. On the fringes of the establishment there were men who goaded the conscience of churchmen and politicians alike: John Collins and Trevor Huddleston attacked apartheid in South Africa and, from 1958 onwards, Collins pressed for Britain's unilateral nuclear disarmament through the activities of CND. But though both these causes were headlined, they did not touch ordinary parish life to any depth.

More dramatic and more astonishing was the success of a young American evangelist, Billy Graham. Into what sort of situation did he step? According to Professor C E M Joad, a convert to Christianity in middle life,

> it is not clear what the Church of England today believes. In particular, there is a feeling that for years she has been fighting a losing battle against science...that the elasticity and vagueness of the Church's creed play no small part in the decline of its influence....as the comparative popularity of the Roman Catholic Church....convincingly demonstrates (Joad, 1952: 238)

Joad's case had been quantified to an extent the year before in an article in the *New Statesman* in which he pointed out that the membership of the Church of England had declined by 400,000 between 1938 and 1951, in a period which included immediate post-war the birth rate boom (Manwaring, 1985: 82). However correct his diagnosis of what he saw as the Anglican malaise, his general views were in line with those of Bishop Chavasse whose report *Towards the Conversion of England* had been published in 1945 and well received. Yet by 1950 little had taken place to fulfil Chavasse's hopes; Chavasse himself gave three reasons for this failure: firstly, insufficient numbers of laity had been able to maintain "that quickened quality of spiritual life" necessary for evangelism - a fault he seems implicitly to have lain at the door of the clergy; second, a generation of men and women grew up between the wars who were ignorant of "their Bible and the fundamental doctrines of their faith" and, third, because the central authority of the Church of England had not implemented that section of the report which was designed to soften up the hard core of British materialism and secularism (Manwaring, 1985: 77). Instead Fisher's mind was preoccupied with the reform of canon law - an important topic no doubt - but described by him as "the most absorbing and all-embracing topic of my whole archepiscopate" (Moorman, 1980; 440) and by raising funds to ensure that, in a decade of rising living standards, the stipends of clergy were not left behind.

Billy Graham therefore arrived to preach to a country where religious and spiritual life was unprepared for an evangelistic revival. Evangelicals, like Chavasse, formed a minority within the Church of England and their zeal, after the failure of *Towards the Conversion of England*, seems to have been flagging. Graham was an American, a Southern Baptist, an emissary of no influential body, young (born in 1918) and theologically a long way from the subtleties of Anglican scholarship. His presentation of the Gospel owed a great deal to the Moody and Sankey revivalism at the turn of the century. There was nothing theatrical about his appeal: the preaching was simple, impassioned, biblical and, to everyone's amazement, seemed to break down British reserve and draw huge crowds. In three months in 1954 Graham preached to 1.3 million people and, at the final meeting in the White City stadium, addressed 65,000 while flanked on one side by the Lord Mayor of London and on the other by no less a person than Archbishop Fisher. Winston Churchill, Prime Minister at the time, is said to have sent for the young evangelist and to have asked him how he managed to fill huge arenas night after night. "I couldn't do it" Churchill is reported to have admitted, "and nor could Marilyn Monroe". Graham attributed the success of his preaching to the work of the Holy

Spirit.

His crusade came at a time when Nonconformity was no longer the force in the land it had been in the heady days of Lloyd George's government. Methodist, Congregational and Baptist membership combined had declined by 27% between the thirties and the fifties. True, Methodist Sunday School attendance rose between 1945 and 1954 and Donald Soper was gaining considerable publicity for his flamboyant socialist-tinged preaching. But subsequent events showed that notoriety and media attention could not stem the decline of a once great group of churches: in the fifteen years from 1960-75 Methodist membership declined a further 24% (Hastings, 1987: 552).

Though evangelicals had great expectations after the Graham crusade, and there were numerous parishes which experienced excitement and growth, especially among the young, the flow of revival subsided gradually while leaving behind a greater general openness to religion than previously. Communication between churches had improved as a result of the crusade because of the co-operation which had been necessary at the planning stages. Co-operation between evangelicals was perhaps overshadowed by the ups and downs of ecumenical dialogue. This took place on a large number of fronts and at many levels. There were Anglican/Methodist talks in 1955; there were contacts between Canterbury and Rome (as a result of the World Council of Churches) and there were negotiations between various church groups within the world-wide Anglican communion.

ASSEMBLIES OF GOD 1950-55

The 1950s were a mixed decade for the pentecostal movement. New buildings were constructed, new churches were opened, the Bible school recovered from the war years, useful administrative changes were made, pentecostal broadcasting began and several large campaigns were held. On the other side of the coin, there were internal disputes, shortages of money, certain pettinesses and troubles in the bookroom. What makes assessment of the solid achievements of the decade more difficult is that reporting and publicity through *Redemption Tidings* became more sophisticated with the result that some of the campaigns which, at the time looked highly significant, may, on reflection, have accomplished less than at first appeared. In addition, with hindsight, it is clear that the pentecostal movement as a whole was unprepared for the charismatic movement of the 1960s. This unpreparedness showed itself in a lack of flexibility and an inability to distinguish pentecostal traditions that were biblical from those that were superficial and arbitrary. In some respects the doctrine of separation, which was equated with holiness, had been used to justify isolation, and isolation prevented the warm relationships and rapid changes associated with the sudden interdenominational burgeoning of the charismatic movement in the 1960s.

The Bible School at Kenley was established by careful and skilful handling of complicated legal and financial arrangements. The Executive Council took charge of day-to-day decisions, and the General Council approved whatever measures had been taken on its behalf. Good will and good sense prevailed and the institutional side of Assemblies of God was seen at its best in carrying out the detailed plans. The site of the School was attractive and Gee's own reputation as a Bible teacher was internationally recognised in pentecostal circles. There was no other man of comparable calibre to take the Principal's job and Gee's support in Britain was extensive because he had not neglected preaching in the United Kingdom. As time passed Gee's annual report to the General Conference continued to show an improvement in Kenley's financial position and student intake; by 1952 Gee had introduced a two year course and by 1953 it was filled by 36 residential students.

Wisely Gee decided to retain the lecturers who were in place when he took Kenley over. Elisha Thompson had worked at the School nearly all his life and he and his wife lived on the premises, which was a convenient arrangement because Mrs Thompson was the matron. L F Woodford and C L Parker were visiting lectures. Gee taught John's Gospel, a series on the Attributes of God, Homiletics and Pastoral Theology; Thompson taught Isaiah, Church History and a course entitled Modern Heresies; Parker dealt with the Gifts of the Spirit and Divine Healing; Woodford covered the Person and Work of Christ and Hermeneutics and a Miss Kelly taught English Grammar. Troubled brewed when word got out that Parker was not teaching according to the fundamentals of Assemblies of God. Parker's position, which is stated in a book he had published at his own expense, was that the Great White Throne judgement described in the Book of Revelation (ch 20 v 11f) will be a place where those who in their normal earthly life have never heard the Gospel may be able to respond affirmatively and so be eternally saved[1]. Parker believed that those who would have accepted the Gospel if they had not had a chance to hear it before death will, at this eleventh hour, accept it. His position was therefore not universalistic, nor does it obviate the preaching of the Gospel at this present time, but it simply suggests that God will not damn people on the basis of their ignorance of the cross of Christ. Instead Omniscience reckons saving faith to exist where it would have existed in other circumstances.

Parker was widely known and respected in Assemblies of God and he had been associated with the School since its very early days. On two occasions (in 1951 and 1953 - see Executive Minutes 133.4e and 150.5f) Parker had tried to sell and advertise his book *Foundation Truths* [1] within Assemblies of God and the Executive had banned it. The ban implies that his book had been read and disliked, though no action was taken against Parker personally. In 1954-5 this changed. The Bible School, having become an institution which functioned within Assemblies of God, was now under the jurisdiction of the General Council. Any member of the General Council - and this included all the recognised ministers - might raise the matter on the floor of the General Conference. In 1954, arising out of the Principal's report, "the Board of Governors was instructed to investigate certain complaints concerning doctrines taught at the Bible School" (General Conference Minutes 1954, 17.a). So, the next year, the Governors reported to the General Conference,

> The General Secretary [John Carter was a member of the Board] presented the special report of the Board of Governors arising out the enquiry into the doctrines taught at the Bible School. It was stated that the Governors have experi-

enced considerable embarrassment owing to the fact that the terms of reference were not clearly specified and the implementing of the GC resolution had proved to be a most difficult and delicate task. In the opinion of the Governors the doctrines taught by C L Parker are contrary to the generally accepted interpretation of our Fundamentals, even though they may not be a denial of the Fundamental Truths, and their unanimous decision was that these doctrines must not be taught in our Bible School. The Governors expressed full confidence in Elisha Thompson. The report was accepted with grateful thanks. The Conference endorsed the decision of the Board of Governors that these doctrines must not be taught in the Bible School and the Principal gave an assurance that he would call for the resignation of C L Parker from the teaching faculty. (G C Minutes, 1955, 17.a)

C L Parker was present at the time and he decided to fight back. He did this by making use of the 12 man Court of Appeal. Within a month Gee had written to Parker asking for his resignation, but by November of the same year a plenary session of the Court had been called to discuss the issues arising out of Parker's appeal. The Executive Council discussed the matter and decided that John Carter should be present at the hearing in order to oversee the "constitutional aspects of the case" (EC Minutes, 163,7). In January 1956, Carter reported to the Executive. He had obviously changed his mind on the propriety of the matter because, in his words, he had "protested against the Court's legality to hear the Appeal, and also against its refusal to allow a representative of the Executive to attend the Plenary Session called to discuss the Constitutional aspect" (EC Minutes, 164, 7).

Parker's defence was slightly technical: he "argued that the Governors had been authorised to investigate 'complaints' and not 'doctrines', also that their mandate was to 'investigate' rather than take action". The Court seem to have accepted part of Parker's plea because "it was the opinion of the Court that the Governors had 'widened the issue at stake' and 'created a precedent that could eventually lead to an unduly restricted interpretation of our Fundamental Truths'" (EC Minutes, 164,7). The Court then decided that the matter should be discussed again at the General Conference. This appeal by the Court of Appeal to the approximately 250 ministers of the Conference went over the heads of the Governors. Among the Governors were at least four members of the Executive Council who decided to bring a counter proposition to the General Conference, namely that the Court of Appeal's terms of reference be clearly defined.

In the 1956 Conference this is what happened. It is not clear what arguments were used, and by whom, but the eventual conclusion of the Conference was that "the Court of Appeal erred in judgment in hearing the appeal of C L Parker and therefore rejected that portion of the report dealing with this matter" - this, however, only taking place after the Court had presented its findings and had asked for a reconsideration of the whole question pertaining to Parker. After finding themselves judged to be in error, the members of the Court placed themselves at the disposal of the Conference and were all given a vote of confidence. As a last ditch stand, Parker made a speech to the Conference as a whole asking that Minute 17.a of the previous year be rescinded. After considerable discussion, Parker was not granted his request. Such are the labyrinthine toils of constitutional procedures when one section of a body fights against another. Nevertheless, Parker did managed to speak to the members of the Court of Appeal and the Conference as a whole and, from this point of view, the constitutional procedures did allow a proper airing of the issues. Parker may have lost his job, but he stated his case at several levels and, had he been able to persuade the majority of the Conference, both the wishes of the Governors and of the Executive would have been overturned. What, of course, was less serious, but anomalous, was that the Court of Appeal, having "erred seriously", should be returned to office with a vote of confidence. But another inconsistency was to follow: in 1963 Parker was elected to the Board of Governors. Parker always explained his removal from the faculty and his election to the Governing Body as an example of the divine sense of humour!

The argument between the Court of Appeal and the Executive Council may be seen as part of the general bureaucratic restructuring which was going on at this period. Though it is easy to criticise such changes as the manoeuvrings of committees, many of the alterations were sensible and helpful. The dispute between the Court of Appeal could be cyncially viewed as a power struggle, but it would not be accurate to do so because the Court only met as necessary and there was no intention in the minds of those who elected men to the various positions on the two committees which function each had. There was never any chance that the Court of Appeal would usurp the role of the Executive or that the Executive would constantly overturn the judgements of the Court.

Admittedly the new General Offices at Newington Causeway

where the General Treasurer, the General Secretary and the Editor of *Redemption Tidings* were all housed did have the effect of centralising the administrative functions of the churches. Yet there were not many administrative functions to exercise. An attempt to set up a corporate pension scheme came to nothing because ministers were not prompt in sending in their contributions. Publishing ventures were fairly unadventurous because money was short. Very often the only large scale investment was in hymn books. Efforts to produce literature for Sunday Schools were never successful and eventually individual churches were asked to order what they wanted directly from the Assemblies of God in the United States - it proved impossible to ship the material over and then print a British cover onto the booklets.

The basic tensions of the period were between those who were prepared to change and those who were not. As an outcome of this tension, there were - often temporary - shortages of money and disagreements on fairly minor matters. The early pentecostals were mould-breaking men and women; many of the post-war pentecostals were either unaware of the pressures and persecutions felt by the previous generation or inclined to accept the status quo unthinkingly. An editorial in *Redemption Tidings* (15 Aug 1952) pointed out how some assemblies made no effort to evangelise or publicise their activities and Nelson Parr in 1954 (*Redemption Tidings* 5 Oct) stressed the use of various methods to attract a crowd and build up a congregation. Such an approach was liable to be criticised as being unspiritual: Harold Horton wrote an article "The Pentecostal Show Goes On" (*Redemption Tidings* 11 Sept, 1953) in which he attacked the use of lurid and dramatic stories of conversion as a means of livening up a presentation of the Gospel and, for good measure, he wrote to the Executive to complain about the use of the title "Rev" in front of the names of some pentecostal ministers; Horton was a believer in the plain unvarnished truth as an advertisment for itself. Parr, on the other hand, was happy to press showmanship into any proclamation of Christ. Oddly enough both men were unconventional in their personal dress and neither could be called a conformist. For Parr, the important thing was "by all means to win some"; for Horton, showmanship disguised a failure to engage in the power of the Holy Spirit and spoke of latent carnality.

When the General Conferences began to change in character after the war as families of ministers began to attend for their holidays, one minister took exception to dancing at after supper meetings and a District Council took exception to unnecessary spending on Sundays.

The Executive on their own initiative decided to ask those using the swimming pool to be modestly dressed (EC Minutes 145 17.e; 168 17). Here are indications of friction between "holiness" as traditionally understood by the earlier pentecostals and the modernity of a gradually prospering Britain. Prospering or not, though, pentecostal ministers could find themselves short of money. Ministerial wages which were not centrally determined, but dependant on the generosity of individual congregations, tended to stick at pre-inflationary levels. The failure of the pensions scheme spoke of a shortage of ministerial funds. Alfred Webb wrote to the Executive asking them to put something in *Redemption Tidings* about the low pay ministers received (EC Minutes 146 16a). Gee wrote a piece for April 10th, 1953, in which he suggested that many men were expected to work for £6, and some for less. As a later financial crisis at the end of the decade showed, it was hard for those who had learnt attitudes to money in the 1930s to adjust to the constant rise in wages and prices which underlay the economy of the 1950s. And, where money might buy less than expected because of price increases, it was hard to be prudent. The church needed to expand, and expansion cost money, so that radio broadcasting, for example, or crusading, or overseas missions - which were all aimed at expansion - might not realise immediate or tangible expansion in one's own back yard. To fail to meet the challenge of broadcasting would be foolish and would put the Assemblies into a ghetto mentality; yet to spend a small fortune on radio might delay the consolidation of local churches. It was a fine balance where faith and prudence struggled for mastery. One of the lasting impressions of the decade is of variety and unevenness. The impact of pentecostal crusades is described below, and perhaps the reason that they received the attention from pentecostal churches that they did was that, in many places, progress was dull and slow. What happened in local churches varied from congregation to congregation. True, W T H Richards was enjoying growth at Slough and Miss Fisher and Miss Reeve were happy with their growth at Hockley. Other pastors spent their efforts on established congregations (like Doncaster) and their most obvious successes were seen in the still-popular Easter or Whitsun conventions. Tell-tale comments in editorials, however, show that there was another side to the picture. "Alas, it is not too common to see a fresh face in our midst....often the advent of a visitor is an 'event' to be talked about with excitement" (*Redemption Tidings* 25 Sept, 1953). How successful, then, were the crusades and conferences?

1. <u>Foundation Truths</u> was published (privately ?) around 1952 with a preface by George Newsholme. In it Parker dismisses the view that the Great White Throne judgement will inevitably be one of condemnation on the grounds that it must address "those who have been born during the Millennium" (p 37). In discussing the principles behind this judgement, Parker states that God will take into account "not only what one did, but what one would have done under happier circumstances" and here he refers to Matthew 11.21-24 where Christ states that the condemnation of Korazin and Bethsaida will be greater than that issued to Tyre and Sidon because these cities *would have* repented if they had seen the miracles and signs performed in the region of Galilee.

The World Conferences

In 1952 the third World Conference of Pentecostal Churches met in Westminster Central Hall, London from June 27 till July 5th. More than 1400 delegates and observers from thirty nations took part.

It was a hot summer. Delegates were busy from morning to night. There were conference sessions in the morning and preaching meetings in the evening. The first Saturday a large open-air service was held in Trafalgar Square and a photograph shows men with their jackets off and women in summer dresses forming a crowd round the fountains as an international party of speakers preached the Gospel. On Monday the business session proper began and after some procedural hesitancy launched into the theme of missions. By Wednesday the plight of pentecostals in Italy was on everyone's lips and a decision was taken to appoint an advisory committee to make representations to various government departments with a view to changing the situation. Catholic priests had broken up Italian pentecostal meetings by using laws against religious freedom dating back to Mussolini's regime. The conference agreed to appoint ten days of prayer and fasting later in the year to buttress the decision, though one delegate, perhaps with typically misplaced spirituality, expressed the opinion that persecution was good for the church and that nothing should be done.

The pressure, prayer and agitation brought about by the conference on behalf of the Italian pentecostals was one of the most obvious success of the entire gathering. Another was less concrete. The *Elim Evangel* reported that what particularly impressed one of their correspondents (R B Chapman) was the breadth and importance of the pentecostal movement in several countries. An ex-Congressman from the USA, doctors and highly competent linguists were as notable to him as the different languages and skin colours of the participants. This implies that British pentecostalism had not reached the governing and academic echelons of society as it had done elsewhere.

There were two other administrative matters of importance. David du Plessis resigned as paid and full-time secretary to the pentecostal movement world-wide. The large number of people in attendance at the conference was largely due to his hard work and extensive travel. He was about to begin his extraordinary ministry among the historic churches in an effort to open Christian eyes to the work of the Holy Spirit today. For such a ministry he felt it necessary to be attached to no official body and to represent no specified grouping. The welcome he received from Episcopalian, Presbyterian and Roman Catholic churches was still future, and there is no doubt that his resignation, though a surprise and disappointment to those who heard him make it in 1952, saved enormous embarrassment to classic pentecostals whose views of Catholicism were in general hardly less apocalyptic than Luther's.

The other thing that occurred was the appointment of a temporary committee to plan the next pentecostal conference at Stockholm in 1955. This was a more delicate task than appeared because of the strongly held belief by the Scandinavian pentecostals that local churches were all that was to be found in the New Testament. Denominational groupings were anathema to the Scandinavians and so they strongly resisted the smallest suggestion that pentecostals might be forming themselves into a megachurch with a headquarters which wielded authoritative control. Five men were selected by ballot: Donald Gee, Lewi Pethrus, Leonard Steiner, Noel Perkin and Roswell Flower. Pethrus was Swedish, Steiner Swiss, Gee was English and Perkin and Flower came from the States (though in fact Perkin was an Englishman originally). Gee was also asked to continue to produce the magazine *Pentecost*, a mark of the esteem in which he was widely held.

The 1955 Conference, held in Stockholm, was more reflective. Among other things it asked speakers to review the history of the pentecostal movement and to ask bluntly what God was trying to achieve through the movement. Gee, in a later review of the gatherings in *Pentecost* (Sept 1955), thought the ten speakers, each from a different country, contributed words of wisdom and knowledge from ripe experience: "minds were enlightened, hearts were inflamed, spirits were subdued, faith was strengthened, hope was increased and love was enlarged". The actual business of the conference was relatively light. The position of Italian pentecostals had improved because they were no longer at quite such a severe civil disadvantage in their own country - though they were still not allowed to officiate at marriages or to propagate the Gospel or to claim charitable exemption from local rates. In Spain twenty pentecostal churches had been shut down and in Columbia 43 pentecostals had been killed and 100 evangelical schools had closed. The committee on religious liberty, therefore, had a continuing task and the improved situation in Italy could be partly put down to its vigilant activity during the three preceding years.

Reports in *Redemption Tidings* (5 Aug, 1955) and in *Pentecost* underlined the size and variety of the crowds which attended. More than 12,000 people filled the vast marquees and even more countries were represented than previously (officially 34). The English delegation seemed to have enjoyed the choral singing and seeing the large church buildings, especially where Lewi Pethrus produced his Christian daily newspaper with a circulation of 60,000.

The conference at Toronto in 1958 was a success, but less fulsomely praised. It was slightly smaller than Stockholm, though this was probably partly due to the greater distances Europeans would have had to travel to attend. About 9,000 people seem to have converged on the National Exhibition grounds and they came from forty countries. There were Eskimos, a Zulu, French, Germans, Swedes, Poles, Ukrainians, Yugoslavs - even a Lutheran bishop from the Latvian church. Both the Sunday services were broadcast and a Canadian MP welcomed the conference on behalf of Prime Minister Diefenbaker. There was a great deal of singing of various kinds and old friends met each other gladly. John Carter reported on the proceedings for readers of *Redemption Tidings* (17 Oct, 1958) and the same issue carried two articles which had originally been preached to the delegates. Carter's report mentions a "fine message" by J A Synan of the Pentecostal Holiness Church. The conference had been called to consider God's purpose "in the pentecostal movement for this hour" and Synan and enunciated the inspiring view that pentecostalism was a divine work, greater in size than the Methodist revival of the 18th century, and more dynamic than the Reformation, that had been raised up to confront the "fearful apostasy of our day" and, at the same time, to prepare the whole church for the millennium. There may have been nothing new in this proclamation, at least nothing new to the veterans of British pentecostalism, but it was refreshing to hear a respected man from another branch of the pentecostal movement come to conclusions so similar to those held by Boddy or Stephen Jeffreys.

On the Tuesday Donald Gee spoke on "the pentecostal experience", and in the afternoon Luther Turner (of the Church of God) expounded the doctrine of the Return of Christ. That evening there was a divine healing service. The following day about 50 pentecostal editors assembled for a men's breakfast. This in itself showed how well established and widespread pentecostal news and doctrine had become. The combined readership of the 50 magazines must have been considerable and, indeed, whenever statistics were collected it was apparent that pentecostalism was becoming the fastest growing section of Christendom. Growth was fuelled by Oswald J Smith's sermon on "literature evangelism" and Douglas Quy's "radio evangelism" two days later.

In summary the conference seems to have concluded that pentecostal churches must continue to grow by any and every means and that the essential doctrines of pentecostalism needed no revision. One of the main benefits of the world conferences was that they helped different branches and sections of pentecostalism to understand and respect each other.

Radio broadcasts

The BBC put a pentecostal service on the air in 1952 (July 2nd). A psychological barrier was broken that morning. Until that time the religious establishment in Britain had shunned pentecostalism. It was rare to read a favourable notice of any kind in the religious press, but when the BBC, which still reverberated with the solemnity of the era of Lord Reith, accepted an ordinary pentecostal meeting as part of mainstream Christianity, the confidence, and perhaps the self-esteem, of pentecostals all over the country grew. Within two years plans had been made to hire air time on Radio Monte Carlo. These plans were overtaken by events because, before they could be put into effect, American Assemblies of God offered their weekly half hour slot on Radio Luxembourg to British Assemblies of God. Despite the similarity of name, the two sets of churches were organisationally and constitutionally quite distinct. The offer was therefore unforced and, when it came, the British perceived it as providential. A hundred pounds a week were needed to finance each broadcast and John Carter, in an appeal to the British assemblies, described it as the biggest thing they had ever undertaken.

From small and slender beginnings the AoG in Britain began to produce programmes of increasing length and quality and by 1957 a Gallup Poll showed that there were up to four hundred thousand listeners to "Revivaltime". In the first two years nearly five thousand letters were received by the station and when, eventually, the programmes came to an end after five years it was because of a change in Radio Luxembourg's scheduling brought about by the new listening habits induced by televison transmissions. As the TV broadcasts closed down at about 11 pm, the hour till midnight became attractive to commercial radio producers, and so religious broadcasts were pushed back till the early hours of the morning when audiences were minimal.

After appointing a Radion Production Committee in 1954 Assemblies of God formed a Radio Council in 1956 to communicate the Gospel in Britain. Radio seemed to suggest a way into the future, it was modern and lively, and reached greater numbers of people than the largest public meeting. If Assemblies of God had failed to accept the financial and technical challenge of making radio programmes, it would have betrayed a failure of nerve and turned its back on one of the things it did best - preaching. Yet, of course, radio is a diffuse medium, and as with all electronic media, there is a danger that the broadcasters will lose touch with the ordinary and everyday life of the church. The scandals surrounding the TV evangelists in the USA in the late 1980s illustrate these dangers. When a new breath of the Spirit blew through the churches in the 1960s, radio was not in the vanguard of these changes, nor did it cause them. It was a tool, a channel of communication, and a signal of the willingness of British AoG to preach Christ in any way it could; but it was not in itself an agent of change.

Sunday School

There was a "baby boom" from about 1945-1948 and these children reached Sunday School age in the early 1950s. Despite an unwillingness to attend church for themselves, many parents were very happy to send their children to Sunday School. The annual events associated with Sunday School like the seaside outings in the summer, or the autumn prize giving service for good attendance, or the carol singing at Christmas time, were seen by the church as an opportunity to create good will in the community and perhaps to preach to the parents. In American Assemblies of God there was an enormous emphasis on Sunday School work in the fifties and huge conferences were held to train Sunday School teachers and to equip writers of Sunday School teaching materials. British AoG attempted to import these materials for their own use, but there were practical problems in placing a British imprint on anything copyrighted abroad. Attempts to solve the problem by making use of overprinted Elim material ran into the same kind of obstacles and eventually local assemblies were encouraged to buy directly from the USA through the AoG bookroom in Luton; but the volume of orders soon put a strain on the bookroom staff, and a 10% handling and administrative charge was agreed by the Executive in 1953.

Sunday School conferences were arranged by District Councils in 1952 and reports appeared in *Redemption Tidings* (24 Oct, 1952). One report noted controversy about visual aid and another highlighted a vigorous discussion on ends and means. Reading between the lines it seems likely that there were different views on the appropriateness of using modern teaching methods in Sunday School classes. The younger men, it seems, were likely to favour new methods while the older ones rejected anything more fanciful than they had known in the 1930s. Where Sunday Schools were made a major part of church life, however, they were large. Dagenham, under Alfred Webb, recruited a staff of 66 who taught an average 350 children per week (*Redemption Tidings* 11 Sept, 1953), and both W T H Richards and Misses Fisher and Reeve largely built their congregations on bursting Sunday School attendance. If the organisation was successful, Sunday School children would graduate to a lively youth meeting and eventually into the church and any keen young men and women could find an avenue for service as School School teachers or youth leaders.

The National Youth Council

In 1953 as a result of discussion at the General Conference of that year the Executive Council started to approach various men to serve on a National Youth Committee. J N Parr, despite his age, was a sensible choice. Bethsham Tabernacle was then probably the most thriving pentecostal congregation in the British Isles and made a policy to attracting young people. Parr, Bethshan's pastor, encouraged the use of drums and saxophonists in his meetings and, although his tactics were occasionally criticised for being worldly, there was no denying his evangelistic success. W T H Richards was also approached. The church at Slough was growing fast and Richards' combination of hard work, spirituality and humour was valued by all those who knew him. L A Cunningham was involved (from a 1952 GC decision) in the setting up of a magazine for young people and so he, too, was an obvious candidate.

Nevertheless the work of the committee did not go entirely smoothly. In 1954 Parr asked the Executive Council if the funds generated by a regional youth rally organised by the Lancashire District Council could be handed over to the new national Youth Committee (EC mins 153 13 c). The Executive declined to overstep what it saw as the legitimate sphere of its authority. When, in 1955, the General Conference voted members onto a National Youth Council, Parr's name was absent from those selected. Richards and Cunningham remained in the work, and three other men were added (E Davies, A F Missen and Colin Whittaker) but Parr either stood down or failed to receive the necessary two thirds majority. The old committee which had been appointed by the Executive was replaced by a larger group responsible to the General Conference. In addition the mandate of the new council was slightly different from that of the old National Youth Committee because, instead of concentrating mainly on youth rallies, the council was intended to foster and encourage Sunday Schools and only to co-ordinate national and regional youth rallies organised by others. It may be that Parr felt himself better employed elsewhere. Early in 1955 Richards resigned from the new council. All this was a pity. Parr and Richards often felt restricted by official councils, and their leadership qualities functioned best in the setting of a local church.

Crusades 1950-55

The most obvious tactic by which to renew the pre-war successes of the pentecostal movement was by holding revival campaigns. The Executive Council of Assemblies of God was aware of developments in the United States and could see that a new generation of "healing evangelists" was coming to the fore. Oral Roberts, William Branham, Jack Coe and T L Osborn were beginning to hold large tent meetings and Roberts, particularly, was known to have attracted enormous crowds on the Californian coast. *Pentecost* (Dec 1950, p 5) carried a report on North America which said, "it is no longer an unusual thing for 15,000 to 20,000 people to turn out to the tent campaigns towards the second and third week of such meetings". By May 1951 an invitation had been sent to Roberts by the Executive Council of British Assemblies of God asking him to come to England (EC mins 133 7d). There was a delay because the message did not seem to get beyond Roberts' manager and finally, when a reply came, it pointed out the difficulties the evangelist would have in transporting his equipment across the Atlantic and the further difficulty he would have in raising financial support for his work outside his home country as a consequence of government restrictions on the transfer of currency from Europe to America.

In the summer of 1952 and at the invitation of the Midlands District Council of Assemblies of God, A C Valdez, a less well-known American evangelist, preached twice a day for a fortnight in Nottingham. More than 2,000 people responded to the Gospel appeals and "it would be impossible to catalogue all the different wonderful miracles; many were instantly delivered from being deaf, and dumb; the blind saw, goitres disappeared, deformed limbs were straightened immediately, internal disorders removed, the lame walked, ruptures disappeared, demons were cast out, etc" (*Redemption Tidings* 18 July, 1952). At the same time, Howell Harris was campaigning in Newcastle-upon-Tyne. Similar results were seen, though on a smaller scale. In both places the local assemblies grew and a picture of twenty-two baptismal candidates all dressed in white appeared in *Redemption Tidings* the following month. In October of the same year, Gordon Cove - once a student at the Hampstead Bible School under Howard Carter - preached for three weeks in a large crowded tent in Birmingham and counted 250 "hands raised for salvation and reconsecration".

In 1953 the same trend continued. In January Valdez preached in Leicester at the Congregational Church, spacious enough to seat 650 people. Photographs show Valdez to have been a stocky dark haired man, probably about forty years old. John Phillips, who was to become a distinguished Bible teacher in Assemblies of God, described what happened,

> satisfying my anticipation, Mr Valdez at last made his appearance. I can't say quite what I had expected, but he was so soft spoken, gentle, unassuming, his whole personality won me at once. The congregation was won too; everybody was at home. As he preached, or perhaps I had better say, talked to them, nothing could have been simpler, no message could have been more easily understood. When the appeal was made the greatest miracle of the night took place. Scores of hands were raised in every quarter of the building. Soon a crowd of almost 200 was standing before the platform. Then they knelt upon the floor whilst the pastor pointed them to the Lord.

After this, Valdez prayed for the sick.

> a deaf person stood before our brother. He laid his hands upon deaf ears, prayed, and then exclaimed, 'There it is!' The sufferer's face lit up. 'Can you hear me' questioned Mr Valdez in a whisper, 'Oh yes, sir' replied the once-deaf man....and so it

went on, case after case. I don't recollect one of these deaf folk leaving the platform undelivered. (*Redemption Tidings* 27 Feb 1953).

More than twelve hundred people made decisions to follow Christ. The AoG Home Missions Council was stirred to make a financial appeal by these scenes and later accounts show it to have begun its own campaigns. Meanwhile, Howell Harris continued his activities. Despite his age, Harris was a persuasive evangelist with a genuine concern for the ill and infirm. In Watford in April there were regularly 200 people in attendance at his meetings. Valdez, however, moving on to Newport, Monmouthshire, began to preach to crowds of 2,000. "Folk who remembered the 1904 revival wept and said 'It is 1904 over again'" (*Redemption Tidings* 10 April, 1943). Many of the 1,600 converts returned to the churches from which they had lapsed, but there was considerable growth in the numerous pentecostal assemblies of South Wales.

News reports in *Redemption Tidings* made encouraging reading. The extraordinary story of the Hebridean revival was given two full pages in the same issue which contained photographs of Valdez at Newport. By the time the General Conference in May was held a proposal had been put forward that a committee of inquiry be set up to investigate "the whole technique of these campaigns" (GC mins, 1953, 22). The proposal was discussed without any decision being reached. A month later the Free Trade Hall, Manchester, and the nearby Albert Hall were packed out by two youth rallies. Altogether more than 4,000 people were congregated in the two halls. The inspiration behind the whole venture can probably be traced to Nelson Parr and a young man, Colin Whittaker who was later lead the way in a new generation pentecostal books, was responsible for much of the organisation.

Harris continued to campaign in Lancashire and Wales and, during the summer, Gordon Cove went to the Shetlands where he saw miracles. A lengthy article by Billy Graham asked the pertinent question, "What is holding back revival ?" (*Redemption Tidings* 14 Aug, 1953). Despite these signs of spiritual life, the long-awaited revival did not come. The desire for revival was an understandable one, but it is not clear whether revival was seen as a short cut to church growth, a sudden windfall of souls, which would make all the uphill pastoral work suddenly run smoothly downhill. To the pastor in a small church, a revival seemed the answer to all his prayers at once. But a quick analysis shows large congregations tended to be gathered round men with organisational and pulpit ability - though Hockley was an exception to this. W T H Richards criticised this sort of impractical dream of revival by writing to *Redemption Tidings* saying

> There has been for some years the preaching of an 'ideal' relative to evangelism. A high sounding ideal, a supernatural and miraculous 'ideal' leaving no room for human initiative or venture. It goes something like the following, 'what we need is a mightly move of Holy Ghost power in our midst. Away with the so called "methods" to attract sinners

but he went on to ask and point out

> Why don't we hear criticisms along the lines of methods relative to Divine healing today ? I have seen sick people who were punched, shaken, massaged, told to march up and down the hall and do exercises, etc. One brother says he has the power of healing in his left hand and another says he has it in the right. Well, we read nothing in the old books to warrant these methods, but if it works then no one seems to mind, but if a preacher adopts unorthodox methods to preach the gospel which work and gets people saved then there is a tirade of criticism against him....men with a passion for souls who have adopted methods and means for preaching the gospel have always been criticised (23 Oct, 1953).

There was, then, a tension between the wish that every blessing, every step forward, every increased congregation, every good sermon should come directly from God and, on the other hand, the desire to adopt methods, techniques and structures which caused the same results. But, as Richards pointed out, methods and techniques in the sphere of divine healing seemed permissible; in the sphere of evangelism, they were frowned on. This does not seem to have been due to any theological standpoint. AoG pastors were not Calvinists when it came to evangelism and Arminians when it came to divine healing. The problems seems to have stemmed from a conception of what was, and what was not, worldly. It was worldly to be systematic or methodical in evangelism. Divine healing, where the preacher claimed divine inspiration for his particular mode of praying for the sick, was spiritual. Some preachers, as Richards pointed out, thought that they could feel the healing power of God in one hand rather than another. Other preachers - notably William Branham - called out by revelation the various diseases that people in a meeting were suffering from and then prayed without asking anyone to leave their seats. Most of the other preachers asked sick people to form a "healing line" or to sit on specially reserved empty chairs at the front.

The debate between methods and divine sovereignty was thoroughly aired in *Redemption Tidings* after Donald Gee had written an article about the much greater success Swedish pentecostal churches had enjoyed as compared with British ones. Returning from the Stockholm Conference in 1955, Gee had dismissed various theories explaining the health and prosperity of Swedish churches. Church government, which admittedly differed slightly from the British norm, could not be held responsible: both countries stressed the autonomy of the local congregation and, though the local assemblies in Britain were more obviously bound together by constitution than the Swedish ones, the differences in practice were small. Nor could the preaching in Swedish churches be nominated as the cause of Swedish growth. British preaching, on average, so it seemed to Gee, was as good as that heard anywhere in the world - and he pointed to the welcome that British preachers almost always received when they preached abroad. Nor could it be said that Swedish pentecostals had avoided opposition and controversy. On the contrary, their difficulties in these directions were at least as great as those experienced by the British. The only answers Gee could accept were these: firstly, the Swedish pentecostals had a much lower tolerance of oddity than the British - church discipline was altogether tighter; and secondly, the Swedes were much more evangelistic than the British, or rather each congregation was evangelistic, and there was less reliance on campaigns and special speakers to do the job.

A series of letters took issue with Gee. George Jeffreys disagreed with Gee's diagnosis in its entirety and stated that the slow growth in Britain could be blamed on pentecostal disunity. Benny Finch said "there is a deplorable number of assemblies that have no outside witness or evangelistic effort at all" (16 Sept, 1955), while Swinburne Smith complained "England is a gospel-hardened country....we need another John the Baptist...a unique visitation of God" (30 Sept, 1955). D H Macmillan also thought that Gee was wrong and that what was required was a period of intense self scrutiny. Keith Munday blamed the dearth of solid expository preaching. George Canty suggested that neither Sweden nor the USA had undergone the horrors and deprivations of war and that this, together with the British national character, had been responsible for unspectacular growth. Alfred Missen thought that the subject was important enough to merit a full day of discussion at the AoG General Conference. Gee later summarised the debate and rounded it off in a separate article. The general unwillingness to accept Gee's original conclusions does indicate the lack of trust that lay under the surface of pentecostalism. Jeffreys' wholesale rejection of Gee's views is sad and Gee may have been referring to him when he pointed out that a number of contributors seemed to have been riding their own hobby horses instead of addressing the question. In the end, it seems, very little of great value came out of the debate. Those who believed in methods continued to use them; those who wanted to wait for a divine visitation, continued to wait.

In 1954 and again in 1955 Billy Graham came to England. Assemblies of God advertised the meetings and carried photographs in its magazine. The size of the whole undertaking completely dwarfed previous evangelistic thrusts and, although pentecostal churches were happy with the direct Gospel preaching, they were not without their own dissenters. In an editorial in *Pentecost* (March 1954), Gee was glad to record that "the writer is one, among other Pentecostal leaders, who has been invited to supply workers for the Campaign. He, and some of his colleagues similarly approached, have been happy to accede to this welcome gesture" especially in view of the fact that "there still remains a hard-core of stubborn prejudice against the Pentecostal Movement in British Evangelical Circles". But, as he also noted, "even this limited participation in Dr Graham's Campaign has met with criticism from a few ardent Pentecostals". The suspicion felt by evangelicals towards pentecostals, and by some pentecostals towards evangelicals was generally swallowed up by the success of the campaign itself. It was apparent, though, that pentecostalism could not rival the massed ranks of the other protestant churches in evangelistic effectiveness. In the USA, Roberts and others could attract crowds as big as those drawn by Graham. In Britain this was not the case and the pentecostals found themselves wondering whether their contribution to Christian life would be as a fervent sub-group within the folds of the major denominations or whether they could still hope to retain their separate identity and outgrow and replace the declining Methodists and Baptists.

Meanwhile Howell Harris and the AoG Home Missions Council continued their own attempts to build congregations and establish churches. Harris was at Plymouth in the September and after a week drew 600 people to the Guild Hall. In November he was in Manchester at the Co-operative Hall and packed it out. Fred Squire collaborated with AoG and preached at Hastings the same month and George Oldershaw in Plymouth. Selwyn Hughes wrote a series of articles on evangelism in the Spring. Peter Scothern campaigned at Sheerness in the summer. The pattern continued. Harris was at Fleetwood, Buxton, Kendal and Glasgow in 1955. Sometimes he started a campaign which other ministers completed. In December 1955 *Redemption Tidings* (9 Dec) reported on the opening of four new pentecostal churches and three new halls. Altogether in the years 1950-55, about twenty-four new places of worship were opened. In the same six year period 113 assemblies were received into AoG, during which time 37 left or closed; in total there were 483 assemblies in AoG by the end of 1955, 332 full ministers and 76 probationers (figures from GC minutes).

Despite spiritual growth when most other Christian groups were diminishing, F R Barnes (then Conference Chairman) firmly believed that the pentecostal churches were often blighted by superficiality. "In every assembly today, there are those who have been with us for 15, 20, and 25 years, and I hang my head with shame as I see the lack of spiritual growth in their lives" (*Redemption Tidings* 19 June, 1953). By implication it was the ministers who carried the greatest blame: "how many sermons preached today", he asked rhetorically, "are based upon a personal knowledge of the Scriptures ?".

Gee, in an anonymous column regularly contributed to *Redemption Tidings* under the name of "Circumspectus", thought that "it is the unspectacular regular ministries that are producing the permanently spectacular results....this is not to disparage the work of the big campaigners...the paucity of permanent accessions to the Church through these immensely publicised efforts is not necessarily or entirely the fault of the evangelists" (21 Jan, 1955). Adding up the balance sheet after half a decade of varied evangelistic campaigning, Gee concluded that the big crowds and the publicity failed to deliver long-term results, or long-term results which could be translated immediately into more and bigger churches.

Creaks and groans

The sober judgements of Barnes and Gee were coloured by their knowledge of the creaks and groans within the British pentecostal assemblies as a whole. They knew of the immobile and often small-minded prayer groups - the "tiny little circle: 'our church, our family, our home and me'" (Barnes, *Redemption Tidings* 19 June, 1953). They also knew of the pettinesses which could mar local assemblies. Trouble in one seaside town occurred when an assembly split in two and both halves claimed the use of the same building (EC mins 150 14). Then there was the occasion when the editor of *Redemption Tidings* (which had a circulation of over 9,600 copies per fortnight) had to ask the Executive Council's permission to buy a typewriter (EC mins 150 5b), which in retrospect, seems a paltry request for the individual concerned to have to make and also to indicate that the Executive's spiritual leadership occasionally descended to the sort of minutiae which in a local church would have been delegated to the diaconate.

There were also other problems. The autonomy of each local church could lead either to a shortage or to an oversupply of trained ministers. Both extremes are reflected in the Executive Council minutes; in January 1950 there were 47 assemblies without leaders and in July 1955 there were 80 ministers (excluding retired missionaries) without pastorates. There was a shortage of money in 1951 (there was not enough money to paint the general offices), but this had gradually improved by 1955 and the overdraft whittled down to £800, equivalent to approximately one annual salary. The General Treasurer, nevertheless, was still asked to travel round the District Councils to acquaint the ministers personally with the situation. Constitutionally, and by virtue of emphasis on autonomy, the Executive Council could not levy a charge on each assembly. Funding for centralised projects had previously been supported by profits made from *Redemption Tidings,* but once this was accounted for in the payment of an editor's salary, it was difficult for the General Offices, and the Executive Council which had the biggest hand in running them, to raise large sums of money. Some pastors, of course, were quite happy about this because they did not wish to see the power of the Executive Council increase and so, when assemblies gave money to ventures outside the local context, it was much more likely to be in the direction of foreign missions or the lively Revivaltime radio broadcasts featuring Nelson Parr than to anything remotely administrative.

Indications that all was not well with the overall linkage in Assemblies of God are to be found in the complaints about failure to attend District Council meetings. In theory these should have taken place about once a month and should have been a useful and encouraging gathering of all the AoG ministers or church representatives in a limited geographical area. At their worst District Council meetings became a drudge, and a divisive drudge at that, while, at their best, they were a genuine expression of fellowship coupled with business likc collaborative efforts. In 1950 one minister resigned because, as a result of a General Conference decision, his non-attendance at District Council meetings would have led to his being excluded from fellowship - presumably he was in danger of losing his ministerial status (EC mins 126 4b). The mere fact that attendance at District Councils - rather than attendance at the General Conference - was elevated to a criterion by which membership of the AoG ministerial list was to be judged shows that some ministers had fallen into the habit of ignoring and avoiding their DCs. Five years later the position had not improved greatly, and the Executive Council placed on the General Conference agenda an item relating to "the difficulty that is being experienced in many DCs of securing the necessary quorum to transact business" (EC mins 164 15). There were two typical scenarios which developed at bad DC meetings. Either one dominant personality ran the proceedings while the remaining ministers sat back in a bored and passive manner or, alternatively, several middle-aged preachers who had emphatic views on a variety of subjects publicly disagreed with each other on matters which, in the long run, were often trivial and about which the younger men cared very little. Procedure was conducted along parliamentary lines and proposers, seconders, resolutions, votes and minutes were all part and parcel of the meeting. Young men, unless they had a peculiar aptitude for the niceties of business, had difficulty in understanding what was going on and a later generation of pentecostal ministers were only too ready to change the format.

Redemption Tidings (30 Jan, 1953) carried a letter under the editorial saying

> In our Movement there are towns where Assemblies have been opened, holding their meetings in very small halls or even private houses. These have never grown and apparently have no vision, yet that town is barred from any effectual witness. In some cases the town contains men and women with a passion for souls, and these are driven to launching out independently or joining a movement with evangelical fervour.
>
> Would it not glorify God for those in charge of any such Assemblies to stand down in favour of younger or more suitable men?
>
> The writer did this and in two years the numbers increased from 35 to 130, and what joy he has when souls are added. The

Righteous Judge will not overlook those who put *Souls* before *Self*.

There are at least two implications of this letter. The first is that there were very many small pentecostal meetings which had stagnated largely because unsuitable men had elevated themselves to positions of leadership. Second, these small churches might well grow properly if the men who hung onto office had the sense to see that they were only motivated by a desire for the limelight. When Fred Newcombe pointed that "one of the problems now frequently being brought to our attention is that of Ministers forbidding any manifestations of the gift of Tongues in certain kinds of meetings, particularly gospel meetings" (*Redemption Tidings* 24 June, 1955) it is evident that pentecostalism in some quarters was feeble and unevangelistic.

Moreover there was sometimes a lack of clarity, even among the leadership of the movement as a whole, about the type of church government it had adopted. Gee (in his anonymous column "Circumspectus") had described AoG as being congregationalist, but Aaron Linford (who was later to become a member of the Executive Council and a long time editor of *Redemption Tidings*) pointed out that there was considerable variety in the method by which local AoG assemblies were governed, and all that could be said to be common to them was that they were self-governing. Some were in the hands of elders, others of deacons, some were looked after by trustees and a few were directly under their District Councils. Yet this self-government was not absolute. A question put to the 1952 General Conference, "Does the autonomy of an assembly preclude the District Council from taking action when the internal policy of government of an assembly permits or condones in its members or officers conduct prejudicial to the testimony of the Fellowship ?" was answered that, in such circumstances, District Councils had the authority to take on the oversight of a wayward assembly.

But disagreement between Gee and Linford, polite as it was, showed that even well informed men could interpret the same Constitution differently. John Carter thought that misunderstandings could be widespread enough to require an article in *Redemption Tidings* (25 Nov, 1955) explaining the beliefs, origination and form of government of Assemblies of God. Thirty years had passed since the 1924 meeting in Birmingham which issued in the formation of the Assemblies of God. A new generation had grown up that was unaware of its roots. What the new generation apparently knew that it did not want was the re-introduction of the permanent office of Chairman such as had been held by Howard Carter (GC mins 1950 6a). The concept of national leadership was still thirty years in the future and anyone who filled Carter's supervising role was feared as someone who might compromise the autonomy of local assemblies. An editorial in *Redemption Tidings* (9 May, 1952) touched the same theme by contrasting the Christian individualists who "must run their own show at all costs" and those who naturally turn to other people in an expression of fellowship. So far as George Newsholme (then editor) was concerned, it was team workers who better fitted the prescriptions of the New Testament.

Divorce

"Divorces reached a peak of 60,000 in 1947, ten times the pre-war figure. The passing of the Legal Aid Act two years later opened the possibility of divorce to many who had previously been deterred by the expense. By the middle fifties there were about 25,000 divorces a year" (Marwick, 1982: 64).

To those who had been brought up before the war, the high rate of divorce was almost personally offensive and indicative of the decline in British morals. Inevitably, the question faced the assemblies. Should pentecostal ministers marry divorced couples in their churches? Should pentecostal ministers themselves be allowed to divorce and remain in the ministry? Should divorced men be appointed as deacons?

Aaron Linford wrote to the Executive Council in 1952 and pointed out that a divorced minister was chairman of one of the District Councils. The Executive Council reacted with due regard for what it felt was constitutional propriety. Linford was thanked for his letter but told that the matter would be better raised by the District Councils themselves rather than an individual. Linford was also told and that some proof concerning general feeling in the movement as a whole on the matter ought to be given (EC mins 143 11d). This is a curious comment because it implies that the Executive were unwilling to act unless propelled into doing so by a ground swell of popular opinion. Yet this implication is probably correct: the Executive wisely did not wish to be contentious or, indeed, to legislate and, as a result, its leadership was occasionally muted.

In 1954 the South Midlands District Council asked that the matter of the divorce and re-marriage of AoG ministers be discussed at the General Conference. As a result a select committee comprising John Carter, Donald Gee, George Newsholme, T S Parfitt and James Salter was asked to bring the matter to Conference the following year. This they did and a copy of the report was presented to each minister for personal consideration. There was deliberately no debate on the document and this must have been in order to prevent potentially disruptive argument. Only in 1968 and 1969 did the subject re-surface. The 1954 document reported "divergencies of personal opinion based on differing interpretations of Scripture". The members of the committee could not agree how the word translated "fornication" in Matthew 5.32 and 19.9 should be understood. Should it refer to pre-marital sexual experience or to adultery ? In the end the committee set out the various views and ended by noting that "there will always be especially involved cases which must be decided upon their own merits".

Overseas missions:
Postwar continuation

Once Hitler had been defeated and life began to return to some sort of normality the Missionary Council farsightedly attempted to lay plans for the post-war world. The Council thought that a greater sense of direction and a closer liaison with the local churches was needed and so invited Donald Gee to fill a new position as missionary overseer, but he turned the offer down (OMC mins 11 May 1945), and the post was never offered to anyone else. The Council therefore streamlined itself by reducing to seven members and ensured that a field survey be given at the start of most meetings. The concentration of missionaries in Britain in the period 1943-47 allowed the Council to take up-to-date and detailed advice about living conditions, climate, problems, possibilities and achievements in each country. By this means the Council could hope to make its judgements on the basis of the best available information.

Remittances to the fields in May 1948 were almost exactly £1400, the lion's share going to China, £621, and India, £244. In May 1938 the overall remittances to the various fields had been just over £250. By comparing the number of places to which money was sent in 1938 and again in 1948, it is clear that the smaller fields had been abandoned during the decade. There is no remittance to Korea, Brazil or Spain in 1948 as there had been earlier. The attempt to plant churches in Brazil had been abandoned, however, mainly because a lively pentecostal work had already been established there by other groups. Spain, of course, was shut up under Franco and Korea was without missionary candidates.

The post-war world was a different shape from the old 1930s world. Commercial air travel made the new world smaller, but the Iron Curtain and the cold war, as well as nationalism in Africa and the Indian subcontinent, produced barriers with which the colonial powers had not previously had to contend. Delegations from the Missionary Council were able to travel out to India and China and, on their return,

> it was agreed that the situation [in Yunnan] called for a fresh lead on the part of the OMC on clear and defined lines. There were distinct weaknesses revealed, characteristic of the work on both the China and India Fields, and these demanded serious attention and the initiation of appropriate steps towards remedying them (OMC Mins 11 March 1949).

In India, however, the Liveseys continued to make progress. Their greatest need was for reinforcements and two couples, the Crooks and the Gilmores, joined them in 1946/47 and took over nearby districts. The Liveseys themselves lived in an isolated area but, apparently by chance, they were asked to dress the wound of a man who had cut himself on a scythe and this led to a string of visitors requiring medical help. Every morning a queue would form outside their home and they would dress abscesses and tend sores and pray for people and, by this means, gain an entrance to the villages where they were then able to preach and teach. Margaret Livesey in her little undated book *Together With God* relates to several outstanding miracles of healing. There is little doubt that the supernatural power of Christ was able to make inroads within Hindu communities which were subject to the all the superstitions attendant upon primitive idolatory. It was the specifically pentecostal character of the work which was the hallmark of all the successful missionary endeavours with which Assemblies of God was connected. W F P Burton and Douglas Scott would have underlined this point in Africa and Europe respectively. Eventually the Liveseys retired in 1954 and left behind churches and Bible schools which function to the present day.

When Gee looked back on AoG missionary work he was able to survey the scene from nearly thirty years of personal involvement. He was a realist and pointed out that Assemblies of God had often demonstrated commendable zeal without equal prudence "it is sad to relate that many thousands of pounds were wasted in ventures doomed to futility for sheer lack of policy" (*Redemption Tidings* 29 Jul 1960). By 1960 the China fields had closed, but those in India, Japan and the Congo remained open. Japan, of course, was affected by the 1939-45 war, and the Congo was to be troubled by the bloodshed which accompanied independence in 1960/61. To Gee the aim of missionary work was to establish self-governing and self-propagating churches under national leadership. Only in the Kalembe field in Congo and in India was this achieved. What happened in China from 1949 onwards was violent and evil. Chairman Mao was a monster on the same scale as Stalin - and the extinction of missionary work there was no fault of the missionaries or their supporting churches in the British Isles. Indeed, it may be that Chinese Christianity has survived the ravages of the Cultural Revolution and the Red Guards and is alive and well, though whether there is any continuity between the efforts of AoG missionaries in the 1930s and 40s and current Chinese Christianity may never be known.

According to Woodford (in an undated taped interview with Alfred Missen c 1965) the success of missionary work in China, however, vindicated the indigenous principle. In his view, only two fields really succeeded in establishing a network of co-ordinated churches under indigenous leadership - these were in Kalembe (where Douglas Scott had been) and throughout the area operated by the Congo (now Zaire) Evangelistic Mission. His analysis of the work in India suggested that, though there had been excellent individual efforts, as a whole leadership on the field had been lacking in the formative years. He saw the early years 1924-31 as being disappointing, even disastrous, and the era 1931-45 as being one of progress and consolidation, while the post-war period saw an increase in all fields[1].

Over the years from the start of Assemblies of God in 1924 there were undoubtedly heroic and self-sacrificing individuals who "forsook all to follow Christ". The early years were haphazard. The HMRC simply attended to affairs at home without trying to exercise a directive function while the missionary worked abroad. Later, when the HMRC became the OMC (the Overseas Missions Council) greater efforts at co-ordination and concentration were made, but, as we shall see, in the late 1970s and early 1980s missionary work diversified and increased, aided particularly by fast travel and a renewal of emphasis on personal financial support for each missionary.

Note to Page 256

1. W F P Burton wrote <u>God Working With Them</u> (London: Victory Press) and it was published in 1933. His account of the extraordinary growth of the Congo Evangelistic Mission emphasises miracles and answers to prayer. There were numerous healings in the Congo, and these healings confirmed the truth of the Gospel to those who heard it.

The relationship between Britain and the Congo missionaries was as follows:

> Let it be clearly understood that all instructions concerning the work, all arrangements as to workers and their duties, all authority and responsibility as to carrying on the testimony, are vested entirely in the missionaries themselves.

> How many hundred missions have been handicapped by the fact that a home council has had the direction of the work. Men in their arm-chairs and their offices have dared to direct the operations of a mission, in a field which they have never seen and under conditions of which they know nothing.

> The CEM missionaries have realised that those on the spot are the ones who know conditions and are best able to meet them. Hence all authority as to the work is vested in those on the field.

> On the other hand, there are many problems as to receiving and training new candidates, preparation of outfits and diretion of missionaries on furlough which cannot be regulated from the field, and these are the matters which have been put into the hands of tried and tested men and women in the home-land, that they may advise and counsel the missionaries on the field.

> To the present all such positions have been honorary. Until his death in April, 1932, Mr Myerscough occupied the post of responsibility in the home office which is now occupied by his son. (Pp 254,255)

The CEM was always independent of Assemblies of God, but it is interesting to see where Burton placed the decision-making function. It was on the field. This leads us to ask whether AoG were mistaken in their methods during the Woodford years.

It is not possible to answer this question properly without taking note of the role played by the Field Councils which did, as far as one can tell, take decisions on the field which were vital to the direction of the work. Burton himself made decisions about the development of the CEM, but Burton was a very exceptional man and it is possible that, in other cases, it was necessary to vest leadership in a Council of Missionaries rather than in a single man.

ASSEMBLIES OF GOD 1956-59

New developments in unexpected places

During the 1950s there were faint indications that the charismatic movement - which held dear the experience of the baptism of the Spirit integral to pentecostalism - was beginning to take shape. Although it was far from clear in the period from 1955 to the early 1960s, there were several unspoken assumptions that underlay both the attitude of the classic pentecostals to the charismatics and the opinion most charismatics entertained of the pentecostals. In general the pentecostals expected Christians in the old denominations who spoke in tongues to be expelled from their own churches and to find a home in the pentecostal churches. After all, this had been the basic cause for the setting up of pentecostal churches in the first place. John Carter, long-time General Secretary of Assemblies of God, wrote in January 1958,

> People from every denomination - Episcopalians, Presbyterians, Baptists, Methodists, Brethren, etc. - hungry for God's best, and, having received, they returned home to witness to their churches and chapels to their new-found experience. They wished others to share in the great joy and blessing that had come to enrich their own lives, but they found, to their surprise and dismay, that, in the main, great opposition greeted them.

> The result is that many of us were forced out of the churches which had given us birth. We were told that 'these things are not for today, they were for the early church', consequently the experience we had received was unscriptural and must be rejected (*Redemption Tidings* 17 Jan, 1958).

Undoubtedly, in some Christian groupings, history repeated itself. Brethren and Salvationists especially, found it difficult to remain in their own denominations. But Anglicans and Methodists had less of a struggle. There came into existence, therefore, a new kind of Christian, and one not seen since the days of Alexander Boddy. Tongues-speaking Christians in non-pentecostal denominations began to be more common. The phenomenon did not gather force till the early 1960s, but what was done in the 1950s set the pattern for the 1960s. If all the

Christians who had received the gift of tongues in the 1950s had immediately joined the classic pentecostals, particularly Elim and Assemblies of God, then there would almost certainly have been an exodus from the traditional denominations in the 1960s. As it was, the men who found themselves speaking in tongues in the 1950s, men like Edgar Trout the Methodist and David Lillie from the Open Brethren, or Don Double and Peter Scothern did not immediately make efforts to join with the established pentecostals. Scothern, it is true, wavered on the brink of Assemblies of God for a while, and applied for ministerial status some time before 1958, but the others were disinclined to make their allegiance with any one denomination. In the case of Lillie this was because of his strong convictions about the shape of the church: he did not want to be part of an ecclesiastical organisation which, in his view, went beyond the bounds of the New Testament. Lillie and Arthur Wallis (who did not speak in tongues till 1962) had hopes for a restoration of full and free congregational life, possibly supervised by apostles, rather than for revived denominations or untidy evangelistic campaigns. In addition Cecil Cousen, who had been a member of the Apostolic Church until he parted company with it in 1953, was unwilling to be involved with any pentecostal group which in his view lacked the power and vitality of the pentecostalism of the 1920s. His disagreement with the Apostolics arose over credence to be given to the north American Latter Rain movement, a movement which emphasised the ministries of contemporary apostles and prophets. Cousen, then, having suffered at its hands was not willing to become entangled with denominational pentecostalism and Lillie and Wallis, because of their Brethren ecclesiology, were also unwilling to join an existing denomination or, in the years that followed, to start their own[1].

The state of Assemblies of God: troubles

While the charismatic movement was barely visible, Assemblies of God continued to grow and develop in the final years of the 1950s. It progressed along the lines laid down previously. It did not change its doctrine or style or methods of work although there were far-sighted individuals, most obviously Gee, who asked questions which implied uncertainty about the fundamental identity of the movement. If we ask whether Assemblies of God could have been more ready to welcome the charismatics, the answer is probably "yes". The trouble was that Assemblies of God (and, no doubt, Elim) were completely unprepared for Christians in the older denominations to start speaking in tongues. There was no time for the classic pentecostals to court the charismatics. The classic pentecostals had problems of their own and had, over the years, become isolated from many other Christian groups. Moreover the charismatics, by and large, tended to be more affluent than the pentecostals and to have ideas of holiness which were vaguer than the separatist tradition of pentecostalism. The old-style evangelicals of the 1930s, of course, were inclined to be stiff and starchy, but the newer recruits of the charismatic movement were freer and easier. Michael Harper, who was converted as a Cambridge undergraduate in the 1951 (See Robinson, 1976: 131) did find his Christianity rather hedged about with a lists of "thou shalt nots...", but as the charismatic movement gained momentum the social attitudes of the charismatics did not easily mix with the more restricted views of the pentecostals. It was not just a matter of social habits - charismatics I knew were quite happy to take a glass of sherry before Sunday lunch; pentecostals would have blanched at such a prospect - but it was also a matter of preferences in worship. Charismatics were accustomed to good organ music, pentecostals tended to reflect the musical tastes of the 1930s, or even the Moody and Sankey revival at the beginning of the century and made do with pianos.

If Gee posed the fundamental questions (as we shall see), others also pointed at weaknesses in Assemblies of God. C Bond, then editor of *Redemption Tidings* wrote "let us beware of the paralysis that is creeping though our ranks today, and stupefying our holiness into mere loyalty" (10 May, 1957); Aaron Linford asked, "how many churches suffer from dictatorship from men whose positions can only be held by force! How many assemblies suffer from irresponsible elements in its membership because it lacks leadership of the New Testament order!" (22 Nov, 1957); less than a year later, Linford made an editorial plea for assemblies to care for their pastors (14 Mar, 1958) and at the General Conference that year John Wallace, the Conference Chairman, saw a need for pentecostals to repent: there were members of pentecostal churches who had not been baptised in the Holy Spirit and who had never heard any of gifts of the Spirit and "there are signs that we are more self-conscious than Christ-conscious". Wallace was perturbed because he saw the pentecostal revival settling down, becoming humdrum, and losing the essential experience which made its doctrinal emphasis real. Keith Munday (1 Aug 58) pointed out that "it is unfortunately true that thousands of Churches have been strangled of their spiritual life by formalism. Organising their worship in such a way that virtually forbids any moving of the Holy Spirit...let us as Pentecostals, however, be ever vigilant lest we unwittingly get entrapped by formalism - yes Pentecostal formalism!". And two years later Linford said editorially

> Doctrinally we are sound, numerically we increase in strength, we cut a finer figure in the ecclesiastical world - but where is the spontaneity, the ebullience, the sparkle, the intensity ? It appears in patches and snatches, but we long for it in fullness once again (*Redemption Tidings* 26 Feb, 1960).

Munday again made the point which gives an indication of where the heart of the trouble lay, "some of our acutest problems in the Church at the present time are not how to get souls saved, or the sick healed, or how we can get the message to the nation. Some of our greatest difficulties are in the relationships between Minister and Minister, worker and worker, Council member and Council member!" (*Redemption Tidings* 27 May, 1960). A picture emerges of a group of churches where relationships in some sections had broken down, or were held in check by strict etiquette, and where, as a result, routine and formality had replaced spontaneity and life.

It was in matters of finance that stresses and strains could become most visible. The late 1950s saw rapid wage inflation. The wages of pastors did not keep pace with the average levels of pay in society. Pastors did not watch wage norms with an eagle eye and the deacons in their churches who settled ministerial pay were rarely business men with an awareness of the speed at which wages and prices were changing. If a local congregation found that its offerings had increased, it was not often that anyone's first thought was to pay the pastor better. It was more likely that the deacons would consider a building programme. In 1955 the general finances of AoG were bad enough for the General Treasurer to have to travel round the various district councils explaining that more money was needed for central projects. But by 1959 the AoG Property Trust had loaned about £14,000 to 13 assemblies[2] for new or extended buildings; the money was never spent on pastoral salaries. In a letter to *Redemption Tidings* Keith Munday pointed out that the AoG was financially hard-pressed and he pleaded for 2 pence per week for each member in order to keep the Revivaltime radio broadcasts on the air[3]. It is impossible to analyse the accounts of each of the 500 or so assemblies individually, but it seems that towards the end of the 1950s, when there was some spare money in people's pockets as a result of the "you've never had it so good" Macmillan years, that various appeals were made to the Fellowship for projects over and above the normal departmental needs. Individual pastors may have suffered from the diversion of funds - certainly there is evidence that some ministers were not sharing in the prosperity of the rest of Britain[4] - while the traditional appeal of missions continued to capture the hearts of mature church members. Over £8,700 was raised in fifteen months to send to the Congo[5] and £2,600 was sent in a Christmas offering to missionaries in 1958[6], while by contrast, only an extra £199 came in to the General Offices as a consequence of the agreement at General Conference that 1% of each assembly's annual offerings should be donated in this way.

In January (24th) 1958 John Carter took the unusual step of writing about AoG finances in *Redemption Tidings*. His analysis makes sense. He pointed out that the General Offices had moved from Luton to London in 1953 and incurred £3,910 of expense that year. Part of this expense related to the purchase of two houses in London, as well as to legal fees and the costs of redecoration and renovation. In addition extra clerical and other staff were employed and office overheads like telephone bills and stationery costs went up. All might have been well but for the printing dispute in 1956 and the increased price of postage. Profits from Redemption Tidings and the Bookroom, which had been earmarked for the bank overdraft, were turned into an unexpected loss. The assemblies were asked to give a minimum for £5 each and this would have realised £2,500 which was half the total sum needed to clear the deficit. The rest could come from contributions by the various departments making use of the General Offices. Of course, the departments did not like this and the levy made on them strengthened the case for decentralisation. It is doubtful, however, whether in the long run decentralisation would have been cheaper because the administration of mail and money could not have been done by an unpaid local church treasurer or secretary. Whichever local church had offered office space to a department would eventually have charged rent to the department concerned and this would have produced administrative costs similar to those engendered by a shared General Office for the Fellowship as a whole.

One problem led to another. The loss made by the AoG publications forced the Bookroom to pay low wages and therefore hire inexperienced staff[7]. Inexperienced staff did the job inefficiently and made matters worse. They also caused problems for other staff whose responsibilities lay with other departments.

The most prolonged, and the most public, dispute within Assemblies of God took place as a result of the appointment of a Select Committee to look at finances. It is not clear from the records when this Committee was appointed, but a reference to its activities occurs in the Executive Council Minutes (8th March 1956, item 6). In this instance the salary level of three centrally paid men was recommended. John Carter, as General Secretary, was to receive £8-10s a week with a rent free house, Henry Jessup, as the editor of *Redemption Tidings* was to receive £8 with a rent free house and Mr Hubble, as General Treasurer, was to receive £8 a week and 30 shillings a week for travel and meals. These salaries can not be said to have been generous, though because of the poor payment of many pastors they may have appeared so. The average weekly earnings for a manual worker in 1956 is reported as £11-17-11[8]. John Carter, with a house for which he was not financially responsible, was probably in receipt of slightly under that of the average manual worker. His wages were certainly below those of the average coal miner (in 1956 at very nearly £15 per week[9]). Considering Carter's age and responsibilities, his remuneration looks low; there were three basic reasons why such payment was tolerated: firstly, the long tail of underpaid pastors found it hard to respect and vote for a man who was paid a great deal more than themselves, secondly, relatively low pay prevented anyone offering themselves for John Carter's job for pecuniary motives, and thirdly, there was a tradition in Assemblies of God, dating back to Howard Carter, that ministers should "live by faith", and this tended in practice to mean on what they received from preaching, and thus John Carter's *guaranteed* income appeared privileged.

At the 1957 General Conference it was decided to appoint a committee of three pastors with experience in business to co-operate with the Executive Council and look at the chaotic[10] state of the AoG Publishing House. The following year Edward Astbury presented their report. He pointed out that some members of the committee wanted to look into the running of the General Offices but they had kept strictly to their terms of reference because objections had been raised to their doing otherwise. Nevertheless as a result of discussion at the Conference a Select Committee of five members was elected to "investigate all the administrative affairs of the General Offices and Publishing House, and that it be authorised to take whatever action it deems necessary" (GC Mins, 1958, 14). This Committee was made up of Robert Barrie, the only member of the Executive, Edward Astbury, A E Friday, Bernard Porter and Joe Richardson[11]. They were given a very wide mandate by the Conference and, of course, the mere fact that they had been appointed had slightly sinister or hostile implications. What was wrong with the General Offices that a special committee needed to give a clean bill of health? Some pastors had an exaggerated sense of congregational autonomy and were therefore disinclined to favour offices and officers who might attempt to gain control over the churches. They were much happier with the prospect of various councils, each running its own affairs, under different roofs. Indeed, there was resistance to the prospect of a General Treasurer who had oversight of all the various accounts in the fellowship, even if this could be shown to be a more efficient and cheaper way of handling the finance. The Select Committee therefore started its work in a polite but frosty atmosphere.

Friction between the Select Committee and the Executive Council was apparent by October that year (EC mins 8th and 9th Oct, 1958, item 7, from which the quotations below are taken). A "special emergency meeting" where representatives of various AoG councils had been present was held on 5th September 1958. The Select Committee had recommended various constitutional changes and *directed* that a temporary General Treasurer should not be appointed. They refused a "united meeting" [which seems to be another meeting between themselves and the Executive and representatives of AoG councils] and, instead, were ready to make themselves available to the Executive for the answering of any questions which the latter had submitted in writing in advance. They expressed amazement at the Executive's "flagrant disregard of our requests concerning the managership of the Publishing House, and view such open defiance of our resolutions with grave disquiet". They also asked for and insisted upon the immediate acceptance of Mr Hubble, the General Treasurer's, resignation and informed the Executive that "the Radio Producer should deal with Revivaltime correspondence and thus eliminate the necessity to employ further staff". For its part the Overseas Missions Council recommended that, in view of the gravity of the memorandum issued by the Select Committee, an Emergency General Conference be called.

The Executive Council meet the Select Committee's demands coolly. The General Treasurer was asked to continue his work till the end of the year and the Committee was "to be informed of the reason why R J Jerrett had been asked by the Executive to become the Manager of the Publishing House". From one of the District Council's (North Lancashire) a letter arrived saying that the Select Committee were "mandate drunk" and urging the Executive to stand up for their own constitutional rights, that is, their rights under the Assemblies of God constitution.

Analysis of this material suggests that the Select Committee were concerned to save money by dispensing with a General Treasurer and by forbidding the Radio Council from employing further staff despite the Producer's unwillingness or inability to cope with his correspondence without secretarial help. Another item in the EC minutes (8th and 9th Oct 1958, item 8b) throws more light on the contention. Mr Hubble, caught in the crossfire between the Executive and the Select Committee, was keen to return to pastoral work. He felt that the Select Committee was acting according to the wishes of the General Conference by asking him to leave. The Executive, on the other hand, argued that it was simply a more vocal section of the Conference which was opposed to Hubble's appointment and that only one man particularly had strongly expressed the view that the Home Missions Council would prefer to manage its own financial affairs rather than pay a percentage towards the support of a General Treasurer.

The Executive met the Select Committee and a report of the meeting is given in the Executive minutes (12th and 13 Nov, 1958, item 9). They agreed to differ over the mandate which the Committee had received from the General Conference. The Executive maintained that there was never any intention that "the internal workings of the office Council were to be interfered with" - a conclusion that does not accord with a strict interpretation of the General Conference minutes which, as we have seen, allowed the Committee to "take whatever action it deems necessary". Both parties agreed to wait till the General Conference to clarify the mandate. They then dealt with other matters. L F W Woodford complained that the Committee had investigated his department (Overseas Missions) while he had been visiting the Congo. The Committee replied that this was not so. Following this the Committee answered John Carter's question about the unnecessary checking of professionally audited accounts; Bernard Porter wondered whether the books had in fact been audited since discrepancies had been discovered. The slight fell on the competency of the auditors; no one subsequently doubted that the books had been audited. The meeting then descended to disagreement. The minutes of the first Select Committee meeting had been sent to the Executive (as a matter of courtesy) but, in the Executive's view, one of the minutes had been incorrect. The Select Committee refused to alter the minute or to discuss the matter. Its members also failed to send any further minutes to the Executive. Instead the Executive was simply notified of the

Select Committee's decisions.

By January of 1958 the North Lancashire District Council had written to the Executive suggesting that a letter be circulated to all the other District Councils with the proposal that the activities of the Select Committee be brought to an immediate close (EC Mins 8 and 22nd Jan 1958). This suggestion was the only way of revoking the General Conference mandate without calling a special or emergency General Conference. There was, however, no unanimity among the Executive on the matter, which does imply that some members of the Executive were in favour of such a step. The EC minutes also record that Edward Astbury, one of the members of the Select Committee, wanted a copy of Mr Hubble's resignation statement sent to every DC to remove unrest. Rumours had circulated that Hubble had been forced out of the General Treasurership by the strong arm tactics of the Select Committee. It appears from the minutes that the Executive simply acknowledged Astbury's letter but did not act on his suggestion.

The Select Committee also gave notice of its intention to investigate every department at the General Offices and pointed out the date when visits would be made. In the meanwhile John Carter reported that he had met Richardson and Friday and "found them in a conciliatory mood" - the implication being that their previous mood had been aggressive.

Eventually the Select Committee report was completed and presented at the General Conference. Much of the Select Committee's concern was with money. Its members were of the opinion that staff salaries at the General Offices should be fixed by a Salaries Committee appointed by the General Conference; they thought that all staff should be paid through a General Wages Book and that staff should clock on and clock off each day; they were in favour of bulk buying to obtain the best rate on stationery and they wanted all orders to be countersigned; they wanted all postage stamps to be bought by the General Treasurer and details of postage to be entered daily into a postage book[12]. The report itself was duplicated and given to each member of the General Conference but, before the Conference as a whole adopted the document, it was decided that everyone who had been implicitly or explicitly criticised should have a chance to express themselves. John Carter spoke to the assembled ministers for some length on "matters affecting the Executive Council and his own Department. As the business session proceeded, it became evident there would not be time for a full discussion" (GC mins, 1959, 16a). At last a resolution to accept the

Select Committee's report without endorsing or condemning it was carried and, at the same time, it was agreed that the Executive and the Select Committee meet once more to implement those items on which they both agreed. After that the period of service of the Select Committee was terminated.

The report is well written and comprehensive and runs to twelve foolscap pages. Despite its clinical tone, there is undoubtedly a thread of criticism against John Carter and L F W Woodford and, to a lesser extent, against the other members of the Executive. For example we are told "it is our considered opinion that the Executive Council erred....."[13] on the appointment of C Bond as editor of *Redemption Tidings* on Henry Jessup's death. There is also criticism of the time keeping at the General Offices: people arrived between 8.55 and 9.35 am and on some days Heads of Departments did not come in at all. On others they came in at lunch time, missed a day in order to lecture at the Bible school, and then returned the following lunch time. The target here was L F W Woodford. But Carter came in for similar flak. His shorthand typist was seen washing the office door and Carter himself, because he sat on so many committees[14], was thought to give insufficient attention to his work as General Secretary for which he was paid. When Woodford was absent abroad on missionary work, Carter stood in for him. The report records verbatim questions and answers between Carter and the Committee. It is clear that the Committee thought that Carter was paid too much, failed to do his work efficiently and had his finger in too many pies. The other way of reading the interview shows Carter to be underpaid for his enormous responsibilities and overworked because he was greatly trusted[15]. Perhaps the kindest reading of the evidence suggests that the Committee came to the General Offices with preconceived ideas about business practice and were appalled to find amateurishness where they expected professionalism. Nevertheless, given the system which produced General Secretaries and General Treasurers from among those who had spent much of their early life as pastors, and who had already demonstrated a clear call to ministerial life, it would be odd indeed if preachers should, at the giving of a Conference vote, suddenly turn into expert desk-bound administrators. Moreover, the running of Assemblies of God had begun in a small, back-room way and there was still the legacy of informality and brotherliness about the whole enterprise.

The implied criticism of L F W Woodford was similar to that of John Carter. Woodford was thought to be paid too much (£11 per week, with an interest free loan on his own private house) and to be doing a job which was not really full-time. The proof of the fact that the Overseas Missions department could be run part-time was that it had been handled by Carter when Woodford was in Africa for sixteen weeks. The Select Committee wanted Woodford to take over the running of his own accounts after the disbanding of the General Treasurership. This Woodford adamantly refused to do, nor did he feel obliged to keep office hours since he was not "an employee of the Movement". Woodford had been looking after Overseas Missions since 1938 and did not take kindly to the prospect of having to alter his working pattern after running things the way he wanted for twenty years. His refusal to accept the changes desired by the Select Committee must be seen as an unwillingness to have his job description redefined by men he felt were going beyond the wishes of the General Conference.

Criticism of the Radio Council Department ran along the same lines. Hedley Palmer, the radio producer, was thought to be doing a job which could equally well be done part-time and for which he probably did not need a secretary. It was only *Redemption Tidings* run by Aaron Linford which escaped the Committee's censure. "We are of the opinion", they wrote, "that considering the appointment is the first of its kind for Mr Linford that he is doing the job conscientiously[16]". Undoubtedly Mr Linford was conscientious, but the point at issue is why the Committee did not apply the same criteria to Mr Linford as to Mr Woodford. After all the, the editorship of the magazine had been done on a part-time basis previously.

The underlying burden of the Committee's anxieties can summarised in their question to Aaron Linford, "Would you not think that for such a Fellowship as ours, being one which is not centrally governed, that our costs are far too heavy for us?"[17]. This was an impossible question for Linford to answer since the costs of a set of central offices could easily have been met if the Assemblies had been willing to send about 1% of their own annual offerings to a general fund. American Assemblies of God seemed to have little difficulty in affording excellent office facilities, but the danger was, as the American experience showed, that bureaucratic red tape could stifle individual initiatives[18]. And a similar tension was remembered nearer home when the Elim Pentecostal Church had been involved in a dispute with George Jeffreys, its earliest leader[19].

In the case of British Assemblies of God, the contention between the Select Committee and the General Offices was not really one between a charismatic committee and a staid and bureaucratic management system[20]. It was really a dispute between two fairly similar groups, both claiming authority from the same Constitution. Although the problems were expressed partly in terms of personalities, it is likely that the General Offices did need reform. The Movement had grown since the days when John Carter had run its affairs from his typewriter. Too little thought had been given to the structure of the administration and to the duplication of effort and resources. There probably was money wasted and the Select Committee did a service in calling attention to shortcomings and muddles. If any criticism can be made of the Committee members, it is that their rationale was too narrow and not theological enough. Their understanding of correct business practice seems to date back to the 1930s rather than forward to the 1960s. They had no conception of "flexi-time", open plan offices or managerial roles[21] that would have been much more appropriate to their recommendations than the book-keeping style of comments which they made. On the other hand, the Executive could have been accused of failing to provide spiritual leadership to the Assemblies and of failing to be radical enough in their idea of how the Fellowship ought to develop. The General Offices were thought to be convenient because they brought all the departments into one building[22], but there is little evidence that communications between departments improved because they could meet daily and there is a general impression that each department did what it wanted without a great deal of regard for the others. Autonomy was the AoG watch word and that was carried over into life at the General Offices. The Committee wrote "in view of the continued insistence of the departments to remain as isolated units within '51' [that is the General Offices] it is the opinion of this committee that the General Council should seriously consider the appointment of an Honorary General Supervisor for the building to hold a watching brief over the whole establishment to see that the wishes of the General Council are carried out so that efficiency with economy is assured" (p 12). This recommendation may be said to have been unconsciously fulfilled in 1988 with the confirmation of Basil Varnam's appointment. He became the first AoG Administrator.

The state of Assembles of God: triumphs

There were three notable areas where Assemblies of God saw progress in between 1955 and 1960. These were in the work among young people, at the Bible College and in the maintenance of the radio Revivaltime broadcasts. The Home Missions department was also successful though this success was less well documented than it had been in the 1940s when the scheme was started. Assemblies of God certainly increased its numbers of churches in the period. The table below expresses this growth

YEAR	NUMBER OF ASSEMBLIES	MINISTERS	PROBATIONARY MINISTERS	DELEGATES
1954	475	338	63	91
1955	483	332	76	100
1956	486	326	77	113
1957	506	372	52	79
1958	506	364	60	75
1959	509	355	68	80
1960	511	384	53	64

(These figures are taken from General Conference Minutes)

In percentage terms, there was an increase of 5.7% in the number of assemblies between 1955 and 1960. Since most other Christian groups were declining in that period, the figures here are notable[23]. Yet, they belie what had taken place at the start of the decade. In 1950 11 assemblies were added, in 1951 there were 16 additions, in 1952 there were 13 and in 1953 there were 11. Growth between 1950 and 1955 was at the rate of 13.9%, which is over double that in the second half of the decade.

The number of ministers and probationary ministers stood at 82-85% of the number of assemblies. This means that roughly 80 of the churches had no full-time minister[24] in the period under review. This figure is reflected in the number of delegates in the table. Under the AoG Constitution each assembly had the right to be represented at District Councils and the General Conference. Usually this representative was the full-time minister, but where the congregation could not afford a full-time minister, or where they were looking for a new minister, a representative could be chosen from the body of the congregation. The 80 or so churches without a full-time minister is indicative of a weakness at the fringes of the pentecostal flotilla. If the growth of AoG had been smooth one would expect the new assemblies added each year to be small and unable to afford a minister for about 18 months. The result would have been that the number of assemblies with delegates would have been approximately equal to each year's growth. But this is clearly not the case. Growth was counteracted by wastage. Some assemblies were disbanded, others merged and others left AoG or, in rare instances, were expelled. There was a hard core of about 350 healthy assemblies and then there was a group of perennially weak assemblies and another group where genuine growth took place. The sudden jump in the number of ministers between 1956 and 1957 is probably explained by the effectiveness of the Bible College in preparing men and women for the ministry.

The National Youth Council

The work among young people was graded according to age. Sunday schools were encouraged and aided by literature bought in from American Assemblies of God. Teenagers were treated separately in the most go-ahead churches and special arrangements were made. Sometimes a Friday night youth meeting was convened. Elsewhere a Junior Church (which was a transitional meeting between Sunday school and adult services) was organised. Some experienced ministers opposed youth meetings on the grounds that these split congregations or pandered to the young. Yet few could deny that the large numbers of children who dropped out of Sunday school and church life in their early teens pointed to a deficiency in the structure of most assemblies.

The National Youth Council advertised and arranged rallies and summer camps and preached a full-blooded Gospel message to the young people they attracted. Adolescents were challenged to surrender their lives to Christ and many did so. At one rally in Newport in September 1958 the veteran Congo missionary Teddy Hodgson spoke. He was a man who had fought in the 1914-18 war, faced lions in Africa and established 163 churches there. His tales of adventure and danger were authentic and he challenged the young to follow Christ bravely. Many responded whole-heartedly to the old man's words and no one could have known how, almost two years later, Hodgson would be martyred[25]. His was the sort of preaching which the young respected and it showed how there was no need to soft pedal the traditional pentecostal approach. As a result of this success, and others like it, the Youth Council introduced the concept of "Christ's Ambassadors" which was a distinctive umbrella name to be given to pentecostal youth[26]. T H Richards was able to write, "Today there is a greater interest in youth and Sunday-school work in our Fellowship than at any time since the formation of Assemblies of God" (*Redemption Tidings* 18 Sept, 1959). Credit for this progress must go to the excellent partnership between Richards and Alfred Missen. In many respects the two men were unalike, but Missen's faith and organisational ability coupled with Richards' charisma struck just the right balance and showed that the post-war generation was ripe for the Gospel.

The Bible College

The Bible College grew steadily under Gee's principalship. In the years 1951-56 163 students had passed through the College[27] and by 1953 the £3,500 debt on the property at Kenley had been wiped out[28]. There were signs that support for the College was not as widespread as Gee and others would have liked. For example in 1956 only 50 out of the 486 assemblies had sent a financial gift, however small, to help with the College's running costs, and the same was true in 1959[29]. Yet the College survived and did good work. A legacy and gift in 1959 enabled a new annexe to be built. Throughout these years the building was filled to capacity[30]. Gee wrote an article explaining how his own views on Bible Colleges had changed. He said,

> Bible Schools are unnecessary. That is exactly what I used to say for many years; and I believed it, too! It is a fitting revenge that in the Providence of God I now find myself installed as the Principal of such an Institution.

> What made me talk like that ? ....Looking back I now know that in my case there was an unrecognised tincture of pride in what I said. I foolishly felt that I was doing pretty well as a pastor....in my heart I was saying 'See what I have done without going to any Bible School'. Perhaps another element was resentment that some of my colleagues who had spent very short terms in Bible Schools should think themselves superior to me (I don't think they ever did) because of that. (*Redemption Tidings* 15 Feb, 1958)

His self analysis is likely to be true for other men also. Those who did well in the ministry without going to Bible College assumed that Bible Colleges were unnecessary, and those who did well after going to Bible College assumed that they would have succeeded anyway.

The curriculum included pastoral theology, church history, religious journalism, teaching on the work of the Holy Spirit and missionary policy, Christology, the epistle to the Romans, homiletics, music and evangelism[31]. Students were expected to take part in summer evangelistic tours (as the Kenley Trekkers) and occasionally enjoyed joint events with Elim students or those at Fred Squire's IBTI[32]. It is possible to detect the nonsectarian hand of Donald Gee here causing his students to look more widely than the confines of their own denomination. As for the long term effects of Bible College education, it is not possible to track down the ministerial lives of all the students who attended Kenley, especially as there was always a sprinkling of overseas students, but there are enough good ministers in Assemblies of God in the 1980s who were at Kenley in the 1950s to demonstrate that the College can not, as its worst critics feared, have shipwrecked the faith of the young.

The radio broadcasts

The AoG Revivaltime radio broadcast on Radio Luxembourg kept going until October 1959, though it became increasingly difficult to bear its cost towards the end. The monthly average cost of maintaining the programme was £520, and there had been a deficit at the end of each month from 1955[33]. By 1959 Revivaltime was in debt to the tune of £763 and its overdraft was only disguised by credit from other departmental accounts which were all held in the same bank. Despite fervent and practical appeals, the money could not be raised. Keith Munday acknowledged the financial burdens that beset many assemblies - his own had to pay £6 a week on interest alone - and still believed it was possible to fund broadcasting adequately. The alternative, that a cult of some sort begin to propagate its views in the slot occupied by Revivaltime, was unthinkable. Yet Revivaltime did go off the air. It hung on for a while in preparation for a new launch. At least one rally was held in the West Midlands in an attempt to rekindle support and interest, but to no avail[34]. The problems, in addition to being financial, were related to the development of television and the consequent rescheduling of commericial radio to gain the maximum benefit from large late audiences.

Revivaltime had a side effect which was not at first intended. It made Assemblies of God more widely known and respected in the evangelical world. John Carter noted,

> for many years we were despised and ostracised by Christian bodies, because they did not know what we believed and taught, and so we were classed with the sects that are heretical and fanatical, but now, mainly through Revivaltime, people have

discovered that we are strictly fundamental, Scriptural, evangelical, as well as pentecostal (*Redemption Tidings* 29 May
1959).

At The 1960 General Conference

The troubles and triumphs of the last years of the decade came to a
head in the General Conference for 1960. Gee had been elected chairman and therefore not only guided the business sessions through their
debates but also gave a keynote address to one of the main public
meetings. He was aware that the experience of the baptism in the Holy
Spirit was beginning to be shared by Christians across the denominational spectrum. He was also aware of the state and condition of British
Assemblies of God both as it compared with the past and as it compared with other pentecostal groups round the world. He started,
therefore, with some questions about the pentecostal movement in
Britain.

Gee's questions centred round the purpose of the pentecostal
churches in relation to the church as a whole. Before he addressed this
issue, he was involved in a public and published disagreement with Eric
Dando on the matter of attendance at mid-week meetings. Gee had
noticed that in many assemblies attendance at the week night prayer
meeting or Bible study was thin - and various reasons for this had been
suggested, ranging from the need for a fresh breath of the Holy Spirit
to the new fangled attraction of television. During the 1920s mid-week
attendance had been high because it was at such meetings that prophecies and utterances in tongues were most often heard. In the 1930s
there was a demand for divine healing and people went to pentecostal
churches to be cured of their illnesses. In the 1950s something new
began to happen. Gee, on balance, thought that this was not altogether
bad. Young families could at least spend time together instead of being
constantly rushed off their feet in order to "get out to the meeting".
Dando, who arrived in Assemblies of God from the Welsh apostolics,
took Gee to task and wrote a powerful letter in which he deplored the
shattering of what he took to be an extremely healthy habit. He put
Gee's remarks down to the fact that Gee was not engaged in full time
pastoral ministry and was out of touch with ordinary church life. From
a historical point of view two things are noticeable: slackness in attendance at mid-week meetings denoted a less enthusiastic set of congregations and the public disagreement with Gee, which Dando headed,
demonstrated that there was a younger generation of men with leader-

ship qualities who were keen to cross swords with the old guard. Gee was sixty-seven years of age and had been on the Executive Council of Assemblies of God since 1925. Was he becoming jaded and ready for retirement ? He certainly carried a heavy workload because, in addition to his duties as Principal of the Bible School at Kenley, he travelled to a different assembly and preached most weekends. And this was because he took no salary for what he did at the Bible School and so his income was entirely derived from royalties and anything the churches cared to give him.

In the autumn of 1957, while on a ministerial visit to Germany, Gee collapsed and rushed to hospital. The surgeon had said to him, "If, as soon as you get back to England, you have the major operation that I advise, you will have *another Springtime*, but if not you will die". The operation (for the removal of the prostate gland ?) was successful and Gee used the metaphor of "another Springtime" to apply to the pentecostal movement. Gee took it as axiomatic that "some new Breath of Revival is needed" but added "to offer you shallow optimism when spiritual surgery may be needed is to be unfaithful to a sacred trust". His diagnosis of the condition of the pentecostal movement took account of health as well as ill-health. The campaigns and conventions, the missionary outlook and the youth rallies, the effort to maintain a radio broadcast and the growth of the Bible College, all spoke of strength and vigour. Yet it was equally plain that there were little assemblies "that are visibly dying. They are living in the past". Of almost equal concern "are misguided folk who turn to artificially-produced emotionalism as a substitute for the genuine work of the Holy Spirit". These two deficiences were symptomatic of decline. The first mistook sentimentality and nostalgia for spirituality, and the second wrongly identified emotionalism with a manifestation of the Holy Spirit.

Gee bluntly reiterated Wallace's call for repentance where this was necessary. He faced the possibility that the pentecostal movement might simply become another denomination where after an early peak there followed a long decline into oblivion. "The ultimate issue", he declared, "is personal". And, more than that, it was an issue of leadership where the mistakes of the early years could be avoided as, and only as, a second and third generation of pentecostals was trained for the future.

In practical terms Gee wanted the AoG Constitution to be revised and brought up-to-date. In spiritual matters, Gee wanted "a bigger vision" and by that he meant that there was a need for a multiplication in the number of churches, especially by the use of the mother-daughter principle where larger congregations gave birth to smaller congregations nearby and supported them until they were strong enough to stand on their own feet. "If we have become content to remain little semi-private meetings for propagating so-called 'deeper truth'; or religious clubs for selfish enjoyment of two or three spiritual gifts; or places of undisciplined emotionalism without concern for the impression upon the outside; or if we regard pastorates as hobbies for men who want to play at being ministers of the Gospel and lack the burning and shining gift that the Holy Ghost puts within a truly Pentecostal servant of the Living God [we are to blame]". Moreover Gee knew that such an outward-looking and evangelistic vision would not of itself produce another Springtime. He said "I believe that another Springtime will only come to us as we restore waiting upon God." It is fatally easy to continue as a denomination and to die as a Revival, he pointed out. And it was here that the issue of identity arose. A revival spreads, spills over to the world and to the ineffective church; it is unpredictable, unorganised, powerful, happy and holy. A denomination is a different kind of animal. Gee wanted the pentecostal churches to remember that they were born in revival and would only continue in revival and that their early evangelism was as a consequence of the revival they enjoyed, not the cause of it. To pray, to wait unhurriedly on God, to be inwardly renewed - this was Gee's prescription and, as he ended his address, he reminded the listeners that "a new era appears to be dawning" in the shape of the charismatic movement. "We must shed our complexes, bred by the ostracism of half-a-century, and boldly take our place alongside our brethren in Christ in the older denominations who may now surprise us by their openness to new movings of God's Spirit".

To what extent was Gee's prescription followed in subsequent years ?

Notes to Pages 259 - 277

1. Much of the information in this paragraph comes from Hocken, P (1986), Streams of Renewal, Surrey: Paternoster. Hocken discusses the genesis of the renewal movement in Britain and presented his findings as a doctoral thesis, Baptised in the Spirit: The Origin and Early Development of the Charismatic Movement in Great Britain, at the University of Birmingham in 1984. Streams of Renewal is the substance of this thesis.

2. See Redemption Tidings (24 Apr,1959) and General Conference Minutes 25th May 1959, item 23.

3. See <u>Redemption Tidings</u> (7 Oct, 1959).

4. There were occasional indications of prosperity. Alfred Webb, the pastor at Dagenham, was presented by his congregation with a car (<u>Redemption Tidings</u> 25 Mar, 1960). Yet lapses from the pension scheme in 1956 and 1957 (General Conference minutes for those years) suggest an inability to find the necesssary premiums. Only about 20% of AoG ministers managed to maintain their contributions, and this threatened and eventually destroyed the viability of the scheme. In a letter to <u>Redemption Tidings</u> (5 Aug, 1960) Gee suggested that the average weekly salary of an AoG pastor might be as low as £5 per week.

5. <u>Redemption Tidings</u> (7 Oct, 1960)

6. <u>Redemption Tidings</u> (21 Feb, 1958)

7. General Conference Minutes (27 May 1957, item 16a)

8. <u>Second Abstract of British Historical Statistics</u>, ed B R Mitchell and H G Jones, CUP, 1971, p 148.

9. <u>Second Abstract of British Historical Statistics,</u> ed B R Mitchell and H G Jones, CUP, 1971, p 149.

10. This word is taken from the General Conference Minutes for 1957.

11. A E Friday was a business man who gave a great deal of time and money to the Revivaltime broadcasts. Joe Richardson, who was noted for his Yorkshire bluntness, was the son of Wilf Richardson who had for a long time been Assemblies God pastor at Wakefield.

12. Nearly £1,500 per year was spent on postage and the money to buy stamps seems to have come from petty cash which was never audited (Report p 4).

13. C Bond, who had been trained at Kenley under Donald Gee, was a man with a university degree. This was unusual at that time in Assemblies of God and and thought to lead to a ministerial approach which was "too academic" and therefore liberal in its view of Scripture. Bond's editorials in <u>Redemption Tidings</u> during the time when he held the editorship are perfectly acceptable and seem no worse, and no better, than those by Henry Jessup, his predecessor, who did not have a university degree. In its criticism of Bond, the Select Committee is probably implicitly criticising Donald Gee who is likely to have been the man to have known of Bond's talents and suggested him as the <u>Redemption Tidings</u> editor.

On page 7 of the Committee's Report they state

> As a Comittee we would strongly protest at the false and erroneous impression current throughout the country, propagated by the General Secretary and countenanced by the Executive Council that Mr G P Hubble resigned as General Treasurer of Assemblies of God because of the activities of the present Select Committee.

These are harsh words. At their worst they imply a campaign by John Carter to undermine the credibility of the Select Committee. At their best, they imply that both the Executive and the Select Committee were telling the truth as they saw it. For this reason the Select Committee quoted at length from Mr Hubble's statement given to the Executive Council in June 1958. This statement is intended to show that Hubble did not resign because of the Select Committee's pressure, but for other reasons. It reads:

> ...It is well to remember in the first place that for more than twelve months from
> September 1953 to the General Conference 1955, the position of General
> Treasurer (as it is now understood, with all the accounts in one man's hands)
> was held by me, at your express wish, but against the wishes of the General
> Conference under sufferance, merely to please the Executive Council, so for
> this reason the position of General Treasurer in a Movement which is not
> centrally governed is to all intents and purposes an untenable one...the position
> also places one under great mental strain, on account of the complexity of the
> work involved rather than on the amount of work itself...the Treasurer is
> accountable to so many different people...firstly to the Executive Council, and
> I must say it has been a pleasure to meet with you...and then there are all the
> other Councils and none of them feel happy about the constant drain upon their
> funds for the upkeep of these premises and the General Treasurer's
> Department...then think of all the Assemblies and pastors, the constant press-
> ing for funds from all and sundry, this also takes its toll. To take the situation
> a step further it should be remembered that I am accountable (please note that
> word) to three separate firms of auditors. Then there is the complexity of the
> accounts themselves. One Council draws Funds from another, explanations
> have to be given, and each auditor in turn has to be satisfied, then there are the
> loans, the debts etc...

14. He was on the Executive Council, the Overseas Missions Council, the Property Trust
Board, the Radio Council and the Home Missions Council. Carter estimated that one day
a week might be taken up with committee work.

15. Carter gave his salary as £11 per week, out of which he paid thirty shillings in rent for
his house. He also received ten shillings a week for out of pocket expenses from the Bible
College. These figures do not match those given in the Executive minutes for 8th March
56, but this is because Carter is referring to his salary early in 1959. What is noticeable is
that Carter's salary had effectively gone down between 1956 and 1959 because in 1956 his
house was rent free and in 1959 it was not. Though he was ten shillings a week better off
in 1959, average salaries had risen considerably. According to the Second Abstract of
British Historical Statistics (B R Mitchell and H G Jones, CUP, 1971, p 148), average
manual weekly wages were at £13-10. Carter was therefore being paid at 30% less than
manual workers.

The Select Committee seemed unable to appreciate this. They asked Carter, "Is it not
true that it costs the Fellowship over £9 per week to maintain these two houses ? [the
editor also had a house]". The implication was that Carter had cheap accommodation at
the expense of the Fellowship.

16. See the Select Committee's report p 11.

17. See Select Committee's report p 11.

18. The era of Thomas Zimmerman's General Superintendency of American Assemblies
of God (1959-85) is often identified with a strengthening of bureaucracy. This view was
put forward in private conversation by various informed AoG ministers in Springfield,
Missouri, in the autumn of 1987.

19. See Cartwright, D W (1986), The Great Evangelists, Basingstoke: Marshall Pickering for an account of George Jeffreys' dispute with the Elim Pentecostal Church, page 138
onwards. Albert Edsor, a long-time associate of Jeffreys, produced an "Open Letter" (July

1986) entitled <u>In Defence of a Man of God Falsely Portrayed</u> in which he bitterly challenged what he took to be the official Elim line on the matter of Jeffreys' resignation at the end of the 1930s. In particular he questioned Cartwright's portrayal of the latter years of Jeffreys' life.

20. This is the classic Webberian conflict. See for example, MacRae, D G (1974), <u>Weber</u>, London: Collins.

21. Flexi-hours imply that a certain number of hours have to be worked, but these take place within a broad time band to be convenient to the worker rather than the office or factory. Open Plan offices produce tend to produce freer relationships within an office. Managerial roles may require "on site inspection". Carter's role was more than that of an administrator. He had a pastoral concern for the Assemblies even if this was not part of his Constitutional mandate.

22. See <u>Redemption Tidings</u> (29th Nov, 1953).

23. The picture of overall decline is slightly more complex than it seems. Between the early thirties and 1955 there was a loss in membership among the principal Free Churches of Sheffield, for example, of 25%. In the whole period 1945-60 Methodism declined slightly but in the middle years there was a small increase, perhaps traceable to the Billy Graham influence in 1954. Yet the general trend for Sunday School members was downward. Between 1921 and 1957, Methodist Sunday Schools took a drop of 54% as against an Anglican drop of 26%. The prospects for the future were not good. See Hastings, A (1986), <u>A History of English Christianity</u>: 1920-1985, London: Collins, p 461, 466.

24. This is a legitimate but not a necessary inference because it was possible for AoG congregations to be pastored by men who did not have credentials with AoG. There were cases, too, where a man had been stripped of his ministerial status by AoG but where the congregation had preferred to keep the man as their minister in defiance of the advice of the District Council or the General Conference.

25. See Whittaker, C, (1983), <u>Seven Pentecostal Pioneers</u>, Basingstoke: Marshalls, p 196-198.
     Alfred Missen and W T H Richards were both born in 1916. In an interview with on 30th June 1988, Alfred Missen told me of the way he and Billy Richards collaborated. Few people expected the partnership to work, but in fact there was never any tension between the two men. They became good friends and held each other in mutual respect.

26. Eg see <u>Redemption Tidings</u> 4 Oct 1957, 24 Oct 1958, 30 Oct 1959. The National Youth Council had also raised a significant amount of money for Operation Advance which was designated to missionary work overseas.

27. General Conference Minutes 10 May 1956 item 18.

28. See <u>Pentecost</u> (June 1953)

29. General Conference Minutes 10 May 1956 and General Conference Minutes 25 May 1959 item 18. The South Wales DC objected to Aaron Linford's being on the Board of Governors and on the Faculty at the same time (Executive Minutes 8 May 1958). Such an objection is difficult to understand if Linford was the best man for the job.

30. There were 36 students (<u>Redemption Tidings</u> 30 May 1960)

31. Redemption Tidings 23 Oct 1959.

32. Redemption Tidings 25 Dec 1958 and 15 April 1960.

33. General Conference Minutes 25 May 1959, item 19b.

34. Redemption Tidings 13 May 1960. John Carter's report on the AoG radio work to the 1960 General Conference opened with these words:

> It was with much regret that the Radio Council was compelled to cease its weekly Revivaltime Programme at the end of October last year. We had been given to understand that all religious programmes over Radio Luxembourg were to be put back one hour, and the Council felt that 12 o'clock was too late for our half-hourly Broadcast. In the course of an interview which two of our brethren had with the London Office of Radio Luxembourg it was learned that the religious programmes were being relegated to 11.30 pm. The reason for this change of policy was given as follows: Religious programmes command a poor listening audience, and this affects the daily average of listeners to Television and the fact that the programme time could be sold over and over again in Germany, Luxembourg had to do some thing drastic. When we applied for an 11.30 broadcast we were informed there was no time available. Our two Representatives came from an interview with the feeling that we should be able to resume our broadcasting in the new year and permission was granted to us to state in our last broadcast that we hoped to resume in the near future. Continual efforts have been made to do this but without success.

THE SIXTIES

General background

Although it is customary to say that there was no clear divide between the 1950s and the 1960s[1], there was a difference between these two decades which is obviously significant. All those who were born after 1945 reached the age of majority in the 1960s. None of this generation had fought in war or been subject to conscription. It was a generation which only had dim memories of post-war austerities and which, by and large, had enjoyed the affluence of the 1950s and assumed that material prosperity was its birthright. Parents might say, "I fought a war so that my son could have a job/buy a house or car" etc. And if they said to their children, "I never had money in my pocket when I was your age", the children were not likely to listen for very long. Either way the young grew up with rising aspirations and burgeoning self-confidence.

The 1960s saw young people make money and become famous. The Beatles started selling hit records from about 1962 onwards. Mary Quant opened her boutiques and even the BBC surprised everyone by *That Was The Week That Was* which satirised old men and old ways. Members of the Cambridge Footlights moved straight from the boards of amateur dramatics to the fringe of the Edinburgh festival to national television. And perhaps it was satire which was indicative of the tensions of the period. Satire can not satisfactorily exist without there being a recognised form of etiquette whose inadequacies and hypocrisies can be exposed and mocked. An age of satire depends on an age of manners, and satire is a means by which manners can be adjusted and a new reality attained. The satirists of the sixties included contributors to *Private Eye*, which was founded in 1962, and they joined forces with the "angry young men" of the novels and the theatre. The common ground between these authors may have existed more in the minds of the media than anywhere else, but the weapons of humour and irreverence and the sheer energy of the young made its impact. Changes were immediately apparent in hair and clothing styles. The short back and sides haircut which had been beloved of army sergeants was replaced by a fringe, hair over the ears - which would have given the old soldiers apoplexy - and no parting. Suddenly respected television personalities, newscasters and announcers, took to the new fashion. The old were made to feel old. They were called "square" and somebody uttered the dictum, "Don't trust anyone over thirty".

Heady talk of revolution led to campus riots in America and to student clamour in Paris in 1968. But politics were not the prime concern in Britain. Morals and mores were the target of the young. Liberation was not seen in terms of throwing off the capitalist yoke because everybody knew that capitalism had delivered the material prosperity which they thoroughly enjoyed. Material austerity was the product of communism, and this was evident enough to anyone who bothered to glance over the Berlin wall. Freedom from sexual constraints, freedom to do what one wanted, freedom if necessary from work, these were the desires of the 1960s breed. And so Parliament legislated: capital punishment was abandoned, divorce reform was carried in 1967 and abortion became legal a year later. The law against homosexuality between consenting male adults in private was repealed.

Overshadowing this liberalisation and the fun-loving attitudes it encouraged - the wild parties, the university rag days, the covert smoking of cannabis, the promiscuity and the hippy cult - came the Cuban missile crisis of 1962. World War III suddenly seemed to loom over the horizon. The virile young American President, John Kennedy, outfaced the older Soviet General Secretary, Nikita Khruschev and demanded, and was granted, the dismantling of missile launch sites on Cuban soil. It was a close-run thing and showed how easily the affluence of the West could have been buried by radio-active rubble. I remember looking out of my bedroom and seeing a red glow in the distance (caused I later discovered by neon lights) and thinking that the bombing had started. Yet the threat of nuclear holocaust was so awesome and the possibilities of protection against it so feeble that there appeared to be nothing one could do to prevent it. "Let us eat, drink and be merry, for tomorrow we die" was a philosophic maxim which combined hedonism, apathy and fatalism in equal proportions. It seemed appropriate for the hour. The Campaign for Nuclear Disarmament, it is true, attracted supporters and marchers[2]. But somehow to march with a placard seemed like whistling in the dark. Even if Britain got rid of its weapons, what guarantee was there that everyone else would bow in admiration and scramble to follow suit ? The missile crisis therefore seemed to encourage demands for consumer freedom and sexual licence.

Music was the atmosphere of the young. New tunes, new types of tune and new technology for making tunes could be recorded and played on a growing number of portable radios and record players. Churches began to sport young men with Beatle haircuts and guitars singing catchy spiritual songs with an emphatic beat. The pentecostal churches here and there blended contemporary sounds with old doctrines. This was intended to interest the young, and to an extent, it worked. Traditionalists shook their heads and thought that the church had become too worldly. And so the young, unless they were born and bred in pentecostal churches, tended to leave. Holy pop music could not compete with the real thing. The more discerning pentecostals realised that only a genuine exhibition of spiritual power and life would attract and retain the young. Gee, for example, warned against emotionalism and at the same time wanted the churches to be renewed spiritually[3]. It was no good trying to be authoritarian with young people or fobbing them off with legalistic precepts. This was the very thing they despised in society at large. Only a challenge like that given by Teddy Hodgson at the National Youth Rally in 1958 or direct Gospel preaching like Billy Graham's at his London Crusades in 1965 and 1966 hit home.

Looking over the wall:
How the Assemblies of God saw Charismatics

A fat person sees those of average weight as being skinny. Assemblies of God saw the charismatic movement as odd. At least that was the first reaction. Gradually, as acquaintance improved, judgement became more discriminating and accurate. AoG itself was not entirely healthy in the sixties and so its initial reaction may have been jaundiced. The condition of AoG was already intimated by Gee's "Another Springtime" address in 1960. Other leaders took up the same theme. Between 1961 and 1966 at least 9 public comments were made which indicated that all was not right with the pentecostal assemblies. It is true that some of these comments were oblique and occurred in the context of other topics. George Oldershaw noticed that in 1961 Assemblies of God had shrunk for the first time in its history[4]. He thought that the remedy would be found if congregations tithed their incomes: shrinkage was caused by a shortage of money which prevented evangelism. Howard Carter who addressed the General Conference for the first time in many years diagnosed the situation differently. "I stand here before you in sackcloth and ashes", he said. Red tape had strangled the life of the Holy Spirit. He recalled how Douglas Scott, a converted dance band leader who had been to the Hampstead Bible School, had travelled to France and, without a good command of the language or the backing of any committee or authorising body, had pioneered about 400 churches which are the backbone of modern Assemblées de

Dieu[5]. Scott had preached and prayed for the sick and had moved from town to town as he felt the Holy Spirit led him. Linford's analysis was different again. In a Chairman's address at the 1963 General Conference he noticed that

> The revolt against centralisation tended to divide and dissipate our efforts. There were periods when 'every man did that which was right in his own eyes'. It was not that we lacked leadership; in fact, we suffered from a plethora of leaders - sometimes leading in different directions.

> With the lessening of the initial impetus that drove us forward in spite of these things, our Testimony began to lose its momentum. The stress of war, the peril of the times, the passing of many of the older generation, the lack of a rallying cry, the absence of of direction - all these played a part in the lethargy that began to grip the Movement[6].

An editorial in 1964 amplified these comments. Linford spoke of a "committee disease" and implied that Assemblies of God had been smitten with this complaint. "The danger of committee-itis is its tendency to restrict creative planning and bold leadership". Yet he could see no way out because, "I must confess some of the alternatives make me shudder. Give me limping democracy to rampant dictatorship"[7]. John Carter added his voice to the general cry. In a Chairman's address for 1964 he spoke of "evidences of deterioration" in AoG for which there was no superficial remedy. "May I suggest that it is not a revision of our Constitution that our spiritual need will be met...the remedy will not be found in better organisation". On the contrary, only heart repentance would be sufficiently radical to prepare the churches for a fresh outpouring of the Holy Spirit. He ended with the words, "we cannot repent as a Movement, but as individuals"[8]. Carter, therefore, struck much the same note as Donald Gee. In 1965 Linford editorially took up the topic again. "As I travel round the Assemblies (and I visit about forty different churches a year) I detect a sense of weariness: not defeatism, but weariness with the toil that is the daily lot"[9]. This observation is all the more pertinent because it is based on first-hand knowledge at the grass roots. The same year Eric Dando gave his first Chairman's address.

Dando was a man of exceptional eloquence and, unlike Gee, the two Carters and Linford, was a relatively new arrival in Assemblies of

God. He was about fifteen years their junior and his comments were not based on any comparison between the past and the present. He was simply struck by the fact that, in order to run the affairs of about 500 pentecostal churches, it was necessary to hold no less than 132 Council meetings per year, and this excluded meetings at local church level. The obvious danger was that the wheels of constitutional machinery would whirr and whirr without any forward motion of the body they were intended to carry. The theme of Dando's address was that Christ must be pre-eminent in every sphere and department of church life. He applied this principle to the mass of pentecostal conciliar activity: if Christ's great concern for evangelism was not being met by multifarious agendas and minutes, they should be scrapped immediately. In proposing an answer to the problems of AoG, Dando insisted on the acknowledgement of Christ's authority, but he also referred to the ministries of apostles, prophets, pastors, evangelists and teachers. The operation of gifted men, who might flourish without let or hindrance, would instil the necessary leadership to guide the churches through and out of their current problems. This was a view which was to become more prevalent in the 1980s. Interestingly, Douglas Quy, who was later to be on the Executive Council of Assemblies of God, made a proposal that "we must make provision for brethren, salaried by the Fellowship, to minister freely to need Assemblies by itinerant ministry"[10]. Dando and Quy's suggestions can be put together in the concept of regional superintendency which allows gifted ministers to work for the strengthening of churches in a defined geographical area.

Throughout the mid-sixties Assemblies of God General Conferences were, in the words of one of its ministers, "soured by the affair of Freddie Bloggs"[11]. Bloggs, [his name has been changed to avoid offence] who was a pastor in Yorkshire, had committed adultery, and had confessed to this and repented of it. Should he be reinstated as the pastor of his assembly and, if so, should his assembly be allowed to remain within Assemblies of God ? This was the crux of the matter. Views of all kinds were expressed. Was the repentance genuine ? If so, for how long should the period of expulsion last ? In essence the conflict boiled down to one between the Yorkshire District Council and the General Conference, with the view of the Executive being parallel to that of the General Conference. It was hard to resolve the conflict because local church autonomy could, in the final analysis, be pitted against the authority of any other Council within Assemblies of God. Yorkshire wanted Bloggs reinstated and his assembly to remain in Assemblies of God. They argued on the basis that grace should always be extended to the penitent. On the other side, it was contended that the high and holy calling of the ministry could not be compromised by slack moral standards[12].

Perhaps it was a good thing that the General Conferences only lasted for a week each year. Some pastors returned from the Conferences in the sixties feeling depressed by the business sessions. Caught up in these problems, there was hardly time for most pastors to consider something which was entirely new. The charismatic movement, when it first began, took established pentecostals by surprise.

Reports of the charismatic movement appeared in *Redemption Tidings* from 1960 onwards. At the time no one knew whether the older denominations would accept spiritual manifestations within their congregations. Would the charismatic movement grow independently, or be a seven day wonder, or would it join up with the pentecostal movement ? Aaron Linford reported

> A strange phenomenon is taking place, both in this country and abroad. Christian ministers and members of churches outside Pentecostal circles are getting baptized in the Holy Ghost with the initial evidence of speaking with other tongues....
>
> What does this mean ? Is it that we are on the verge of a new era, and that the testimony for which we have stood so long, and for whose sake suffered obloquy and ostracism, is now overreaching the bounds of our Fellowship as Joseph's fruitful vine ?...
>
> The baptism of the Spirit is not the exclusive possession of the Pentecostal people; the Pentecostal Movement is not the proprietor of the Holy Ghost. His baptism is the heritage of *all* God's people *everywhere*. (*Redemption Tidings* 6 May 1960, original emphasis).

Linford's reaction is thoughtful. He wonders about the significance of charismata in the older denominations and considers the possibility that a new era may be dawning. He is aware that the overt activity of the Holy Spirit ought to be the hallmark of all Christian groups. Yet, it does not seem from his comments that he has met or talked with charismatic Christians.

In 1960 David Petts wrote a report in *Redemption Tidings* indicating that there were pentecostal manifestations among some of the students at Oxford University. This was about the last place that pentecostals would have predicted there would be speaking with tongues. Oxford seemed too intellectual and too inter-denominational for anything remotely glossolalic. Petts related his call to the ministry while attending a Baptist Union Summer School and his subsequent successful search for the baptism in the Holy Spirit a month before becoming an undergraduate[13]. Gradually the Oxford pentecostals - one of whom, Andrew Parfitt, in teacher training at Culham, was the son of an AoG pastor - organised the Students' Pentecostal Fellowship which was intended to function like the Inter-Varsity Fellowship and disseminate pentecostal doctrine and experience in the Christian Unions. Richard Bolt became its first travelling secretary[14]. Bolt's story is interesting in itself. He told it in *Redemption Tidings* (16 Sep 1960). He was the son of a London doctor and had been educated in expensive boarding schools. After National Service he went Oak Hill to train for the Anglican ministry, but while on a degree course at Durham a spiritual crisis in November 1957 led him to wander the cobbled back streets of the Cathedral city until he unexpectedly stumbled across a small Assembly of God. The pastor prayed and laid hands on him with the result that Bolt had an overwhelming experience of the presence of God and spoke in tongues. About eighteen months later Bolt was given two days notice to leave a theological College at Clifton and his involvement with Anglicanism came to an abrupt end. He was accepted into the Assemblies of God ministry soon afterwards and pastored a church in Colchester while campaigning wherever he was invited and preaching at Universities and Colleges around the country[15]. Regular reports of SPF activities were given by John Miles[16].

David du Plessis spoke at the 1961 AoG General Conference. Du Plessis had become a key figure in the spread of pentecostal doctrine and practice to sections of the church previously untouched by pentecostalism. His life was remarkable and its impact is still being fully assessed[17]. He was born, lived and worked in South Africa until 1937. In 1936 Smith Wigglesworth, then visiting for a preaching tour, burst into du Plessis' office, pinned him against the wall and prophesied. The substance of the prophecy has been reported in detail[18] several times. In it Wigglesworth told du Plessis that "through the old-line denominations will come a revival that will eclipse anything that we have known throughout history.... you will have a very prominent part"[19]. This is what happened. Du Plessis preached at the World Pentecostal Conference in Zurich in 1947 and was elected its secretary in 1949 in Paris but resigned in London in 1952. By 1954 du Plessis had been invited to attend the Evanston gathering of the World Council of Churches and two years later he was regularly speaking to ecumenical leaders about the work of the Holy Spirit. To his own amazement the message which du Plessis preached - that Jesus was the baptizer in the Holy Spirit - was warmly received and, where received, often followed by speaking in tongues. Elderly and revered church leaders whose own ministries were sometimes in a state of crisis found a new lease of life and power in the simple spiritual experience du Plessis was able to communicate.

Both Gee and du Plessis saw the pentecostal experience as the foundation of the true unity of the Spirit for which the World Council of Churches struggled by misguided institutional means. Pentecostalism, which had been branded as being horribly divisive, was beginning to be seen as marvellously unitive. Gee, partly because of his temperament and partly because of his wide experience in all over the world, had a breadth of sympathy which would have surprised his contemporaries[20]. Gee and du Plessis were friends and, because Gee edited *Pentecost* the quarterly World Pentecostal Conference magazine, all du Plessis' activities were regularly reported.

On the Monday evening of the 1961 Conference du Plessis told his story. It is hard to assess what impact his address had. The report in *Redemption Tidings* (14 July) is very matter-of-fact and gives the impression that the full import of what was being said was not grasped. In fact it was not until 1966 that a discussion was held at Conference on the topic, "The Problems of Fellowship with Other Christian Bodies".

It looks very much as if the pentecostal movement was sluggish in its response to what was happening over the wall. An article in *Redemption Tidings*, reprinted from the *Church of England Newspaper*, gave an impressionistic survey of some parishes[21]. Linford devoted an editorial to "pentecostal episcopalians" in November 1962 in which he quoted occurrences in the States and approved of them. In April 1964 Keith Munday wrote a perceptive article about what was happening in Britain. He compared the small pentecostal movement with the insignificance of Israel in relation to the superpowers of its day. Through Israel had come the Scriptures which were destined to change the world; through the pentecostal movement had come doctrine and experience which was to be of value to the world-wide church. It was true that "some of our own number had thought that the outpouring for which have long prayed would have boosted our own numbers, until we became an expanded mammoth Movement with thousands of Pentecostal assemblies replete with a marble headquarters just off the M1". What mattered was that the current outpouring of the Spirit might be the prelude to a great revival of religion across the country.

Perhaps as a preparation for this revival *Redemption Tidings* carried a large number of articles about specifically pentecostal teachings. C L Parker, for example, wrote a series on the gifts of the Spirit in 1 Corinthians 12 in which he followed the line both Horton and Howard Carter had drawn earlier. Parker, being Parker, had to attract controversy: he questioned the truth of the widely held view in pentecostal circles that healing for Christians was accounted for in the atonement of Christ. As he pointed out the Greek word translated "atonement" in Romans 5.11 is translated "reconciliation" in every other place. Since reconciliation between God and man is only necessary where sin has taken place, it is completely inappropriate to think of sickness as having to be atoned for. Parker's view drew some critical letters but did not blow up into a major row. Linford himself in an editorial (18 May 1962) took a less dramatic and supernatural view of healing than was pentecostally common. He noted the importance of such factors as diet, physical rest and mental tranquility to the overall health of the individual.

In 1962 (2 June) Linford asked whether utterances in tongues were directed towards God or the congregation. This was a question which was to aired at about twenty year intervals among pentecostals. The argument was relevant to ordinary church life: if utterances in tongues were Godward, then manward interpretations were invalid and forty year old customs were wrong. If these were wrong, could others be wrong also ? It was a worrying prospect. After considering the options Linford defended the traditional view, that is, that tongues in private prayer were Godward but as an utterance during congregational worship were manward. In 1963 (21 May) a complete issue of *Redemption Tidings* was devoted to tongues and the Holy Spirit. The distinctive position of Assemblies of God, namely that the baptism in the Holy Spirit was evidenced initially by glossalalia, was firmly argued. A classic Donald Gee article was reprinted, together with two American contributions which were equally persuasive. The need for this restatement of the AoG position almost certainly arose from a realisation that the experience of the baptism in the Holy Spirit could, in the context of other denominations, become more vague and ultimately, in a maze of hedging about and qualification, disappear altogether.

Three years later Linford began a thorough and impressive series on spiritual gifts which, though it said little that was altogether new, cogently and coherently expressed the best of past teaching on the subject.

Pentecost, with a circulation of 2,500 copies[22], (December 1965) reported on the publication of Michael Harper's book *As At the Beginning*, which told the little known story of the pentecostal movement round and the world and since the turn of the century, and contained reference to the Full Gospel Business Men's convention in London where the Albert Hall, Westminster Central Hall and the Metropolitan Tabernacle had been booked. Circulation of *Pentecost* among Assemblies of God and Elim ministers is hard to ascertain, but the bulk its copies went to Britain and America. *Pentecost* would have informed those pentecostal readers with the widest interests. Most AoG ministers in Britain seem to have stood on the sidelines and watched the charismatic movement unfold in front of their eyes. Richard Bolt, who was then an AoG minister, was crossing denominational boundaries and, in his own way, so was Donald Gee, but Gee fell foul of his co-pentecostals when he accepted an invitation to attend the World Council of Churches meeting in Delhi and, after consultation with his peers in Britain and pressure from the American Assemblies of God, Gee decided not to attend. Strength of feeling against liberal protestantism was understandably still high and Gee's visit would have been seen as compromising the doctrinal truths for which pentecostals stood. Within the USA, where Gee was widely known, it was thought far more important that Assemblies of God should continue to gain the respect of fellow evangelicals rather than form links with liberals. Missen's talk at the 1966 General Conference was a logical development of the classic pentecostal position. He dealt with the ecumenical movement and the charismatic movement. "Ecumenism is bedevilled with two evils: the evil of Romanism and the evil of liberal theology" and yet he did not want to stand back from the church as a whole. "Abstention does not necessarily mean isolation. One can have influence upon groups without being formally united with them" - and it was here that Missen, who as we shall see had taken over the General Secretaryship from John Carter, showed his unwillingness to stand aloof from other Christians. Yet, when it came to the charismatic movement, he had to say that "it has been said with some truth that to speak with tongues has almost become fashionable, but to be a pentecostal is as unfashionable as ever.... Brethren in the new *Charismatic Awakening are in the main holding aloof from the recognised Pentecostal bodies*" (original italics).

This led him to consider the divisions within the pentecostal movement and to argue that it was more necessary than ever to try to bring about their healing. He had in mind the Elim/AoG division and perhaps hinted at the factions that existed, as we have seen, within the Assemblies of God.

We can not say what would have been the effects on the pentecostal movement, or on the church in Britain, if the pentecostal movement in the 1960s had managed to bury the hatchets which were so often being brandished. The constitutional wrangles and arguments, no doubt perfectly legitimate in their own way, distracted energy and faith from the relationships and tasks to which the pentecostal churches should have dedicated themselves. Where relationships were good, the Assemblies of God saw life and growth. The National Youth Council was a clear example of this and it was Missen's own association with the obviously successful NYC which led to his being elected as General Secretary in 1963 against Aaron Linford who was himself an excellent candidate[23].

Notes to Pages 283 - 293

1. See, for example, Hastings (1986) page 507 or Briggs (1983) page 302.

2. Britain acquired the Hydrogen bomb in 1957 and CND gained momentum. Christians like Canon Collins and Humanists like Bertrand Russell combined in its ranks and influenced the Labour Party. The largest march took place in 1961 and went from Aldermaston where nuclear research was conducted to a rally in Trafalgar Square. Thereafter the movement declined until the 1980s.

3. Writing in Redemption Tidings 1 Apr 1960 and 10 Mar 1961.

4. See Redemption Tidings 7 July 1961.

5. See Stotts, George R (1981), Le Pentcôtisme au pays de Voltaire, Viens and Vois: Craponne.

6. See Redemption Tidings 21 June 1963.

7. See Redemption Tidings 14 Feb 1964.

8. See Redemption Tidings 5 June 1964.

9. See Redemption Tidings 29 Jan 1965.

10. See Redemption Tidings 26 Feb 1965. Of course the idea of itinerating salaried ministers was dependant on there being money available within the District Councils or through the Executive to fund such a project. Aaron Linford wrote an editorial (1 April 1966) in which he strongly made the point that pastors should be paid properly. The editorial was entitled "Worthy of Double Honour" and said "We should see that those who serve in the Word receive adequate support both spiritual and financial". The mere fact

that Linford needed to write such an editorial implies that a large quantity of pentecostal churches were supporting their pastors inadequately. If there was insufficient money being paid to local pastors, it was highly unlikely that there would be surplus money for the support of itinerating ministers. And Quy's scheme never seriously got off the ground in the 1960s or 70s.

11. Ray Hall at York expressed this opinion to me privately 6 July 88, but is happy for his remark to be attributable.

12. Bloggs (not his real name) had resigned from AoG ministry in 1958, but at the 1960 General Conference he was expelled (Minute 9) - presumably because it was felt that his resignation had been in order to forestall expulsion. In the Executive Council (5th and 6th Oct 1961) a letter from the South Lancs District Council was read out. South Lancs had heard that the Rotherham Assembly, whose pastor was the forcible David Powell, had allowed Bloggs to "minister from the platform" and they requested the EC to take whatever action it deemed necessary.

The EC wrote to Rotherham to ask what was going on and received a letter saying that "Mr Bloggs has been attending this assembly for the past 10-12 months and his activities in the church are no more than we allow any of the members". This reply seemed evasive to the EC and so a letter was sent to the Yorkshire District Council asking that the matter be investigated. The point was that, according to the AoG Constitution, ministerial discipline was a local matter and not one on which the EC had any direct powers.

Further complications arose when the Yorkshire DC wrote to the EC asking for a definition of "expulsion" (EC Minutes 3/4 May 1962). The term "expulsion" was then defined at the 1962 General Conference. In a proposition brought by the EC,

> Expulsion from the Fellowship is the severest form of discipline that can be exercised against any member of the General Council. It should be reserved for the gravest offences. It allows of no conditions: no question of reinstatement or period of time can be entered into at the time of expulsion.
>
> No expelled person should be allowed to minister at, or take part in any form of divine service in connection with any of our ministers or assemblies without express permission from the District Council concerned with the expulsion and the Credentials Committee. (GC Mins, 1962, 10.b)

The General Conference minutes then specifically stated "A proposal was carried that this motion be applied prospectively in the case of Mr Bloggs and the Rotherham Assembly". That should have been that. But it wasn't. The following year complaints were aired at the General Conference that the Rotherham assembly (with David Powell as its pastor) was ignoring the ban on Mr Bloggs. A meeting between the Council of Representatives and the pastor and delegates of the Rotherham assembly was to arranged to discuss the matter (see GC Mins, 1963, 27). In 1964 the matter was reported on and as a result the term expulsion was redefined. It was now to read

> If after a period of not less than six months a local pastor may wish to restore an expelled person, who has show fruits meet for repentance, to the means of grace, he may with the approval of his own District Council which shall consult with the District Council concerned with the expulsion allow him to break bread and to take part in Divine service. No expelled person shall be allowed to minister at or to convene any such service without express permission both from the District Council concerned with the offence and the District Council in which he is residing and the Credentials committee. (GC mins, 1964, 11.b)

In 1967 (GC Mins 14.d) we read

> Reinstatement. A proposal that an expelled Minister shall be given no promise of reinstatement and where such reinstatement is granted it shall under no circumstances be under five years was not carried. It was resolved to appoint a Committee of five members to state the issues involved in and the Scriptures relating to reinstatement of expelled ministers.

Earlier in the same year, "The Conference was informed that Mr Bloggs was pastoring the Handsworth Assembly. A proposal that this matter be tabled for twelve months was not carried. It was resolved that the Executive Council shall meet with the Credentials Council and a delegation of the Yorkshire District Council to discuss the matter" (9).

In fact the matter was altogether more heated that this decision suggests. Item 10.b for the 1968 General Conference records the twists and turns of discussion.

> A report of the meeting of the Executive Council, the Credentials Council and a delegation from the Yorkshire District Council was read. D S Quy was subsequently appointed to the Chair for this item. It was resolved to go back to the circumstances prevailing after the first meeting with Handsworth Assembly and to ask this General Conference to deal with the Handsworth Assembly and Mr Bloggs. A proposal that the General Conference restore to full fellowship the Handsworth Assembly and take note of the report regarding Mr Bloggs and pass on was not carried.

How many hours of debate lie behind this statement ? I have not been able to find out, but at one Conference the first four days of the business sessions were taken up with this discussion. The minutes go on

> A proposal that Mr Bloggs be asked to resign the pastorate of the Handsworth Assembly but be granted the privilege to minister the Word of God was not carried.

So deadlock seemed to have been reached. Two proposals, each of which would have been fully debated, were not carried. The minutes continue

> After prophetic utterance it was resolved that this General Conference disagree with Mr Bloggs pastoring the Handsworth Assembly but constrained by the Spirit of God through prophecy to commit this matter into the hands of God. It was then resolved that the report of the joint meeting between the Credentials Council, the Executive Council and the delegation from the Yorkshire District Council regarding Mr Bloggs and Handsworth issue be accepted as having been read.

Prophetic utterance broke into the situation and solved it. There was no way the matter could be deferred or referred to another committee or combination of committees. The matter was left to God. What is interesting is that charismatic gifts were applied in the business session. At last the pentecostal movement made use of the riches of its heritage.

Would that the matter had ended there! It came up again, with a slightly different emphasis, in 1969 and 1970. The focus of the problem now became the status of the Handsworth assembly where Mr Bloggs pastored. In 1969 there was disagreement between the Yorkshire District Council and the Executive over the meaning of "committing into the hands of God". The Yorkshire DC considered that this meant expulsion; the

EC thought that this did not mean expulsion. The EC's proposal supporting their interpretation was not carried. A further proposal that the matter be left was also not carried. Eventually the Yorkshire DC interpretation received the necessary majority.

In 1970 there were further debates because the Court of Appeal had been consulted. Had the expulsion of Handsworth been illegal - and this seems to mean "illegal" according to the law of the land ? A further group was set up to arbitrate. (item 10.c). To end on a positive note: Bloggs was re-admitted to AoG's ministerial list just before he died.

13. David Petts was to go on to become Principal of the Assemblies of God Bible College at Mattersey and a member of the AoG Executive Council.

14. Richard Bolt had been travelling round the universities before the formation of SPF and it was logical that he should become its first travelling secretary. Don Underwood, a graduate of Trinity College Dublin and a member of the Army education corps, became the first SPF General Secretary. Underwood was in London at the time. The students belonging to SPF were largely drawn from Assemblies of God, though there were connections with Elim, particularly when Alex Tee was selected to be another travelling secretary.

15. Bolt went on to pastor an independent church in London attended by Terry Virgo (who was to become a leader of the Restoration movement) while he was a student at London Bible College. It was generally agreed that Bolt was a man of extraordinary spiritual gifting under whose ministry genuine miracles were seen. Unfortunately Bolt's character was somewhat eccentric and this reduced the acceptability of his ministry.

16. Miles went on the mission field to French speaking Africa and then returned with his American wife to the States. He took a doctorate in languages and is now a Professor at Wheaton College, Illinois.

17. At least one esteemed evangelical theological college on the west coast of the United States has named part of its building complex after du Plessis in recognition of his unique contribution to twentieth century Christianity.

18. Eg Hocken (1986), chapter 1.

19. Quoted in A Man Called Mr Pentecost, 1977, by David du Plessis (as told to Bob Slosser), New Jersey: Logos International, p 2 and 3.

20. For example he corresponded cordially with Bendedict Heron, a Roman Catholic priest and monk of the Order of St Benedict (Olivetan).

21. See Redemption Tidings 13 Oct 1961.

22. See Executive Council Minutes (11 Jan 1962).

23. Alfred Missen told me that his wife had been taken on one side by John Carter and told not to be upset when Aaron Linford was elected General Secretary. Missen, however, was voted into office on the second ballot with a distinct majority.

A closer look at Assemblies of God

What sort of men (and women) were pastoring churches in Assemblies of God ? No statistics of average age or training have ever been collected. There is, however, one source which does give some suggestive information about the backgrounds of AoG pastors. A series entitled "pentecostal pulpit" was run in *Redemption Tidings* from February 1959 for several years. A central double page was devoted to a sermon article by an AoG minister. Each piece had a photograph of the author and a fairly full biography. Unfortunately the biographies omitted the writer's date of birth and other crucial dates like the year he entered the ministry full-time. However, by collecting the first 138 of these biographies, several statistics can be deduced. Each writer mentions with more or less detail the circumstances of his (or her) conversion.

CONVERSION CIRCUMSTANCES	NUMBER
Assemblies of God	37
Methodist	33
Church of England	17
Jeffreys campaigns	12
Elim	10
Salvationist	8
Brethren	6
Pentecostal (Independent)	6
Congregationalist	4
Strict Baptist	1
Presbyterian	1

At least 10 of these men were Welsh, and probably rather more though it is impossible to be precise from the biographical material given. In several instances, dramatic healings either to the man or woman concerned or to a close member of the family led to a ministerial call. This is particularly so where the Jeffreys brothers were active. In the figures above the campaigns of George and Stephen Jeffreys have been treated together and have been kept separate from Elim backgrounds.

Not surprisingly, it is the Assemblies of God which comes top of this list. Either campaigns by AoG ministers or upbringing within an AoG assembly could be decisive. Methodism is the background in 33 cases and very often it is Wesleyan or Primitive Methodism. Perhaps surprisingly there was a significant number of men who had started life in the Church of England - C L Parker being the most obvious example. The 10 men with Elim backgrounds show that there was certainly transfer between the two main pentecostal bodies. Salvationists provide a predictable background for AoG ministers. The open air meetings and the emphasis on evangelism would have been easily applicable in both denominations.

It would be unwise to place too much weight on these figures because the sample from which they are drawn is not necessarily a representative one. Nevertheless, because there were about 350-400 ministers during the time when these figures apply, it is clear that we have an insight into the lives of about one third of the total number of pastors.

Other statistics are given in the General Conference minutes.

YEAR	NUMBER OF ASSEMBLIES	MINISTERS	PROBATIONARY MINISTERS	DELEGATES
1954	475	338	63	91
1955	483	332	76	100
1956	486	326	77	113
1957	506	372	52	79
1958	506	364	60	75
1959	509	355	68	80
1960	511	384	53	64
1961	511	397*	47*	70*
1962	517	400*	50*	78*
1963	522	405	54	62
1964	530	394	58	58
1965	534	402	61	52
1966	535	412	45	57
1967	535	416	38	62
1968	530	419	49	62
1969	525	423	50	34
1970	531	435	46	58

*This figure is estimated because it is not given in General Conference minutes

Taking the table as a whole it is immediately clear that the growth in the number of assemblies within Assemblies of God levelled off in the 1960s. No growth at all occurred between 1960 and 1961 and there was actually a decline between 1965 and 1970.

To off-set this, it is also clear that the number of AoG ministers increased in the same period and even in the years 1968/69 where there was a drop in the number of assemblies, there was an increase in the number of AoG ministers.

This trend can be seen when calculating what percentage of assemblies had an AoG minister. In 1960 75% of assemblies employed an AoG minister; in 1970 81% of assemblies employed an AoG minister, but this figure had been as low as 74% in 1964. Since it was normally the AoG ministers who were in full-time employment with their assemblies, the figures show that there was always a cluster of about 50 assemblies which were unable or unwilling to support their pastor. In most instances these assemblies would have been too small to generate enough income for the pastor to live adequately. In a few cases, these assemblies would have had a preference for unpaid leadership and could have supported a pastor if they had so wished.

The total size of Assemblies of God during this period can be calculated from an estimate made by Keith Monument in 1960[1] that the average assembly was about thirty strong. This would have given a membership of just over 15,000 people in 1960. Alfred Missen collected more accurate statistics in in 1966. In his report to Conference that year he stated that 245 assemblies had sent figures in to him. From these he had estimated that the "Fellowship has a membership of 28,000" and a Sunday School membership of 31,000, giving it a total size of 66,000. This last figure, of course, is a unrealistically high because Sunday School children cannot be included in any calculation about the manpower available for evangelistic or missionary work or in any assessment of the total financial resources of the Fellowship.

Figures are also available for General Conference attendance. During the war years, the Conference had been entirely ministerial and had been held in one of the larger assemblies. After the war the Conference was opened out and, although the ministers continued to hold their business sessions in camera, visitors attended the evening meetings.

AoG GENERAL CONFERENCE

YEAR	MINISTERS PRESENT	TOTAL ATTENDANCE	PLACE
1960	309	1300+	Skegness, Butlin's
1961	346	1600+	Prestatyn Holiday Camp
1962	362	2000+	Morcambe, Middleton Twr
1963	311	?	Morcambe, Middleton Twr
1964	332	2603	Clacton-on-Sea, Butlin's
1965	335	3732	Clacton-on-Sea, Butlin's
1966	362	3526	Clacton-on-Sea, Butlin's
1967	377	4321	Pwllheli, Butlin's
1968	363	3457	Bognor Regis, Butlin's
1969	379	?	Bognor Regis, Butlin's
1970	373	?	Bognor Regis, Butlin's

(Figures taken from General Conference Minutes or Redemption Tidings)

In both columns there is a steady drift upwards. One of the most exciting facets of General Conferences for those who attended them in the sixties was that more and more visitors swelled the main evening meetings, that whole families attended - dad took the kids off school and enjoyed drawing his holiday pay packet at the same time thanks to improved working conditions - and that a sense of fun as well as a spiritual vitality was generated by the whole occasion. Pentecostal families began to feel that they mattered and the presence of children and young people brought the more esoteric and mystical individuals down to earth. Was it really important to discuss the finer points of eschatology when the children in the next chalet were crying ? Was it unholy to laugh in the swimming pool ? Camp life loosened everyone up and the sense of a large happy outing, which often started when the party-booked coach left the church to take everyone to Clacton, or Pwllheli or Bognor, continued into the serious rallies. Pentecostalism could be *happy* and so, while the heavyweights argued in the business sessions - and it is perhaps no coincidence that the most rigorous arguers at Conference were often not family men - good things happened despite the frictions which, with a truer sense of perspective, could have been glossed over or cheerfully and willingly solved.

The good things about Assemblies of God in the 1960s, the exciting work of the National Youth Council, the continued broadcasting, the faithful activities of the Home and Overseas Missions Councils and the gradually improving financial position has to be seen in parallel with the bad things: the constitutional wrangling and the sense of flatness which, if we are correct in our deductions from the Chairman's addresses in this period, pervaded large sections of the movement.

It was a period when the old guard left office. At the age of 70 John Carter retired from the General Secretaryship in 1963. L F W Woodford retired from his post looking after Overseas Missions in the same year. George Oldershaw retired in 1967. In 1962 Gee had retired from the Executive Council after 37 years continuous service. As we shall see, Gee's period as Principal of Kenley also effectively came to an end around 1963. The veterans were moving aside and undercurrents within and outside Assemblies of God often surfaced in the area where the old leaders had held their courses. The transition between one generation and the next was constitutionally smooth but it was hard for the younger men to make changes. The old men were still active. Carter and Gee, for example, were emeritus members of the Executive Council and, if they wished, could speak at the General Conference on any issue and be sure of carrying weight.

Alfred Missen (born in 1916) became General Secretary in 1963 at the age of 46. His work on the National Youth Council had been extremely successful and he was replaced by the first salaried member of the NYC, Mike Jarvis. There had been youth rallies in the late 1950s and early 60s. Missen continued, after he had become General Secretary, to attend the summer youth camps and was sometimes to be seen trudging through the rain in Wellington boots adjusting guy ropes and fly sheets. The NYC rallies could attract 2,800 people[2] and their magazine, *Pentecostal Youth*, edited by Colin Whittaker, had a monthly circulation of over 4,000 copies[3].

While the NYC attracted crowds, the Home Missions Council continued its efforts to establish churches all over Britain. The method was basically to hold a campaign in a town, shepherd the converts together into an assembly, buy a building, supply a pastor and wait for growth. The trouble was that it was hard going. Finding a hall could be tiresomely difficult. Who was to organise the distribution of leaflets publicising a campaign ? When the campaign was held, the number of converts registered might prove insufficient to form the necessary nucleus and, even if such a nucleus had been established, an unsuitable person might assume unhealthy dominance and prevent further growth. Keith Monument, the full-time Home Missions Secretary, travelled up and down the country and was open to new ideas. W T H Richards, for example, encouraged "doorbell evangelism"[4]; Clifford Rees argued that campaigns to fortify and enlarge small churches should be held[5]; Keith Munday suggested do-it-yourself campaigns which would not require a specially imported speaker[6]. Howard Carter, whose work in the 1930s had been similar to that of Home Missions, pleaded for New Testament principles of evangelism and church planting[4]. Alfred Webb said the need was for more men and more money[7]. George Oldershaw (who is usually credited with founding Home Missions) thought that many of the problems would be solved if congregations tithed their incomes[8]; if they did this then every ten wage earners could support one full-time pastor and a full-time pastor could devote himself to evangelism. When all was said and done, it was obvious that gifted evangelists were a rarity. Howell Harris continued to hold successful meetings until at least 1965 and Richard Bolt in the early sixties seemed to be inheriting the mantle of the great evangelists of the past. Monument used two evangelistic deaconesses to prepare the ground for one of Harris's campaigns in Brixton[9] and then found Clifford Beasley as a man who was willing to tour in a caravan and both prepare for campaigns and follow up after them[10]. Arthur Barratt campaigned in Chesterfield in 1961 and Peter Scothern at Maltby in the same year. That year, too, a deliberate attempt was made to ensure there was effective liaison between Home Missions and the Bible College because ex-students seemed the obvious candidates to take on new, small assemblies. Periodic round-ups of Home Missions news in 1961-62 included mention of efforts at Staveley, Loughton, Retford, Crawley, Lichfield, Kelvedon, Oswestry, Chesterfield, Eastwood and Derbys. Gradually progress was made.

Broadcasting was similar in some respects; great efforts did not always issue in tangible results. Assemblies of God had heroically kept the Revivaltime broadcasts going till 1960. Nelson Parr - the man who had called together the original meeting which issued in the founding of Assemblies of God - had become its silver haired radio evangelist, a return from the cold for a man whose ardour for Gospel preaching lasted till his death in 1979[12]. After a two year interval it was decided that nothing further could be done without appointing a salaried man. Hedley Palmer, a Welshman skilled in the arts of male voice choirs, became AoG's full-time radio producer in 1962 and in 1966, using a variety of radio stations including Radio Caroline, was reaching 11 million people a week. In fact in 1967 Keith Munday reported that the Radio Caroline broadcasts had elicited more than 600 letters, clear evidence that the programmes were hitting home. Programmes made by AoG were taken by the Far Eastern Broadcasting Company, the Central Africa Broadcasting Company, Radio WIVV in Vieques, Puerto

Rico.

Overseas Missions were also continued in the sixties, but it would require a separate study to deal adequately with their successes and failures. Financially, Assemblies of God made its largest commitment overseas. In 1967, for example, the OMC budget was £30,732 which was about three or four times that spent on either radio work or Home Missions. The effect of missionary work was to remind ministers, especially at the General Conference or when a missionary on furlough travelled round the home assemblies, that the world was bigger than their little corner. There were, of course, psychological double binds with missionary work: there was the problem of giving generously to overseas work and being mean to the pastor at home; and there was the problem of being unsure by any valid criteria whether the money spent on missionary work had actually been fruitful. Missionaries did not like to have to show that their wages had produced converts - that put an intolerable pressure on the man or woman battling with the problems of a new language and a new culture. By the same token, it seemed a waste of sacrificially given money to pay the travelling expenses of an overseas missions secretary (Walter Hawkins was elected on L F W Woodford's retirement); yet, if one did not do so, how could any proper information about what was happening on the mission field be properly collected ?

Notes to Pages 297 - 303

1. Redemption Tidings 25 March 1960.

2. Redemption Tidings 13 April 1962.

3. Executive Council Minutes 11 Jan 1962 (item 9b). Pentecostal Youth's circulation was given as 4,100.

4. See Redemption Tidings 14 July 1961 at the General Conference.

5. See Redemption Tidings 8 Nov 1963.

6. See Redemption Tidings 8 Nov 1963.

7. See Redemption Tidings 31 Mar 1961.

8. See Redemption Tidings 7 Jul 1961.

9. See Redemption Tidings 15 Jan 1965.

10. See Redemption Tidings 15 Mar 1963.

11. See the Conference Report 1966.

12. Parr retired from Bethshan Tabernacle, Manchester, in 1965 at the age of 78. He was another of the veterans who left office in the mid-sixties. Parr had been active with the National Youth Council only four years previously. <u>Redemption Tidings</u> (7 Apr 1961) reported on a South Lancs Youth Day at Bethshan when 1,250 were gathered. Parr, of course, took a leading part.

The Going of Donald Gee

Donald Gee lived at the Bible College in Kenley. It was a beautiful place, large enough to be a small hotel and with a wide slightly ornamented lawn at the back. Under his Principalship the College had prospered. Student numbers increased, a minibus was bought, and eventually it was necessary to build an annexe to extend the facilities[1]. He worked without taking a salary apart from being given his board and lodging. His name was widely enough known to attract students from European countries (like Holland or France) which had a pentecostal movement but no Bible College of their own. His own sane and level-headed exposition of Scripture, as well as his practical knowledge of pentecostal missions all over the world, ensured that students received unparochial and broadly based teaching. It was Gee who ensured that Kenley took part in United Bible College demonstrations at the Metropolitan Tabernacle in London, and this allowed students to see across into other pentecostal denominations in Britain[2].

Most of the churches in Assemblies of God seemed indifferent to the College. The 1960 General Conference was told that less than 50 assemblies had sent even the smallest gift towards the running expenses at Kenley. Here was a difficulty. If the Faculty took no pay, if the students fees were as low as possible and if it was clear to a man like Gee who knew what pentecostalism world-wide was like that British AoG needed trained ministry, then how disheartening it was that only a tenth of the assemblies felt any necessity to give. It is all the more remarkable, then, that the College went from strength to strength.

Gee had been born in May 1891 and approached retirement age in the 1960s. In 1962 the General Council minutes reported that "the Conference unanimously confirmed the re-appointment of Donald Gee as Principal of the Bible College". The appointment was for a two year term and would have expired in 1964 when Gee was 73 years of age. All seemed well. In 1963 there was a furore at the Conference. The Governors attempted, sensibly enough, to ensure that there was a smooth transition between Gee and his successor. They therefore proposed that Robert Barrie work for a year alongside Gee as his Vice Principal until Gee's term of office was completed. After this, Barrie should become Principal.

After this proposition had been agreed upon, but a little while before the 1963 Conference, Gee asked if he could retire on 31st December 1963. This was because he had been asked to Chair the World Pentecostal Conference at Helsinki in the summer of 1964 and he felt that he would like a full six months to make the detailed preparations. Presumably Gee assumed that Barrie would become Principal on 1st Jan 1964 and that they would simply have two terms working together rather than three.

At the General Conference in May 1963 the Governors' proposition, after prolonged discussion, was not carried. This was a shock. Robert Barrie, who was due to be re-elected to the Governing body, immediately withdrew his name from the ballot paper and Eric Dando and A E Mellors, as those who felt that their advice had been spurned, resigned. The Conference, taken aback by what had happened, asked Barrie, Dando and Mellors to reconsider their decisions, but the three "felt unable to withdraw their resignations, due, they affirmed, to the present administration of the College"[3.] This is an enigmatic statement. Why did they feel they had to resign ? Was the administration so bad they could not give their names to it unless a Vice Principal expert in administration be appointed ? A new proposal - intended to prevent the Governors' resignations - that Aaron Linford instead of Robert Barrie be asked to act as Vice Principal until the 1964 Conference was also defeated. Gee himself, in a private letter four months later, wrote "my chief uncertainty has been a fear that there may be a lingering objection to my continuance in the office because of what transpired at the last General Conference. The last thing I desire is to be the centre of any further storm in that matter"[4]. These words suggest that Barrie's proposed appointment rested upon dissatisfaction with administrative aspects of College life, and these would have been within Gee's province.

What are we to make of all this ? It has been suggested that a faction in the Conference was ambitious to get control of the College and to lever Gee out[5]. This interpretation of what happened does have in its favour Gee's being well beyond retirement age. He appeared to be hanging onto office beyond 70, even though John Carter had retired at that age and Woodford at the conventional 65. By modern standards Gee does not seem particularly old, and his mind was vigorous and alert. He was a widower and had no home: why should he give up work before he absolutely had to ?

The resignation of three quarters of the Governing Body ensured that three new Governors were elected. All appeared to be well, though there was a little friction between Ernie Crew, who had just joined the Faculty on a full-time basis, and Elisha Thompson who had been there since the early days. The Governors made it clear that, in Mr Gee's absence, Mr Thompson was second in command. Trouble brewed in January 1964 at a Representatives' Conference. This was a gathering of various men in Assemblies of God who were chosen on a regional basis. Their job was to consider matters for the provisional agenda of the General Conference. Any public statement made at the Representatives' Conference would be sure to get back to the DCs all over the country.

Ernie Crew asked what had been decided about the nomination for the Principalship in 1964. Chas Wishart quoted the Board of Governors' decision to invite Gee to stand for a further year, that is, until 1965; Gee, after hesitation, had accepted because his work load had decreased with the arrival of Crew at the College. Crew, however, told the Representatives that Gee's health was poor - that he was showing signs of forgetfulness and had fallen down, perhaps because of a temporary black out, while preaching at Cardiff. In a letter to the Board on January 27th, Crew wrote

> At a recent Representatives Council Meeting held at Leicester I raised the question of Mr Donald Gee's nomination for another term of office. Although the period has been changed to one year in the nomination I feel as I pointed out in the council that he really is not physically fit enough to carry the burden for another term of office. For a man of his age his mental capacity is quite wonderful, but we have to remember that our brother doesn't only serve as Principal of the College. He edits *Pentecost*... ...the Matron remarks quite frequently lately how much Mr Gee is failing physically. He staggers far more than I like to see him, and confesses to often getting up with reluctance...I have been to have a talk with Mr Gee, and told him what I have done. I humbly apologise for embarrassing the members of the Board who were present at the conference, but I really believe I am right about his health. He is far more weary than he likes to show.

In answer to an enquiry about his health Gee wrote to the Board on 4th February

> The simple facts are that my health is good, especially for a man of 72. People continually remark on how well I look. The Lord be praised.

But he went on to admit that on one occasion not long before he had needed help to get out of the bath. Nevertheless he felt his mental powers to be unimpaired. "I can only say that I have recently completed a broadcast on a most difficult subject to the complete satisfaction of the BBC. This is no mean test". In order to make a more informed decision about whether to stay on or not at the College, Gee underwent a medical examination and reported on the doctor's findings to the Board. His arteries were hardening and his blood pressure was slowly rising. "I shall try to cut down my travelling...I may need to reduce my preaching appointments at a distance...I often regret the hill up from the station, but I take that with due respect!"[6] As a result of these considerations, Gee said "it does seem to me that the Governors will be wise to begin to consider a successor, but without treating the matter as urgent"[7].

The Governors took Gee's advice and proposed Elisha Thompson as the next Principal at the 1964 General Conference. Elisha failed to attain the two-thirds majority he needed[8]. The Governors asked the Conference if Gee could stay on a further year while they considered matters, but they were asked for a name to be proposed before the end of the session. Robert Barrie was therefore put forward, and he was voted into office.

All appeared to be well. The 1963 proposal came to fruition in 1964. But there was more to come. Barrie was a married man and needed more spacious accommodation than the Principal had been previously allocated. The Conference was asked to raise money for the purchase of a house for Barrie and, after a final but unsuccessful proposal by the Governors that Gee be Principal Emeritus, it was resolved that the Executive Council and Gee consult together about where Gee should live: he had nowhere to go.

Soon afterwards Jean and Doreen Wildrianne at the IBTI offered him a room[9]. A taxi came to the door at Kenley and, without a formal farewell or any proper recognition of his thirteen years of free service to the College, Gee left.

Consultation between the Executive and Gee took place, but Gee was obviously sore at the way events had turned out. The Executive made a grant to Gee of £250. In September of 1964, the Executive learnt of Gee's plans to re-marry but considered that, in view of precedents which might be set, any pension Gee should receive ought to be in the hands of the Governors. The Governors agreed to pay £3 per week[10].

A proposal at the 1965 General Conference that Gee be paid the same amount in pension as John Carter and L F W Woodford, who each received £6 per week, was not carried. Instead Gee was given an illuminated scroll which had been produced by one of the students.

It is very difficult to find anything good to say about this sorry episode. Assemblies of God was at its worst. Gee had given his time and talent to the College and it had benefited from his ministry. Even today, twenty years after his death, royalties from his books are paid into a Needy Student Fund. And to cap it all, when the Executive Council attempted to put matters a little more right by paying Gee a gratuity on his retirement, two district councils wrote in to complain about the way the money was spent[11]. Moreover when, after Gee's death, it was suggested that a pension be paid to his widow, this was not agreed to. Many years before Gee had written a little pamphlet entitled *Giving and Worship* pointing out the connection between these two activities. It was a pity that so few people seem to have have read it.

Eighteen months after taking office, Robert Barrie died. He was 56[12]. Much had been made of Gee's health, but it was the old man who stood at the younger man's graveside.

The Aftermath

John Carter was appointed by the Governors as acting-Principal, an ironical twist because Carter and Gee were almost the same age - though sensible enough because Carter did not need married quarters, and this appointment was confirmed at the 1966 General Conference. Ernie Crew returned to pastoral ministry, Robert Barrie's widow gave up her work as matron, Elisha and Mrs Thompson stayed on, but Barbara Warwick, who had for a long time run the correspondence courses and done secretarial work, left. And the College remained full. Carter was not a gifted lecturer because he tended simply to dictate his notes on systematic theology, but the curriculum remained more or less as Gee had established it, and the visiting lecturers stayed on. Missen taught Acts and Pauline Epistles, Aaron Linford pneumatology and Elisha Thompson the Old Testament. W T H Richards came in for a day or two a term and spent time on evangelism.

There was an unexpected arrival on the scene during Carter's Principalship. His brother Howard became a full-time tutor and he brought with him, to act as matron, the wife he had married a few years before. The old Hampstead Bible School team of the 1930s was re-assembled, though it is difficult to discover what the students thought of a Faculty composed largely of septuagenarians!

Gee lived only twenty months after his second marriage. He took his bride (a widow from Scotland who was about seven years his junior) to Germany where he preached and then they bought a small place in Sussex from which he wrote articles and travelled on preaching tours. He was active and happy. In July 1966 Gee went to the funeral of an old friend in Bedford and shared in the tributes. Taking a taxi from St Pancras to London Bridge on the way home, he suffered a heart attack and was dead on arrival at Guy's Hospital.

The funeral was held in the spacious Metropolitan Tabernacle, London and over 500 people gathered. It was an interdenominational occasion and fittingly indicative of Gee's considerable influence. Percy Brewster from the Elim church, Gilbert Kirby of the Evangelical Alliance and John Carter and Alfred Missen from Assemblies of God spoke appreciatively of the man they had known. Kirby said of him

> We have a Theological Study Group presided over by John Stott and one of the original members and one of the most faithful attenders was Donald Gee - no one more beloved. Everyone who came in touch with him realised they were in touch with a man of God. A great bridge builder. He moved in wide circles. Not a contentious man, but a gracious man, full of grace and truth: a Christian gentleman[13].

These words were echoed in a printed memorial in *Redemption Tidings*

> The Pentecostal Movement as a whole is bereaved, for his name and influence are known and felt throughout the world. The truth of this was impressed on me when, as a member of the Advisory Committee, I accompanied Brother Gee to the World Conference in Toronto. People everywhere literally queued up to shake his hand and have the privilege of a word with him. They had heard him minister at this Camp Meeting or that church, or had read one or other of his books. I had never seen anything like it, he could scarcely move about without people accosting him[14].

It was Carter who had known Gee longest, for exactly fifty years, and he preached, concluding with the words,

> A gifted writer has laid down his pen. An eminent Bible expositor will teach no more. A distinguished Editor has

vacated his chair. A renowned author has concluded his last volume. A veteran leader has left our ranks. A great warrior has fought his last battle. Our friend Donald has fallen asleep. Divine awakening will bring about joyous reunion.

Notes to Pages 305 - 311

1. See Executive Council Minutes 6 Sept 1962, item 9.

2. See Redemption Tidings 15 Apr 1960 and 31 March 1961.

3. See General Conference minutes 1963, item 16.e. Swinburne Smith did not resign along with the other Governors because he disagreed with them.

4. A letter written by Gee to Keith Munday, who was then Secretary to the Board of Governors, 4th Sept 1963.

5. Made by someone who would wish to remain anonymous since such a construction of events is speculative. According to Swinburne Smith (in an opinion expressed to Keith Munday), there was a general feeling that Gee should have resigned when he was 70 years of age.

6. A private letter from Swinburne Smith to Keith Munday, 18th Nov 1963. "Brother Gee came over to see me last Friday and seemed concerned about what he called 'a little tension'. He wishes it to be made quite clear to Brother Crew that Brother Thompson is second in command, and should be acting as Principal in his absence".

7. Letter to Keith Munday, Secretary of the Board, dated 20th Feb 1964.

8. Elisha Thompson himself did not seem worried by this. He would have been happy to continue with Gee as Principal Emeritus, but it appears that what really made him an unacceptable candidate to at least one DC was the suspicion that he entertained doctrines similar to C L Parker's about judgment after death. Thompson wrote to the Governors in March 1964, "my nomination as Principal, by the Board of Governors, is not just what I could have wished. Still it could well be for the best for the time being".

9. Jean Wildrianne remembers that Gee lectured two or three times a term at IBTI, and had done so since the days of Fred Squire. Sitting in their lounge, and feeling upset, Gee had said, "I don't know where to go". The Wildriannes, who were joint directors, with J-J Zbinden of the training institute were able to act quickly.

10. Keith Munday had decided not to stand for the Governing Body at the 1964 Conference.

11. Executive Council Minutes 8 Jan 1964. The two complaining DCs were Kent and Midlands. These complaints are all the more disgraceful because it had been made clear at the General Conferences in 1960 and 1961 that Gee gave his services unpaid to the College.

John Carter's book Donald Gee - Pentecostal Statesman (Nottingham: AoG Publishing House, 1975) omits any reference to the trouble which preceded Gee's departure from Kenley. It is, of course, a matter of personal judgement whether one should put the best face on things or tell the whole truth, however hurtful that might be.

12. I am grateful to Desmond Cartwright for supplying this information from his astonishing resources. Barrie died on 16 December 1966.

13. Quote from Colin Whittaker's Seven Pentecostal Pioneers, Marshalls Paperbacks, 1983, p 98 and 99.

14. These are John Carter's words in Redemption Tidings 19 Aug 1966.

Charisma and constitution

Assemblies of God had from the beginning been a revivalist movement and the Bible College was simply a means for training men and women to preach the Gospel so that the revival could be spread more widely. Each step in AoG's development had resulted from a broadening concern. The founding of the magazine, *Redemption Tidings*, was designed to propagate pentecostal doctrine; the founding of the Overseas and Home Missions had exactly the same end in view, though with the scriptural aim of planting new churches; the Broadcasting Council was also established for the same reasons. Each step was evangelical, but with the conscious proviso that the Gospel could and should be preached in the power of the Holy Spirit. The Gospel was seen primarily in terms of the atonement offered by Christ to the individual sinner. A "social Gospel" which stressed the improvement of society by reformist measures, by education or political means, was always viewed with deep suspicion by pentecostals. Let society be improved as individual drunkards and criminals found new life in Christ; any attempt to circumvent the sin of the sinner was bound to fail because, in the final analysis, society was composed of thousands upon thousands of individuals, and each individual a sinner.

The founding of pentecostal eventide homes, or centres for drug addicts, or hotels[1] was theologically radical. But as the pentecostal movement continued its existence, there were more and more elderly men and women who had lived all their lives as members of pentecostal churches. A pastoral initiative was required to help the lonely and infirm. Despite the possibilities for heated debate about the extent to which a Gospel dealing with sin and salvation had room for practical or institutional good deeds, there quite suddenly - and without any public discussion - appeared within Assemblies of God various Eventide Homes. The Eventide Homes began in 1960 and, though one of them caused a rumpus in Yorkshire[2], there were five such establishments by 1985.

The story of David Wilkerson, an American AoG minister, became hot property in the 1960s. A best-selling paperback book, *The Cross and the Switchblade*, told of his phenomenally successful work among drug addicts and armed teenage gangsters in New York. Assemblies of God in Britain sold large numbers of copies of the book and then invited Wilkerson over to Britain to hold meetings. Anyone who heard Wilkerson preach immediately recognised a man who combined intense compassion with an old-time evangelism - in fact Wilkerson came from two generations of American AoG ministers. The Executive Council paid Wilkerson's air fare to Britain and booked halls and arenas for him. The response of the Christian press was warm and the crusade meetings in London and Glasgow were crowded and exciting[3]. Unfortunately, the BBC, which at that time was even more inclined than it is today to sneer at anything remotely enthusiastic in the realm of religion - despite the fact that it thought the Proms were wonderful and football merited all kinds of drunken excesses, produced a biased programme and doused public support. Had that not happened, it is possible that Britain's drug problems in the 1980s would have been far less extensive. Moreover the link between drug abuse and AIDS, which was not known in the 1960s, would have not had such deadly repercussions. Various Christian drug agencies came into being (among them Vic Ramsey's New Life Centre) and a spin-off of Wilkerson's American Teen Challenge which was under the auspices of British Assemblies of God, but they never went half way to solving the problems of the nation[4].

The invitation to Wilkerson was issued by the Executive after Alfred Missen had become General Secretary. He and Eric Dando were keen there should be better co-operation between British and American AoG[5]. Both groups of churches were independent of each other, but there were doctrinal and ethical similarities, and each stressed the autonomy of the local church. As a result an invitation to Tom Zimmerman, the General Superintendent of AoG in America, was issued and he preached at the General Conference in 1966. Zimmerman was an expert organiser and a powerful committee man and liked the idea of founding a European Assemblies of God. With his encouragement, the European Pentecostal Fellowship was initiated, but it also included non-Assemblies of God personnel; eventually after constitutional manoeuvres, this was renamed PEK and revised so that it could run along the same lines as the Pentecostal World Conference[6]. However one of the important outcomes of the ministry of the European collaborations was that a delegation of Rumanian pentecostals came to Britain and, in 1969, a British delegation of Missen and Dando visited Rumania. The odd thing about this story, of course, is that an invitation to an American General Superintendent should issue in British ministry to Rumania. Invitations have unexpected consequences!

In addition to the strengthening of links with the States, there was also the matter of relations with Elim. Squabbles had arisen in 1961 over the campaigning by Elim in an area near to an Assembly of God congregation. This was a problem capable of an endless variety of permutations: Elim might accuse AoG of opening churches on its doorstep, AoG might accuse Elim of campaigning so close to one of its congregations that there was a danger that some members might drift across the invisible dividing line into the other camp. How close was close ? When was a congregation not a congregation ? Did three AoG (or Elim) people meeting in an old hut prevent a bright new crusade in the town hall ? These were the sorts of bones of contention which might be gnawed at for hours in committees. And what if, as happened in this case in 1961, Elim had spent money on preparations for the crusade before AoG got to hear of it and complained ? Letters would pass from a locality to the two Executive Councils and they would then write to each other and make decisions at their bi-monthly meetings. It all took time and was bothersome and cumbersome[7]. Surely the sensible decision would be to amalgamate the two fellowships - as in fact had been suggested as far back as 1923 or 1924. In October 1963 a joint meeting took place between representatives of the two groups. They were similar in size, though Assemblies of God was slightly larger. Each group had its own magazine and Bible College, its own Home and Overseas missions councils. These could all be merged into one: one magazine, one Bible College and one missionary council could be formed. It looked promising, but the discussions foundered on a single word: the word "initial". Assemblies of God believed that the baptism in the Holy Spirit was indicated by the "initial evidence" of speaking in other tongues. Elim believed that the baptism in the Holy Spirit was evidenced by "signs following". As Alex Tee, an Elim preacher explained, speaking in tongues was, for Elim, the "invincible evidence" because someone filled with the Spirit *might* prophesy rather than speak in tongues, or prophesy *before* speaking in tongues.

And so the discussion failed. One member of the AoG Executive said afterwards that, in his experience, whenever discussion in favour of unity failed, the two bodies concerned tended to drift further apart. This must not, he affirmed, happen in this instance. And so, as deliberate policy, the two Executives meet more rather than less frequently than before, and relations between the two churches have continued to be cordial - like a long courtship which is never quite consummated in marriage[8].

Any merger with Elim would have required fundamental reform. Constitutional reform was under discussion in the sixties. As early as 1961, a proposal had been put forward to change the one-minister-one-vote ballot system at Conference. In theory Assemblies of God considered itself a fellowship of assemblies rather than a fellowship of ministers. Some assemblies were not represented at the General Conference, but this could be overcome, it was suggested, either by postal votes or by the use of block votes cast by the chairman or secretary of each district council. Mercifully, this idea was not carried. Had it been accepted two results would almost certainly have followed: firstly, ministerial attendance at the General Conference would have tailed off and, secondly, there would have been arguments about the correctness of allowing district councils of different sizes to have the same voting power[9].

At the General Conference in 1967 the Lincolnshire DC proposed that a committee be appointed to examine the AoG constitution with a view to remodelling it. This was done and the following year it was resolved that the matter be deferred[10]. The General Conference minutes then record, following a prophetic message and a time of waiting upon God, the Executive Council requested D Powell to read a paper on 'Reducing our Machinery to a Minimum'. It was resolved that the Executive Council together with D Powell and the Committee for remodelling the Constitution meet to consider this paper and endeavour to submit to the 1969 General Council an amended Constitution more in keeping with the spirit expressed in this General Council (item 10.j).

What happened was this: John Phillips, a respected member of the Executive Council, prophesied. The business meetings in those days were not tape recorded and so various views exist of what exactly was said and what exactly was meant. Aaron Linford, recalled some of the wording, "Forty and six years this house has been in the building...but I will raise it in three days...."[11]. There are echoes here of the words of Jesus in relation to the temple at Jerusalem (Jn 2.20), but the application was clearly in this instance to the Assemblies of God because it has been founded approximately forty-six years previously. Did the prophecy mean that the AoG Constitution had taken forty-six years to be formulated, but that it would be re-written more or less over night ?

After consideration by the Executive and a time of prayer, David Powell was asked to read a paper he had brought along to the General Conference and which he had originally presented to the Yorkshire District Council of which he was a member.

Powell's paper runs to five sides of quarto. It begins by asserting that "the progress of the movement is not keeping pace with the progress of our machinery. We are making more cogs which tend to grind us to a halt rather than to gear us to advance" and that there was a "growing tendency to central control" and that "we are in a state of decline". At the same time, there was evidence of "a great spiritual upsurge among many of the members of the established denominations". Assemblies of God should therefore consider "dispensing with all our offices, committees and the whole of our constitutional minutes as we now have them". The work carried out by these means could be done by alternative methods: the publishing interest would be carried on by a body of trustees who could, if necessary, appoint talented laymen; district councils could be replaced by the enlarged ministry of large local churches; church planting at home could be done by gifted individuals; the Bible College would revert to friendly independence as in the days of Howard Carter; the General Conference could be regionalised and overseas missionary work could be done "as they did it in Bible days" - which is the vaguest and least well thought out section of the proposals.

Both Powell (a Welshman weighing about twenty stone who was prepared to stand *contra mundum*) and his friend W T H Richards had been impressed by the Swedish pattern of pentecostal churches where all Christian activity was very directly rooted in the local church. Broadcasting, Bible Schools and publishing were adjuncts of the ministry of large city-wide assemblies. Powell's paper has a Scandinavian ring to it. Had his proposals been accepted, it is interesting to speculate on the interaction between pentecostals and charismatics in the 1970s. Almost certainly it would have been easier for charismatic Christians to accept a non-denominationalised pentecostal church and, moreover, when the restoration movement began it would have found large ready-made congregations available which could have been easily linked together into a new network of assemblies by itinerant men with ministerial ability. In other words the hallmark of restorationist teaching - which I take to be apostolic governance of Spirit-filled churches - could have been rapidly stamped on existing churches. Some pentecostal assemblies, of course, would have defended their autonomy and continued their orientation to a less well defined Assemblies of God.

But others would have moved into other alignments and the restoration movement would probably have been able to take place more easily within a loosely structured Assemblies of God and, in some cases, used ordained Assemblies of God ministers.

In the event, Powell, the members of the Executive and the remodelling committee met in June 1968 for two days and secured agreement on a range of changes in the direction of simplifying the Constitution. The Executive minutes (June 12th and 13th 1968) record that Powell's paper was carefully and sympathetically considered but "it was felt his approach went far beyond the idea of a simplified Constitution as laid down by Conference". It is the phrase "as laid down by Conference" which is interesting because it shows that there was an unwillingness to cut the umbilical cord between Conference and Constitution. There would have been no reason to prevent the Conference from radically amending the Constitution, even to the extent of abolishing the Constitution altogether. As it was, a modification of the Constitution was proposed and three factors were built into the new model:

- there be an Assembly and ministerial list

- there be two official councils (Executive and World Missions Councils)

- declarations about pacifism, clerical attire, religious titles, scholastic degrees and the theory of British Israelitism be retained.

The new model was carefully worked out, but in many respects it had neither the advantages of the completely new concept advocated by Powell nor the advantages of the old Constitution which had, at least, grown and adapted to the contingencies of practical debate and circumstances.

In 1969, George Jeffreys Williamson - perhaps the most brilliant chairman and constitutionalist Assemblies of God ever produced - presided over the General Conference. The first step was easy. The "Report concerning the Amendment to the Constitution was taken as read". Then trouble began. There was a proposal that Powell's minority report be circulated. This was refused. Powell's report outlined the steps by which, as he saw it, there had been a retreat away from his ideas[12]. A proposal that Powell meet again with all the various parties was also defeated. A new and completely unexpected proposal was accepted that "in order to give the Chairman and the Conference greater flexibility in discussion, Standing Orders and all Constitutional procedure be suspended for a period of one hour and that prayerful discussion proceed under the guidance of the Chairman". This was a strange, but perfectly sensible decision. The Conference, which was to decide about the structure of its Constitution, suspended its Standing Orders so as to allow discussion. There could hardly have been a more potent admission that the Constitution, which of course was a product of Standing Orders and which required them at General Conference business sessions, prevented rational and spiritual debate. Furthermore, this decision showed that the Constitution could be dispensed with by the Conference. There is a kind of Alice in Wonderland logic in all this. Some men wanted the Constitution abolished; others wanted it retained; therefore it was suspended while a decision was made; any decision made while the Constitution was suspended was still constitutionally valid since the suspension of the Constitution was itself constitutionally valid!

The discussion is recorded in the minutes,

> whilst feeling the constraint of the Spirit of God, and recognising the need for some simplification of the Constitution, the General Council proposes that no item involving Constitutional change shall be considered at either this, or next year's General Conference and that in each of these Conferences at least two days shall be given for spiritual discussion and unhurried waiting on God.

Effectively, then, change was deferred and the nature of the business sessions was altered, at least temporarily, to allow time for preaching or discussion of topics related to ministerial or church life. The "three days" of John Phillips' prophecy had, by that time, been interpreted as referring to "three years"; change was discussed for three years, but in the end very little was altered.

In the years which were to follow, those who were opposed to the Constitution very often felt that Assemblies of God had missed its way and lost opportunities in the debate surrounding constitutional change because, as the events of the 1970s turned out, nothing seemed to alter much. The trouble was that, while a minority of AoG ministers felt strongly that the Constitution was an obstacle to progress and another minority felt that it was a safeguard to doctrinal rectitude and ministerial propriety, a third group of ministers felt that the problems which beset the movement would best be solved by a change of heart - that constitutional reform was an irrelevance.

An historical judgement about which of these groups of ministers was correct is complicated by one's view of the prophetic utterance given by John Phillips at the 1968 General Conference. The Executive minutes (12th June 1968) contain this contemporary assessment:

> A letter from the Secretary of the South West DC asked if any directive would be given by the Executive Council to the Fellowship as a whole in the light of the prophecy at the General Conference. It was decided to place on record that we as an Executive Council accept the fact that God spoke to us through the gifts of the Holy Spirit and that this was in harmony with the addresses given in the Public Meetings. Any ensuing discussion has been based upon the whole tenor of the Conference and not upon any one manifestation [of the Holy Spirit]. The greatest effect of the prophecies given in the business sessions was to bring us to our knees, and during the time spent in waiting upon the Lord our hearts were moved with desire and determination to free ourselves from any procedure and machinery that might impede us as a Fellowship from making a real impact upon our generation.

The Executive's view was that the prophecy should not be considered in isolation from the rest of the Conference: it supplemented but did not override the preaching at the public meetings. This balanced view of the value of prophecy is admirable, but its detractors, some of whom thought that it was *only* the prophecy which should have been regarded, considered that the Executive had failed to listen to God. Others took the view that the prophecy itself was tinged by the conscious or unconscious leanings of the man who brought it[13]. These are sensitive issues. A man who prophesies in a pentecostal gathering does so in the knowledge that his words may be accepted or rejected by those present. If they are rejected, question marks about his ministry inevitably arise. To reject a man's words is to reject the man. Yet a pentecostal gathering which tries to solve all its problems without recourse to the charismatic gifts is in a state of acute declension.

A separate, but related, matter brought up at the 1969 Conference was tabled till 1970. This was the proposal that "elders or comparable church officers" attend the business sessions. This would have introduced a large number of new people whose votes would have undoubtedly made a massive difference to the conduct of AoG. The relatively closed circle of full-time ministers would have been broken open. Elders, particularly those who held responsible secular jobs in commerce, education or industry, would have been impatient with many of the Conference debates and the most long-winded of the speakers, and would have made their dissatisfaction known.

Taken as a whole the three Conferences 1968, 1969 and 1970 indicated that the pentecostals were in good heart. Aaron Linford commented editorially on each one: "What mighty meetings! What great ministry!" (of 1968); "there were times when waves of glory broke over our souls as more than 300 ministers and delegates vociferated their praises" (of 1969); "in a conference of such brilliant blessings it is difficult to pick out highlights at all" (of 1970). The perplexities of the business sessions were not a complete guide to the condition of the assemblies. The basic issue was not that of health but that of direction. Which way forward ?

Notes to Pages 312 - 320

1. Haldon Court in Devon is interdenominational in its clientele, but it was begun through a pentecostal Christian who was involved in the Youth Camps of the 1950s.

2. It was symptomatic of the rows and bad feeling which marred the early sixties. One member of the Yorkshire DC accused another of lying about the payment of the builder used for the Eventide home and the Executive Council was called in to arbitrate. All this took time and generated correspondence and various ministers stood on their dignity or walked out of meetings before a satisfactory resolution could be achieved. The Executive Minutes for 1960/61 tell the tale.

3. Edward England (1982), The Spirit of Renewal, Eastbourne: Kingsway reports that Wilkerson's meetings at the Royal Albert Hall were billed between "the Rolling Stones, a folk blues festival and boxing". Significantly, Wilkerson was heard and accepted by the charismatics and strengthened their position within the churches where they belonged.

4. I worked in Vic Ramsey's drug hostel in Bromley, Kent, for a while. It was not well organised and, so far as I know, did very little useful work. Vic Ramsey (an ex-AoG minister) is now interested in health foods.

Comment on Wilkerson's visit is given in Redemption Tidings 6 Jan 1967 by Alfred Missen. A young couple, Brian and Josee Downward, went round Britain with a Teen Challenge film, "Teen Revolt" before Wilkerson's visit and prepared the ground for him.

5. According to an interview with Alfred Missen 30 June 1987.

6. The Swedish pentecostals were opposed to any organisation which took decision making processes away from the local church. The European Pentecostal Fellowship had

a rudimentary Constitution, but it was not rudimentary enough for the Swedes. The World Pentecostal Conference does not make decisions or vote on matters of international policy. PEK is similar: it is designed for discussion and teaching rather than for legislation.

7. See, for example, Executive Minutes 29th June 1961 item 5c and 5 Oct 1961 items 3e and 3h.

8. Alfred Missen described the negotiations and discussions with Elim in his interview of the 30th June 1987. Mention is also made of them in the Executive Minutes for 15 Oct 1963 and 4 Feb 1964.
    Keith Munday has compared Elim and AoG's relationship to a prolonged courtship.

9. The proposal for a block or postal voting system was put forward by the South Wales District Council. I have said "in theory" Assemblies of God was a fellowship of assemblies because it was very difficult for an assembly in, say, Cornwall to have a great deal of practical shared life with an assembly in Edinburgh. It was the ministers who formed friendships with each other and these friendships were much more in the nature of New Testament fellowship.
    At the same General Conference there was discussion of the procedures to be used by the Court of Appeal (see GC mins 1961 item 22d)

10. John Carter, Aaron Linford, Alfred Missen, Hedley Palmer and G J Williamson were chosen.

11. In a telephone conversation 25th July 1988.

12. At some point later that year the Executive convened a meeting with representatives of all the AoG official councils to sound out opinion within the movement as a whole. This procedure, while it was cautious and would possibly have saved time at the 1969 General Conference, was strictly speaking unnecessary by virtue of the fact that the Conference had already asked a fairly large group (Powell, the remodelling committee and the whole Executive) to make up its mind on the shape of a new Constitution. When a new meeting between Powell, the Executive and the remodelling committee took place in January 1969, the decision to retain the old Constitution had in essence been made - or at least this was Powell's view. This was the view he expressed in his uncirculated minority report which is dated May 1969.

13. On 18th August 1988 John Phillips recalled the occasion in an interview with David Allen and myself. He had had, until the time that he prophesied, no fixed views on church government. He had thought God would bless any form of Christian church or group if it fulfilled certain basic conditions unconnected to its governmental structure. The matter of the AoG Constitution was debated during a morning session at the General Conference. At the lunch break Phillips had walked back to his chalet and felt deeply "wrought upon" by the Holy Spirit. He had not taken lunch, but prayed and paced his room for two hours until the start of the afternoon session. During a short time of worship before the business started, Phillips brought his prophecy. He felt completely taken aback by his own words, which made a powerful impact on the ministers present. The Executive had gone aside to judge the prophecy and deemed it "from the Lord".

    Others of those present, however, while accepting the genuineness of the prophecy, thought that it was open to various interpretations, and indeed that the man who prophesied was not the best person to suggest what it meant. This is because it has been argued that prophecy can be manipulative and the means by which some individuals give added status to their own predilections. It should emphatically be said that the Executive went out of their way to record their view that the 1968 prophecy was genuine. John Phillips spent the three years 1968-71 looking hard at the New Testament guidelines for church government and he came to the conclusion that AoG needed to emphasise ministerial gifting more strongly. When, however, everything was picked up in 1971 more or less where it had been left off three years previously, Phillips wondered what he should do and, on the advice of others, remained a member of the AoG Executive, but with increasing discomfort. He and AoG parted company in 1988.

THE SEVENTIES

Politically, this was a decade of varied governments. There were general elections in 1970, 1974 (twice) and 1979; there were four prime ministers - Edward Heath, Harold Wilson, James Callaghan and Margaret Thatcher. Economically, Britain suffered, like the rest of the western industrialised world, from a quadrupling of oil prices in 1973-4 after the Yom Kippur war. Inflation reached 20% for a time in 1980. Wage claims by the big Trade Unions soared to anything up to 30%. House prices climbed in the same period and unemployment rose through 1.4 million in 1977 to an apparently unacceptable 2 million by 1980.

The combination of inflation and economic stagnation - aptly described by the ugly word "stagflation" - summoned similar political solutions. The Labour Party introduced a "social contract" in the mid-seventies in an effort to mitigate wage claims, and the Conservatives attempted to control Trade Unionism by statute. The Industrial Reform Bill of 1971 was opposed fiercely by most factions to the left of centre in British politics and when the miners struck in the same year and again in 1974, the Conservatives seem to have been dealt a shattering blow. As Lord Blake (1985: 311) commented of that period, "the outlook of commentators, economists, intellectuals, journalists - the opinion formers in general - was anti-conservative".

Running alongside these conflicts in British society were racial issues. Enoch Powell had made his famous "Tiber foaming with much blood" speech in 1968 and the 100,000 largely supportive letters he received indicated that he had hit a sensitive spot in the popular consciousness. West Indians and Asians had arrived in the 1950s when the economy seemed healthy. When the economy turned sick in the seventies, working class whites thought their jobs were being taken by interlopers; five thousand dockers struck in favour of Powell's speech, and the matter was rekindled by the arrival of Ugandan Asians in 1972. Compared with the heat generated by immigration, the revival of Welsh and Scottish nationalism was more sober - although Welsh arsonists destroyed several holiday cottages bought by wealthy English at prices beyond the pockets of the locals - and solved by referendums in 1979 which came out solidly against devolution.

Trouble in Ireland became sectarian, bitter, violent and evil. The failure of the Peoples' Democracy movement in the mid-sixties and the inability of Terence O' Neill to reform and moderate Ulster Unionism eventually gave an excuse for the resurgence of the IRA and the suspension of Stormont (in 1973)[1]. The Irish Sea protected the great mass of the British people from the civil disturbances which bloodied the Falls Road and turned the shopping centres of Belfast into shuttered enclosures. Eventually the IRA campaigned in mainland Britain and pub bombs and car bombs occupied the attention of the media. Images of strikes or riots filled TV screens and the heady, idealistic days of The Beatles faded into the background. Yet, throughout this period, living standards gradually rose - at least, they rose for those who were employed. Telephones, deep freezers, central heating systems, health foods, common market wine, radios, hi-fis and cars were bought by growing percentages of the population. A new social underclass appeared. The long-term unemployed, often living a short distance from the closed or streamlined steel works or mines where their fathers and grandfathers before them laboured, were unable to learn new skills or to move south to the High-Tech de-unionised industries beginning to mushroom on the outskirts of towns like Basingstoke and Slough which benefited from a proximity, by motorway, to London.

Crime and divorce rates continued to rise. Each side of the political spectrum blamed the other for the social and moral ills which strained the welfare services and surfaced in a school system traumatically adjusting to the rigours of the Comprehensive ideal. There were 23 thousand divorces in England and Wales in 1963 and by 1980 there were over 150 thousand. There were 750 thousand one parent families by 1976 and 600 thousand alcoholics in 1979. Abortions continued at 120-140 thousand a year. (Hastings, 1986: 597)

The churches hardly distinguished themselves. The search for rapprochement between Anglicans and Roman Catholics assumed a far greater importance in the minds of churchmen than it did among the general public, and even if relationships between Canterbury and Rome had become cordial to the point of intimacy, it is doubtful whether secular man in what was dubbed "post-Christian" Europe would have changed his habits and attitudes overnight and become once more a loyal communicant[2]. The average young person thought religion a private matter and religious doctrine a matter of personal preference quite devoid of rationality[3]. In fact, anyone who talked to young people in the mid-seventies soon discovered that many of them shared the misconception, fostered by the media, that the sectarian murders which bereaved Ulster were to be laid at the door of Christianity[4].

Hastings (1986: 603f) quotes the dismal figures. Church buildings closed - at one point in 1976 the Church of England was demolishing a building every nine days - and christenings dropped, by 1970, to below 50% of births and, by 1980, to below 40%. Even in theory, then, the Church of England did not command the adherence of a majority of the nation's future. Methodism lost 20% of its membership between 1969 and 1977. The United Reformed Church dropped from 192 thousand in 1973 to 132 thousand in 1984. Roman Catholicism also experienced decline, but its influence was strong in certain parts of the country in the context of more rapid decay among Protestant bodies.

Among Protestants in the Church of England evangelicals reorientated themselves at a well-attended conference in Nottingham in 1977. Social issues henceforth would be permissible areas of concern and, perhaps more important in the short term, charismatic anglicans - nearly all of whom were evangelicals - decided that they were anglicans first and evangelicals second. This decision prevented a charismatic drift away from the Church of England and probably made contacts between pentecostals and anglicans slightly more difficult than they would otherwise have been[5].

So far as the classic pentecostals were concerned, the most important development on the British churchscape was the growth and development of the House Churches (or Restoration movement). These were congregations whose doctrine of the baptism and gifts of the Holy Spirit was identical with that of the pentecostals. There were few disputes on these matters. Differences arose on two other fronts: the House Churches stressed the grace of God in the life of the Christian and this expressed itself most obviously in standards of dress and behaviour. Whereas pentecostals would frown on commercial or sporting activities on Sundays, House Churches took a much more relaxed view of Sunday football or jeans. Theologically more fundamental was the restorationist insistence on the contemporary existence of apostles and prophets within the body of Christ. The practical result of this insistence was to ensure that the co-ordination and cohesion of restorationist groups of congregations was effected by *ministerial relationships* rather than a written constitution. While Assemblies of God laboured to reform itself constitutionally, the House Churches, free from tradition and red tape, were able to act and react much more rapidly to changing situations and demands. As a consequence, too, of the importance of recognised apostolic ministries within their own growing congregations, the payment of restorationist ministers was very much superior to that common in both Elim and Assemblies of God. Such an economic difference between the two groups was facilitated by the middle-class background of many restorationist congregations. No precise figures are available, but personal impressions certainly suggest that, whereas the pentecostal movement had its centre of gravity in the mining communities of the north of England, the House Churches were at home in the affluent south[6]

Notes to Pages 323 - 326

1. See for example Rose, R (1971), Governing Without Consensus, London: Faber & Faber. Whyte, J (1978), Interpretations of the Northern Ireland Problem, Economic and Social Review, 9.4 257-282 is also helpful, as is Darby, J (1976) Conflict in Northern Ireland: The Development of a Polarised Community, Dublin: Gill and Macmillan.

2. Wilson (1966: 130) explains the clergy's enchantment with ecumenism in terms of the advancing power of secularism. "Only ecumenism, and it now has a long history in the experience of English denominations at home and overseas, could justify the compromise with the secular society, under the guise of compromise with fellow Christians".
    The designation of Europe as "post-Christian" was applied to Britain by Gilbert in the title of his book. See Gilbert, A D (1980) The Making of Post-Christian Britain, London: Longman.

3. See M H Duke and E Whitton (1977), A Kind of Believing, London: General Synod Board of Education.

4. I was a school teacher at this time and worked in four large comprehensive schools in the south of England. This was a common observation among pupils hostile to Christianity.

5. By "charismatic" I mean those whose experience of the Holy Spirit was similar to that of classical pentecostals; those who had experienced speaking in tongues and some or all of the charismata mentioned in 1 Corinthians 12. These observations about the degree of contact between pentecostals and charismatics are based on personal communications with evangelical anglicans, some of whom were charismatics.

6. The story of the rise of the House Churches is well told in Andrew Walker's (1985) Restoring the Kingdom, London: Hodder & Stoughton. An enlarged and revised edition came out in 1988.

AOG: TWENTY YEARS OF CHANGE

The constitutional arguments and debates which took place in AoG at the end of the 1960s continued, with perhaps less urgency, into the 1970s. There continued to be a section within AoG which thought that the Constitution had become an obstacle to progress. Where was democracy in the New Testament ? Was there any indication that any member of a congregation in the New Testament voted on any topic at all ? And, beyond this, was the arrangement of New Testament congregations into a co-ordinated group achieved by a written statement of beliefs and procedures ? The answer to these three questions was clearly negative. On the other hand, it was argued by those who took a positive view of the AoG Constitution that it embodied principles of justice which prevented dictatorial self-styled apostles, bishops or archbishops from ruling churches without let or hindrance. What undermined the fears of those who defended the Constitution was the fact that Swedish pentecostals had for years only recognised the primacy of the local church and refused to band themselves together into anything which had the formality of a denomination. Much more recent and closer to home, and therefore in a sense more relevant, the House Churches were characterised by apostolic oversight of networks of churches. Both these instances provided a model, and a working model, to encourage reform.

John Phillips' prophecy at the 1968 General Conference led to a period of reflection and abstention from discussion of constitutional issues. In 1971 he was asked to present a paper at the start of the General Council sessions on "The Principle of Government in the Local Church and Administration in the Fellowship". Alfred Missen presented a paper on the same topic and it was understood that Phillips would give a reformist view and Missen a conservative view. The two papers were given. No discussion followed. The business of the Conference was picked up where it had been left off two or three years before.

Phillips was stunned and, in his own words, "felt that something had died" that morning. Only later, at an Executive Council meeting, did he learn that the veteran John Carter, a staunch defender of the Constitution, had felt the same way[7].

In 1971 George Jeffreys Williamson was Chairman of the General Conference. He was an able debater and consummate in the art of thinking constitutionally. He dealt with reports from the various AoG councils and then asked the assembled ministers to consider the revision of the Constitution. A proposal that the Constitution be left untouched for two years was not carried. This proposal, of course, expressed the opinions on the most entrenched sector of AoG. It was implicitly a rebuttal of the committee which had laboured since the 1967 Conference to produce a remodelled Constitution. A new proposal that the work of the 1967 committee (issued in booklet form) be used as the basis of a new Constitution after consultation with all the various AoG official was not carried. The failure of this second proposition showed that there was opposition even to moderate reform. Whether this opposition stemmed from the ultra conservatives or from the radicals (who wanted no Constitution at all) is not clear; possibly they both voted against the parliamentary group who comprised the constitutional reformers.

Lengthy discussion then followed because an impasse had been reached. It was eventually decided to place confidence in the Chairman who would lead discussion according to his discretion. Williamson, who had been among those who had produced the booklet outlining the proposed revision of the Constitution, set out a procedure by which the agreement might be reached[8]. The booklet containing the draft version of the new Constitution had been circulated before the conference. He suggested that the General Council deal with amendments to the old Constitution first (and these had been conveniently summarised in the agenda) and then vote on other amendments as they were brought up from the floor of the conference. Finally, a vote could be taken "upon a composite motion which would include the original proposal as thereby amended"[9]. This method of progress was slow and cumbersome, though eminently fair. As the earlier voting had made clear, unanimity was in short supply among the ministers. Moreover the problem with Williamson's plan was that amendments could be agreed on (because they formed part agenda) and then amended again. Thus the General Conference minutes record

> It was resolved that the word 'two' in the final sentence of 2:2(c) be replaced by the word 'both'. (The whole section was later amended). (24.b)

It required superhuman patience and concentration to cope with the niceties of amendment on amendment. Some changes were made. For example, it was agreed that the Governors of the Bible College should inspect the premises regularly. It was also agreed that elections to office in AoG councils should be by a two-thirds majority of those present, while other matters could pass with a simply majority. Decisions affecting personalities should be by ballot. But such changes were hardly earth shattering and unlikely to inspire faith; the following year, there was a slight decline in the number of ministers attending the General Council.

In his report on the conference in *Redemption Tidings* (1 July 1971), Alfred Missen put a brave face on what had happened. "A good start", he wrote, "was made with the revision which will be continued next year". Considering that attempts to reform the Constitution had started at least four years before, this description was decidedly positive. In fact, as the minutes for the 1972 conference show, there was an attempt to undo the little that had been done in 1971. A proposal that the procedure adopted in 1971 was "unconstitutional and therefore invalid" failed, but the mere fact that it was brought showed that the ultra conservatives were not prepared to give up easily. Eric Dando, who was Chairman in 1972, was given the same powers as Williamson had been given in 1971 to guide discussion as he saw fit. In the event "it was resolved to leave the whole matter of the Constitution on the table until called for" (GC mins, 1972, 10.b). No one seemed to have the heart for further constitutional battles, and perhaps the reformers realised that spiritual renewal and revival could come despite, rather than because of, the Constitution. Indeed, Eric Dando's in his Chairman's address to the conference implicitly conceded this point; ultimately spiritual life and power mattered far more than minute books, standing orders and logical procedures[10].

In 1973 AoG held its fiftieth General Conference and, to mark the Jubilee occasion, there were backward as well as forward glances. Keith Monument suggested that one afternoon be devoted to a discussion of the Fellowship's future. From this discussion it was resolved that consideration be given to a presidium that would oversee the churches. This was a novel idea. It brought leadership to the fore and recognised that local autonomy had its dangers as well as its strengths. The Executive Council however, in a meeting in January 1974, thought the proposed presidium "would not further the interests of the Fellowship" (15 Jan, item 3f). Inevitably a presidium would have encroached on the Executive's traditional area of authority. Yet, as we shall see, a similar proposal was eventually, and without acrimony, accepted and brought other changes in its wake.

As an indication of the stage through which Assemblies of God was passing, something new happened to the younger generation of pentecostals. The sons of pentecostal pastors began to penetrate the institutions of higher education. Valentine Cunningham took first class honours at Oxford, stayed on to research for his doctorate, and eventually became Dean at Corpus Christi[11]. His father was the pastor of the AoG assembly in Rugby. Cunningham's brother-in-law was Bill Spring, a man with a Master's degree and a strong social conscience. Steven Crisp completed his doctorate at London University in 1968, and his father had been a pentecostal pastor in Yorkshire during the war. Andrew Parfitt completed his teacher training in the sixties and eventually became a Deputy Headmaster. His father had been for a long time the pastor of one of the the AoG congregations in Maidstone. These men, and others like David Petts who had a Baptist background, began to publish their opinions in *Redemption Tidings*. Not unnaturally, they were gently critical of the taboos of their parents and unafraid to disagree with even the most venerable of the old preachers. Cunningham, perhaps the most outspoken of the younger generation, took W P F Burton to task for dismissing Catholic pentecostals (*Redemption Tidings* 16 July, 1970). It was Cunningham again who, in his personal impressions of the 1975 General Conference, poked mild fun at the pentecostals' preoccupation with pornographic magazines on news stands and their distrust of academic qualifications. He pointed out that the organisation of the General Conference was not what it should have been. People got lost, could not easily find those they needed to find, found themselves on awkward sittings for meals and misused the amplification equipment. In impressive articles, Cunningham said things that no one else would have thought of or have dared to say. He pointed out how AoG is the inheritor

> not only of the Protestant, but of the sectarian, nonconformist tradition....we not only stand in a line of spiritual descent from Wesley, through the Salvation Army and Holiness movements which Wesley generated, but, as our insistence on adult baptism, and the Congregationalist government of Assemblies of God reveal, we are aligned with traditional dissent from the Church of England. Even physically: many of our Assemblies worship in ex-Methodist, Congregationalist, Countess of Huntingdon's Connexion, Bible Christian, and so on, chapels. (*Redemption Tidings* 31 Dec, 1970)

He noticed which way the wind was blowing by comparing the

charismatics and the pentecostals.

> Where others are now, widely, bring the 'layman' back into the ministry, seeking to blur that old distinction between clergy and laity, we have developed a distinct pastor-layman mentality. In our recruiting and training of pastors, in the activities we assign to pastor and congregation as the proper sphere of each, in the generally current expectations we assume about what each should do, we assume a fairly sharp gap between clergy and laity. Yet there is no such division in the New Testament.

The pentecostals, who prided themselves of their biblical orthodoxy, suddenly found themselves moving in a sacerdotal direction while the older denominations were moving the opposite way.

> On every hand, the ground we've fought for is being conceded. The principles of the local church as a body of Spirit-baptised and filled believers ministering to each other and to the world....we now find Christians who once were locked into a view of Christianity that held hierarchies, priests, cathedrals, and all the rest, to be vital necessities, going in for de-structured, de-centralised gatherings in homes, where ministry is provided by the Holy Spirit's men, irrespective of whether they be lay or cleric. (Redemption Tidings 5 Dec, 1974)

This analysis of current trends was earlier used by Cunningham to assess the role of pentecostals in relation to the older denominations (*Redemption Tidings* 2 March, 1972). Invoking Troeltsch's church/sect distinction, he accepted the argument that the real pressure for ecumenical ventures - and these turn sects into churches (as sociologically defined) - comes from ministers rather than laymen, and that this pressure is a subtle result of the erosion of ministerial responsibilities by the advance of psychologists, psychiatrists, welfare workers and the like, all of whom took over ministerial functions and reduced the social status of the minister. To Cunningham "no Christian sect has arisen by accident" and mergers and ecumenism have nothing to do with the essential spiritual unity which exists within the local congregation. Sectarianism, therefore, should be seen as a good thing and not, as it is often painted, an example of arrested development or intolerance.

One of Cunningham's most scathing and amusing pieces was

entitled Eratosthenes Butterscotch. The article occurs in an issue of *Redemption Tidings* (20 July, 1972) alongside worthy articles on "The preacher and his hymnbook" and "words of light and love". Cunningham certainly knew how to put the cat among the pigeons. He had gone to the porter's lodge at his college and noticed, among a pile of dead letters, one from the T L Osborn evangelistic organisation addressed to Eratosthenes Butterscotch. This was clearly a spoof name and so Cunningham opened the letter and found there an invitation to contribute to the funds of Osborn "on the grounds that God would uniquely reward such gifts with health, prosperity, and marital success". This invitation led Cunningham into a reflection on the ministries of Osborn and his fellow American Oral Roberts. The Madison Avenue jargon, the complete preoccupation with money, the implication that *only* if Christians give to these glossily packaged preachers can any good accrue either in evangelism or in missionary work, the re-cycling of money (giving to Oral Roberts University so that students can go out and earn more money to give to Oral Roberts), the virtues of personal capitalist aggrandisement and the overall equation of prosperity with divine blessing would have, as Cunningham reminds us, been laughed at in the partially persecuted early church and made nonsense of the life of Christ himself.

Of course, about a month later, a letter followed from the Oral Roberts Evangelistic Association in which a representative defended the academic standards and valid accreditation of Oral Roberts University, though she had greater difficulty in providing a convincing defence against the other charges. Sadly, however, Christians in local churches, pestered by mail shots from evangelists, continued to send their hard earned pounds to they knew not where and ignored the needs of their local pastors[12].

Bill Spring wrote several articles in *Redemption Tidings* under the title "Pentecostal Periscope" on social issues. He interviewed the media sage Malcolm Muggeridge who had then recently converted to Christianity and had not at that time entered the Church of Rome and found common cause with him on the subject of abortion. Some of Spring's views might have struck most pentecostals as either left wing or trendy, but his passionate attack on abortion, and the well argued case he mounted against it, aligned pentecostal thinking with spontaneous moral protests which were arising at that time: the National Festival of Light, Mrs Mary Whitehouse, Lord Longford's report on pornography and Muggeridge's own increasingly despairing and cynical assessments of modern society[13].

Stirrings of change in pentecostalism are detectable in the photographs of meetings at this time. Young Christians with guitars, ministers with fashionable beatle fringes and hair over their ears and slightly off-beat check jackets become visible. These deliberate attempts to be modern, and to appeal to the young, were found in the more progressive ministers. George Jeffreys Williams, for example, dressed in style, though he was older than the undergraduate generation of pastors' sons, but his concern for educational issues stemmed from a solidly responsible Christian conscience. He became a governor of several schools in the town where he pastored and organised conferences specifically for Christian teachers who worked in the state sector of education[14].

It was Williamson who became Principal of Kenley after the interim period overseen by John Carter. The departure of Gee had required a respected and experienced figure and Carter, who had lectured since the 1920s, kept Kenley ticking over. But Williamson was a driving force who did not suffer fools gladly - and for this reason made enemies on the Conference floor - and when, in 1970, there was an election for the Principalship, neither Hedley Palmer, who had been active in the expansion of AoG broadcasting, nor Aaron Linford, who was a skilled and experienced lecturer, took the position.

Williamson was inducted at Kenley in the autumn of 1970, and he found the accounts in a less than satisfactory state. He devoted himself and his wife and the students to a policy of expansion and ministry. He took the students out to churches all over the country nearly every weekend[15] and advertised the work of the college and was able to increase the student intake and boost the flagging finances. He turned the deficit into a profit and by October 1971 had a record number of students (61) from 14 countries. He completely altered the Faculty by inviting in new and younger men, and he was not afraid to employ those with academic as well as pastoral qualifications. David Allen, David Petts, Paul Howe (a General Practitioner) and George Forester had degrees and John Phillips, Keith Munday, John Phillips, Aeron Morgan, Alfred Missen, J W Foster and Barry Benney were all men of proven ability as Bible teachers. Williamson's stated policy was to invite the best speakers he could from all over the country. Previously costs had been reduced by asking only local pastors to become visiting lecturers. By April 1972 Kenley was buzzing with life and at the General Conference a few months afterwards Williamson was speaking on "The Need for and Nature of Bible College Training", a subject about which there were still lingering reservations in the minds of a proportion of AOG ministers.

Less than a year later, Williamson was saying a sad farewell. Two things happened: first, he had begun negotiations for the sale of Kenley to larger premises outside London. Property prices were rising rapidly in the late sixties and early seventies and, in any case, London prices were significantly higher than they were elsewhere in the country. From the profit on Kenley the Board of Governors intended to buy a property purpose-built for education and with room for expansion. In his negotiations Williamson acted on behalf of the Board. At the time the Principal was not a member of the Board and so was placed in an invidious position between the Board and any Contractor or Estate Agent with whom he might enter into discussions.

Second, Williamson had been accused by a student, in a letter to the Executive Council, the Board of Governors and all the chairmen and secretaries of the Assemblies of God District Councils of having done things which were "very far from the testimony of Christ". The student was later suspended for six months by the Governors.

The Governors investigated the student's claims and agreed that Williamson had made no immoral approaches to any person, and though "the Principal may have acted frivolously, we are convinced that no reflection should be placed on his character" (as a statement read by the chairman of the Governors to all the students put it). Two days later, on the 7th December 1972, Williamson suffered a heart attack, partly brought on by overwork and partly by shock. A further two days later Williamson decided to resign as Principal, and it was planned that his resignation would take effect from the end of July 1973. In the event, the resignation date was brought forward to the 21st February, 1973, because Williamson's health, and that of his wife - who was the College matron - continued to be bad. Two of the Governors pressed Williamson to take extended leave of absence and then return, but Williamson's health had clearly taken a turn for the worse and, to add to his problems, his wife soon afterwards required major surgery. As a token of the College's recognition for Williamson's services, a farewell meeting was arranged by the Governors and the appropriate tributes were paid by them and others associated with the College including, of course, the students themselves.

The Governors' report to the General Conference that year was not very informative[17]. It should be noted, however, that at no point was Williamson subjected to ministerial discipline or reprimand, and his standing in the movement was not diminished. After a rest of a few months Williamson was fit enough to return to work and he became a pastor and a District Council chairman. In 1979 Williamson resigned from AoG and went to minister overseas.

From early 1973 the sale of Kenley was suspended. John Carter was asked by the Governors to act as Principal. Various men, among them

David Powell, were drafted in for a few weeks at a time to supervise the students. At the General Conference in 1973, when little thought had been given to a suitable successor, a prophecy was given to the effect that the new Principal should walk forward and declare himself to the assembled ministers. In the electric atmosphere David Powell came to the microphone. He explained how he had sensed some months before that he would be at the College and the arrangements he had made to cover the pastoring of his large assembly at Rotherham. David Petts, then pastor of the Basingstoke assembly, and a much younger man, also walked forward with great trepidation and explained how, in the middle of the night, he had woken up, read his Bible and come across 2 Kings 22.14 (in the Authorised Version) through which he believed God had spoken to him about living at the College. At the vote, the Principalship went to Powell.

Powell therefore tried to handle the sale of the Kenley property. A decision had been taken to buy an old preparatory school in north Nottinghamshire. When the summer term of 1973 ended, Kenley was vacated. Williamson had been in contact with a firm of developers and, in February 1973, a price of £106,000 had been verbally agreed, though nothing had been signed. Powell, when he took office, spoke to the firm again and, in June 1973, managed to raise the offer to £126,000[18]. At that time, however, the Principal was not *ex officio* a member of the Board of Governors. The Board objected to Powell's negotiations although according to a minute of the Board (16 May, 1973) "it was agreed that Mr Powell and Mr Finn [one of the Governors] make some local enquiries and then arrange for the sale by auction".

On 22nd June 1973, the Board met. David Powell was asked to attend at 7pm but was not called in till 8.15pm. He was astonished to be told that the Board had decided to refuse the offer before them. He objected vehemently but was told that the decision was outside his province. The Board had been told that the property would fetch a higher price, especially if it had planning permission. From where did the Board get its incorrect advice ? A relative of a member of the Board worked for a London firm involved in development and architecture and it was his influence which prevailed[19]. Within days, largely because of the quadrupling of oil prices, the property boom had subsided and prices dropped drastically. Kenley was left unattended and unsold and vandals broke in and eventually a fire gutted part of one of the buildings. Because the buildings were underinsured, the financial loss was never made good. Kenley was eventually disposed of for about £60,000 and the new Bible College at Mattersey laboured under an unnecessary debt for approximately the next fifteen years.

There are three lessons which this saga should teach Assemblies of God: first, it is imperative to the smooth running of any Christian organisation that relationships between the various branches, committees and people involved be gracious, open and sweet. Had David Powell and the Board been able to see eye to eye, important difficulties might have been resolved amicably; the Board would have been able to appreciate Powell's position as the man charged with the responsibility of setting up the new premises at Mattersey within the short space of three months, and the pressing financial needs he had to do this job. Conversely he might have appreciated their duty to obtain the highest price for the property they were required to sell. Second, Assemblies of God at this time relied excessively on the advice of so-called experts. It is clear that the experts were not expert enough and, while with hindsight, it seems obvious enough that property prices go down as well as up, the Board failed to realise the risks they were running in refusing a good offer. Considering that Assemblies of God has made enormous play on the validity of the gifts of the Holy Spirit and the supernatural in general, it is ironical in the extreme that, at a moment when divine prescience would have stood them in good stead, the Board failed, so it would appear, to pay any attention to the guidance of God. Third, despite the failures which were so obviously apparent in the transition from Kenley to Mattersey and from Williamson to Powell, the Bible College did recover in the long run and expanded and flourished. But Powell only stayed at Mattersey three years and most of the credit for the College's recovery must go to the ministry of David Petts. It is true that an attempt to retrieve the situation was made at the 1974 General Conference. John Carter insisted that Assemblies of God apologised to the firm which had made the offer to Williamson and, so far as he personally was concerned, Assemblies of God should have accepted the original £106,000 because, contract or no contract, the word of a Christian should be binding; failure to keep one's word would invoke God's judgement. Carter, normally a mild man, was angry in the extreme with the turn events had taken and the Conference formally agreed to write a letter of apology to the property developers[20]. The letter was written, but by then it was too late.

As a postscript to these events, a Constitutional change was made and the Principal became an *ex officio* member of the Board of Governors[21].

Change also came through the inexorable thinning of veteran pentecostal ranks. Howard Carter died in 1971, Leonard Jenkins in

1973, E J Phillips (a senior Elim minister who had liaised with John Carter for many years) and Ernie Crewe in the same year, Elijah Thompson in 1975 and, in 1976, Nelson Parr. Leadership fell on younger shoulders, though one of the men whose ministry and personality was most respected, Billy Richards, died suddenly, and probably from overwork, in 1974. But in general the old order was changing and giving way to the new. There were new names, new problems and new initiatives in the seventies. The winds of change brought doctrines from the charismatic and restorationist wings of the church floating over the pentecostal camp. Could a Christian have a demon, or be demon possessed ? This was a question which troubled classical pentecostals at this time. The neo-pentecostals, by and large, said yes, and the classic pentecostals, after some debate, said a firm no. Once men and women spoke in tongues and became aware of the supernatural, they also became sensitised to the occult. If a convert who had spoken in tongues continued to sin, what possible explanation could be given ? A demon somehow worming its way into Christian's body was thought to be the answer. To those who refused this explanation, it important that no place in the New Testament once referred to this problem among members of the early Church. And, given that the early Church was called out of a largely pagan culture and environment, this evidence seemed conclusive[22].

A similar problem arose over the "Jesus Only" issue. This was essentially a dispute about the correct verbal formula to accompany water baptism. The Jesus Only faction believed that baptism should not use the trinitarian formula "in the name of the Father, the Son and the Holy Spirit" because this was nowhere found in the book of Acts. Moreover, the name of Jesus only was said to include and incorporate the names of the Father and the Holy Spirit. If this had been the full extent of the controversy, it might have been easily solved, but inevitably the Jesus Only formula led to a pentecostal unitarianism, or at least to a modalistic doctrine of the Trinity which denied the co-eternity of the Three Persons, and it was for this reason strongly resisted by the classic pentecostals. To complicate matters, a unitarian pentecostal group in the United States had split from American Assemblies of God in the 1920s and there was a fear, among those who knew of American pentecostalism, that the heterodox group would become established in the United Kingdom as it had in the States[23].

Less far apart doctrinally, but more influential socially, the charismatic movement as a whole concerned classic pentecostals in the 1970s. Pentecostal leaders varied in their approaches: G J Williamson and Alfred Missen both attended Fountain Trust conferences - though Missen walked out at Guildford in '71; Aaron Linford kept abreast of charismatic literature and responded sharply whenever classic pentecostalism was devalued (*Redemption Tidings* 31 Oct, 1974). None of these three men appeared tempted by the Church of England ministry, and all found the anglo-Catholic fringe of Anglicanism quite alien. The upsurge of charismata in the older denominations, however, and the sense that pentecostalism was being drawn out of its isolation may have a beneficial influence on relations between Elim and Assemblies of God. The two Executives met regularly several times a year and discussed various joint projects. Nothing practical came out of the meetings, except that they were valuable in preventing friction and dissension.

Less easy put one's finger on, but real to those who worshipped regularly in pentecostal churches in the seventies, was a burst of new music for worship and praise. The most widely used pentecostal hymn book, *Redemption Hymnal*, dated from 1951 and contained the best of the Wesleyan, Salvationist, Moody & Sankey years with a sprinkling of Isaac Newton, Fanny J Crosby, John Newton together with some pentecostal writers like L F W Woodford, Harold Horton and H Tee. Some of these hymns belonged to the camp meeting and the evangelistic crusade. Their tunes usually went with a swing and some of the best had been sung on the music hall stage. Choruses to hymns, sung between each verse, were rhymed and interwoven with biblical metaphors ("we have an anchor..."; "we're marching to Zion..."; "the Comforter has come...") which were unintelligible to visitors. Gradually slower devotional songs, often verbatim verses of Scripture, came to be popular and easily disseminated by cheap and portable tape cassettes. The new songs represented a mini-reformation. They were "Scripture in song" rather than poetry in song and they encouraged worship. In order to teach congregations the new songs, and perhaps 30 new songs a year were introduced in lively churches, competent musicians, both keyboard and vocal, were needed. The old-style of pounding pastor who tried to stir up his congregation with lusty singing found musical ministries emerging among his flock. Lead singers, aided by microphones and electronic keyboards, began to teach churches to worship. A subtle change in atmosphere took place. The old hymns were still sung, but the new music, often written only a few years before, came to take a larger and larger place in the meetings. Leading a meeting was no longer a matter of choosing five hymns and a passage from the Bible to read and setting these in a sequence. Suddenly the permutations of possibility in each meeting increased. Prophecies and other spiritual gifts flowered in the flow of the new music: people were healed in the middle of meetings instead of waiting for the evangelist to lay hands on them after the sermon. Overhead projectors became more important than hymn books and the new style of worship, with its implications for multi-ministry church life, became associated with the radicalism of restorationism.

There were abuses in the new music. Some young men foolishly came to believe that it was impossible to worship God by singing a hymn and others that, in order to experience pentecostal liberty to the full, it was necessary to dance in the aisles. Congregations were exhorted to clap during some musical passages and others insisted that everyone raised their hands in the air in the mosaic prayer posture. The beauty in the new music was overlooked and immature men thought that they could force congregations to change the musical habits of a lifetime overnight. There was even an attempt to find a theology for the new worship by exploring the "fallen tabernacle of David" mentioned in Acts 15. But, abuses apart, the new music was thoroughly beneficial: it washed away the mechanical side of the old hymn singing and, indeed, it brought a powerful sense of the presence of God to Christians whose lives were all too predictable.

The overall health of British Assemblies of God can be partly estimated from its numbers of churches and ministers.

(Refer to the table on page 340)

The increase 1970-80 of 27 assemblies amounts to 5%. In the same period the number of ministers increased by 16 or 3.5%. The number of delegates decreased by 9 or 15%. In figures not given here the number of retired ministers rose by 30 or 81%. Taken as a whole the growth in Assemblies of God was gradual in the 1970s but the growth in the number of full-time ministers even more gradual. This suggests that many of the new assemblies were small and unable to support a full-time pastor. Meanwhile, the number of retired ministers reached a peak in 1978, and the decline thereafter suggested that the list was reduced by deaths more rapidly than it was added to by retirements; the old guard's ranks were being thinned.

But who would predicted a growth in the number of assemblies 1980-85 at a higher rate than in any period in the previous decade? The vitality of the churches which was manifested in music and worship finally resulted in the addition of 35 assemblies in five years.

YEAR	No. OF ASSEMBLIES	MINISTERS	PROBATIONARY MINISTERS	DELEGATES
1966	535	412	45	57
1967	535	416	38	62
1968	530	419	49	62
1969	525	423	50	34
1970	531	435	46	58
1971	534	430	51	52
1972	549	428	64	51
1973	549	418	59	46
1974	551	427	51	46
1975	541	416	46	52
1976	541	413	63	56
1977	544	414	61	68
1978	550	417	61	59
1979	554	435	65	56
1980	558	446	67	47
1981	571	463	76	50
1982	580	478	79	42
1983	584	501	64	38
1984	591	505	50	38
1985	593	513	67	58

[Figures for 1971, 1977 and 1984 have been taken from two sources which differ slightly. The two sources are: General Conference minutes by adding and subtracting from the names listed there, and figures supplied by Basil Varnam the AoG Administrator. The greatest variation is between the number of ministers in 1977. This figure may be 419 or 414. The figures adopted smooth the general trend].

Of course, the new congregations which came into existence through the evangelistic efforts of established churches - the mother/ daughter system of church growth - was only part of what was happening. The Home Missions section of AoG continued to work hard. It had started at the end of World War II and in a retrospective series of articles former Home Missions secretaries considered those early days (*Redemption Tidings* 9 Nov 1972). They had tried to organise large, well advertised campaigns, but had difficulty in finding gifted evangelists, suitable premises, competent "follow-up workers" and sufficient funds. But several churches were established nearly every year and some of these like the one at Newcastle-upon-Tyne, where Herbert Harrison the follow-up worker became the pastor who stayed for thirty years, grew very large. There were adventures and struggles in the work: George Holmes, for example, wrote about 500 letters a year in addition to pastoring a church and raising funds. Cecil Jarvis recalled spending three days giving out 10,000 handbills. Billy Richards gave two days a week to travel and often campaigned himself - he and his cousin Bill Mitchell took a piano through Basingstoke on a cart playing music to attract a crowd and then hired the local Haymarket Theatre for a campaign. By 1959 it was clear that, unless the Home Missions secretary was properly paid for his services, a succession of men would pass through the office, each one lasting as long as he could cope with the pace. In 1959 Keith Monument was elected as AoG's first full-time Home Missions secretary. Between 1959-72 he organised 100 crusades, nearly one a month on average. His biggest problem was in supporting the converts from crusading. He attempted to enlist the help of the AoG District Councils and to stir up interest with regional rallies, but what he need was a good supply of pastors who were willing to take on tiny congregations till they grew financially self-supporting. There were casualties and failures. Campaigns which seemed overwhelmingly successful might, within a year or two, leave little trace behind. At Crewe, for example, where Ron Hicklin preached there were 150 decisions for Christ in the first week, but just over ten years later there were barely a dozen in attendance at the assembly (*Redemption Tidings* 1 Aug, 1974). In Basingstoke Melvin Banks crusaded in the autumn of 1970. The Town Hall was packed for fourteen nights, several healings took place, the local paper ran a favourable article and provided photographs, but a year later only two families remained in the assembly (*Redemption Tidings* 21 Jan, 1971).

Undoubtedly the greatest success was reported by Melvin Banks. There were 1000 decisions for Christ in Clapton, 150 in Exeter, 500 at Caephilly, 700 at Market Deeping, 300 at Aspley and 400 in the Rugby ground at Wigan (*Redemption Tidings* 6 May, 1971, 11 May 1972, 3 Aug 1972, 18 Oct 1973, 4 Nov 1976, 4 Aug 1977). Admittedly a letter to *Redemption Tidings* (27 Sept, 1979) questioned the validity and meaning of the figures quoted in crusade reports.

> It matters very much that there is often a considerable discrepancy between the reported numbers of decisions and the remaining numbers of disciples. It matters very much that

people can testify to a physical healing (albeit in circumstances in which they would feel embarrassed to say 'nothing has happened') and be so obviously unconcerned about their spiritual welfare.

One might retort that it was not the evangelist's fault if people slipped away after his departure. But that was not the point of the letter. If genuine "decisions for Christ" had been made, surely those who had made those decisions would be firm enough to continue as Christians in the absence of a well-known preacher ? If those who had made "decisions" were absent from church, was the "decision" worth reporting in a magazine?

In fact Banks rarely worked with Home Missions - he was too much of an individualist, and he took little part in the affairs of British Assemblies of God, though he remained on its ministerial list.

By 1980 Monument was able to report to the General Conference that 34 congregations of various sizes were linked with the Home Missions Council. And many of the "heralds" (young men or women who gave up a year of their lives to help in crusades) had entered full-time pastoral ministry; in fact there were 39 men who had entered the AoG ministry in this way. In 1978 the Home Missions budget topped £50,000 per year and it continued upwards after a dip in 1979. This money covered the entire Home Missions operation: preparation of campaigns, publicity and follow-up. It was a huge undertaking and hampered by the distances which Keith Monument had to travel to keep in touch with all his concerns. In the mid-1970s Clifford Rees joined Monument as AoG set itself the target of 1000 assemblies by 1990. There were often petty tragedies because, despite long journeys and sacrificial funding, it was sometimes hard to prevent churches closing as fast as others were opening. On one occasion Clifford Rees travelled to a small church in mid-Wales. A woman of 80 was in charge and there were three other people in attendance at the meeting. Home Missions offered to pay for a pastor to come to live in the area to revive the work. The elderly quartet met and decided that they could not accept the offer in case they did not like the young man supplied by Home Missions. That work, with its building, has now closed and joins the list of derelict churches which litter the British landscape.

Large crusades were popular and AoG was pleased to sponsor Hans Koornstra, a Dutchman who had been trained at Kenley, Arthur Williams, Ron Hicklin, Stan Hyde, Paul Walker, a visiting American pastor, and Douglas Quy, all of whom held successful during the 1970s.

Yet, Clifford Beasley and Brian Downward pioneered churches without the campaign method. Beasley worked in Chester and *Redemption Tidings* (9 Jun, 1977) reported on how he had started in his home and, within three months, had 60 people crammed into his living room every Sunday afternoon. Within six months he had 86 converts and within a year and with only one newspaper advertisement, Beasley set up a functioning church in its own building. Brian Downward, in two years at Newtown in mid-Wales, saw his congregation grow rapidly and a large modern building erected and paid for. It required a special kind of faith to find land, negotiate with town councils and order bricks and mortar without a huge sum of money in the bank. But once the site was bought and the congregation inspired the people of the assembly gave their labour free of charge and the experience of collaborating on the site developed Christian character. Men who found singing hymns tedious, rose to the challenge of using their hands for the glory of God. Newtown was opened in 1978. In 1985 Bennie Finch opened Halton Pentecostal Church in premises which had once been a railway shed and an enormous iron foundry. The church contained a bookshop, offices, a school, a recording studio, a sports hall and a large auditorium and it was the congregation which gave up its free time and sometimes its holidays to reach the moment of completion.

Overseas missions also occupied the attention of pentecostal churches. The long standing association between AoG and the Congo (or Zaire) Evangelistic Mission, the travels of Howard Carter and Donald Gee, the regular furloughs of missionaries and the sporadic missionary reports in *Redemption Tidings* over sixty years had made pentecostals aware of the mission fields beyond Dover.

At each General Conference the largest item in the financial reports was always Overseas Missions. Its income reached £100,000 in 1979 and was over £200,000 in 1982. And, as we shall see, a great deal more was almost certainly given of which no accounts were kept.

There was no settled procedure for the selection of missionaries. Each missionary was expected to hear "the call of God" and to make appropriate preparations for service. It is true that the PMU training schools had been set up before World War I to give a rudimentary preparation in biblical doctrine to men and women who wanted to evangelise overseas. Once the PMU was joined to the Assemblies of God, missionary work continued in China, India and Africa. But no set of procedures or training methods or cultural acclimatisation was arranged in Britain. Those who offered themselves for missionary work were interviewed and then accepted or rejected. Local problems on the field were handled by Field Councils (which were similar to the District Councils in Britain) and the overall policy of the AoG General Conference was carried out by the elected Overseas Missions Council which was made up of men elected from the floor of the General Council, that is, from the list of AoG accredited ministers.

Funding from assemblies was raised by individual missionaries before embarking on their travels, but during World War II, as we have seen, the system was changed. Not all missionaries were equally good preachers and it was thought fairer to equalise the distribution of cash so that each missionary received similar amounts from a common pool. The equal distribution system gave the Overseas Missions Council (OMC) considerable control over missionaries because it could withhold money from enterprises with which it disagreed. In the 1970s, as part of the changes happening in the British assemblies, there was a successful move to alter the funding of missionary work back to the previous system, or to one like it. According to Walter Hawkins, this move was entirely generated by the home churches and not at all desired by the missionaries themselves; according to Colin Blackman the changes were generated by the more progressive members of the OMC[25]. It is, however, doubtful whether many of the ministers at the General Conference realised the implications for the two funding systems. The personalised support scheme appealed to the churches because it allowed them to take a much closer interest in the men and women to whose ministries they were making a financial contribution. To give into a common pool was uninspiring; to give to an individual whose needs were known, whose prayer letters were received and who returned every two or three years with news of what was happening on the other side of the world, was attractive. Theologically, too, the personalised scheme seemed a great deal nearer to the pattern of missionary work found in the Acts of the Apostles. In Acts 13 Paul and Barnabas, on the first ever missionary journey, were sent out by the church at Antioch, and returned to the church at Antioch after successfully completing an evangelistic task. Aaron Linford was unhappy with the new system because he thought that there were few assemblies in the British Isles which had the financial capacity or the manpower to send men overseas for either short or long periods of service (*Redemption Tidings* 7 Oct, 1976). In his view, there was nothing in the AoG Constitution to stop a church, or a group of churches, sending people overseas and supporting them. But, though in theory he was correct, in practice it did not work out like that. The Spanish Pentecostal

Mission was set up by E J Shearman and others from the Denton assembly before the OMC conceived of Europe as a mission field. The result was that Shearman was criticised for appearing to circumvent official councils[26].

After five years of discussion, the AoG Constitution was finally changed. The work of the OMC was defined as (a) informing AoG of "the challenge and opportunities of world evangelism" (b) assisting local churches and District Councils in sending missionaries out (c) receiving applications from would-be missionaries and recognising approved overseas workers (d) receiving and distributing missionary offerings, with permission to deduct up to $2\frac{1}{2}\%$ for administration (e) granting ministerial status to workers overseas unconnected with a District Council and (f) ensuring the missionary policies and principles of the General Council are carried out[27].

Funding, as might be expected, was complicated by the fact that missionaries who had been sent out prior to the constitutional changes in 1981 were on the old equal distribution support system while and others came onto the personalised support system. Churches switched their giving to named missionaries and the common pool was depleted. The OMC found itself hampered by cash shortages in the mid-1980s. The money was being given to the missionaries, but because much of it did not pass through the OMC account, it was impossible to know exactly how much was being given; and, of course, no deduction for administration could be made on unaudited money.

Yet, there was a considerable expansion of missionary work as a result of an alteration to the structure of the OMC that was logically coupled with emphasis on local churches. Instead of letting the OMC direct its missionaries to fields where a co-ordinated effort was being made, Global Action areas were set up. These areas were very broad: Europe, Africa, Asia, South America, and the members of the OMC themselves travelled extensively encouraging missionaries to various types of Christian work and attempting to place preachers and teachers in countries which had hitherto been closed or unworked by British AoG. The OMC was flexible in its strategy. As far as the African field was concerned, it collected funds for Bible Colleges in Nairobi and at Kalembe (*Redemption Tidings* 18 Mar, 1971; 11 Apr, 1985). In the Far East, it worked with Malaysian Assemblies of God and joined missionaries sent out from the USA or other pentecostal groups from elsewhere. Missionary work was likely to be a denominational synthesis. Bickering between missionary groups could and did take place, especially over the ownership and control of property which had been built by funds from one or other group. The Nairobi Pentecostal Bible College, begun by Cyril and Barbara Cross, attempted to prevent such friction by ensuring the College's governors were drawn from representatives of the groups supporting it. British AoG had seats on the Board, but they shared them with local church leaders and the American Elim. This sort of arrangement institutionalised co-operation between Christians and minimised denominational empire building[28].

Illustrative of a different kind of missionary work was that of David Newington. As an extroverted and unconventional Englishman, converted in a pentecostal church in the 1930s, he worked in the Congo from 1945 until he moved to South Africa and there became involved with correspondence courses. As honorary director of the Emmanuel Press he sent out literally millions of tracts and lessons each year. He was joined by missionary "lifeliners" who took secular jobs in African countries but aided in the distribution and tuition of respondents to the literature.

Some idea of the extent and expansion of British AoG missionary work can be gauged from statistics. In 1970 there were workers of various kinds in twelve countries. Of these 68 were certificated workers (including 24 with the Congo Evangelistic Mission (CEM)) and a further 70+ lifeliners. By 1980 work was being carried on in at least nineteen countries and by 1987 in 29 countries. The actual number of fully-supported missionaries did not alter greatly over this period. There were 66 missionaries in 1987 and 13 with the CEM. Also included on the AoG list were associate missionaries who were either wholly or partly supported by church groups of various kinds[29].

Perhaps the general thrust of AoG ministry into the poorer countries of Europe reveals the type of help the British assemblies could offer. After Alfred Missen visited Rumania in 1969, a consignment of Bibles had been dispatched to the Christians in that country. These were returned and Missen contacted the Rumanian ambassador in England to complain. The political Constitution of most of the Iron Curtain countries guaranteed religious freedom, but laws designed to prevent civil disobedience or sedition were often invoked to suppress religious activities[30]. Missen's complaint, therefore, would almost certainly have had a legal force and been the sort of thing Rumanian authorities would want to keep out of the western press. In March 1975, Missen reported on the European Pentecostal Fellowship (PEK) and the contributions which Christians in the non-communist section of Europe tried give in Rumania, Poland, East Germany, Hungary and Russia itself. Money for Bibles was given. Later, in 1978, British pentecostal preachers began to hold seminars behind the Iron Curtain. According to Jean Wildrianne there were 150,000 pentecostals in Rumania and close on 1,000 pentecostal churches. In Bulgaria there were at least four pentecostal churches with more than 300 members (*Redemption Tidings* 28 Sept, 1978). Keith Munday reported on a visit he, Jean Wildrianne and Ron Hibbert made to East Berlin and Warsaw, calling in on Czechoslovakia on the way to Vienna. Their trip was a teaching one and some of those who attended the meetings remembered having heard Donald Gee at Danzig before 1939. They taught on pentecostal subjects and, as Munday pointed out, it is not very easy to prophesy through an interpreter! (*Redemption Tidings* 26 Apr, 1979). In the 1980s this trend continued and a variety of AoG ministers took cars, vans or lorries across to these countries. Medical supplies and, occasionally, second-hand medical equipment (X-ray machines, for example, that were being replaced by newer models in British hospitals) were all transported and given to pentecostal Christians who then passed them on to their government authorities, but with a tacit understanding that local police chiefs would allow believers to go about their business unmolested.

The more mobile ministries of AoG pastors was partly the product of multiple changes at home. Yet pastors who had been abroad were also more likely to introduce changes at home, and so the two effects reinforced one another. Both Ray Belfield and E J Shearman travelled across the world and reported the results of their trips in *Redemption Tidings* (3 Jun, 1976; 22 Jan, 1981). The dynamics of change at home, however, were complex. Adjustments to doctrine or social emphasis, or freer exchanges with other Christians, tended to have knock-on effects into other departments of church or ministerial life.

Barry Benney gave up the editorship of *Redemption Tidings* in August 1978 and, immediately Colin Whittaker took over, there was an improvement. The range of articles widened and became more relevant and immediate. Interviews with speakers to Home Missions or General Conferences were published and their impressions and remedies were clarified and made more accessible. Louis Palau was interviewed (26 July, 1979), Ralph Mahoney a little later (22 Nov, 1979) and Andrew Evans, who had seen Australian Assemblies of God revived, on 5th May 1983. Speakers, often those from pentecostal churches where fresh life had appeared, were able to encourage British pentecostals to accept new practices. House meetings, for example, had been considered divisive in the 1930s. At a time when pentecostals were

leaving home groups to buy their own church buildings, subtle alterations took place in the quality of Christian life. Home groups fostered
caring and sharing, intimate personal relations, unhurried conversations, and symbolically linked home and church. The large church hall
destroyed the fabric of relationships, or put relationships on a different
footing. The church became an evangelistic outpost, a preaching station, a place with hard chairs and loud noise. Quite unexpectedly home
groups began to re-appear. Herbert Harrison, a man who had been
brought up under the powerful evangelistic ministry of Nelson Parr,
wrote favourably about house groups (*Redemption Tidings* 15 Sept,
1977). Harrison had seen his own Bethshan Tabernacle in Newcastle-
up-Tyne grow to several hundred very much on the model of Parr's
congregation. But Harrison also realised that a single pulpit, one-man-
band style of ministry had its limitations. Bethshan, Manchester, had
enormous difficulties in finding a successor to Parr when he finally
died. The multi-talented preacher-cum-teacher-cum-organiser was a
rarity and the New Testament pattern set out a variety of ministries,
each of which complemented the others. House meetings, each led by
an elder or an aspiring elder, offered enormous advantages over the old
system. For a start the single pastor was less likely to work himself to
death and then to leave the church searching for someone else they
could put on a pedestal. Furthermore, the house meeting provided
finer grain pastoral care. Problems which had been swept under the
carpet by the big meeting format could now be attended to. Marital
problems or problems in families between parents and their reluctantly
Christian children could be solved before reaching crisis point. Women
could participate in home meetings where they might have been deterred from public participation in large gatherings. There were a host
of advantages to the house meeting, and the only drawback - the
possibility of a split occurring as a house group leader took his little
flock elsewhere - could be counteracted by ensuring that relationships
between pastor, or pastoral team, and house group leader were strong.
Within ten years of Herbert Harrison's article house groups had been
introduced into the majority of pentecostal churches.

This change, although it might have appeared superficial, had far
reaching effects. Young men who might have expected to fill a pew for
forty years found themselves and their wives actively involved in unpaid
pastoral work as house group leaders. Their own talents developed,
their commitment increased and the most discerning of the older
church members liked what was happening. When the proliferation of
house groups is taken in conjunction with the musical revolution which

was taking place at the same time, it is obvious a new wave - and pentecostals would have said it was a wave of the Holy Spirit - was passing across the land.

To some extent the new format, the pastor assisted by house group leaders - some of whom were elders, was copied from the restorationist groups. Many of these groups were growing faster than AoG or Elim in the 1970s, and many were gaining as disaffected pentecostals transferred their allegiance to the newer meetings. Many of those who went to the restorationist churches were long-standing Christians and had been brought up in Baptist, Brethren or classical pentecostal congregations[31]. The classic pentecostals had to reform or die[32].

Reformation was encouraged by the ministers brought into the AoG conferences. Yongi Cho, who spoke at the 1980 General Conference, had built the largest pentecostal church, and probably the largest church of any kind in the world, by using house groups and, where men failed to rise to the challenge, of appointing female house group leaders. Cho pastored in Korea and in an eastern culture women were less liberated than was common in the west. Yet Cho succeeded and his congregation of half a million people (and the number was constantly being revised upwards) were looked after and remained under his overall supervision. There was no pentecostal pastor in Britain who could argue with Cho's success and it took an obscurantist indeed to insist that the old ways of doing things were the only ways.

Ralph Mahoney's insights also generated excitement (*Redemption Tidings* 22 Nov, 1979). Mahoney was an American Assemblies of God minister whose ministry had been transformed from local to international. He believed "we are on the verge of the greatest harvest in the history of the church", in other words he had nothing to say about the tribulationist view of church history which chilled Christian hearts with the expectation that anti-Christ was around the corner. Mahoney's view of the activity of the Holy Spirit in the life of the church raised levels of discussion and hope. He saw prophetic and apostolic ministries as being able to solve practical church problems in towns and districts. He expected such ministries to proliferate as the twentieth century church grew stronger and stronger. He had little time for a defeatist mentality or powerless eccentricity. Though theologically his message was unoriginal, his experience and the extent of his vision were a revelation to those who heard him. When he predicted a spate of church growth in Britain, he was heard with delighted astonishment. Restorationists had often said that God had finished with the denominations - among whom AoG was reluctantly numbered.

Mahoney swept all this away: God could renew leadership, pour out his Spirit and transform the landscape.

The issue of the end-times, of the exact order of events in the eschatological scheme given by the New Testament, was psychologically important. AoG had, since its inception, taken the stance, popularised by the Schofield Bible, that there would be a rapture of the church prior to the Great Tribulation; in other words the church would be snatched supernaturally from the earth just before a final devastating persecution of the Jews. These events were taught with an unwarranted dogmatism, but where trouble loomed on the horizon, it was possible to assume that the rapture would, in fact, take place in the middle of the Great Tribulation or at its end and, if this happened, the church itself would be the object of the most malicious and effective attack in its history[33]. Such an outlook was dark and, when taken in conjunction with church life which had become dry and mechanical, was depressing and paralysing. Restorationists, by and large, were far more optimistic in their interpretation of the end-times than classic pentecostals, and it was partly for this reason that their churches seemed to exude a confidence the pentecostals had lost. Mahoney did not take a restorationist position, but he believed that evangelism would succeed and be effective. When Andrew Evans was able to report how Australian Assemblies of God had become the fastest growing section of the church in Australia, opening one new church a day, it became evident that the restorationist movement was not taking on where the pentecostals had left off (*Redemption Tidings* 5 May, 1983). The view, implied or stated by restorationist preachers, that classic pentecostalism was a spent force could be seen to be incorrect[34]. Classic pentecostalism which had lost its fervour and become pentecostal in name alone was indeed a dead organism, but pentecostalism repentant and revived had quite another future. If the pentecostals would be open to the full range of the Holy Spirit's power, they could once again experience a phase of growth and life. Evans explained how they had introduced regional superintendency to their churches so that ministers had a senior minister to whom they could turn with a problem. Prophetic ministries, which had been frowned on in the early days of AoG because of abuses, were once more released, but released in conjunction with other ministries which could restrain any imbalances. Praise and worship were allowed to well up from the body of the congregation. New music was written and songs were integrated into charismatic manifestations. All this was in line with what was already happening in Britain. Music, largely under the influence of Chris

Bowater, who had been a Head of Music in a Comprehensive school, was already leaving traditional hymn singing behind, or at least richly supplementing it. House groups were part and parcel of the new structure of churches all over the world which were growing - and evangelical Anglican and Baptists were also introducing them - and so it was logical enough to re-structure the support systems for pastors.

Both Bernhard Johnson in 1978 and Reinhard Bonnke in 1979 preached to AoG Conferences and said that they felt a new sense of divine activity (*Redemption Tidings* 16/23 Nov, 1978; 14 Jun, 1979). "Now is God's time for Britain" was Bonnke's message. He had begun a series of extraordinary campaigns in Africa and bought a huge tent in which to conduct Cape-to-Cairo gatherings. Eventually the tent was outgrown and his 1988 crusade in Nairobi attracted over 100,000 people[35]. He spoke with authority to his British audience because his ministry in South Africa had had extremely unpromising beginnings.

During the late 1970s/early 1980s AoG consciousness of the message and influence of restoration teaching became more acute when several AoG ministers transferred to "Bradford"[36]. Both Clifford Beasley and Ian Jennings who had served on AoG councils - Beasley on the HMC and Jennings on the NYC - left AoG. Both men were talented and effective preachers and there was, among several leading AoG ministers, sympathy with the non-bureaucratic method by which restoration churches made decisions and carried them out. For example, the Basingstoke Community Church decided to start a Christian school and, within about 18 months, had raised over £100,000 and installed its first pupils. AoG would have taken much longer to have implemented such a project, which would have attracted open enthusiasm as well as open criticism. Ministers in restoration churches emphasised the value of personal relationships. The word "official", which had crept into AoG almost unnoticed, was not popular with restorationist preachers, and their image of AoG was one of a lumbering group of churches, legalistically bonded together, in themselves unaware of the extent to which New Testament grace prevented isolationism, and run by inefficient committees[37]. John Phillips, John Shelbourne and Herbert Harrison held seminars among AoG ministers in which they showed what the restoration movement had to teach AoG[38]. Undoubtedly, there was often a coldness among AoG ministers. Some District Councils were a disgrace and there were churches that were run more like working men's clubs than Spirit-filled congregations. Pastors all too often were hampered by elders or deacons who, in turn, were hampered by a small trickle of money. If the pastor offended the deacons, they pulled the purse strings shut and thereby brought him back to their own way of thinking. Restoration teaching stressed the authority vested by Christ in those he had called to the ministry. It was the job of the deacons to carry out the wishes of the pastor, not to thwart him at every turn. This needed to be said and Phillips, Shelbourne and Harrison said it. On the other hand, the authority of the minister could be, and sometimes was, abused. So called "heavy shepherding" was warned against and some of the older or more traditional AoG pastors preferred what they were used to. Brian Hewitt, in an attacking article, implied that the shepherding movement was a "doctrine of demons" both because of its teaching about absolute submission to certain ministers and because it was associated with the view that Christians often needed deliverance from demons (*Redemption Tidings* 21 Feb, 1980). Herbert Harrison replied to Brian Hewitt, and their exchange was symptomatic of the debate inside AoG about the "new thing".

This "new thing" was argued about by the "trads" and "rads" (traditionalists and radicals) at General Conference and ranged over important and practical theological topics: what should the nature of the church be, what was the task of the church and what was in store for the church ? The radicals had a higher view, though not a sacramental view, of the church and crucial to the church's development was the proper function of ministry gifts. Without apostles and prophets, as well as evangelists, pastors and teachers, the church would never attain its full maturity or glory. The radicals tended to be amillennial in their eschatology and to talk in terms of "the kingdom". Such talk was anti-denominational by implication because the kingdom, as described in the Gospels, transcended denominational boundaries and attitudes. A thoughtful article on kingdom theology by Paul Newberry contrasted the kingdom of God as a here-and-now entity with salvation theology which stressed individual experience and an individual entrance to heaven (*Redemption Tidings* 13 May, 1982). Kingdom theology stressed relationships. Warm, personal relationships were seen as vital to a proper functioning of the church. If there were two poles in the psychology of the "old thing" and the "new thing", they could be summarised by the words "relationships" and "official". The new emphases of the kingdom wanted Christians to be honest and real with each other. It was more important to get to know members of the congregation by playing games or going on holiday with them than it was to observe the niceties of minute books and regulations. The two sets of attitudes associated with the old and the new touched every aspect of church life. Accusations and counter accusations could quickly fly from one side to the other. If the radicals were so strong on relationships, why did they bulldoze their way into situations and ignore the ordinary conventions of politeness; if the traditionalists were so holy, why did they lack the power of the Holy Spirit?

The bone of theological contention which was chewed most publicly concerned the millennium[39]. Assemblies of God's Constitution ensured that all its ministers accepted the premillennial Second Coming of Christ. If premillennialism could be shown to be unbiblical, AoG ministers would have to resign or change their Constitution, with all the trauma that that would involve. Keith Munday had addressed the issue in 1978 at a joint conference in Swanwick for Elim and AoG ministers (*Redemption Tidings* 16 Feb, 1978). "There is an a-millennial school of thought which denies the millennium and seems to be attracting adherents", he wrote, and he then set out fully and clearly the reasons he had for believing in a literal millennium. In particular he stressed the promises in Scripture relating to the nation of Israel and the impossibility of the fulfilment of these promises unless a millennial state ensued. Various AoG ministers wavered and at the 1985 General Conference several pointed out the impracticability of asking each minister to sign the fundamental truths annually. What happened, it was asked, when a man found it difficult to make up his mind on a matter and sometimes veered one side of a doctrinal dividing line and sometimes another ? Would he come in to AoG one year and go out the next ? What happened if witch hunts were started against ministers whose doctrinal position on the millennium was considered suspect ? Would they have to face an inquisition to ensure doctrinal orthodoxy ? And, most important of all, could it really be argued that belief or disbelief in the millennium was a matter of *fundamental importance* ? Matters reached a climax when the Executive Council of AoG was asked by its General Conference to meet the Bradford restorationists (GC mins 1982, item 11). Attempts to meet the Bradford men before the Conference had been attempted, but despite a willingness on the AoG side to discuss matters of mutual interest - especially the transfer of Beasley and Jennings to Bradford - no dates were forthcoming from the Bradford side (EC mins 16 Feb 1982, item 3c). Eventually the Bradford group stipulated that they would meet the AoG Executive on the basis of individual fellowship and not as denominational officials. It was axiomatic to the position of restorationists that they were not founding new denominations and, indeed, that denominations were a scourge upon the face of the church and should be dismantled forthwith. The meeting, therefore, took place and afterwards a ministers' conference was called to communicate to AoG what had been established. The conference brought matters out into the open and allowed both "trads" and "rads" in AoG to recognise their differences and points of agreement. A mass exodus to restorationist churches was never a probability, but the special conference had the effect of shutting this possibility off because it was made clear that AoG had something to learn from restorationism. AoG would change rather than die[40].

The discussion over the effects of restorationism on AoG, as we have said, was as much on social as on theological matters. The restorationists saw nothing wrong with the wearing of trousers by women, with well-paid preachers and they saw nothing much right with female headcoverings or inflexibility as to the timing or content of spiritual meetings. When Ray Belfield went on a world tour and was away from Britain for a year he returned to be interviewed by Colin Whittaker, then editor of *Redemption Tidings* (22 Jan, 1981).

His comments were outspoken. He thought it pathetic that British AoG with approaching 600 churches should support only 30 missionaries or that "our touchiness about money" should be allowed to continue. He brushed aside the reserve of the British about charismatic Roman Catholics and television evangelism. And so far as hats for women were concerned, he thought the matter trivial.

> In the rest of the world these are small issues, but here they become major issues and our separation and commitment as a Christian is so often judged by the way we dress and our validity as a Church is often judged by the time and type and style of our services. This is not the case in other parts of the world.

In the realm of spiritual gifts he pointed out how meagre were the manifestations in most pentecostal churches in Britain. Only tongues, interpretation and prophecy were common and the other charismata listed in 1 Corinthians 12 were hardly ever evident. Marriage guidance was more or less absent from British pentecostal churches and in Australia there was a far stronger emphasis on the training of young people; more, not fewer, Bible Colleges were needed in Britain. And, on the matter of the government of the movement, Belfield was indifferent: it was not the presence or absence of voting which mattered, but the concentration on inessentials which destroyed whichever system was employed.

Letters began to arrive commenting on what Ray Belfield had said. Some were mildly cautionary, others strongly antagonistic. "I travelled both Islands [of New Zealand] and noticed that many ladies do not wear hats. This to me is a travesty of truth", wrote one correspondent. Another blasted the Roman Catholic church and stated that the "issue is whether such a person having been genuinely converted would STAY IN the Catholic fold" (original capitals). Another wanted nothing to do the customs of other cultures: "God made us BRITISH and I'm not sure I want to be typically AMERICAN or anything else" (original capitals). Yet none of the letters was from anyone strongly influential in AoG. Leaders appear to have recognised the truth of Belfield's comments and the backlash came from the pews.

Yet, on one matter, there was agreement. Teetotalism - not mentioned in Belfield's world view interview - was hammered home by the American preacher Dave Wilkerson and supported by Benny Finch (*Redemption Tidings* 28 Feb; 17 Apr 1980). The mere fact that teetotalism needed to be passionately defended showed how far the pentecostals were in touch with restorationists and charismatics both of whom, by and large, were in favour of moderation rather than abstinence. Fears that "things would go too far" and that the loosening up in pentecostal behaviour would lead to gross worldiness lay behind the reassertion of traditional positions.

Pressures for change, therefore, were exerted on Assemblies of God both from within its own ranks by ministers whose vision of the church had broadened and from outside by the activities of the restoration movement. One simple example of the feebleness of AoG at its worst was found in the report of the Salaries Committee for 1978. This Committee had the job of writing round to the churches to recommend a salary for pastors. Since the churches were self-governing, the letter had no force and the deacons or church officers could, if they wished, throw it in the bin. But at least it indicated to them the sort of level they should aim at when paying their pastors. In 1978 the Salaries Committee wrote

> Over the period under review, the Committee has endeavoured to be, perhaps, a little more realistic in its approach to the question of Pastors Salaries (sic). Our Assemblies vary considerably in numerical strength which obviously reflects on their income. It was therefore realised that many of our smaller Churches were out of their depth when the soaring National average was quoted. As a result, there were cases, where our

advice was just filed, consequently it became imperative that we should suggest a bare minimum, which in our opinion a Minister of the Gospel ought to have in these days. (General Conference Reports 1978).

The report presumes that church offerings will not rise as fast as the national average wage and that, in a time when wages are rising, pastors should effectively take a drop in salary. There is neither business acumen nor spiritual principle to support this view. If it were taken to a logical conclusion, AoG pastors would become poorer and poorer because when wages were steady or falling, it would argued that pastors should not receive a pay rise against the trend of their congregation. Thus the poor pastor is condemned to become endlessly poorer. It was against this sort of folly that radicals in AoG privately fulminated. Certainly the restorationists would have had none of it.

As a further example of the sort of muddle pentecostals could get themselves into, there was the matter of the Test cricketer Alan Knott. Knott had been converted to evangelical Christianity and interviewed by the AoG Broadcasting Council. It was a neat piece of work by Ken Calder, the man responsible, and one would have thought that he would have been praised for it. But not a bit of it! A letter in *Redemption Tidings* (15 Mar 1979) written more in sorrow than in anger wondered how any Christian could admit to playing cricket on a Sunday. Tom Woods, who wrote the letter, was a gracious and godly man, and there was no malice in his pen, but he could not understand how any Christian could devote himself to sport. The blank incomprehension with which older pentecostals faced new values could hardly be better exemplified by this incident. The old pentecostals had learnt what they had been taught very well and they were not able to assimilate new ideas and situations. Tom Woods had been a Methodist local preacher before becoming a pentecostal and sabbatarianism had, for him, been a form of holiness. What was especially odd in this instance, but the same sort of tension can be seen in the life of Howard Carter, was that Tom Woods regularly prophesied and fervently believed in the dynamic life of the Holy Spirit within the believer. Thus, a mixture of pentecostal unpredictability co-existed with what looked like vestigial legalism in the same man[41].

The debate over divorce, which went back to the 1950s, demonstrated a parallel type of pentecostal tension. As early as 1952, as we have already seen, Aaron Linford wrote to the Executive Council about a divorced man being chairman of a district council. A committee of selected AoG ministers reported on the matter in 1955 and explained the tenable scriptural positions on the subject, and there the matter rested. But in 1957 Aaron Linford put forward his view on marriage and divorce in an editorial in *Redemption Tidings* (25th Oct). His contention was that the clause in Matthew's Gospel which allows divorce on the grounds of "fornication" (Mat 5.32) means that the binding betrothal among Jewish people engaged to be married could be undone if one party was sexually immoral. The Matthean "exceptive clause" refers to engagement and not to marriage and there is therefore no sanction in the Gospels for divorce. "I am afraid that through the years my own opinion has hardened. I consider that marriage cannot be annulled except by death".

In 1961 the General Conference adopted the following paragraph to express its feelings,

> Whereas the present state of society is marred by moral and sexual laxity, and low standards of marriage and divorce are current, it is hereby urged upon all our assemblies and ministers that we discourage divorce by all means at our disposal and seek to establish scriptural standards by sound teaching.

This was an uncontentious statement. Everyone could agree that moral standards needed to be higher. "After further discussion", the minutes continue, "it was decided that the whole matter should be tabled". No decision was to be made. It was felt that agreement would be hard to reach.

Redemption Tidings ran a regular column dealing with questions sent in by readers. Eddie Durham was asked whether he would allow a divorcee to hold office in a church. Durham's answer was no. He would allow church membership to divorcees but, while a previous partner lived, and even after conversion, he would not allow office (25 Aug 1961). Though Durham was an individualist, his answer did not provoke controversy and was therefore probably representative of a wide spectrum of Assemblies of God opinion.

In 1968 the pace hotted up. John Carter and Aaron Linford spoke to the ministers on the subject of divorce and discussion followed both at the Conference and later at District Councils. Carter's position was that "fornication" - the only evangelical ground for divorce - meant more than "pre-nuptial unchastity", and this he concluded after looking at the various New Testament usages of the Greek word "porneia" and its cognates. Porneia included adultery, but it was wider than this. Carter then took the logical step of insisting that divorce on the grounds of porneia allowed for re-marriage. At the end of his paper, however, Carter insisted that divorcees could not hold office in church life because 1 Timothy 3.2 said that a bishop/overseer should be the husband of one wife. This could not, he argued, be a reference to polygamy since, if it were, it implied that polygamy was permitted in the church for all except those in leadership positions[42]. Nor could it refer to a second marriage contracted after a divorce since Paul's argument in Romans 7 precluded this. Therefore, though divorce on the grounds of fornication was permissible, no remarried divorcee could be in a position of pastoral responsibility.

Aaron Linford advanced the view he had outlined more than ten years previously. He believed that *porneia* was quite distinct from adultery and that there was no ground for the dissolution of marriage.

In 1969 Carter and Linford, together with Alfred Missen, were asked to define their areas of agreement and to report back to the Conference. They agreed that fornication was the only ground for divorce (though they did not attempt to harmonise their divergent meanings for *porneia*) and also that Assemblies of God ministers who remarried while a former partner was alive should cease to hold status. They then recommended,

> Those people whose marriage relationships are tangled before conversion and are divorced, or divorced and remarried, should be assured that the past is forgiven and it is better to let the status quo prevail rather than embark on hurtful endeavours at reparation. While such persons may, upon true repentance, be received into the fellowship of the church, it is recommended, in order that the testimony be protected from reproach, that they do not be allowed to serve as church officers.

This is an extraordinary paragraph. One wonders how a man or woman who had been divorced before conversion - and Assemblies of God laid enormous store by the reality of dramatic life-changing conversions affecting the eternal destiny of the individual - could really believe that "the past is forgiven" if exclusion from church office was inevitable. How could the convert properly feel a full member of an assembly ? Why should the homosexual or the drug addict be allowed, after conversion, to become a minister whereas the divorcee be perpetually excluded?

In 1976 the Assemblies of God Constitution was altered to prevent divorcees from holding ministerial status, although divorcees who held status at the time when the Constitution was altered were allowed to continue in office and those who had resigned as a result of the change were offered reinstatement in 1979.

A lengthy letter by G J Williamson (*Redemption Tidings* 10 Feb, 1977) argued strongly that the New Testament taught divorce should be allowed on the grounds of adultery or desertion and that divorce always presumed the possibility of a perfectly legitimate and blameless remarriage. No one replied to Williamson's case.

An attempt by the Birmingham DC at the 1981 General Conference to get rid of the divorce minute failed. It was eventually resolved that

> no person after conversion having divorced and remarried, or who is joined in matrimony to a person divorced after conversion during the lifetime of a former partner, shall hold status or be a leader in an assembly of our Fellowship[43].

No cognisance was taken of guilt or innocence in divorce proceedings and the exceptive clause in Matthew was either ignored or applied to Jewish betrothal. As a result of this ruling several men who had been divorced before conversion were unable to continue as AoG ministers when marrying for the second time. Needless to say, there were members of the General Conference who found such a ruling repugnant, but they did not form a two-thirds majority and had to be content with the appointment of yet another select committee which reported the following year, but without changing the constitutional position.

The first part of the constitutional minute passed in 1981 was, however, interpreted by the Executive Council (14 Nov 1988) to mean that only those who divorce and remarry after conversion are debarred from AoG ministerial status. This represents a slight liberalisation of the previous minute.

But the divorce debate was not only a matter of social attitudes. It was also a matter of hermeneutics, and hermeneutics had never been fully discussed as a topic in itself in Assemblies of God. The motives behind the divorce debate were pure. All sides wanted to do what was right in the light of Scripture, and there was a fear that, if the pentecostal ministry was threatened by unsuitable candidates, the entire movement would come to a juddering halt.

While the divorce debate was taking place, a simple and compassionate letter to *Redemption Tidings* (10 Mar, 1977) from Gerald Chamberlain set in train a chain of events which showed pentecostal ministers at their best. In 1977, in response to Chamberlain's appeal, a group of ministers met informally at the General Conference and agreed to do something, they did not quite know what, for children whose problems were being handled by the social services. After the Conference an anonymous gift of £1000 was handed in to the AoG General Offices in Nottingham. This gift was the first deposit in the Pentecostal Child Care Association's account. A few ministers - Gerald Chamberlain, Warwick Shenton, Alfred Missen and Mike Godward - then wrote to Redemption Tidings (25 Aug, 1977) to put their plans and concerns before the Fellowship. Gradually, and not without financial struggles, the PCCA came into operation, acquired property and began to care for battered, abandoned and molested children (*Redemption Tidings* 19 Apr, 1979). It built up a reputation among local authorities and survived without appeals for money or grabbing headlines in the press. It was a quiet miracle in an era which needed them.

There were other acts of compassion, too, which resulted in one AoG minister, John Wildrianne, being awarded with the decoration of Cavaliere of the Order "Al Merito della Repubblica Italiana" for his organisation of relief work after an earthquake in Italy (*Redemption Tidings* 23 Sep, 1982; General Conference Reports 1981). Over £70,000 was donated from British AoG along with tents, sleeping bags and camping equipment. What particularly stimulated the appeal in Britain was that many of those affected were Italian pentecostals whose lives had rarely been easy. Wildrianne as part of the AoG Action Europe team had seen the disaster first hand and, with the blessing of the Executive Council, he had ensured that lorry loads of supplies had been driven to the point of need.

If the pages of *Redemption Tidings* are an accurate reflection of the concerns of British AoG in the early 1980s, then it is clear that there was a broadening and deepening of the pentecostal movement's outlook. Two articles on human rights stressed the plight of those imprisoned for conscience[44]. The Siberian Seven - a group of Russian pentecostals who took refuge in the basement of the American embassy in Moscow - were also featured (4 Feb, 1982). Concerns of a different kind rose to the surface at the prospect of a Pope on British soil. In May 1982 a Pope visited Britain for the first time and Assemblies of God found itself almost alone among Protestant groups in voicing concern. The 1981 General Conference had issued a statement pleading with Anglican and Free Church leaders to refrain from any public involvement with the Head of the Roman Catholic Church which would deny or contradict the Protestant Heritage. Redemption Tidings printed the replies of various denominations to this statement and all of them begged to differ with the AoG position. "The Methodist Church already has very close relations with the Roman Catholic Church"; the United Reformed Church "welcomes the Pope's visit and prays that this may be the occasion for genuine ecumenical encounter". Dr Runcie replied courteously from Lambeth Palace saying, "it is my judgement, and also I understand that of the leadership of the Free Churches, that some involvement in the visit would not contradict what you call our Protestant Heritage". After the printing of these replies a record postbag had rolled in to *Redemption Tidings* (1 Oct, 1981) expressing grassroots opinion: "The Protestant martyrs would 'turn in their graves' if they knew such an event was taking place..."; "it has long been the plan and purpose of Rome to bring the Protestant Church back under the papal umbrella". One letter, however, put the other point of view "I feel we should welcome and show friendship to such a devout man as the present Pope when he visits out land". Later an official invitation to attend the service at Canterbury Cathedral was extended to AoG leaders but, at the 1982 General Conference, this was turned down flat on a point of principle. It was one of the matters over which there was no difficulty in obtaining a majority!

If we ask why pentecostals found it easy to agree on attitudes to the papacy even after the changes brought about by Vatican II and by the emergence of Catholic pentecostals, the answer must almost certainly be found by looking at interpretations of parts of the Book of Revelation which go back to Luther. As Bridge (1985) points out the rejection of the miraculous by Reformed and generally Calvinistic sections of the church is explicable on the grounds that the unreformed church, the papal church, had been riddled with bogusly miraculous reliquaries, ossuaries and shrines, and the new Protestant church turned its back on any such miraculous attestation of its Gospel. As a result a dispensational theology was constructed which confined miraculous events to the early church and denied the possibility of miracles after about AD 180. Pentecostalism had accepted the theology of the Reformation on most points apart from a completely different attitude to the supernatural and with a stress on evangelism which tended to be Arminian in emphasis. Catholicism was seen, therefore, as fulfilling the role of the Scarlet Woman, the apostate church, in Revelation 17. It was also, as the experience of Italian pentecostals indicated, seen as the perpetrator of considerable persecution or injustice in those parts of the world where it was entrenched.

Colin Whittaker commented editorially on AoG's 1981 General Conference by saying,

> this Conference will be remembered as the one at which the wind of God commenced to blow at gale force. Four years ago the warm, soft, gentle breeze of God melted us to tears and we experienced a deep and lasting renewal in our hearts. The evidence of the depth of work done in them, has been manifest in the wonderful spirit that has prevailed in our Conference Business Sessions (*Redemption Tidings* 11 June, 1981)

The earlier changes in Assemblies of God came from pressures from within the movement and pressures from outside. Whittaker's description suggests a modification to this balance of forces: *because of changes within*, Assemblies of God took a more confident view about its contribution outside to other church groups, other sections of society and other countries. Certainly Whittaker himself wrote Seven Pentecostal Pioneers, published by Marshalls in 1983, and thereby broke into a realm which had been closed to classical pentecostals from the beginning of the century; nearly all pentecostal publications in Britain had come through a recognisably pentecostal publishing house, but such was the impact of the charismatic movement in Britain by the early 1980s, that an important mainline Christian publisher was prepared to risk an overtly pentecostal book. *Seven Pentecostal Pioneers* went through several editions and Whittaker himself went on to write a string of well received books on pentecostal and revival themes.

Redemption Tidings, which Whittaker edited, had been printed regularly since 1924. It was designed primarily to provide balanced pentecostal doctrine and to unite the scattered pentecostal churches. By the mid-1980s, it was ready to take a new tack. Whittaker had taken its weekly circulation up to record levels beyond 10,000, but he found it impossible to go any higher and economically an impasse had been reached. Price rises caused the circulation to dip, whereas a drop in the price failed to cause a corresponding rise in the circulation. The time was felt to be ripe for a new venture and *Redemption Tidings* became *Redemption* in 1985 as a result of a General Conference decision that year. *Redemption* became a monthly magazine and it was intended to reach beyond the borders of Assemblies of God into Christian bookshops and other denominations. Unfortunately after three years and an expensive publicity campaign progress had been disappointing. Sales had dropped badly because the few additional readers from non-AoG backgrounds could not compensate for the cancellations of some of the customers who had regularly subscribed to *Redemption Tidings*. What is significant, though, is not the circulation failure of the new magazine since, all things being equal, circulation is likely to pick up again eventually. Rather the willingness of AoG to produce a magazine intended largely for readers outside its assemblies marks an outward looking and positive attitude.

Several of the AoG assemblies in the 1980s took on a wider range of functions than previously. The Widnes assembly (under Bennie Finch) opened a school, as did the Nottingham assembly (under the Shearmans), and Widnes also included a sports hall in its complex. The Bedworth assembly (under John Partington) attempted to alleviate unemployment in its area and others, like the Scunthorpe assembly (under Paul Weaver), opened tea or coffee shops in their towns as a method of evangelistic outreach. Under George Ridley at Milton Keynes old people's flats were planned, and many churches ran bookshops, telephone ministries or bought Christian books to present to the libraries of local schools. The old idea of an assembly hall which was used for a few hours a week and then locked up was seen to be economically wasteful as well as theologically narrow. The new style of assemblies were firmly committed to the concept of a multi-purpose building, often with a suite of pastoral offices, a playgroup or kindergarten and direct contact with the public on a daily basis.

The Bible College began a slow upward climb in the late seventies and early eighties. In 1977 David Powell threw the Conference into confusion by declining at the last minute to stand for re-election as Principal - the Principal's post, like other full-time and central jobs in AoG being subject to a two thirds majority every two years at the General Conference. There were two other names on the ballot paper, David Petts and Ernest Anderson, but had Powell's decision been known earlier one minister (wrongly as it turned out) suggested that other nominations would have been forthcoming. The Conference broke into district council groupings meeting separately as was convenient to them in various parts of the Butlin's complex and produced no less than nine propositions about the composition of the Governing Body and other related matters. The Conference then returned to a plenary session but all of these propositions failed to carry and eventually a tenth proposition delineating the Principal's role and duties was passed, as well as a decision to place the principalship for that year in the joint hands of the Governors and the Executive. These two bodies chose three men, each to do one term, for that year[45]. In 1978 David Petts and Alfred Missen, who had resigned from the General Secretaryship, stood for the post. By a slight margin Petts received a majority and became the youngest Principal since Howard Carter[46].

The College's facilities may have been suitable for a boys' preparatory school, but they were certainly inadequate for adult education. The heating system was temperamental and there was only dormitory accommodation with very little space for private study. If the College was to make any significant contribution to ministerial training in the latter part of the twentieth century, it was imperative that radical changes be made. At the instigation of the young Principal, the Governors agreed to build a completely new block and, with the support of the Executive and the endorsement of the 1980 General Conference, a plan for 120 study bedrooms with a new kitchen and dining room was drawn up. Gradually, and not without financial tight corners and moments of unhappiness, the College increased in student numbers, in its staffing levels and in the range of courses it offered[47]. Moreover students continued to apply from all over the world. What was new, however, was that the College began to attract students from charismatic and restorationist backgrounds. In a very real way the College became inter-denominational, though firmly associated with Assemblies of God. But the ministry of the College, both in its domestic and in its international activities, exemplified the changing role of Assemblies of God.

The outward looking Assemblies of God of the 1980s was led by a new enlarged Executive Council. Ever since the Restoration movement had begun to impinge on pentecostal consciousness, there had been a subdued cry for leadership. No one wanted dictatorship, and no pentecostal leaders of national standing wanted to be dictators, but there was a general recognition that an annual conference at which too little conferring on matters of substance took place was a failure. Someone had to take a lead by making choices about the priorities facing AoG as a whole. Somehow, too, care and guidance had to be provided for young ministers who were the most vulnerable and precious human asset the Fellowship had. As early as 1973, in an unscheduled discussion on AoG's future at the Conference, the idea of a presidium was put forward[48]. At the 1974 Conference the proposal that

> twelve brethren full of faith and of the Holy Ghost, whose ministry has been clearly attested by God, be charged with the

overall responsibility of the spiritual oversight of the Fellowship, answerable to the General Council, and empowered to co-opt personnel they deem necessary to discharge the work of the Kingdom of God through the Fellowship (item 10a)

... was deferred for three years.

By 1976, the Executive seemed to have changed its mind, or at least to have realised the urgency of the situation. Alfred Missen, surveying the various activities of AoG in a centre page article, explained that the Executive now devoted "less and less time to finding the way out of our problems and more and more time to discerning the way ahead" (*Redemption Tidings* 30 Sept, 1976). By 1983 it had been resolved that "a committee be formed to examine the role, purpose and composition of the Executive Council" and that this committee "identifies all possible areas within the Fellowship requiring spiritual leadership and considers how this leadership could best be expressed by the Executive Council" (GC mins 1983 item 10). The call for leadership was becoming more insistent and the wording of the resolutions shows how the Executive itself was being expected to alter its role.

The Executive and an eight man committee met for four days, two of them with prayer and fasting. Their report ran to less than two sides of A4 paper, but this would have made its contents more easy to assimilate and agree upon. They suggested a simple Constitutional change in the role of the Executive: it should be asked to "promote and safeguard the general welfare of Assemblies of God". The word "promote" was crucial since it would immediately give the Executive enormous scope to lead the Fellowship in various unspecified ways and directions. In order to cope with the work load these increased responsibilities would bring, the Executive should be increased to twelve men who should address themselves to the following areas of need: doctrinal matters, theological trends, church practices, functions of District Councils, fellowship and care of ministers, relations between assemblies, official council activities, youth work and day-school ministries, the media, music, worship, ethnic groups and Christian education programmes. Moreover, the existing members of the Executive were willing to stand down from office in order that a new enlarged Executive could be chosen from scratch[49].

At the 1984 Conference the proposition dealing with the changed role of the Executive was accepted. Discussion then centred around the composition of the new body. Some people wanted a delay of twelve months "for prayerful consideration of nominations" and others wanted nominations from the Conference floor. Both these proposals failed and so nominations were taken from the many which had been given by district councils before the production of the final agenda. Normally there were only a few nominations for the Executive, but once it had been realised that extra places were likely to be created, there were about forty names to choose from and it took six ballots to decide between them and so fill the twelve vacant seats.

In the autumn the Executive got down to work on its task. Each EC member was asked to write down what he considered to be the priorities for the council. These are recorded in the EC minutes (5 Sept 1984, item 8) and make interesting reading. They range from "to find our role in God" to "leadership training" to "build strong relationships between EC members" to "encourage district councils to function as outlined and suggested in the Constitution". The importance of harmonious relationships was stressed, and it was emphasised that these relationships should not only be found between members of the EC but between the EC and the district councils so that younger ministers might be encouraged and cared for. There was also a stress on the need for the Executive members to pray together. All in all, though the priorities were not expressed identically, a pattern emerged - a pattern, it is true, partly dictated by the areas of responsibility marked out by the earlier report. The district councils needed to be revitalised. Ministers needed training, in-service or otherwise, and inspiration; restructuring was necessary; relationships had to be improved; prayer, private and collective, was a condition of blessing. There is no mention of evangelism here, or of missionary work and this is because the EC members understood that such activities would follow naturally from a healthy set of churches. The churches needed to be taught and mobilised. They did not need fresh rules or more money or higher moral standards or even greater charismatic manifestations, though no doubt all these things would be welcomed and would occur once the basic remedies had been applied.

One might have expected that the transition to an enlarged and more effective Executive would have appealed to the most go-ahead of the churches in AoG. The Constitutional changes of the mid-80s were progressive rather than reactionary, restorationist in tone rather than traditionalist, and indicative of AoG's desire to be at the forefront of church life in the British Isles. At long last the hopes of Donald Gee's address "Another Springtime" - and the other reforming messages of the late 1960s - were beginning to come to fruition. Yet in 1985 the large assembly in Slough founded by Billy Richards left Assemblies of God. This was not because the Slough assembly regretted the changes taking place in AoG. Quite the reverse; the leading pastor at Slough, Wesley Richards, had been a member of the eight man committee which had discussed the role of the Executive. Wesley was known to be talented and in favour of change. He wrote a letter to all the ministers in AoG just before the 1985 Conference explaining what he was doing. The letter was restrained in its vocabulary and understated its criticisms of AoG as a whole. In brief it said that the denominational label, "Assemblies of God", was an obstacle to church growth and co-operation and confusing to the man-in-the-street who was looking for simple Christianity rather than the specialised set of doctrines associated with a particular denomination. The Slough assembly, it was said, was not leaving Assemblies of God to join any other denomination. It was leaving Assemblies of God to be able to collaborate with all those in the kingdom of God[50].

So Slough left and attracted criticism for doing so. It was hard for AoG ministers to understand how Wesley Richards could take an active part in thinking about the future of AoG's new Executive and, indeed, how he could be willing to stand for this Executive and then, within a year, when he was not elected onto the new body, to take his church out of the movement his father had so carefully placed it in. Billy Richards had used a Trust Deed for the property at Slough which tied it in as tightly as possible to Assemblies of God. The extrication of the Slough assembly from AoG, despite the willingness of the Executive to be as helpful as possible, proved to be legally tiresome and complex.

Legal tangles also lay strewn across the path of the assembly at Lincoln. This was a big and impressive congregation which seemed to have everything it could want. The excellent teaching ministry was provided by John Shelbourne and John Phillips (popularly known as "Big John and Little John") and the music was in the hands of Chris Bowater, probably one of the most creative and talented church musicians in Britain at the time. At some point, as part of the booming growth of the church, a smaller congregation of charismatic Methodists amalgamated with the Lincoln assembly and the leader of this congregation joined the ministry team of the existing pentecostal assembly. For a time all went well. There were occasional tensions because the charismatic Methodists, having painfully left Methodism, were unwilling to join themselves to any other denomination. Matters began to come to a head when the deed of covenant scheme in Assemblies of God delayed its repayments to individual churches.

The problem arose because the Inland Revenue started to clamp down on all charities which were funded by covenanted gifts, and all the more so if the rebates given by the Revenue amounted to more than one million pounds per year. The scheme demanded that a donor promise to give a certain sum annually to a registered charity and, at the end of the year, the charity could claim the income tax which had been paid on the gift. When the sums involved were small, the Inland Revenue was willing to accept an "open plate" system whereby covenanted money was given without any proof of payment through the collection plates used in church services. But, inevitably, there were a few, and they were very few, occasions when people covenanted money which they did not give. The result of tougher government policy at first led to Assemblies of God being asked for £4,000,000 by the Inland Revenue. The covenant repayments, which were handled by the General Offices at Nottingham, were delayed while negotiations between AoG and the Inland Revenue took place. Eventually, after the previous AoG treasurer Mr Gigg, a man in his eighties, had taken part in the discussions, it was shown that the Inland Revenue had, at some point in the past, accepted the validity of "open plate" collections and the sum demanded in repayment from Assemblies of God therefore shrunk to £300,000. At Lincoln, however, the delay in the payment from the General Offices to the assembly - and because the assembly was large the amount involved was large - seemed to highlight the inefficiencies of a denominational system. Lincoln looked for a covenant scheme which could by-pass the General Offices and discovered to its horror that the previous amalgamation of the Assembly of God at Lincoln and the independent Methodist group had no existence in law. Both groups had different Trust Deeds and, after legal advice, it seemed that only if the Lincoln assembly withdrew from Assemblies of God could a new integrated church group be formed which would exist as a legal entity and to which covenant payments could be made.

At the same time, John Phillips had been struck by the verses in John's Gospel 17.22,23 in which Christ prays for the unity as the Church, a unity which the world will see. This prayer, coupled with teaching which largely emanated from restorationist circles about the kingdom of God (an inter or non denominational concept if ever there was one), led the Lincoln Oversight to recommend to its members that the church withdraw from Assemblies of God. Because of the magnitude of the issue, and because the Lincoln Oversight rejected democracy as a means of church government, the congregation was informed about the withdrawal rather than consulted about its wishes[51].

This decision shocked Assemblies of God more than the departure of Slough. The two Johns were well known and loved and John Phillips had served on the Executive for 24 years continuously. As is often the case in such schisms, matters turned nasty when a group which had been within the Lincoln assembly claimed that it still wished to belong to Assemblies of God and that it should legally be taken as "the continuing assembly". This move had repercussions with regard to the property owned by the church at Lincoln. If the group which wished to belong to Assemblies of God had, in reality, never left Assemblies of God, then the assets of the church belonged to them. So about forty people claimed the assets which had been purchased by about 500 people.

Bad feelings were generated both within the Lincoln District Council to which the two Johns still belonged and at the General Conference. The Assemblies of God Property Trust was bound, as it had been in the case of Slough, to honour the terms of the original Trust Deed. However much it might have been deemed fairer to let the majority of the congregation to take the assets it had largely paid for, the Trust on the building was made in favour of Assemblies of God; this was a standard procedure and enacted to prevent buildings being hijacked by heterodox individuals or segments of a congregation. At the General Conference, perhaps surprisingly, feelings ran against the group which wished to remain in Assemblies of God. At least this is how it appeared. There were those who felt that the "continuing assembly" which was being pastored by the elderly David Powell had acted "unrighteously" in its dealings with the main congregation which had left Assemblies of God[52]. Unfortunately, too, John Phillips knew the members of the Executive who were asked to deal with the mess very well, and it was easy for him to feel let down by them - even if they were acting blamelessly. In March 1988, just before the General Conference, he sent a letter round to all the Assembly of God ministers in which he stated his wish to resign from the denomination. His reasons boiled down to the words "when 'the law' takes over from 'fellowship negotiation'....I can no longer be part of the 'system' which has developed".

For many years John Phillips had been unhappy with voting and committee legislation in AoG and this letter brought all his doubts to a climax. His letter, which circulated the General Council in March 1988 just before a vote on whether or not he and John Shelbourne should be allowed to retain their status as AoG ministers, was proba-

bly instrumenta l in clinching the final result. He and John Shelbourne were voted for on the same proposition and failed by a smallish
margin to retain their status. It was sad, and indeed strange, that both
John Phillips and John Shelbourne were named in the same proposition since the former had resigned and the latter had not. Although a
majority of those present at the Conference wished to retain the two
Johns on the ministerial list, the two thirds majority was not attained.
Tragically, John Shelbourne died of a heart attack a year later.

For Assemblies of God, therefore, the 1980s brought losses as
well as gains. The total number of churches in the denomination grew
by 22 (nearly 4%) in the four years 1981-85, which was almost as much
as the decade 1970-80. There was new growth, and some of it was
attributable to young men who had passed through Kenley in the
Jeffreys Williamson era. Equally, and the figures are hard to compare,
some growth was due to the determined evangelism of the Home
Missions Council. It may have been that the trauma caused by the
departure of Slough and Lincoln, a trauma cutting two ways and
affecting both the congregations and the Fellowship they had left, may
have deterred other assemblies from following suite. Little seemed to
be gained by leaving AoG: local autonomy really did allow successful
pastors to do more or less as they liked, provided they put in the
occasional appearance at a district council meeting. So perhaps the
lesson of Slough or Lincoln was not "are you in or out ?" but "are you
going on or not ?"[53]

Assemblies of God went on to make what was, for it, a revolutionary decision. In 1987 the first AoG General Superintendent, Aeron
Morgan, was appointed. The autonomy of the local church had been
sensitively guarded since 1924 and the whole idea of superintendency
would have been thrown out for fifty years after that date. Yet the
proposition which created the post specified that it should apply to a
named individual. Aeron Morgan was known and trusted. Churches
felt confident that he would not attempt to impose himself upon them
and therefore the implication of the proposition creating his post was
that a successor would not necessarily be found when he gave up. The
administrative load of the General Secretary was devolved upon Basil
Varnam, which left Aeron Morgan free to visit councils and churches
and exercise an itinerant ministry wherever he wished though still, at
the same time, maintaining a position on the pastoral team at one of
the larger churches. The General Superintendent was thought of as a
pastor's pastor, though his ministry was influential across the range of
AoG activities. He was a preacher, and he had to be, because he

constantly needed to bring help, inspiration and teaching to full-time ministers and church officers. By his ministry the needs of the Fellowship as identified by the new Executive in autumn 1984 were to be largely met. Yet, as he travelled, he realised the scope of the task and there was talk of regional superintendency or of complementary superintendency carried out by other members of the Executive.

Superintendency was intended to release ministry, not to restrict it. Australian experience, for example, showed that a good superintendent produced fuller and more effective ministries in those he superintended. Among those under the aegis of the Executive were women. Although AoG from its inception had accepted women pastors, the main outlet for female ministry was either on the mission field or through the Women's Missionary Auxiliary, a locally organised network of women who raised money and materials for missionary work. Some of the most active of these women, as it happened, worked in local churches as the wives of pastors, but the degree to which this happened depended not only on the theological position of the pastor and his church but also on the inclinations of the wife concerned. There was, as other sections of the church also demonstrated, a resistance to female ministry at a deep level. Only teaching and encouragement could expect to change the situation. A new Women's Ministries section was formed within Assemblies of God in 1988 with the intention of of doing just this. So far it is hard to assess how successful this has been.

The altered format and timing of the AoG magazine must be seen as part of these changes. And, as with the alteration to Women's Ministries, judgement on the magazine must be held in abeyance. More obviously measurable will be the restructuring of the General Conference. A 1988 Conference decision was made to banish the business sessions from the Conference and, instead, to hold a family Bible week. Though this change might seem small, there was a freshness and excitement at the 1988 Sonrise Celebration at Minehead and this was communicated to the assemblies. The event was deemed a success. The ministers who until 1988 tended to find themselves overworked and wearied by the demands of many hours of discussion and voting were free to spend time with their families or churches after attending one of a great variety of seminars of different sizes. Business was conducted at a separate conference in the autumn and this was not open to the general public. The division of business from ministry can only be to the benefit of both.

At the 1989 business conference at Scarborough the Executive

Council presented its plan or vision for the future structure of the assemblies in their relations with one another. The old District Councils, which on average had about 25 congregations, were to be replaced by Regional Councils, each with about 60 congregations. The logic of the larger groupings stems partly from the improved transport system throughout Britain. Motorways allow rapid travel over long distances and ministers are expected to drive and own cars. But the conglomeration of 60 congregations also places considerable resources at the disposal of a region if each congregation makes a financial contribution to local initiatives. In particular, it should be possible to support a full or part-time Regional Superintendent who, while retaining links with a home church, will be able to encourage, strengthen and co-ordinate all the others nearby. In addition, the regular meeting of such superintendents will have a centripetal effect, that is, it will create a natural cohesive force within the Movement. At the same time, a reduction in the number of groupings within Assemblies of God should give missionaries and Executive Council members better access to the resources and needs of an area.

As these multiple changes permeate Assemblies of God there will be pockets of reaction and pockets of accelerated progress. There will be variety within the churches of AoG towards the end of the twentieth century, but we can also expect a general movement in the same direction; diversification will accompany multiplication. In a Conference message in 1987 Colin Warner compared Assemblies of God to a divinely planted tree. What matters ultimately is not the shape of the tree, nor its position in the orchard, but whether the tree bears fruit. And if it bears fruit its fruit will correspond with the nature of the tree. The changes of the 1980s are designed to produce a fruitful pentecostal fellowship: that is the test of whether it has all been worthwhile.

7. John Phillips told David Allen and myself this at an interview at Mattersey on 18th August 1988.

8. The other members were John Carter, Aaron Linford, Alfred Missen and Hedley Palmer. In general the 1967 committee simplified the old Constitution by cutting out historical material referring to the formation of Assemblies of God, by putting Definitions and Standing Orders in a section on their own before material relating to each of the sections of Assemblies of God and by removing verbosity, outmoded expressions and repetitions.

9. See GC minutes (1971) item 24.b.

10. The Constitution, in a muted way, continued to be the focus for debate. Douglas Quy in his impressions of the conference in Redemption Tidings (16 June, 1977) said that
> "an ageing and restrictive Constitution struggled for its existence in the face of a call from God to release the Fellowship to do His will".

A month later Aaron Linford wrote a lengthy letter to Redemption Tidings (14th July 1977) defending the Constitution.

> "In fact our Constitution is the custodian of our liberties, guaranteeing the autonomy of our local Assemblies and maintaining their sovereignty in all matters except those that are laid down to foster fellowship, preserve unity and restrain anarchy....for ten years we have been impeded by radicals who are out to abolish the very instrument that originally made 'Assemblies of God' possible. I prefer the reasonable restrictions of an agreed Covenant of Fellowship (for so our Constitution is) to a free-for-all that borders on anarchy".

The two positions could hardly be stated more sharply. Quy felt the Constitution was restrictive, Linford thought it guaranteed freedom.

11. One of Donald Gee's daughters had read history at Oxford some years before.

12. The scandals which stemmed from the fall of Jimmy Swaggart and the Bakkers in 1987 showed that the same kind of prosperity teaching continued, and with renewed force, through American TV into the next decade. Roberts was one of the American TV evangelists and, like the others, his payment for air time necessitated the expenditure of huge sums of money. The only way to raise this money was to appeal for it over TV. Buying air time to appeal for money to buy more air time became a vicious circle. Men who had begun as simple Gospel preachers found themselves under enormous financial pressure and several of them capitulated by losing the original simplicity of their faith.

Certainly British pentecostals were a target for postal solicitations of money. I heard about an old lady who had sent Morris Cerullo £50 and was delighted to receive a "free" Bible as a result! And this example could be multiplied many times over. According to Cunningham's original article T L Osborn raised £109,000 in the year ending December 1970 from the UK alone.

13. I knew Bill Spring at this time. The National Festival of Light was an amorphous, largely evangelical, protest against social mores established in the 1960s. Meetings were held in Trafalgar Square and Westminster Central Hall. The media were at first

astonished with the event and then bored by it. I met a BBC radio reporter, dressed *à la mode,* in Westminster Central Hall who was disenchanted by what he saw. He had hoped for a popularist revolutionary demonstration.

Mrs Whitehouse wrote Cleaning up TV: From Protest to Participation (Blandford Press) in 1967. The American Report of the Commission on Obscenity and Pornography was published in 1970.

14. See EC Minutes 13 Jan 1970 (item 9a).

15. According to David Allen who had worked as Williamson's assistant at Bury and then been asked on to the Faculty as a visiting lecturer when Williamson took over the college. The Saturday night College rallies were expertly organised all over the country and both Faculty and students participated. Williamson worked prodigiously hard.

16. The letter said that Williamson had done things which were "very far from the testimony of Christ".

17. The doctor attending Williamson had told the Board that Williamson's life would be threatened by any further stress. It was for this reason that the Board's comments at Conference were muted.

18. Details of this correspondence is kept at the archives at Mattersey Hall.

19. Letter to the author from Robert Fairnie, then secretary to the Board, dated 7 Nov 1988. At the fatal meeting where the decision to refuse £126,000 was made, Eddie Durham was absent. Mr Fairnie expressed the view in his letter that Eddie Durham's shrewdness might have saved the situation.

David Powell, in a document (held in the Mattersey archives) which he later presented to the Executive Council, expressed the opinion that the Solicitor, M T Vincent, who acted for Assemblies of God also advised against the sale of Kenley in the summer of 1973.

20. See 1974 GC Mins item 17.b. There was a row at the 1974 Conference about the sale of Kenley. Yet the Conference also made a point of placing on record the belief that the Board had acted "in good faith and for the best interests of the Fellowship".

21. See 1976 GC Mins item 12.b. Clifford Rees proposed the change. Rees had been one of those drafted in by the Board after Williamson's departure. He found uproar among the students on his arrival and great difficulty in restoring peace.

22. Val Cunningham wrote a series of articles in Redemption Tidings (1973) in which he took Derek Prince, one of the chief protagonists of the doctrine, to task. Billy Richards also wrote on the subject in Redemption Tidings (11 Oct, 1973) and strongly urged the impossibility of the co-existence of the Holy Spirit and a demon within the same person. Lawrence Livesey, respected missionary to India, also wrote on the subject in Redemption Tidings (24 Jan, 1980). The whole matter lay dormant for a while but cropped up from time to time in the years following. The Yorkshire District Council of AoG found it necessary to discuss Christians and demons in 1988.

23. See Blumhofer E (1985), Assemblies of God: A Popular History, page 44 following. The matter of baptism in the name of Jesus Only was discussed at the Executive Council meeting of 10 Sept 1970. At least one well-known AoG minister, George Deakin, accepted the Jesus Only baptismal formula, though he never became unitarian (EC Mins

11 Jul 1974, item 4g).

24. The PMU council (of five) accepted an equal number of AoG presbyters for one or, at the most, two years. The enlarged Council came into existence on 9th January 1925. Thereafter the interests of the PMU were looked after by AoG, and that legal arrangement obtains to the present day.

25. In an interview at his home on 10 Nov 1988. Walter Hawkins was the full-time secretary of the OMC 1963-79.

I telephoned Colin Blackman on 23 Nov 1988.

According to Massey, R D (1987) *'A Sound and Scriptural Union'. An examination of the origins of the Assemblies of God of Great Britain and Ireland during the years 1920-1925*, PhD dissertation, University of Birmingham, p 141, the Highbury Conference held in May 1924 by which Assemblies of God was finally constituted agreed that the component assemblies should take a monthly missionary offering which should be sent to the Missionary Treasurer (Thomas Myerscough) "to avoid unequal distribution" of such funds. It is very hard to know what proportion of missionary giving was designated to individual missionaries and how much was given for general and equal distribution. Certainly the Preston assembly where Mr Myerscough pastored very consistently supported the ZEM because W P F Burton was local to that area. What Massey, however, does show very clearly is that the missionary vision of Assemblies of God can in a large measure by attributed to the inheritance it received from the PMU; or, to put it another way, the PMU grafted a missionary vision into the new young AoG at the Highbury Conference.

25. In an interview at his home on 10 Nov 1988. Walter Hawkins was the full-time secretary of the OMC 1963-79.

26. E J Shearman said this in an interview at Central Church, Nottingham, on 10 Nov 1988.

27. The 1976 GC mins (item 12.f) record that "it was resolved that we adopt the principle that, in the future, missionaries be adopted, sent forth and supported from a local church or churches" and further that "a committee of seven be appointed to examine this matter". Changes were not implemented till 1981. Points a-f above are taken from the 1981 GC mins (item 16). It will be seen that the principle of sending missionaries out from churches rather than from a national network of churches or from a Council was granted.

28. Barbara and Cyril Cross, Assemblies of God missionaries, began the Nairobi school in rented premises in 1966. In 1969, after being forced to leave Nairobi itself, they bought a 5 acre piece of land a few miles away. Money was raised in Britain through a KEE, Kenya Extra Effort project. The College opened in 1973.

29. The 1970 figures are taken from the Conference report of that year. The 1987 figures are taken from the AoG yearbook of that year.

30. After the 1939-45 war the Soviet Constitution granted some freedom to religious groups, especially the Russian Orthodox Church. Propagandists of Soviet Communism prior to the *glasnost years* denied persecuting the church and would point to the relevant articles of the Constitution as if this settled the matter. I speak from personal experience. Equally, it is very clear, especially from the number of prisoners of conscience released after 1987 and from the information supplied by Amnesty International, that a large number of men and women were imprisoned for their faith behind the Iron Curtain.

Rumania followed the Moscow line and, indeed, KGB operations in Britain were often run through Rumanian surrogates.

31. The Community Church in Basingstoke contained ex-Salvationists, an ex-Anglican minister, several ex-AoG or Elim, ex-Brethren and ex-Roman Catholics. Those who left the classic pentecostals did so, among other reasons, because they had found church life dreary and inflexible. In this they were distinct from others who came into the Community Church after speaking in tongues. Salvationists and Brethren, especially, took an anti-tongues line.

32. There was an argument in the mid-1970s over the scope of pastoral discipline. Carlos Ortiz, a south American pentecostal, had written a book of that title on discipleship in which he had contended for a strong pastoral hand. Alfred Missen had attacked this emphasis as being an aberration, but Peter Kay in a long cogent letter (Redemption Tidings 24 June 1976) had refuted Missen and pointed out that church life of New Testament quality depended on more than a casual attitude either to God or to fellow Christians. Ortiz believed in house groups.

The Bible Society began to publish statistics at this time and these showed that the classic pentecostals were being rapidly overtaken by the house churches. However, subsequently, once the AoG had begun to collect its own data, it was found that the size of AoG had been underestimated and the house churches figures had been based on estimations and projections.

33. W P F Burton and John Carter exchanged letters on the subject when Burton altered his views and denied the rapture, or at any rate denied that the church would escape tribulation or a period of apostasy. Carter maintained that the events of the Book of Revelation applied largely to the world from which the church had been removed and that the 24 elders in heaven in chapter 4 symbolised the church in its entirety. Burton believed that the church was bound to be subject to the plagues and troubles graphically portrayed in the central part of the book. Redemption Tidings (27 Jan 1977) published an article entitled "Will the church go through the Tribulation ?" putting both sides of the question.

34. I remember hearing Ern Baxter preach in about 1973 saying that the pillar of fire had moved on. Classical pentecostal churches were being left in the wilderness.

35. The figure was given by an eyewitness, Peter Kay, in personal conversation during the summer of 1988.

36. The section of restorationism which was associated with Bryn Jones had its main buildings at Bradford at this time. Clifford Beasley left AoG in 1982 (see EC mins 15 June 1982 item 5e). Ian Jennings left AoG in 1984 (see EC mins 5 Sept 1984).

37. These are the sorts of comments made to me by preachers in the restorationist movement.

38. See EC Mins (22 April 1980) item 5j. The EC arranged five regional seminars around the country at which John Shelbourne and others spoke (Redemption Tidings 18 Mar 1982)

39. Keith Munday wrote an article critical of team ministry (Redemption Tidings 25 March 1982) and Herbert Harrison (3 June 1982) attacked Munday. Linford then wrote attacking Harrison (1 Jul 1982). In 1984 Ian Jennings wrote an article in Solid Rock, the AoG youth magazine where he argued that the church had to be "restored" before the return of Christ. David Allen preached on the millennium at the 1987 General Confer-

ence and restated the accepted AoG position, but with the support of the church fathers as well as Scripture. He was able to show that millennialism at least went back to Augustine, and was strongly suggested by Christ in Acts 1.

40. See a report by Keith Munday Redemption Tidings 6 Jan 1983.

41. Tom Woods is a man I know and for whom, before his death, I had a very considerable respect. These remarks, therefore, are not derogatory. Perhaps, the sort of comparison I wish to draw might be best made by asking whether Donald Gee would have had a problem with a cricketing Christian. The answer surely, no. Gee's theology was wide. He understood Spirit-filled Roman Catholics. Others, without the ability to work from basic biblical principles found it hard to apply their faith to changing social and ecclesiastical situations. Letters in Redemption Tidings (26 Apr 1976), one from a school teacher, put the other side of the matter and pointed out that not every Christian was called to pursue exactly the same vocation.

42. This is a logical blunder. We might by the same token say that all church members are allowed to be drunkards, violent, quarrelsome, lovers of money, unable to manage their own homes etc, since these qualifications are also part of the list in 1 Timothy 3.
    Carter's paper, so cogent in answering Linford's views on the meaning of *porneia*, is oddly self-contradictory in regard to the remarriage of ministers. Other Christians, according to Carter, may legitimately and without bigamy remarry if their partner is guilty of *porneia*, but spiritual leaders, it seems, are effectively bigamous if they remarry.

43. The 1976 minute (item 12.d) stated that "no person having been divorced and remarried or who is joined in matrimony to a divorced person during the lifetime of the former partner shall hold status or be the leader in our Fellowship".

44. One by Peter Kay (Redemption Tidings 25 March 1982) and the other by William Kay (Redemption Tidings 15 Apr 1982)

45. These were Keith Munday, Alfred Missen and David Petts.

46. Alfred Missen resigned from the General Secretaryship and let his name go forward in the ballot for Principal. David Petts had been nominated by the Governors. At the election Missen was nine votes behind, but immediately proposed a vote of confidence in Petts saying that he had foreseen the result and that he wished to avoid the confusion caused by last minute withdrawals.

47. In the 1986 General Conference the College was severely criticised for being in a financially tenuous position. The criticism was unfair because the Conference itself had agreed the building project which was partly the cause of the financial deficit. In addition it was very difficult to budget accurately when student intake for any one year could vary to the extent of £20,000 in fee income.

48. This was at the 50th Annual General Conference of AoG. Keith Monument, who was due to introduce a session suggested that, instead of his contribution, the ministers as a body discuss the Fellowship's future. While there was a danger of nostalgia in the 50th year, Monument was keen to safeguard the future. See GC mins 1973 item 2.

49. The EC mins (14 Feb 1984, item 8.2) throw another sidelight on the matter. At the EC meeting of this date the Executive ratified the decisions made by the eight man committee and the Executive combined. All existing members of the EC were wiling to stand down in mid-term or to relinquish their constitutional right to stand for re-election automatically. Three members, John Phillips, Paul Newberry and Colin Whittaker, indicated that,

if the proposals of the revising committee (ie the EC and the eight co-opted men) were not carried at the General Conference, they would either not stand for re-election or resign from the Executive. This shows that these were the three members of theExecutive most committed to change. On the other side of the coin, two members of the Executive, Keith Monument and Aaron Linford, were only willing to stand down if asked to do so by the General Conference.

50. Wesley Richards took the view that the denominational label "Assemblies of God" was an obstacle to church growth and co-operation with neighbouring churches.

51. I have seen, but do not possess, a copy of the letter sent out to church members by the Lincoln Oversight. The letter set out four reasons why the congregation should withdraw from Assemblies of God. They are, as I remember them, (a) the kingdom concept (b) the requirements of the covenant scheme (c) the desire for legal existence (d) the unanimous wish of the Oversight.

52. This was raised or implied from the Conference floor in 1988. As a result an investigation of the conduct of the group within the Lincoln Assembly was carried out by the Executive Council of AoG and a report to the ministers in 1989 concluded there was no reason to oppose the acceptance of this group as an assembly within British AoG. "The Lincoln Pentecostal Church [was] received into fellowship of Assemblies of God" (GC mins 1989 9b).

53. This is how Paul Newberry put it to me.

BIBLIOGRAPHICAL REFERENCES
AND FURTHER READING

Adams, A (undated), Stephen Jeffreys, The Covenant Publishing Co.

Argyle M and Beit-Hallahmi, B (1975), The Social Psychology of Religion, London: Routledge & Kegan Paul.

Barratt, T B (1927), When the Fire Fell and An Outline of My Life, Norway: Alfons Hansen & Sonner.

Bebbington, D (1979), Patterns in History, Leicester: Inter-Varsity Press.

Berger, P L (1975), Invitation to Sociology: A Humanistic Perspective, Harmondsworth: Penguin.

Blake, R (1985), The Conservative Party from Peel to Thatcher, London: Fontana.

Blumhofer, E (1985), Assemblies of God: A Popular History, Springfield: GPH.

Boulton, E C W (1928), George Jeffreys: a ministry of the miraculous, London: Elim Publishing House.

Bragg, M (1976), Speak for England, London: Book Club Associates.

Bridge, D (1985), Signs and Wonders Today, Leicester: Inter-Varsity Press.

Briggs, A (1983), A Social History of England, London: Book Club Associates.

Burton, W F P (1933), God Working With Them, London: Victory Press.

Carter, H (undated) New York...Tokyo...Moscow!, Twickenham: Hampstead Publications.

Carter, J (1971), Howard Carter: Man of the Spirit, Nottingham: Assemblies of God.

Carter, J (1979), A Full Life, Nottingham: Assemblies of God.

Carter, J (1975), Donald Gee: Pentecostal Statesman, Nottingham: Assemblies of God Publishing House.

Cartwright, D W (1976), *Pentecost in Britain*, Elim Evangel Sept 25th.

Cartwright, D W (1981), *From the Back Streets of Brixton to the Royal Albert Hall. British Pentecostalism 1907-1926,* Unpublished paper read at Leuven Dec 28-29, 1981.

Cartwright, D W (1986), The Great Evangelists, Basingstoke: Marshall Pickering.

Croft, W J (1929), The Lord Working With Them, Stockport: The Edgeley Press.

Cole G D H and Postgate R (1938), The Common People: 1946-1938, London: Methuen.

Collingwood, R G (1980), The Idea of History, Oxford, OUP.

Curtis, S J (1961), <u>History of Education in Great Britain</u>, London: University Tutorial Press.

Darby, J (1976), <u>Conflict in Northern Ireland: The Development of a Polarised Community</u>, Dublin: Gill and Macmillan.

Dunn, J D G (1984), Models of Christian Community in the New Testament in <u>Strange Gifts ?: A Guide to Charismatic Renewal</u> (eds) Martin, D and Mullen, P. Oxford: Basil Blackwell.

Duke, M H and Whitton, E (1977), <u>A Kind of Believing</u>, London: General Synod Board of Education.

England, E (1982), <u>The Spirit of Renewal</u>, Eastbourne, Kingsway.

Evans, Eifion (1969), <u>The Welsh Revival of 1904,</u> London: Evangelical Press.

Fisher, H and Reeve O (undated), <u>Still it Flows.</u> (Printed privately ?)

Frodsham, S H (1949), <u>Smith Wigglesworth: apostle of faith</u>, London: Assemblies of God publishing house.

Gee, D (undated), *Pentecostal Pilgrimage: World Travels of a Bible Teacher*, unpublished typescript.

Gee, D (1948), <u>Bonnington Toll: the story of a first pastorate,</u> London: Victory Press.

Gee, D (1967), <u>Wind and Flame,</u> Croydon: Heath Press.

Gee, D (1980), <u>These Men I Knew</u>, Nottingham: Assemblies of God Publishing House.

Gilbert, A D (1980), <u>The Making of Post-Christian Britain</u>, London: Longman.

Gill, R (1975), <u>The Social Context of Theology</u>, Oxford: Mowbrays.

Harper, M (1965), <u>As At the Beginning,</u> London: Hodder & Stoughton.

Harrington, W and Young, P (1978), <u>The 1945 Revolution,</u> London: Davis-Poynter

Hart, B L (1970), <u>History of the First World War,</u> London: Pan.

Hastings, A (1986), <u>A History of English Christianity 1920-1985,</u> London: Collins.

Hill, C P (1966), <u>British Economic and Social History 1700-1939,</u> London: Edward Arnold.

Hocken, P (1986), <u>Streams of Renewal</u>, Surrey: Paternoster Press.

Hollenweger, W J (1972), <u>The Pentecostals</u>, London: SCM.

Horton, H (1934), <u>The Gifts of the Spirit,</u> Letchworth: Letchworth Printers.

Inge, W R (1926), <u>Lay Thoughts of a Dean,</u> London: G P Putnam's Sons

Inge, W R (1928), <u>The Church in the World,</u> London: Longmans, Green & Co

Iremonger, F A (1948), <u>William Temple,</u> London: OUP.

Jeffreys E, (1946), <u>Stephen Jeffreys: The Beloved Evangelist</u>, London: Elim Publishing

Johnson, P (1976), <u>A History of Christianity</u>, London: Weidenfeld and Nicholson.

Manwaring, R (1985), <u>From Controversy to Co-existence</u>, Cambridge: CUP.

Marwick, A (1982), <u>British Society Since 1945,</u> Harmondsworth: Penguin.

Massey, R D (1987 (8?)), '*A Sound and Scriptural Union*'. *An examination of the origins of Assemblies of God in Great Britain and Ireland during the years 1920-25.* Unpublished PhD dissertation, University of Birmingham.

Missen, A F (1973), <u>The Sound of a Going</u>, Nottingham: Assemblies of God Publishing House.

Mitchell, B R and Jones, H G (1971), <u>Second Abstract of British Historical Statistics</u> Cambridge: CUP.

Moorman, J R H (1980), <u>A History of the Church in England,</u> London: Adam & Charles Black.

Nelson, D J (1981), *For Such a Time as This*. Unpublished PhD dissertation, University of Birmingham.

Norman, E R (1976), <u>Church and Society in England 1770-1970</u>, Oxford: Clarendon Press.

Orwell, G (1937), <u>The Road to Wigan Pier</u> reprinted in (1983) <u>The Penguin Complete Longer Non-Fiction of George Orwell</u>, Harmondsworth: Penguin.

Orwell, G (1962), <u>Inside the Whale and Other Essays,</u> Harmondsworth: Penguin.

Parker, C L (undated), <u>Foundation Truths</u>, (printed privately ?)

Parker, C L (1969), <u>The Mystery of God</u>, Croydon: Assemblies of God.

Parr, J N (1972), <u>Incredible,</u> Fleetwood: John Nelson Parr.

Pollock, J C (1955), <u>The Cambridge Seven,</u> London: IVF.

Poole-Connor, E J (1966), <u>Evangelicalism in England</u>, Worthing: H Walter.

Prestige, G L (1935), <u>The Life of Charles Gore: A Great Englisman</u>, London: Heinemann.

Roberts, J M (1980), <u>The Pelican History of the World</u>, Harmondsworth: Penguin.

Robinson, M (1976), *The Charismatic Anglican - Historical and Contemporary: A Comparison of the Life and Work of Alexander Boddy (1854-1930) and Michael C Harper*. Unpublished M.Litt dissertation, University of Birmingham.

Rose, R (1971), Governing Without Consensus, London: Faber & Faber.

Ross, B R (1974), *Donald Gee: In Search of a Church; Sectarian in Transition,* unpublished PhD thesis, Toronto Canada.

Rowntree, G S (1901), Poverty, a study in town life, London: Macmillan.

Saxby A E (undated), God's Ultimate, London: Stockwell Ltd.

Slosser, R and du Plessis, D (1977), A Man Called Mr Pentecost New Jersey: Logos International.

Stotts, G R (1981), Le Pentcôtisme au pays de Voltaire, Craponne: Viens and Vois.

Stevenson, J (1984), British Society 1914-45, Harmondsworth: Penguin.

Squire, F (1958), Operation Relief, Britain: FSP.

Sumrall, L F (c 1939), Adventuring With Christ, Marshall, Morgan and Scott.

Taylor, A J P (1985, revised bibliography 1975), English History 1914-1945, Harmondsworth: Penguin.

Thomson, D (1981), England in the Twentieth Century, Harmondsworth: Penguin.

Trevelyan G M (1944), English Social History, London: Book Club Associates.

Tugwell, S (1971), Did You Receive the Spirit ?, London: Darton, Longman and Todd.

Turnbull, T N (1959), What God Hath Wrought, Bradford: Puritan Press

Walker, A (1985), Restoring the Kingdom, London: Hodder & Stoughton.

Whitehouse, M (1967), Cleaning up TV: From Protest to Participation, Blandford Press.

Whittaker, C (1983), Seven Pentecostal Pioneers, Basingstoke: Marshalls Paperbacks.

Whyte, J (1978), Interpretations of the Northern Ireland Problem, Economic and Social Review, 9.4, 257-282.

Wilkinson, A (1986), Dissent of Conform ?, London: SCM.

Williams, C (1981), Tongues of the Spirit, Cardiff: University of Wales Press.

Wilson, B R (1961), Sects and Society: a sociological study of the Elim Tabernacle, Christian Science, and Christadelphians. Berkley: University of California Press.

Wilson, B R (1966), Religion in a Secular Society, London: C A Watts & Co

Young, M and Willmott, P (1975), The Symmetrical Family, Harmondsworth:Penguin

ACKNOWLEDGEMENTS

In the course of this research I have conducted formal, taped interviews as follows:

1.	Tom Billsborough/Ruth Parry (and others at Preston)	17 Jan 1988
2.	Mrs Gee (Donald Gee's daughter-in-law)	30 May 1987
3.	Jim Gibson (Kilsyth)	27 Nov 1988
4.	Willie Hacking	14 Nov 1984
5.	W Hawkins	10 Nov 1988
6.	A Linford	9 Nov 1984
7.	A J Lucas (Doncaster elder)	25 June 1986
8.	A Missen	3 June 1985
9.	A Missen	30 June 1985
10.	J Phillips	18 Aug 1988
11.	D Powell	12 Aug 1985
12.	Wesley Richards	autumn 1984
13.	E J Shearman	16 Nov 1988
14.	T Woods	21 Sept 1985

On the phone I consulted:

Colin Blackman	Aaron Linford	Paul Mercy
Alfred Missen	John Morgan	Keith Monument
Keith Munday	David Powell	Clifford Rees
Warwick Shenton	Jean Wildrianne	J J Zbinden

Documentary material concerning Sunderland was kindly made available to me by Charlie Douglas and Steve Fozzard and other information came from Clyde Young.

I was also given access to the earliest minutes of the Yorkshire DC and the Preston assembly. The OMC gave me access to their minutes relevant to the Woodford era. In addition I read the minutes relating to the formation of the Broadcasting Council and the minutes of the Govenors of the Bible College for the 60's and 70's.

Ken Calder and David Littlewood kindly made recordings of old interviews or sermons available to me. And various other people in Assemblies of God also sent or lent old photographs, letters and magazines in response to an advertisement in *Redemption Tidings*. Paul Mercy lent me his own copy of the *Latter Rain Evangel*.

To all these my thanks are due.

Notes

Notes